MONOPOLY CAPITAL

*An Essay on the American Economic
and Social Order*

MONOPOLY CAPITAL

An Essay on the American Economic and Social Order

PAUL A. BARAN
and
PAUL M. SWEEZY

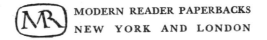

MODERN READER PAPERBACKS
NEW YORK AND LONDON

Library of Congress Catalog Card Number: 65-15269

First Modern Reader Paperback Edition 1968
Sixth Printing

Monthly Review Press
116 West 14th Street, New York, N.Y. 10011
33/37 Moreland Street, London, E.C. 1

Manufactured in the United States of America

For Che

PREFACE

Early in 1962 Robert F. Kennedy, then Attorney General in his brother's administration, traveled around the world as a sort of good-will ambassador of the United States. On his return he addressed the annual luncheon of the Associated Press. In his talk, printed in the *New York Times* of April 24th, he related the following incident:

> I was introduced in Indonesia to another large student body and a boy at the end of my speech got up and asked a question. In the course of this question he described the United States as a system of monopolistic capitalism. And when he said that expression, half the student body applauded.
>
> So I said, "Well now, I'd like to find out. I am a representative of the United States here. What is it that you mean by monopolistic capitalism. What is it that defines that description in the United States? You said it in a derogatory sense. What is it that meets the description in the United States? What do you mean by monopolistic capitalism?"
>
> And he had no answer. And I said, "Well now, anybody who clapped, anybody who applauded when this gentleman used that expression—what is it that you understand by monopolistic capitalism?" And not one of them would come forward.

If Kennedy thought that the refusal of his audience to debate the subject of monopoly capitalism indicated a lack of knowledge, he was surely very much mistaken. Indonesian students, like their counterparts in the underdeveloped countries all over the world, know a great deal about monopoly capitalism, having seen its ugliest face and suffered the consequences of its global policies in their own lives. But it is hardly surprising if they feel that it is too serious a subject for glib definitions or clever debating points.

Kennedy's questions remain, however, and we may pay him the compliment of assuming that they reflect a state of genuine ignorance which is shared by most of his countrymen. This book is addressed to any of them who are really interested in answers and are willing to put in the necessary time and effort to gain some understanding of an extraordinarily complicated and difficult subject. We hope too that it will be of use to the students of Indonesia and all the other countries of the underdeveloped world in achieving a fuller and clearer comprehension of a reality whose importance they already recognize.

One type of criticism we would like to answer in advance. We shall probably be accused of exaggerating. It is a charge to which we readily plead guilty. In a very real sense the function of both science and art is to exaggerate, provided that what is exaggerated is truth and not falsehood. Anyone who wishes to claim that we have overstepped the bounds of this proviso should be prepared to present his own version of the truth about American society today. Such efforts we welcome. For the rest the final test of truth is not anyone's subjective judgment but the objective course of history.

This book has had an unusually long period of gestation— almost exactly ten years from the first tentative outline to the date of publication. Factual material for illustrative and narrative purposes was gathered and used as needed, but there has been no systematic attempt at updating, nor have we tried to take account of all the significant works bearing on one aspect or another of our subject as they have appeared. This is, as the subtitle states, an essay, not a treatise, and it makes no pretense to comprehensiveness.

Most of our intellectual debts will be clear from the text and footnotes and call for no special mention here. For careful editing and innumerable improvements in presentation and style we are indebted, as both of us have been on many occasions in the past, to John Rackliffe.

«««««««»»»»»»»

The foregoing is a reconstruction from notes jotted down some two years ago of what we intended to include in the

Preface. To my profound sorrow, it now falls to my lot to attach an addendum—and to sign the Preface alone. Paul Baran died on March 26, 1964.*

Though Baran never saw the final form of the manuscript which went to the typist and the printer, I must emphasize that this in no way diminishes the joint character of the book. The ideas and the structure we worked out in a continuous interchange beginning long before the first outline was set down on paper. Whatever was drafted by one of us was criticized at length by the other, and in most cases redrafted and recriticized more than once. Everything now in the book had been through this process before Baran's death. Apart from putting the entire manuscript into finished form, the only thing I have done has been to leave out what would have been two additional chapters. This material was in rough draft at the time of his death, but in each case one or the other of us had raised important questions which still remained to be discussed and resolved. Since neither chapter was essential to the theme of the essay as a whole, the best solution seemed to be to omit them altogether. I reached this conclusion the more easily since even without these chapters the book turned out to be longer than I had expected or we had originally intended.

Paul M. Sweezy

New York City
January 1, 1966

---

* A year after his death *Monthly Review* published a special memorial issue, *Paul A. Baran: A Collective Portrait* (March 1965), edited by Leo Huberman and myself, which later appeared in book form. This includes three selections from Baran's work, two essays on his work and life, 38 statements by people from all over the world, and a bibliography of his writings.

CONTENTS

LIST OF TABLES

LIST OF CHARTS

The truth is the whole.—Hegel

Two centuries ago, a former European colony decided to catch up with Europe. It succeeded so well that the United States of America became a monster in which the taints, the sickness, and the inhumanity of Europe have grown to appalling dimensions.

—Frantz Fanon

1

INTRODUCTION

The situation in the social sciences in the United States today is paradoxical. The number of research workers and teachers is rapidly rising. Their training and command of their disciplines, including the ability to use precise mathematical reasoning and sophisticated statistical methods, are far above the levels attained by their predecessors of even one generation ago. Universities, foundations, and governments organize research projects and dispense grants on an unprecedented scale. Books, reports, and articles are turned out in a never-ending stream. And yet all this high-powered intellectual activity has yielded few important new or fresh insights into the way our society works and where it is headed.

To be sure, we know that our society is working anything but well. But only a few years ago, during what C. Wright Mills aptly called the Great American Celebration, social scientists were assuring us that everything was fine. That the opposite is true—that idle men and idle machines coexist with deprivation at home and starvation abroad, that poverty grows in step with affluence, that enormous amounts of resources are wasted in frivolous and often harmful ways, that the United States has become the symbol and defender of reaction all over the world, that we are engaged in several wars and clearly headed toward more and bigger ones—the knowledge of all this, and much more, did not come to us from the social sciences but from the observation of unavoidable facts. One can even say that social scientists, assuring us for so long that all was for the best in what they took to be the best of all possible worlds, did what they could to keep us from looking reality in the face.

How can we account for the paradox of more and better trained social scientists failing ever more glaringly to explain social reality?

Part of the answer no doubt lies in plain opportunism. Who pays the piper calls the tune, and everyone knows who the payers are and what tunes they prefer. In a capitalist society, an effective demand will always call forth its own supply.

But it would be both wrong and libelous to leave the matter there. Among American social scientists there are men and women of the highest integrity who are motivated by a genuine passion for truth. If they too have failed to throw light on the great social issues of our time, the reason is not opportunism but the inherent limitations of their outlook and methodology. These they have partly inherited from the past and partly shaped in response to their own environment. This environment is above all one of increasing complexity calling for more and more specialization of every kind and at every level. Following this road, social science has become more and more compartmentalized, with its practitioners turning into ever narrower specialists—superbly trained experts in their own "fields" but knowing, and indeed able to understand, less and less about the specialties of others. As for society as a whole, which in the past has been the chief preoccupation of the great social thinkers, since it transcends all the specialties, it simply disappears from the purview of social science. It is taken for granted and ignored.

And yet the dictum of Hegel which we have chosen as an epigraph for this book retains its undiminished validity: "The truth is the whole." To be sure, there are also an infinitude of small truths which American social scientists have been diligent, and often successful, in pursuing. Having borrowed liberally from their findings, as the reader will discover, we would be the last to belittle them. But just as the whole is always more than the sum of the parts, so the amassing of small truths about the various parts and aspects of society can never yield the big truths about the social order itself—how it got to be what it is, what it does to those who live under it, and the directions in which it is moving. These big truths must be pursued in their own right and for their own sake. And here bourgeois social science has abdicated all responsibility.

2

The same cannot be said of Marxian social science. Its focus is on the social order as a whole, not on the separate parts; and it embodies a methodology and a theory, or perhaps more accurately a number of theories, which go far toward explaining how our society works and where it is going. But here too there are grounds for dissatisfaction. Important works of Marxian social science have been rare in recent years. Marxists have too often been content to repeat familiar formulations, as though nothing really new had happened since the days of Marx and Engels—or of Lenin at the latest. As a result Marxists have failed to explain important developments, or sometimes even to recognize their existence. The Great Depression of the 1930's accorded admirably with Marxian theory, and its occurrence of course greatly strengthened the belief that similar catastrophic economic breakdowns were inevitable in the future. And yet, much to the surprise of many Marxists, two decades have passed since the end of the Second World War without the recurrence of severe depression. Nor have Marxists contributed significantly to our understanding of some of the major characteristics of the "affluent society"—particularly its colossal capacity to generate private and public waste and the profound economic, political, and cultural consequences which flow from this feature of the system.

The stagnation of Marxian social science, its lagging vitality and fruitfulness, cannot be explained by any simple hypothesis. Both objective and subjective causes are involved, and to disentangle them and give each its proper weight would be a difficult task. But there is one important factor which we believe can be identified and isolated and hence (at least in principle) remedied: the Marxian analysis of capitalism still rests in the final analysis on the assumption of a competitive economy.

Those, whether Marxists or not, who are familiar with the theoretical works of Lenin may find this statement surprising. For it was Lenin who wrote: "If it were necessary to give the briefest definition of imperialism we should have to say that imperialism is the monopoly stage of capitalism."[1] And there is no doubt that Lenin, in analyzing the domestic and international politics of the period which culminated in the First World War, gave full weight to the predominance of monopoly in the advanced capitalist countries. This was indeed a decisive advance in Marxian theory and goes far to account for the tremendous power and undiminished relevance of Marxism in its Leninist—and Maoist—forms. And yet it remains true that neither Lenin nor any of his followers attempted to explore the consequences of the predominance of monopoly for the working principles and "laws of motion" of the underlying capitalist economy. There Marx's *Capital* continued to reign supreme.

Not that Marx was unaware of the existence of monopoly in the British economy of his day—the real historical system from which he distilled his theoretical model. But like the classical economists before him, he treated monopolies not as essential elements of capitalism but rather as remnants of the feudal and mercantilist past which had to be abstracted from in order to attain the clearest possible view of the basic structure and tendencies of capitalism. It is true that, unlike the classicists, Marx fully recognized the powerful trend toward the concentration and centralization of capital inherent in a competitive economy: his vision of the future of capitalism certainly included new and purely capitalist forms of monopoly. But he never attempted to investigate what would at the time have been a hypothetical system characterized by the prevalence of

[1] *Imperialism: The Highest Stage of Capitalism*, Chapter 7.

large scale enterprise and monopoly. Partly the explanation is
no doubt that the empirical material on which such an investigation would have had to be based was too scanty to permit
reliable generalization. But perhaps even more important, Marx
anticipated the overthrow of capitalism long before the unfold-
ing of all its potentialities, well within the system's competitive
phase.

Engels, in some of his own writings after Marx's death and in
editorial additions to the second and third volumes of *Capital*
which he prepared for the printer, commented on the rapid
growth of monopolies during the 1880's and 1890's, but he did
not try to incorporate monopoly into the body of Marxian
economic theory. The first to do this was Rudolf Hilferding in
his important work, *Das Finanzkapital*, published in 1910. But
for all his emphasis on monopoly, Hilferding did not treat it as
a qualitatively new element in the capitalist economy; rather
he saw it as effecting essentially quantitative modifications of
the basic Marxian laws of capitalism. As we have already
noted, Lenin, who was strongly influenced by Hilferding's
analysis of the origins and diffusion of monopoly, based his
theory of imperialism squarely on the predominance of monopoly in the developed capitalist countries. But as also noted,
neither he nor his followers pursued the matter into the fun-
damentals of Marxian economic theory. There, paradoxically
enough, in what might have been thought the area most immediately involved, the growth of monopoly made the least
impression.

We believe that the time has come to remedy this situation
and to do so in an explicit and indeed radical fashion.[2] If we

[2] In our own previous writings on capitalism, both of us have attempted to take account of the impact of monopoly on the functioning of
the capitalist economy. See, for example, Paul M. Sweezy, *The Theory of
Capitalist Development*, New York, 1942, especially Chapters 14 and 15;
and Paul A. Baran, *The Political Economy of Growth*, New York, 1957,
Chapters 3 and 4. In this sense the present book is a direct continuation
of our earlier work. It should also be interpreted as reflecting our dissatisfaction with that earlier work.

are to follow the example set by Marx and make full use of his powerful analytical method, we cannot be content with patching up and amending the competitive model which underlies his economic theory. We must recognize that competition, which was the predominant form of market relations in nineteenth-century Britain, has ceased to occupy that position, not only in Britain but everywhere else in the capitalist world. Today the typical economic unit in the capitalist world is not the small firm producing a negligible fraction of a homogeneous output for an anonymous market but a large-scale enterprise producing a significant share of the output of an industry, or even several industries, and able to control its prices, the volume of its production, and the types and amounts of its investments. The typical economic unit, in other words, has the attributes which were once thought to be possessed only by monopolies. It is therefore impermissible to ignore monopoly in constructing our model of the economy and to go on treating competition as the general case. In an attempt to understand capitalism in its monopoly stage, we cannot abstract from monopoly or introduce it as a mere modifying factor; we must put it at the very center of the analytical effort.[3]

Now Marx derived his theoretical model of the competitive capitalist system from study of Britain, by far the richest and most developed capitalist country of his day. This was necessary and unavoidable.[4] And on the same principle a theoretical

[3] Throughout this book, except where the context clearly indicates otherwise, we use the term "monopoly" to include not only the case of a single seller of a commodity for which there are no substitutes, but also the much more common case of "oligopoly," i.e., a few sellers dominating the markets for products which are more or less satisfactory substitutes for one another.

[4] In retrospect one cannot help regretting that Marx did not strongly emphasize from the outset that the developed capitalism of Britain (and of a handful of other countries of Europe and North America) had as its counterpart the exploitation and consequent underdevelopment of much of the rest of the world. He was fully aware of this relationship, as witness the following statement: "A new and international division of labor, a division suited to the requirements of the chief centers of modern

model of the monopoly capitalist system must be based on study of the United States, which is today as far ahead of other countries in terms of capitalist development as Britain was in the nineteenth century.

3

The purpose of this book is to begin the process of systematically analyzing monopoly capitalism on the basis of the experience of the most developed monopoly capitalist society. This statement, however, needs to be clarified; for in science, as in art, a beginning can be of two kinds: a sketch of the overall conception, to be elaborated and filled in later, or the actual commencement of the final work. Our effort is in the nature of a sketch, a fact we have sought to underline by labeling it an "essay." We hope that our success or failure will be judged accordingly—not by errors or shortcomings of detail in fact or reasoning (though naturally we want such errors and shortcomings to be pointed out and criticized with all necessary severity), but by the extent to which we have effectively focused attention on the need to study monopoly capitalism as

---

industry, springs up and converts one part of the globe into a chiefly agricultural field of production for supplying the other part which remains a chiefly industrial field." (*Capital*, Volume 1, Part 4, Chapter 13, Section 7.) Furthermore, Marx's treatment of primary accumulation stressed the crucial part played by loot from the colonies in the emergence of full-fledged capitalism in Europe. However, we can now see that Marx's omission to extend his theoretical model to include both the developed and the underdeveloped segments of the capitalist world—an omission which he might well have repaired if he had lived to finish his work—has had the unfortunate effect of focusing attention too exclusively on the developed capitalist countries. It is only in recent years that the decisive importance of the dialectical interrelation of development and underdevelopment has begun to be fully appreciated.

(All our references to the first volume of *Capital* cite chapters according to the numbering of the original German edition. The Kerr edition of the English translation converts two sections of Chapter 4 into independent chapters and turns the last two chapters in the volume into a separate part comprising eight chapters. There is hence no method of citation which is valid for all editions.)

such, and have pointed to its crucial problems and the ways in which they may be most fruitfully tackled.

Our essay-sketch makes no pretense to comprehensiveness. It is organized around and attains its essential unity from one central theme: the generation and absorption of the surplus under conditions of monopoly capitalism.[5]

We believe that this is the most useful and enlightening way to analyze the purely economic functioning of the system. But, no less important, we also believe that the modes of utilization of surplus constitute the indispensable mechanism linking the economic foundation of society with what Marxists call its political, cultural, and ideological superstructure. In some societies this mechanism is relatively simple and its effects easily accessible to analysis. In a true feudal society, for example, the surplus is forcibly extracted by feudal lords from the labor of serfs and directly consumed by the lords and their retainers without significant mediation of traders and other types of middlemen. Under these circumstances, the determinants of the size of the surplus, the way it is used, and the relation between these matters and the politics and culture of the society are readily understandable. In other societies the connecting mechanism between economic and noneconomic phenomena is vastly more complicated and may come to play an important role in the functioning of both the foundation and the superstructure. We believe that monopoly capitalism is a society of the latter type and that any attempt to understand it which omits or slights the modes of utilization of surplus is bound to fail.

We do not claim that directing attention to the generation and absorption of surplus gives a complete picture of this or any other society. And we are particularly conscious of the fact that this approach, as we have used it, has resulted in almost total neglect of a subject which occupies a central place in Marx's study of capitalism: the labor process. We stress the

[5] For a discussion of the concept of the economic surplus, see Paul A. Baran, *The Political Economy of Growth*, Chapter 2.

crucial role of technological change in the development of monopoly capitalism but make no attempt to inquire systematically into the consequences which the particular kinds of technological change characteristic of the monopoly capitalist period have had for the nature of work, the composition (and differentiation) of the working class, the psychology of workers, the forms of working-class organization and struggle, and so on. These are all obviously important subjects which would have to be dealt with in any comprehensive study of monopoly capitalism.

Our neglect of the labor process does not, however, mean that this book is not concerned with the class struggle. For a number of reasons, some of which are analyzed in Chapter 7, the class struggle in our time has been thoroughly internationalized. The revolutionary initiative against capitalism, which in Marx's day belonged to the proletariat in the advanced countries, has passed into the hands of the impoverished masses in the underdeveloped countries who are struggling to free themselves from imperialist domination and exploitation. It is the exigencies of this international class struggle which, as we attempt to show, play an increasingly decisive part in determining the utilization of the surplus, and therewith the whole character of the society, in the leading imperialist power. We also deal in Chapter 9 with the racial problem in the United States, which is one of the critical links between the international class struggle and the internal balance of social forces within the United States.

4

The economic surplus, in the briefest possible definition, is the difference between what a society produces and the costs of producing it. The size of the surplus is an index of productivity and wealth, of how much freedom a society has to accomplish whatever goals it may set for itself. The composition of the surplus shows how it uses that freedom: how much it invests in expanding its productive capacity, how much it consumes in various forms, how much it wastes and in what ways. It would obviously be highly desirable to have a full statistical record of the development of each country's surplus over as long a period as possible. Unfortunately, to the best of our knowledge, no such record exists for any country, even for a short period of time. There are various reasons for this, of which perhaps the most obvious are lack of familiarity with the surplus concept and the absence of reliable statistics. But even where, as in the United States, a reasonably large body of statistical material does exist, it is very difficult to arrive at accurate estimates of the magnitude of the surplus and its various components.

To attempt a full explanation of these difficulties would be to anticipate. Suffice it to say at this point that in a highly developed monopoly capitalist society, the surplus assumes many forms and disguises.[6] Part of the problem is to identify the most important of these theoretically, and the rest is to extract a reasonable estimate of their magnitudes from statistics which have been set up and prepared for entirely different purposes. In this book we have concentrated our efforts on the theoretical task, introducing quantitative data mostly for explanatory or illustrative purposes. But it also seemed desirable to present systematic estimates of the surplus and its major components. Having a poor opinion of our own knowledge of statistical sources and skill at avoiding statistical pitfalls, we asked our friend Joseph D. Phillips, for whose knowledge and ability in these respects we have the highest regard, to prepare these

[6] It is for this reason that we prefer the concept "surplus" to the traditional Marxian "surplus value," since the latter is probably identified in the minds of most people familiar with Marxian economic theory as equal to the sum of profits + interest + rent. It is true that Marx demonstrates—in scattered passages of *Capital* and *Theories of Surplus Value*—that surplus value also comprises other items such as the revenues of state and church, the expenses of transforming commodities into money, and the wages of unproductive workers. In general, however, he treated these as secondary factors and excluded them from his basic theoretical schema. It is our contention that under monopoly capitalism this procedure is no longer justified, and we hope that a change in terminology will help to effect the needed shift in theoretical position.

estimates. After reading a draft of the relevant chapters and giving thought to the problem of sources, he concluded that the task was a feasible one and accepted our invitation. His estimates of the United States surplus and its major components for the period 1929-1963 are presented in the Appendix beginning on p. 369. Though subject to qualifications and *caveats*, as Phillips makes clear, they are, we feel confident, reliable as indicators of the orders of magnitude involved.

Some of the statistical categories used are intelligible only in the light of the theory yet to be developed. But it is relevant to cite two of Phillips's major findings since they lend support to the methodology of this work.

First, the magnitude of the surplus in the United States amounted to 46.9 percent of Gross National Product in 1929. This figure declined in the early years of the Great Depression and of course rose sharply during the Second World War. Apart from these interludes, the trend has been steadily upward, reaching 56.1 percent in 1963. The importance of the surplus as a subject of study is here illustrated in a striking way.

Second, the portion of the surplus which is usually identified with surplus value (profits + interest + rent = Phillips's "property income") declined sharply in the same period. In 1929 property income was 57.5 percent of total surplus, and in 1963 it was only 31.9 percent. Clearly, not only the forces determining the total amount of surplus need to be analyzed but also those governing its differentiation and the varying rates of growth of the components.

5

Marx, analyzing the most advanced capitalism of his day, was emphatic in telling those living in less developed societies, "De te fabula narratur"—of you the story is told. And again: "The country that is more developed industrially only shows to the less developed the image of its own future."[7] Should the

[7] Both quotations are from the Preface to the first edition of Volume 1 of *Capital*.

analyst of American monopoly capitalism today address the same message to the less developed parts of the capitalist world?

As we look back on the history of the last hundred years, we can see that what Marx said to the less developed countries actually applied to only a few of them—those which never fell under, or had escaped from, the domination of more developed countries and therefore could emulate the latter rather than being exploited by them and hence having their development stunted and distorted to suit the needs of the dominant economy.[8] Certainly a similar limitation applies today: only a few countries—most of Western Europe (including Britain), Japan, Canada, Australia, New Zealand, possibly South Africa—can conceivably follow in the footsteps of the United States. In the rest of the capitalist world scores of colonies, neo-colonies, and semi-colonies are doomed to remain in their degraded condition of underdevelopment and misery. For them the only road forward leads straight out of the capitalist system.[9]

Our question, then, boils down to the relevance of American experience for perhaps a dozen or so countries which are capitalistically developed but less so than the United States. Do the

[8] Marx probably intended his message only for this group of independent and actually developing capitalist countries. "De te fabula narratur" was specifically addressed to Germans who might think their country could escape the fate of Britain; and when he spoke of industrially less developed countries seeing the image of their future in the more developed, he probably had in mind countries which were developed by the standards of the time, only less so than Britain. It seems doubtful that he intended to include among the industrially less developed countries the underdeveloped colonial and semi-colonial dependencies of the advanced capitalist powers.

[9] This of course is not the view of bourgeois social science which ever since the Second World War has been busily propagating recipes for the capitalist development of underdeveloped countries. For a critique of much of this literature and a demonstration of the virtual impossibility of capitalist development of underdeveloped countries in the present world context, see Paul A. Baran, *The Political Economy of Growth,* Chapters 6 and 7. Everything that has happened in the decade since that book was written has confirmed the accuracy and relevance of the arguments advanced on this crucially important question.

theoretical considerations set forth in this book apply to these "second-echelon" capitalist countries as well? Can these countries see here at least the outlines of the image of their own future? Or have they entered, as we are often told, a stage of "neo-capitalism" characterized by the liquidation of old imperialist ties, the adoption of rational planning by the state in close partnership with Big Business and organized labor, and the transcendence of the contradictions and conflicts which have always beset capitalist development in the past and are still so much in evidence, even if the forms are not always the familiar ones, in the United States?

We cannot claim to answer these questions out of any detailed study of the recent history of the countries in question. But we can express our own strongly held opinion that the burden of proof rests not on those of us who expect capitalist countries in comparable stages of economic development to have similar experiences, but on the prophets of a new dispensation. In our lifetime the United States has been through two periods during which the problems of capitalism were widely believed, and proclaimed to the whole world on the highest authority, to be on the way to final solution—the New Era of the 1920's and the American Celebration of the 1950's. The fact that both turned out to be short-lived illusions should make people in other countries very cautious about accepting similar assurances today.

2

THE GIANT CORPORATION

Scientific understanding proceeds by way of constructing and analyzing "models" of the segments or aspects of reality under study. The purpose of these models is not to give a mirror image of reality, not to include all its elements in their exact sizes and proportions, but rather to single out and make available for intensive investigation those elements which are decisive. We abstract from nonessentials, we blot out the unimportant to get an unobstructed view of the important, we magnify in order to improve the range and accuracy of our observation. A model is, and must be, unrealistic in the sense in which the word is most commonly used. Nevertheless, and in a sense paradoxically, if it is a good model it provides the key to understanding reality.

There are no rules for model-building, and, as the literature of economics attests, it is much easier to build a bad one than a good one—a bad model being one which abstracts from essentials and therefore leads to neither insight nor understanding.[1] Nor are there any simple *a priori* tests by which a model can be judged. The proof of the pudding is in the eating. We can only start with certain hypotheses and ideas; we can use them to separate the unimportant from the important; out of the residue of the important we can shape what look like the parts and elements of a system; we can assemble the parts and elements,

[1] As Duesenberry rightly says: "Knowing how to simplify one's description of reality without neglecting anything essential is the most important part of the economist's art." James S. Duesenberry, *Business Cycles and Economic Growth*, New York, 1958, pp. 14-15.

refining and polishing as we proceed. When we finally get our model, there is one test to which we must subject it: does it help to make sense of the real world? Or, to put the matter in another way, does it help us to see connections to which we were previously blind, to relate effects to causes, to replace the arbitrary and the accidental by the regular and the necessary? In a word, does it help us to understand the world and act in it intelligently and effectively?

These are the general ideas and aims by which we have been guided in constructing a model of the monopoly capitalist economy. It is intended to put at the center of the stage and play the spotlight on those features which, despite all diversity and underneath whatever overlay of detail, make the system what it is. And in order to accomplish this, we start, for reasons which have been indicated in the preceding chapter, with an analysis of the typical unit of Big Business, the modern giant corporation.

Once again: we are not interested in realism of a photographic kind. There undoubtedly are corporations which correspond closely to the "ideal type"—to use Max Weber's expression—with which we shall be concerned, but the analysis would lose none of its relevance even if there were not. The point is that the decisive units of the economy are unmistakably moving toward a definite, recognizable pattern, and this pattern itself is much more important than any of the concrete approximations to it. A model of which the major component parts are corporations of the ideal type will display with sharpness and clarity what may appear in everyday economic life in a disguised form, difficult to recognize and easy to misinterpret.

2

The corporate paradigm on which we wish to focus attention has a number of characteristic features, of which we may single out the following:

(1) Control rests in the hands of management, that is to say,

the board of directors plus the chief executive officers. Outside
interests are often (but not always) represented on the board
to facilitate the harmonization of the interests and policies of
the corporation with those of customers, suppliers, bankers,
etc.; but real power is held by the insiders, those who devote
full time to the corporation and whose interests and careers are
tied to its fortunes.

(2) Management is a self-perpetuating group. Responsibility to the body of stockholders is for all practical purposes a
dead letter. Each generation of managers recruits its own suc-
cessors and trains, grooms, and promotes them according to its
own standards and values. The corporate career recognizes two
characteristic forms of advance: rising from lower to higher
positions within a given company, and moving from a smaller
company to a larger one. The acme of success is the presidency
or board chairmanship of one of the biggest corporations.

(3) Each corporation aims at and normally achieves financial independence through the internal generation of funds
which remain at the disposal of management. The corporation
may still, as a matter of policy, borrow from or through financial institutions, but it is not normally forced to do so and
hence is able to avoid the kind of subjection to financial control
which was so common in the world of Big Business fifty years
ago.

Before we investigate the behavior of giant corporations of
this type, a few words of explanation and clarification may be
useful.

In the first place, there is no implication in our description of
the corporate paradigm that great wealth, or family connections, or large personal or family stockholdings are unimportant in the recruiting and promotion of management personnel
—that, for example, the chances of a David Rockefeller's getting a job at the Chase Manhattan Bank and rising to the top
position are the same as those of anyone else with similar personal and intellectual attributes. On the contrary, wealth and
connections are of the utmost importance, and it may indeed be

taken for granted that they are normally decisive. What we are implying is something quite different: that stock ownership, wealth, connections, etc., do not as a rule enable a man to control or exercise great influence on a giant corporation from the outside. They are rather tickets of admission to the inside, where real corporate power is wielded. Mills put the essential point in a nutshell:

> Not great fortunes, but great corporations are the important units of wealth, to which individuals of property are variously attached. The corporation is the source of, and the basis of the continued power and privilege of wealth. All the men and the families of great wealth are now identified with large corporations in which their property is seated.[2]

What needs to be emphasized is that the location of power inside rather than outside the typical giant corporation renders obsolete the conception of the "interest group" as a fundamental unit in the structure of capitalist society. In traditional usage, an interest group is a number of corporations under common control, the locus of power being normally an investment or commercial bank or a great family fortune.[3] Thus a Morgan company was one under the control of the investment banking firm of J. P. Morgan & Company, a Rockefeller company one under the control of the Rockefeller family, and so on. The members of an interest group would naturally coordinate their policies; and in the case of conflicts, the interests of the controlling power (or of the whole group as interpreted by the controlling power) would prevail.

A whole series of developments have loosened or broken the ties that formerly bound the great interest groups together. The power of the investment banker was based on the urgent need of the early corporate giants, at the time of foundation

[2] C. Wright Mills, *The Power Elite*, New York, 1956, p. 116.

[3] An analysis of interest groups in the American economy as of the mid-1930's will be found in Appendix 13 to Part 1 of the National Resources Committee's well-known report *The Structure of the American Economy*, Washington, 1939 (reprinted in Paul M. Sweezy, *The Present as History*, New York, 1953, Chapter 12).

and in the first stages of growth, for outside financing. Later
this need declined in importance or disappeared altogether as
the giants, reaping a rich harvest of monopoly profits, found
themselves increasingly able to take care of their financial
needs from internally generated funds. At the same time, the
domineering founders of family fortunes were dying off, leaving their stockholdings to numerous heirs, foundations, chari-
ties, trust funds, and the like, so that the ownership unit which
once exercised absolute control over many enterprises became
increasingly amorphous and leaderless. Thus the larger corporations gradually won more and more independence from both
bankers and dominant stockholders, and their policies accordingly were geared to an ever greater extent each to its own
interests rather than being subordinated to the interests of a
group.

We are not of course maintaining that interest groups have
disappeared or are no longer of any importance in the United
States economy. We do hold that they are of rapidly diminishing importance and that an appropriate model of the economy
no longer needs to take account of them. It is not the purpose
of the present work to support this view with empirical evidence, despite its ready availability. But since belief in the
crucial importance of interest groups is a deeply rooted tenet
of left-wing thought, it seems wise to cite one specific example
of the dissolution process as it has affected what would once
have been generally admitted to be one of the two most powerful interest groups, the Rockefeller group.

The core of the Rockefeller interest group was the original
Standard Oil Company which, after its break-up in 1911 under
the Sherman Antitrust Law, became a number of separate
companies operating in different regions of the country. There
is ample evidence that these companies remained in one interest group under firm Rockefeller control through the 1920's.
They respected each other's marketing areas and generally
worked together against the rapidly rising independents. An
attempt by the President of Standard of Indiana in 1929 to

wrest control of his company from the Rockefeller family via a proxy contest for stockholder support was decisively defeated and the would-be rebel was unceremoniously fired.

In the years after 1929, great changes came to the oil industry: the international cartel was formed; the rich Middle Eastern fields were opened up; domestically, the depression-born prorationing system brought what amounted to government enforcement of monopoly prices; the tripling of the number of motor vehicles in three decades and the widespread substitution of fuel oil for coal sent demand and production skyrocketing. How did the old Rockefeller companies react to these developments? Did they continue to act as a team, all doing their best to promote the interests of the group as a whole, as the interest-group theory would lead us to expect? Or did each seek to exploit the new opportunities in its own interest?

The record leaves little doubt about the answer. California Standard, getting into Middle Eastern production in a big way but without adequate marketing outlets, teamed up internationally with Texaco rather than with one of the "brother" companies, and invaded the New England market, traditional stronghold of Jersey and Socony, even at the cost of depressing gasoline prices. The others were not long in following California's example, and by now the various Standard companies have completely broken away from the 1911 marketing areas and are busily stealing markets from each other as well as from the non-Standard companies.

Meanwhile Indiana Standard which in the early days, no doubt at Rockefeller behest, had excluded itself from the foreign field began to hunger for the fantastic profits which the international cartel companies were making on their Middle Eastern operations. Indiana therefore joined the Italians and Japanese, as well as certain smaller American independents, in scabbing on the cartel by offering Iran and other Middle Eastern producers a 25-75 profit split rather than the standard 50-50.

It is possible that the old Standard companies may still be

subject to Rockefeller influence, perhaps even control: publicly available information is not conclusive one way or the other. But if they are, one can only infer that the Rockefellers have decided that the best way to promote their interests is to allow, or perhaps encourage, each of the companies to promote its interests. In these circumstances the issue of Rockefeller control becomes irrelevant to the behavior of the companies or the *modus operandi* of the system of which they form constituent parts. This is the point which we wish to take into account in constructing our model: we abstract from whatever elements of outside control may still exist in the world of giant corporations because they are in no sense essential to the way it works.

This does not of course mean that each giant corporation operates in isolation, that there are no alliances and alignments, no agreements and groupings. On the contrary, these forms of action—like their opposites, competition and struggle —are of the very essence of monopoly capitalism. All that we are asserting is that the relevant line-ups are determined not by ties to outside control centers but by the rational calculations of inside managements. In the oil industry, for example, Standard companies are as ready and willing to ally themselves with or fight against non-Standard companies as with or against other Standard companies. It all depends on where the maximum profit lies.

But we are getting ahead of our story.

3

What pattern of behavior can we expect from huge, management-controlled, financially independent corporations?

Formal economic theory has largely ignored this question, continuing to operate with the assumption of the profit-maximizing individual entrepreneur who has occupied the central role in theories of the capitalist system since well before the time of Adam Smith. Retaining this assumption amounts in effect to making another: that in all respects that matter to the functioning of the system the corporation acts like an individual entrepreneur.

If one stops to think about it, this seems unlikely on the face of it. Furthermore, while economic theorists have largely ignored the corporation, other social scientists have devoted much time and energy to its study. So far as we know, none of them has ever supported the proposition that the modern corporation is merely an enlarged version of the classical entrepreneur. On the other hand, there is a voluminous literature dating back to the turn of the century and reaching its culmination in the famous work of Berle and Means which argues most emphatically that the modern corporation represents a qualitative break with the older form of individual enterprise and that radically different types of behavior are to be expected from it. According to Berle and Means:

> It is conceivable—indeed it seems almost inevitable if the corporate system is to survive—that the "control" of the great corporations should develop into a purely neutral technocracy, balancing a variety of claims by various groups in the community and assigning to each a portion of the income stream on the basis of public policy rather than private cupidity.[4]

What Berle and Means described as "conceivable" a quarter of a century ago is taken for granted as an accomplished fact by many present-day observers of the business scene. Thus Carl Kaysen, in a paper delivered at the 1956 annual meeting of the American Economic Association, speaks of "the wide-ranging scope of responsibility assumed by management" as one of the "characteristic features of behavior" of the modern corporation, and proceeds as follows:

> No longer the agent of proprietorship seeking to maximize return on investment, management sees itself as responsible to stockholders, employees, customers, the general public, and, perhaps most important, the firm itself as an institution. . . . From one point of view, this behavior can be termed responsible: there is no display of

[4] *The Modern Corporation and Private Property,* New York, 1932, p. 356.

greed or graspingness; there is no attempt to push off onto workers or the community at large part of the social costs of the enterprise. The modern corporation is a soulful corporation.[5]

According to this view, which is certainly very widespread nowadays, the maximization of profits has ceased to be the guiding principle of business enterprise. Corporate managements, being self-appointed and responsible to no outside group, are free to choose their aims and in the typical case are assumed to subordinate the old-fashioned hunt for profits to a variety of other, quantitatively less precise but qualitatively more worthy, objectives.

The implications of this doctrine of the "soulful corporation" are far-reaching. The truth is that if it is accepted, the whole corpus of traditional economic theory must be abandoned and the time-honored justification of the existing social order in terms of economic efficiency, justice, etc., simply falls to the ground. This has been most effectively pointed out by Edward S. Mason:

> But if profit maximization is not the directing agent, how are resources allocated to their most productive uses, what relation have prices to relative scarcities, and how do factors get remunerated in accordance with their contribution to output? Assume an economy composed of a few hundred large corporations, each enjoying substantial market power and all directed by managements with a "conscience." Each management wants to do the best it can for society consistent, of course, with doing the best it can for labor, customers, suppliers, and owners. How do prices get determined in such an economy? How are factors remunerated, and what relation is there between remuneration and performance? What is the mechanism, if any, that assures effective resource use, and how can corporate man-

[5] Carl Kaysen, "The Social Significance of the Modern Corporation," *American Economic Review*, May 1957, pp. 313-314. See also M. J. Rathbone, President of Standard Oil of New Jersey, in the *Saturday Review*, April 16, 1960: "Managements of large companies must harmonize a wide span of obligations: to investors, customers, suppliers, employees, communities and the national interest. Thus the large organization may actually have a narrower range for its decision-making than the small, closely held corporation which is not so much in the public eye and hence not so exposed to criticism."

agements "do right by" labor, suppliers, customers, and owners while simultaneously serving the public interests?[6]

Economists have made no attempt to answer these questions, and indeed it is doubtful whether it even makes sense to ask them in relation to an economy such as Mason postulates, that is to say, one made up of or dominated by a few hundred soulful corporations. Prices and incomes would be indeterminate, and there would be no theoretically definable tendencies toward equilibrium. To be sure, economic life in such a society might settle down into routines and patterns which could be analyzed by historians, sociologists, and statisticians, but it seems reasonably clear that today's economic theorists would be out of a job.

One school of thought, associated especially with the name of Herbert A. Simon of Carnegie Institute of Technology, seems already to have drawn these conclusions and is attempting to study the big corporation and its implications by means of what Simon calls "organization theory." According to this theory, corporations do not try to maximize anything but merely to achieve "satisfactory" results. Thus, to the maximizing behavior which was assumed to characterize the old-fashioned entrepreneur, Simon contrasts what he calls the "satisficing" behavior of modern corporate managements. At the annual meetings of the American Economic Association in 1956, a paper by Simon expounding this view was answered by James Earley of the University of Wisconsin who had been engaged for a number of years on a study of the management policies of a sample of large and successful American corporations. Summing up a wealth of carefully collected and analyzed empirical material, Earley had little difficulty in disposing of Simon's theory; what is more significant from our point of view is that he went on to give a most useful and illuminating description of how modern corporate managements really be-

[6] Edward S. Mason, "The Apologetics of 'Managerialism,'" *The Journal of Business*, January 1958, p. 7.

24 MONOPOLY CAPITAL

have. This statement is so good that it seems worthwhile to
rescue large parts of it from the untitled obscurity of the Economic Association's *Papers and Proceedings*. After noting some
points of agreement and others of minor disagreement with
Simon, Earley proceeds as follows:

> I have more serious reservations concerning what appears to be
> the major economic theorem Simon arrives at; namely, that the busi-
> ness enterprise looks for merely satisfactory solutions of its problems
> and specifically seeks merely satisfactory profits. That his approach
> has led so directly to this conclusion is one of the facts that makes
> me especially doubt that it is a satisfactory one. Whatever may be
> true of individuals or of other types of organization, I cannot square
> Simon's "satisficing" behavior with the behavior of the large-scale
> American business firm. I agree that the conventional notion of
> profit maximization and of general "optimization" must be modified.
> I contend this is carrying the change much too far. Let me briefly
> catalogue the main types of evidence that lead me to reject the
> "satisficing" postulate.
> (1) As a part of my research, I have made a study of recent
> management literature, both general and specialized, one of my
> hypotheses in doing so being that this literature will reveal the
> frames of reference and mores of advanced business management. A
> striking characteristic of this literature (except where public rela-
> tions is an evident objective) is its systematic focus on cost reduc-
> tion, the expansion of revenue, and the increase of profits. There is,
> of course, much reference to standards and to the need of remedy-
> ing unsatisfactory situations. The drive is always toward the better
> and frequently the best, not just the good. Like Samuel Gompers'
> ideal union leader, the exemplary man of management seems to
> have "More!" for at least one of his mottoes.
> (2) Secondly, my questionnaire studies of the practices and poli-
> cies of leading so-called "excellently managed" companies lead
> me toward generally similar conclusions. I have published the major
> results of the first of these studies and will not review them here.[7]
> (3) The third fact that makes me doubt Simon's postulate as
> applied to the firm is the rapidly growing use of economists, market
> analysts, other types of specialists, and management consultants by

[7] The author's reference here is to James S. Earley, "Marginal Policies
of 'Excellently Managed' Companies," *The American Economic Review*,
March 1956.

our larger businesses. The main function of most of these people is
to help the firm reduce costs, find superior methods, choose the most
profitable alternatives, and uncover new profit opportunities. As
these sophisticated gentlemen gain in influence in business councils
—and I confidently believe they will—profit oriented rationality is
likely to be more and more representative of business behavior.

(4) Most of all I am impressed by the rapid development of
analytical and managerial techniques that both stimulate and assist
the business firms to find the least costly ways of doing things and
the most profitable things to do. Operations research and mathematical programming are only the more fancy of this growing
genus. There are also greatly improved forms of accounting and
budgeting, improved methods of market analysis, refinements in
business forecasting, and interesting types of nonmathematical programming. The unifying character of these new techniques is that
they seek to apply the principles of rational problem-solving to
business planning and decision making.

Let me conclude by briefly sketching the notion of business behavior that seems to be emerging from my own studies. It falls
somewhere between the old postulate of profit maximization and
Simon's "satisfactory profit." It fully recognizes the limited informational and computational resources of the firm. It also incorporates
his suggested concept of the "aspiration level" and a modified principle of "viability." My behavioral postulate could best be briefly
described as "a systematic temporal search for highest practicable
profits."

The theory underlying it runs, very briefly, as follows:

The major goals of modern large-scale business are high managerial incomes, good profits, a strong competitive position, and
growth. Modern management does not view these goals as seriously
inconsistent but rather, indeed, as necessary, one to the other. Competitive strength and even survival, management believes, require
large innovative and substantial growth expenditures in the rapidly
changing technical and market conditions of the present day. Since
growth by merger is hazardous and frequently impossible, large and
more or less continuous capital expenditures are necessary. For well-
recognized reasons, management wishes to minimize outside financing, so the funds for most of these expenditures must be internally
generated. This requires high and growing profits above dividend
levels. So, too, do high managerial rewards. High and rising profits
are hence an instrument as well as a direct goal of great importance.

With these goals and needs in view, advanced management plans for profit through time, using coordinated programs stretching as far ahead as practicable. The profit targets incorporated in these programs are sufficient to finance not only good dividends but also desired innovative and growth expenditures. The programs are revised frequently, as experience accrues and new opportunities are discovered.

The tendency toward profit maximization (i.e., highest practicable profit) appears in this system along several dimensions. In the process of revising and reformulating programs, more expensive and less profitable activities are pruned or dropped and cheaper or more profitable ones are added. Less costly processes and the more profitable product and market sectors serve as the standards toward which others are expected to converge or be replaced. By steadily selecting those methods and sectors that promise better returns, these standards are kept high and, if possible, rising. Finally, the overall profit and growth targets of the enterprise as a whole are raised through time, unless adversity prevents.

These goals and programs and standards, it is true, represent at any time certain "aspiration levels," and the efforts to satisfy them receive prime attention. But the two major points about them are that (1) they are likely to be hard to reach and (2) they will ordinarily recede (i.e., grow larger) through time. Even in good times the firm's aspiration levels, therefore, are fairly taut, and they are highly elastic upward. On the other hand, there is great resistance to adjusting profit and other standards downward, so that in bad times the business firm tries even harder to make the highest practicable profits.

I readily agree that I have sketched the behavior of what might be called the "exemplary firm" rather than the firm that is quantitatively representative of the present business population. But my main point is that the management techniques and the *expertise* that can validate my notion are developing rapidly, are increasingly being made available to business, and are being rapidly adopted by leading firms. Consequently, I suspect, the exemplary firm will be the representative firm of the future. If so, its behavior will be more rather than less appropriately analyzed by some of our time-honored theoretical notions, such as profit maximization. . . .[8]

Two aspects of this admirable statement call for comment. First, it introduces a healthy corrective to what Earley calls "the conventional notion of profit maximization and general 'optimization.'" This conventional notion has been tied to a

[8] *American Economic Review*, May 1957, pp. 333-335.

more or less explicitly stated assumption that the maximizing entrepreneur has complete knowledge of all alternatives open to him and of the consequences of choosing any combination of them. Given this assumption, he can always select the combination of alternatives which yields an absolute maximum. Further, if it is assumed that his knowledge remains equally complete in the face of changing conditions, it follows logically that he can always make instantaneous and appropriate adjustments to new circumstances. What is involved here is an assumption of omniscience on the part of the entrepreneur, which, far from being a useful abstraction, is of course an absurdity. In practice, to be sure, economists have usually given a more sensible meaning to the maximization principle, but by failing expressly to repudiate the omniscience postulate, by failing to spell out what is and what is not involved in the assumption of profit maximization, they have left themselves vulnerable to attacks of the kind mounted by Simon. It is therefore valuable to have Earley's carefully considered statement. By stressing the "limited informational and computational resources of the firm," he makes clear that no assumption of complete knowledge is involved, and his entire argument is based on the rejection of any idea of an absolute maximum or optimum. The firm (whether individual entrepreneur or corporation makes no difference) always finds itself in a given historical situation, with limited knowledge of changing conditions. In this context it can never do more than improve its profit position. In practice, the search for "maximum" profits can only be the search for the greatest *increase* in profits which is possible in the given situation, subject of course to the elementary proviso that the exploitation of today's profit opportunities must not ruin tomorrow's. This is all there is to the profit maximization principle, but it also happens to be all that is necessary to validate the "economizing" behavior patterns which have been the very backbone of all serious economic theory for the last two centuries.

The second aspect of Earley's statement which we want to emphasize, and the one most relevant to our present purpose, is the convincing demonstration that the big corporation, if not

more profit-oriented than the individual entrepreneur (he
quite properly leaves this question open), is at any rate better
equipped to pursue a policy of profit maximization. The result
is much the same: the economy of large corporations is more,
not less, dominated by the logic of profit-making than the economy of small entrepreneurs ever was.

It might be thought that this is enough to dispose of the
soulful corporation and at the same time to justify the procedure of those economists who have altogether ignored the rise
of the corporate form of enterprise and continued to reason in
terms of the individual entrepreneur. This is not so, however,
and for two reasons: First, the alleged soulfulness of the corporation relates not only to its attitude toward the acquisition
of profits but also to its attitude toward the utilization of
profits, and there is still much to be said on the latter subject.
Second, there are undoubtedly differences between individual
enterprise and corporate enterprise which have little to do with
the goal of profit maximization but which still are of great
importance for economic theory. But before we take up these
topics it will repay us to probe somewhat more deeply into the
motivational and behavioral patterns of corporate managements.

4

The big corporation came into its own in the second half of
the nineteenth century, first in the fields of finance and railroads, spreading to industry around the turn of the century,
and later invading most other branches of the national economy. In the typical case, the early corporate giants were organized by—or, as a result of merger, failure, or other emergency,
soon fell under the control of—a class of financier-promoters
who have become famous in American history as "robber
barons," "moguls," or "tycoons"—all terms reflecting the popular feeling that the American Big Businessman of that period
resembled the feudal lord in his predatory habits and lack of
concern for the public welfare.

The center of the business world in those days was not the corporation but the tycoon, who typically controlled a collection of corporations in various lines of activity.[9] A very wealthy man, the tycoon nevertheless did not believe in tying up his funds permanently even in corporations under his own control. The corporation's assets for the most part represented "other people's money" which the tycoon managed with a view to his own profit, not theirs. Apart from methods such as stealing, fraud, milking one company for the benefit of another, etc.—all celebrated in the muckraking literature of the day— his primary interest lay in capital gains made through buying securities cheap and selling them dear, an objective which could be promoted at times by building up a company and at others by wrecking it. To quote Veblen, who may be regarded as the classical theorist of this kind of business enterprise:

With a fuller development of the modern closeknit and comprehensive industrial system, the point of chief attention for the business man has shifted from the old-fashioned surveillance and regulation of a given industrial process, with which his livelihood was once bound up, to an alert redistribution of investments from less to more gainful ventures, and to a strategic control of the conjunctures of business through shrewd investments and coalitions with other business men.[10]

The present-day corporation manager is a very different type from the tycoon of fifty years ago. In one respect he represents a return to pre-tycoon days; his chief concern is once again the "surveillance and regulation of a given industrial process with which his livelihood is bound up." On the other hand, in another respect he is the antithesis of classical entrepreneur and tycoon alike: they were both individualists *par excellence*, while he is the leading species of the genus "organization man."

There are many ways to describe the contrast between

[9] The word "tycoon" entered the language around the middle of the nineteenth century as a title which foreigners (incorrectly) applied to the Japanese Shogun.

[10] Thorstein Veblen, *The Theory of Business Enterprise*, New York, 1904, p. 24.

tycoon and modern manager. The former was the parent of the giant corporation, the latter is its child. The tycoon stood outside and above, dominating the corporation. The manager is an insider, dominated by it. The loyalty of the one was to himself and his family (which, in its bourgeois form, is essentially an extension of self); the loyalty of the other is to the organization to which he belongs and through which he expresses himself. To the one the corporation was merely a means to enrichment; to the other the good of the company has become both an economic and an ethical end. The one stole from the corporation, the other steals for it.[11]

All of this has been aptly summed up by a modern manager who is the grandson of one of the most famous entrepreneurs of the past. In a speech before the American Newspaper Publishers' Association on April 28, 1955, Henry Ford II said:

> The modern corporate or joint-venture capitalism has largely replaced tycoon capitalism. The one-man-band owner-manager is fast being replaced by a new class of professional managers, dedicated more to the advancement of the company than to the enrichment of a few owners.

Actually, managers are not professionals in the sense that doctors and lawyers are—there are no recognized standards, training, etc.—but on the main point Mr. Ford is unquestionably right. The tycoon was interested in self-enrichment: he

---

[11] Popular sentiment condones the latter but not the former. This is presumably the reason for the widespread impression, which has by now attained the status of axiomatic truth among those who describe and comment on the American scene, that the businessman of today is a highly moral person by comparison with his predecessor of a half century ago. There seems to be no good reason for accepting this view; indeed, the extent of executive criminality in furtherance of company aims which was revealed by the late E. H. Sutherland in his important but much neglected work *White Collar Crime* (New York, 1949) would seem clearly to point to the opposite conclusion. What undoubtedly has changed is the pattern of executive criminality, though no one, including Sutherland himself, seems to have appreciated the importance of this fact to an understanding of recent American history. See also J. G. Fuller, *The Gentlemen Conspirators* (New York, 1962): this is the story of the famous price-fixing case in the heavy electrical equipment industry.

was an individualist. The modern manager is dedicated to the advancement of the company: he is a "company man."[12]

None of the foregoing is intended to imply that the tycoon has altogether vanished from the American scene. The long inflation of the 1940's and 1950's produced a whole crop of promoters and operators conforming exactly to the sociological type of the tycoon. But nowadays they operate around the periphery and in the interstices of the American economy, and they are looked down upon with a mixture of disdain and contempt by the *real* Big Businessmen of today, the managers of the giant corporations. In this connection we are fortunate to have a record of a direct confrontation of the two types. The latter-day tycoon is Cash McCall, hero of the novel of the same name by Cameron Hawley, himself a Big Businessman turned writer. The corporate manager is Frank Abrams, retired board chairman of Standard Oil Company of New Jersey, in terms of assets America's largest industrial corporation. The confrontation was arranged by *Business Week,* which queried a number of businessmen of varying backgrounds about their reactions to Cash McCall and his methods of operation.[13]

Cash McCall is a man of almost superhuman skill and daring who possesses an infallible Midas touch. He specializes in buy-

[12] Mr. Ford's statement was later borrowed and characteristically embellished by a Big Business public relations man. J. C. McQueen, Manager of Employee and Plant Community Relations at the Evandale Plant of General Electric, at the Tenth Annual Teachers' Institute of the Cincinnati Public Schools, August 29, 1956, made a speech in which he repeated without attribution the above statement of Henry Ford II from "The modern corporate or joint-venture capitalism" through "class of professional managers." The final clause, however, reads as follows: "dedicated to serving the balanced best interests of all contributors to and claimants on the goods and services of the business." (Mimeographed release.) Here we meet the soulful corporation again—and also get a glimpse of its origins in the fertile minds of the public-relations fraternity.

[13] "How Good an Operator Is Cash McCall?" *Business Week,* December 17, 1955. Among those queried, Cash McCall's most enthusiastic supporter was Louis E. Wolfson, perhaps the best publicized of the real-life Cash McCalls of the postwar decade.

ing companies, doctoring them up, and selling them at a big
profit. For this purpose he has a string of high-powered
retainers—lawyers, management consultants, spies, etc. He has
no interest in holding onto or developing any of the properties
which come into his control, and for this reason he is con-
trasted throughout the book with the "company man" (the
term is Hawley's) whose first loyalty is to the company he
works for and who is represented as becoming increasingly the
normal American businessman. Here is the gist of Frank
Abrams's opinion of Cash McCall (the insertions and omissions
are *Business Week's*):

> The individualist seems [in Hawley's book] to be the man of
> ideas who performs miracles in reorganization, and the company
> man the plodder who makes little or no contribution to the larger
> scheme of things. My experience is quite to the contrary. The com-
> pany man, I have found, is the man who likes to serve a good cause
> to the best of his ability, and is content to prosper with [his com-
> pany]. The individualist is quite apt to be a self-seeker . . . he will
> switch allegiance from company to company, and seems mainly
> concerned with personal power and the trappings of wealth.
>
> My business experience has been . . . relatively free of the tax
> manipulations and promotional shenanigans that seem the chief
> concern of the principal characters of this book. Perhaps I have been
> insulated from some of the facts of smaller business life, and if so I
> can now, in retirement, appreciate how fortunate I have been.

This is the voice of the genuine aristocrat, one who is firmly
established in his station in life, secure and confident. He is
proud to identify himself with his company, to share in its
prosperity. He has little use for individualists: they are unreli-
able and their insecurities lead them into the vulgarities of
power-grabbing and conspicuous display. Above all, he is conscious of living in the world of *Big* Business, the rulers of
which, like the feudal nobility of old, have learned to live gra-
ciously, "insulated from the facts of smaller business life."

This last phrase speaks volumes about present-day American
society. Cash McCall is no petty shopkeeper. He owns one of
the largest hotels in Philadelphia and occupies a whole floor of

it; he flies his own private plane and maintains a great country
estate; he spends millions of dollars on the impulse of the
moment. By Hollywood standards, in fact, Cash McCall is the
very model of a Big Businessman. And yet to Frank Abrams—
who may or may not have as much money as Cash McCall is
supposed to have—all this is merely vulgar display and cheap
shenanigans. To the aristocracy of company men, Big Business
is Standard Oil and a few score similar corporate giants which
collectively control the nation's economic destiny—all the rest
is unceremoniously relegated to the limbo of "smaller business." "In the United States today," writes one of the aristo-
crats, a Vice President of the Pittsburgh Plate Glass Company,
"135 corporations own 45 percent of the industrial assets.
These are the companies to watch. Here lies managerial
power."[14] Clearly, the exercise of power is matched by the
consciousness of power.[15]

<h1 style="text-align:center">5</h1>

Big corporations, then, are run by company men. What kind
of people are they? What do they want and why? What position do they hold in the class structure of American society?

[14] Leland Hazard, "What Economists Don't Know About Wages,"
Harvard Business Review, January-February 1957, p. 56.
[15] No attempt can be made here to explore the ramifications and
implications of the transformation of the Big Businessman from tycoon
to company man. Nevertheless, we cannot leave the subject without
noting that it has made its mark on serious literature (*Cash McCall* is to
be rated rather as a tract for the times in novel form). "In the fifty-four
years since Frank Norris created the prototype of the modern capitalist in
The Pit," writes David Dempsey, "the approach of American novelists
toward the world of business has undergone a complete revision. Norris,
and subsequently Dreiser, saw the rise of the corporation as a one-man
affair; their focus was on the individual who dominated business for his
own ends, but whose actions affected society at large. Norris' wheat
speculator Curtis Jadwin, like Dreiser's nineteenth-century capitalist,
Frank Cowperwood, is molded in the classic tradition of the hero who
builds an empire at the cost of his own integrity. Since few American
corporations at present are dominated by a single individual, the novelist
has been compelled to reorient—actually, to invert—his point of view.
Today, it is the corporation itself . . . that has become the villain; it is the

There is a widespread impression, and much literature to support and propagate it, that the managements of big corporations form some sort of separate, independent, or "neutral" social class. This view we have already encountered in an elementary form in the "neutral technocracy" of Berle and Means and the "soulful corporation" of Carl Kaysen; it is developed more elaborately in such works as James Burnham's *The Managerial Revolution* and Berle's *The 20th-Century Capitalist Revolution*. Most of the variants of this theory have interesting and enlightening insights to contribute, but in our view they all share a common defect: the basic idea is wrong.

The fact is that the managerial stratum is the most active and influential part of the propertied class. All studies show that its members are largely recruited from the middle and upper reaches of the class structure; they overlap with what C. Wright Mills calls the "very rich"; with few and negligible exceptions, they are wealthy men in their own right, quite apart from the large incomes and extensive privileges which they derive from their corporate connections.[16] It is of course true, as we have emphasized, that in the typical big corporation the management is not subject to stockholder control, and in this sense the "separation of ownership from control" is a fact. But there is no justification for concluding from this that managements in general are divorced from ownership in general. Quite the contrary, managers are among the biggest

---

individual caught in the corporate structure, rather than the public, who is the victim. . . ." Review of *From the Dark Tower* by Ernest Pawel, *New York Times* (Sunday Book Section), June 23, 1957.

In one important respect, this analysis seems to us not quite accurate. The crux of the matter is not that "few American corporations at present are dominated by a single individual." There are plenty of them, even among the biggest. The point is that the company man, even when he rises to a dominant position in his company, as often happens, is a very different type and plays a very different role from the old-fashioned tycoon. For the tycoon, the company is merely a means, while to the company man it has become an end.

[16] By far the best treatment of these subjects will be found in C. Wright Mills, *The Power Elite*, especially Chapters 6, 7, and 8.

owners; and because of the strategic positions they occupy, they function as the protectors and spokesmen for all large-scale property. Far from being a separate class, they constitute in reality the leading echelon of the property-owning class.

This is not to argue that managers have no distinctive interests *qua* managers. Like other segments of the propertied class, they do. But the conflicts of interest that arise in this way are between managers and small property owners rather than between managers and large property owners. The clearest case in point has to do with dividend policy.

It is generally assumed that the desire of managers, noted earlier, to generate the largest feasible volume of internal corporate funds leads to an interest in a low dividend payout rate, while stockholders' concern to maximize their disposable cash income leads to an interest in a high payout rate. Actually, this is much too simple. Most managers are themselves big owners of stock (in their own and other companies) and as such have the same interest in dividends as other big stockholders. This interest is neither in a minimum nor a maximum payout rate but somewhere in between: stockholdings should yield a reasonable cash income (for managers this is particularly important as a guarantee of family security after they retire or die); on the other hand, they should also steadily appreciate in value. The first requirement calls for dividends, the second for plowing back of earnings. Nevertheless, the special managerial interest in a low payout rate does exist and is undoubtedly important. But the point to be emphasized is that this makes managers the allies of the very largest stockholders for whom a minimum payout rate is also a desideratum. The reason of course is that the very rich save a large part of their incomes in any case, and it is to their advantage for the corporations in which they own stock to do the saving for them rather than pay out dividends from which to do their own saving. Corporate saving results in an increase in the value of their stock. If at any time they need the cash, either to spend or for some other investment, they can sell part or all of their shares, realizing the increment of value in the form of a capital gain taxable at the maximum rate of 25 percent. On the other hand, if they receive more in the form of dividends they have to pay taxes at the much higher rates applicable to their brackets, which of course cuts down their effective rate of saving.

Pressure for higher payout rates generally comes from small stockholders. Only rarely is it effectively exerted on managements via the formal corporate voting machinery, but this does not mean that the small stockholder is without influence. Socially the seven million or so small stockholders in the United States are an important group: they are quite likely to be solid citizens, leaders of public opinion with local political influence. Since the tiny upper echelon of the propertied class (including its leading element, the managers of the big corporations) is always politically vulnerable, it naturally wants to have the support and loyalty of the small stockholder. A moderate, and perhaps even more important a steady, dividend policy is the most effective way of insuring this support.

In practice, dividend policies are the outcome of a compromise between the desire of managements and large stockholders for a low payout rate and the desire of small stockholders for a high rate. Moreover, as would be expected, there is considerable variation from one company to another. Those which are largely owned by a few rich individuals or families tend to have the lowest payout rates; while the highest rates of all are likely to be paid by companies which both have a large number of small stockholders and are also situated in what may be called "public-relations-sensitive" areas of the economy. As would also be expected, managements as a rule hold the upper hand in determining the terms of the compromise, maintaining payout rates of 50 percent or less in most management-controlled industrial corporations. When profits rise, moreover, managements deliberately delay the adjustment of dividends to the new profit level, so that in time of prosperity the actual as distinct from the target payout rate tends to decline.[17] All of which testifies to the combined power of management and the very rich: the two are in fact integrated into a harmonious interest group at the top of the economic pyramid.

6

The company man is dedicated to the advancement of his company. This does not mean, however, that he is any more or less *homo economicus,* any more or less selfish, any more or less altruistic than either the tycoon or the individual owner-enterpreneur before him. All of these conceptions are at best irrelevant and at worst misleading. The problem is not one of "psychology" of any kind but of the selective and molding effects of institutions on the personnel that operates them. It might seem that this is too elementary to require mention, but unfortunately it is not possible to take for granted such a degree of enlightenment among economists. Economic theory is still heavily permeated by the "psychologizing" tradition of nineteenth-century utilitarianism, and economists need continually to be reminded that this tradition leads only to confusion and obscurantism.

To be a going concern, a social order must instill in its members the ambition to be a success in its own terms. Under capitalism the highest form of success is business success, and under monopoly capitalism the highest form of business is the big corporation. In this system the normal procedure for an ambitious young man must be to work himself up to as near the top as possible of as big a corporation as possible.[18] Once he enters a given corporation, he devotes himself to two ends:

[17] For more complete quantitative data, see the excellent study of John Lintner, "Distribution of Incomes of Corporations Among Dividends, Retained Earnings, and Taxes," *American Economic Review,* May 1956.

[18] "The way to achieve and retain greatness is always to be striving for something more." Osborn Elliott, *Men at the Top,* New York, 1959, p. 40. This book contains much useful information on American business leaders.

ascending the managerial ladder and advancing the relative
status of his company in the corporate world. In practice these
two ends are indistinguishable: the young man's rise in the
company depends on his contribution to improving the position of the company. This is the crux of the matter, and this is
why we can say without qualification that the company man is
dedicated to the advancement of his company: he is dedicated
to the advancement of his company precisely to the extent that
he is dedicated to advancing himself.

This remains true even after he has reached the top of a
given company. If he makes a good record, he may be "called"
to a larger company. And even if he is not, or has no hope of
being, he is still just as much interested in improving the position of the company he heads; for standing, prestige, and
power in the business world are not personal attributes but
rather are conferred on the individual businessman by the
standing, prestige, and power of his company and by his posi-
tion in that company. If true co. won't see need to recruit a man keydn't crave jobs

These propositions are vividly illustrated in *Cash McCall*.
Grant Austen, one of the main characters, is owner and president of a small company. During the Second World War the
company becomes enormously profitable, but Austen soon dis-
covers that his position in the business world remains unchanged. "Earnings leaped to a level where he could have paid
himself an annual salary of $100,000—the hallmark of a *Big
Business* president—but Grant Austen knew from his increased
contact with the world of Washington, New York and Detroit
that the Suffolk Moulding Company was a painfully small
example of what was referred to as *Small Business*. His standing in the world of industry was the sociological equivalent of
an underprivileged sharecropper." His daughter is refused
admission to an exclusive girls' school on the pretext that there
are no openings. "Grant Austen knew better. There were other
men whose daughters had applied afterward and been accepted. There was only one possible explanation—he wasn't a
big enough man to count. The Chadwick School was like so

many of the men he met in Pullman club cars—they had never heard of the Suffolk Moulding Company. Being president of a small company didn't mean a thing." The best week of Grant Austen's married life is spent at a National Association of Manufacturers convention in New York where he and his wife give a dinner party. "Their guests were other presidential couples, all of whom outranked them in net worth, but Miriam held her own. . . . During the days while he was attending convention sessions, she managed to get acquainted with two women whose husbands were both officers of companies that had their securities listed on the New York Stock Exchange." The end of Austen's business career drives home the main point with an ironic twist. Harassed and frustrated by the problems of small business, he finally decides to sell out. He gets two million dollars more than the company is worth—only to discover that now all at once, unattached to any company, he is a nobody even in those business circles which had formerly accepted him as an equal.

But size is not the only index of corporate status: this is an oversimplification. Other important indexes are rate of growth and "strength" as measured by such standards as credit rating and the price of a company's securities. Thus, assuming equal size, one company will rank ahead of others if it is stronger and growing more rapidly; and strength and rapid growth may even offset a big size differential if the larger company is stagnant or declining. The primary objectives of corporate policy—which are at the same time and inevitably the personal objectives of the corporate managers—are thus strength, rate of growth, and size. There is no general formula for quantifying or combining these objectives—nor is there any need for one. For they are reducible to the single common denominator of profitability. Profits provide the internal funds for expansion. Profits are the sinew and muscle of strength, which in turn gives access to outside funds if and when they are needed. Internal expansion, acquisition, and merger are the ways in which corporations grow, and growth is the road to size. Thus profits, even though not the ultimate goal, are the necessary means to all ultimate goals. As such, they become the immediate, unique, unifying, quantitative aim of corporate policies, the touchstone of corporate rationality, the measure of corporate success. Here is the real—the socio-structural as distinct from individual-psychological—explanation of the kind of profit-maximizing behavior so ably described by Earley in the passage quoted on pages 24-26.

Nothing has yet been said about whether corporate executives strive to maximize their salaries and/or personal incomes.[19] It is probably safe to assume that they do, for two reasons. For one thing, there is a selective process at work which tends to draw the people who are most interested in making money into business and to divert those less interested into other pursuits. As Veblen said, "men whose aim is not an increase of possessions do not go into business."[20] And second, within any given business milieu, relative salary or income is an important badge of standing. William H. Whyte, Jr., inquiring into executives' attitudes toward taxes, found the following to be true:

Unhappy as executives are about high taxes, to them the key aspect of salary is not its absolute but its relative size. And the relative size does depend on the income *before* taxes. The part of the pay stub that shows gross salary may be cause for hollow laughter, but it is still the part that is critical, and the man who gets $30,000 a year finds very little comfort in pondering the thought that his $37,000-a-year rival takes home only $892 more than he does.[21]

[19] The two are of course not identical. Mainly for tax reasons, the corporate world has devised a variety of methods for compensating executives in addition to the old-fashioned salary and bonus. Taken over the whole life of the executive, these "fringe benefits" may be even more important than salary. "In these days of profit-sharing benefits, retirement plans, and stock options," says an advertisement of the Guaranty Trust Company in *Business Week* of November 24, 1956, "the present and future capital assets of the average business executive are far greater than his bank balance and salary check seem to indicate."

[20] *The Theory of Business Enterprise*, p. 20.

[21] *The Organization Man*, New York, 1958, pp. 144-145.

There can thus hardly be any doubt that corporate managers do normally strive to maximize personal income. But nothing in the theory of corporate behavior would be changed if we were to make the opposite assumption: that company men are unconcerned about the size of their incomes, that they go into business and work hard at it because they like to rather than for the money it brings in. There certainly are some business-men who feel this way; and indeed they might all be of this type, and might be paid accordingly, without changing any-thing in their behavior as company men.

One way of clarifying this is by an analogy. A professional baseball player makes his living by playing ball. He may detest the life and stay with it solely for the money. Or he may love the game and be quite willing to play for nothing if necessary. It makes no difference at all when he gets out on the playing field. There his objectives are no longer dictated by his per-sonal feelings and preferences; they are laid down for him in the baseball rule book. Whatever his likes and dislikes, what-ever his inner urges, his actions must be directed to the single, measurable aim of getting more runs than the other team. If he won't or can't play the game according to the book, he is dropped from the team and loses his job. If his contribution to his club's success is inadequate, he is benched or sent down to the minor leagues.

Baseball, it is said, is America's national game. It would be more accurate to say that business is America's national game: there are many more people engaged in it and the stakes are much higher. But the two operate on similar principles. In baseball the objective is to get to the top of the league; day-to-day policies are directed toward winning games by getting more runs than opposing teams; players are judged by their cumulative day-to-day performance. In business the aim is to get to the top of the corporate pyramid; day-to-day policies are directed to making the most possible profits; as in baseball, men are judged by their cumulative day-to-day performance. In both, those who refuse to play according to the rules get thrown out. Those whose performance is substandard sink toward the bottom. In neither are personal motivations important except insofar as they may contribute to effectiveness in action, and in this respect they play their part along with many other factors such as physique, intelligence, skill, training, and the like.

To sum up: Business is an ordered system which selects and rewards according to well understood criteria. The guiding principle is to get as near as possible to the top inside a corporation which is as near as possible to the top among corporations. Hence the need for maximum profits. Hence the need to devote profits once acquired to enhancing financial strength and speeding up growth. These things become the subjective aims and values of the business world because they are the objective requirements of the system. The character of the system determines the psychology of its members, not vice versa.

One corollary of this analysis requires particular emphasis. "At the historical dawn of capitalist production," Marx wrote, "avarice, and desire to get rich, are the ruling passions. . . . Accumulate! Accumulate! That is Moses and the prophets."[22] But he was careful to point out that this ruling passion was not an emanation of human nature but rather was the product of the system in which it played so crucial a role:

[The capitalist] shares with the miser the passion for wealth as wealth. But that which in the miser is a mere idiosyncrasy, is, in the capitalist, the effect of the social mechanism of which he is but one of the wheels. Moreover, the development of capitalist production makes it constantly necessary to keep increasing the amount of the capital laid out in a given industrial undertaking, and competition makes the immanent laws of capitalist production to be felt by each individual capitalist, as external coercive laws. It compels him to keep constantly extending his capital, in order to preserve it, but extend it he cannot, except by means of progressive accumulation.[23]

[22] *Capital*, Volume 1, Chapter 22, Section 4.
[23] *Ibid.*

We have come a long way since the historical dawn of capitalist production, and even since Karl Marx wrote *Das Kapital*. Nowadays the avaricious capitalist, grasping for every penny and anxiously watching over his growing fortune, seems like a stereotype out of a nineteenth-century novel. The company man of today has a different attitude. To be sure, he likes to make as much money as he can, but he spends it freely, and the retirement benefits and other perquisites which he gets from his company enable him to take a rather casual attitude toward his personal savings. Noting the contrast between the modern businessman and his earlier counterpart, one might jump to the conclusion that the old drive has gone out of the system, that the classical picture of capitalism restlessly propelled forward by the engine of accumulation is simply inappropriate to the conditions of today.[24]

We can now see that this is a superficial view. The real capitalist today is not the individual businessman but the corporation. What the businessman does in his private life, his attitude toward the getting and spending of his personal income—these are essentially irrelevant to the functioning of the system. What counts is what he does in his company life and his attitude toward the getting and spending of the company's income. And here there can be no doubt that the making and accumulating of profits hold as dominant a position today

---

[24] Schumpeter made this very mistake. "The bourgeoisie worked primarily in order to invest, and it was not so much a standard of consumption as a standard of accumulation that the bourgeoisie struggled for and tried to defend against governments that took the short-run view. With the decline of the driving power supplied by the family motive, the businessman's time-horizon shrinks, roughly, to his life expectation. And he might now be less willing than he was to fulfill that function of earning, saving and investing even if he saw no reason to fear that the results would but swell his tax bills. He drifts into an anti-saving frame of mind and accepts with an increasing readiness anti-saving *theories* that are indicative of a short-run *philosophy*." J. A. Schumpeter, *Capitalism, Socialism, and Democracy*, New York, 1942, pp. 160-161. That none of this applies to the corporate capitalist seems to have escaped Schumpeter altogether.

as they ever did. Over the portals of the magnificent office
building of today, as on the wall of the modest counting house
of a century or two ago, it would be equally appropriate to find
engraved the motto: "Accumulate! Accumulate! That is Moses
and the Prophets."

7

The replacement of the individual capitalist by the corporate
capitalist constitutes an institutionalization of the capitalist
function. The heart and core of the capitalist function is accumulation: accumulation has always been the prime mover of
the system, the locus of its conflicts, the source of both its
triumphs and its disasters. But only in the infancy of the system could accumulation be said to exhaust the obligations of
the capitalist. With success came also responsibilities. In the
words of Marx:

> When a certain stage of development has been reached, a con-
> ventional degree of prodigality, which is also an exhibition of
> wealth, and consequently a source of credit, becomes a business
> necessity to the "unfortunate" capitalist. Luxury enters into capital's
> expenses of representation.[25]

These expenses of representation have traditionally taken
the form of conspicuous waste on the one hand and philanthropy on the other. Both have always had what would nowadays be called a public-relations purpose: the one to dazzle
and overawe the public, the other to secure its loyalty and
affection. Both have been borne by the capitalist in his private
capacity.

One of the most striking changes in the American scene in
recent years has been a marked decline of both types of expenditure by the aristocracy of the business world. The great
estates of Newport and Southampton, the regal yachts of the
Morgans and the Astors, the debutante parties costing half a
million dollars or more—one now reads more about these

[25] *Capital*, Volume 1, Chapter 22, Section 4.

things in history books than in the society pages of the daily
paper. The Big Businessman of today (Texas oilmen excepted,
as they should be) lives if not modestly at least in decent obscurity: the last thing he wants is to make a big splash with his
wealth. Similarly, individual philanthropy seems to play a de-
creasingly prominent role—so much so that one of the country's biggest businessmen, writing about the problems of the
corporate world, feels justified in titling one of his chapters
"The Vanishing Philanthropist."[26]

These developments do not mean, however, that capital's
expenses of representation have somehow been abolished. Like
other aspects of the capitalist function, responsibility for meeting capital's expenses of representation has been institutionalized. Nowadays it is the corporation itself that has to maintain
a high standard of living before the public, and it does so by
erecting grandiose headquarters buildings, providing its functionaries with offices which grow plushier by the year, trans-
porting them in fleets of company-owned jet planes and Cadil-
lacs, granting them unlimited expense accounts, and so on and
on.[27] Most of this is the sheerest kind of conspicuous waste, cor-

[26] Crawford H. Greenewalt, *The Uncommon Man: The Individual in
the Organization*, New York, Toronto, London, 1959, pp. 113 ff.

[27] Consider the new sixty-story Chase Manhattan Bank building.
"Tall enough at 813 feet to throw the early morning sun back at itself,"
says a brochure issued by the bank under the title *A New Landmark for
New York*, "the Chase Manhattan Bank building represents the fulfillment of an architectural ideal and a high water mark in modern management. It was designed not just to function but to express—its soaring
angularities bespeaking an era rather than a transient need. . . . When the
building was in an embryonic state, it was decided that the decorative
element which would best complement the stark simplicity of its modern
architecture was fine art. Accordingly, the bank recruited the services of
a committee of art experts to select works which would contribute to a
warm and stimulating environment in which the employees would work
and at the same time express the bank's concern with those things man
holds dearest. The works chosen to adorn private offices and reception
areas range from the latest in abstract impressionism to primitive Ameri-
cana and connote the bank's rich role in American history as well as its
global interests. . . . 1 Chase Manhattan Plaza is really many things in
one—a product of an age when reaching for the stars is no longer a

related negatively, if at all, with productive efficiency; yet no
corporation with serious claims to Big Business standing would
dream of neglecting this aspect of its operations. Size, success,
strength—the desiderata of corporate policy—must be not only
achieved but also displayed for all the world to see. The need
to dazzle and overawe is as great as ever, and the costs which it
entails have certainly grown along with the growth of capital.
What have changed are the form and method of conspicuous
waste, not the purpose or content.

Much the same can be said about philanthropy. This too is
being institutionalized, and though up to now foundations
have taken the lead, the corporations themselves are playing an
increasingly important role, especially in the field of providing
private support for institutions of higher learning.[28] Doubtless
those observers are right who see here a trend that will continue into the indefinite future; the end may well be that the
cost of nearly all private philanthropy will be directly borne by
corporations.

It is in this area of philanthropy, and the public-relations
efforts which accompany it and are closely related to it, that

---

figure of speech and men pierce the ocean depths as blithely as they cross
the street—a bench mark in architectural history—a staggering complex
of machinery—an art gallery unlike any other in the world—a towering
symbol of Chase Manhattan's confidence in the future of the storied
financial district." All Americans can share a legitimate pride in this
monument to what man holds dearest, the more so since as taxpayers
they pay about half its cost.

[28] One should not assume that this is all pure philanthropy. "Business
corporations," writes William M. Compton, President of the Council for
Financial Aid to Education, "are not benevolent institutions. But they
can be 'benevolent' when considered benevolence is in the interests of
their owners." *Association of American Colleges Bulletin*, March 1954.
Presumably Mr. Compton knows from personal experience how corporations feel about these matters. Or to cite again Crawford Greenewalt,
President of Du Pont: the continued progress of American industry
depends on the nation's having "a balanced research program, which
means that it must supplement its applied research with an amount of
fundamental research sufficient to provide the basic information upon
which all scientific progress depends. . . . A substantial amount of such

we find a genuine kernel of truth in the "soulful corporation" idea. In criticizing this notion earlier, we rejected the view in Kaysen's paper "The Social Significance of the Modern Corporation" that profit maximization has ceased to be the guiding principle of corporate conduct. But when Kaysen says that the modern corporation's "responsibilities to the general public are widespread" and lists among them "leadership in local charitable enterprises, concern with factory architecture and landscaping, provision of support for higher education, and even research in pure science," there is no reason to cavil. Having maximized their profits, corporations do feel called upon to engage in activities of this sort and almost certainly will do so to an increasing extent. If these are emanations of the corporate soul, then the existence of that metaphysical entity can be taken to be a fact. But it is a familiar soul, not a new one. Escaping from the dying body of the capitalist philanthropist, it has migrated to the capitalist corporation. For the system as a whole, there has been no net increase of soulfulness.

8

We have tried to show that the giant corporation of today is an engine for maximizing profits and accumulating capital to at least as great an extent as the individual enterprise of an earlier period. But it is not merely an enlarged and institutionalized version of the personal capitalist. There are major differences between these types of business enterprise, and at least two of them are of key importance to a general theory of monopoly capitalism: the corporation has a longer time horizon than the individual capitalist, and it is a more rational calculator. Both

---

research is now being done by industry. The major responsibility, however, must rest with our universities, for only they can provide the atmosphere in which truly fundamental scientific inquiry can flourish. The problem is not so much one of persuasion as of finance; it is here that industry, by supporting academic fundamental research, can at the same time serve its stockholders and supply a public need." *The Uncommon Man*, pp. 137-138.

differences are fundamentally related to the incomparably larger scale of the corporation's operations.

The corporation is in principle immortal and inculcates in its functionaries a long time horizon, not because of its special legal form (after all, a corporation can be wound up just as easily as a proprietorship) but because what it "incorporates" is a vast and complex capital investment the value of which depends on its being maintained as a going concern. Similarly, the size of the corporation's operations enforces a far-reaching specialization and rationalization of the managerial function. "Perhaps the best analogy to an executive's job," writes Crawford H. Greenewalt, President of the Du Pont Company, "is that of the symphony conductor under whose hand a hundred or so highly specialized and yet very different skills become a single effort of great effectiveness."[29] And as to the rationalistic ethos of the big corporation there could hardly be more eloquent testimony than the rapid spread of methods (and the personnel to work them) of the kind so strongly emphasized in the statement by Earley quoted on pages 24-26—cost accounting, budgeting, data processing, management consulting, operations research, and much else besides.

The long corporate time horizon and the rationalization of management generate certain characteristic attitudes and modes of behavior. Of these perhaps the most important are (1) a systematic avoidance of risk-taking, and (2) an attitude of live-and-let-live toward other members of the corporate world. In both respects the change from the old-fashioned individual enterprise is so great in quantity as to amount to a change in quality.

(1) With regard to risk-taking, the difference is not so much that the individual capitalist was inherently more of a gambler than the corporation (though very likely he was) but rather that he had neither the capability nor the habit of calculating risks. He was like the little fellow who keeps on playing the

[29] *The Uncommon Man*, p. 64.

numbers game either not knowing or not caring about the certain odds against him; while the big corporation is like the professional gambler who takes good care that the odds are in his favor. The time horizon factor also plays a role here: the corporation, being under no pressure to realize quick returns and disposing over ample resources, approaches a new development with care and circumspection and does not make a final commitment until the relevant investigations and preparations have been carried out. Finally, and in a sense ironically, the corporation knows how to use for its own ends the very weaknesses of the small enterprise which it has outgrown. When a new industry or field of operations is being opened up, the big corporation tends to hold back deliberately and to allow individual entrepreneurs or small businesses to do the vital pioneering work. Many fail and drop out of the picture, but those which succeed trace out the most promising lines of development for the future. It is at this stage that the big corporations move to the center of the stage. Referring to the electric appliance field which he knew from long experience, T. K. Quinn, formerly a Vice President of General Electric, wrote: "I know of no original product invention, not even electric shavers or heating pads, made by any of the giant laboratories or corporations, with the possible exception of the household garbage grinder. . . . The record of the giants is one of moving in, buying out and absorbing the smaller creators."[30] Though no general information on this subject seems to be available, there is reason to believe that Mr. Quinn's statement holds true of many other industries.

[30] T. K. Quinn, *Giant Business: Threat to Democracy*, New York, 1953, p. 117. After this chapter was published in the July-August 1962 issue of *Monthly Review*, we received a letter from Mr. Morrison Sharp of Racine, Wisconsin, which reads in part as follows: "Mr. Quinn might consult either his own legal department, or the Racine Chamber of Commerce, or even the In-Sink-Erator Company of Racine, which invented and perfected the household garbage grinder. Common gossip has it that the giant GE makes its own brand-name machine under rights from the In-Sink-Erator Company after the settlement of a long and successful lawsuit." Alas for illusions!

(2) The attitude of live-and-let-live which characterizes Big Business likewise derives from the magnitude of the corporation's investment and from the calculating rationality of its management. By and large, this attitude is reserved for other big corporations and does not extend to the smaller businessman. For example, the big three automobile companies behave toward one another in a way that Schumpeter appropriately called "corespective,"[31] while their behavior to the scores of thousands of dealers who sell their products to the public is notoriously overbearing and dictatorial. The reason, of course, is that each of the big ones recognizes the strength and retaliatory power of the other big ones and as a matter of deliberately calculated policy avoids provoking them. But corespective behavior is by no means limited to competitors. If one big corporation is not a competitor of another, it is quite likely to be either a customer or a supplier; and in this realm of corporate relations the sovereign principle is reciprocity, which enjoins corespective behavior as surely as competition does. In addition, the Big Business community is numerically small, comprising perhaps 10,000 or so people for the entire country, and its members are tied together by a whole network of social as well as economic ties. Conscious of their power and standing in the larger national community, they naturally tend to develop a group ethic which calls for solidarity and mutual help among themselves and for presenting a common front to the outside world.

It wasn't always so. In the early days when Big Business was emerging from the jungle of small-scale competition, corespective behavior was rare indeed. Even the railroads had to go through a series of exhausting rate wars before they finally got it into their corporate heads that roadbeds and tracks and locomotives and cars would go on being used to carry passengers and freight whatever might happen to security owners or rival managements. The original tycoons, faced with the conse-

---

[31] *Capitalism, Socialism, and Democracy,* p. 90n.

quences of cutthroat competition, sought a way out through a policy of ruthless monopolization. The victims of this drive, however, were numerous and not without influence. By entering into a temporary alliance with dissatisfied farmers and workers, they succeeded in getting the antitrust laws passed, which, though far from achieving their avowed aim of preserving (or restoring) free competition, nevertheless put very real roadblocks in the way of full monopolization. For this reason, as well as others of a technological and economic nature, there were few cases in which one corporation or even one financial interest group succeeded in establishing effective control over an entire market.

It was under these circumstances that Big Businessmen began to learn the virtues of corespective behavior. The process of learning was hastened as the highly individualistic tycoon passed from the scene and the company man gradually took his place as the typical representative of corporate business. Today there are probably fewer genuine monopolies than there were at the turn of the century, but there is also infinitely less cutthroat competition. And this brings us straight to the problem of the *interaction* of the corporate giants.

3

THE TENDENCY OF SURPLUS TO RISE

Monopoly capitalism is a system made up of giant corporations. This is not to say that there are no other elements in the system or that it is useful to study monopoly capitalism by abstracting from everything except giant corporations. It is both more realistic and more enlightening to proceed from the outset by including, alongside the corporate-monopoly sector, a more or less extensive smaller-business sector, the reason being that smaller business enters in many ways into the calculations and strategies of Big Business. To abstract from smaller business would be to exclude from the field of investigation some of the determinants of Big Business behavior.

One must, however, be careful not to fall into the trap of assuming that Big Business and smaller business are qualitatively equal or of coordinate importance for the *modus operandi* of the system. The dominant element, the prime mover, is Big Business organized in giant corporations. These corporations are profit maximizers and capital accumulators. They are managed by company men whose fortunes are identified with the corporations' success or failure. They—and here the pronoun stands for both the corporations and the men—look ahead and calculate with care. It is their initiative that sets the economy in motion, their power that keeps it moving, their policies that get it into difficulties and crises. Smaller business is on the receiving end, reacting to the pressures of Big Business, to a certain extent shaping and channeling them, but without effective power to counter them and still less to exercise an independent initiative of its own. From the point of

52

view of a theory of monopoly capitalism, smaller business should properly be treated as a part of the environment within which Big Business operates rather than as an actor on the stage.

2

Within the corporation, relations are direct, hierarchical, bureaucratic. Here genuine planning holds sway, with directives flowing from the top down and responsibility from the bottom up. For the system as a whole, however, such relations are absent. Not even the largest corporations produce more than a very small fraction of society's total output. Take General Motors, for example, which, measured in terms of sales, is the biggest industrial corporation in the country. In 1957, GM's total of wages, overhead costs, and profits, which corresponds closely to the company's contribution to the Gross National Product, amounted to just over $4 billion, about 1 percent of GNP for that year. It is of course true that several giant corporations often act in concert, but they do so for the purpose of serving their own ends rather than for the purpose of influencing, not to say controlling, the functioning of the system as a whole.

Overall, monopoly capitalism is as unplanned as its competitive predecessor. The big corporations relate to each other, to consumers, to labor, to smaller business primarily through the market. The way the system works is still the unintended outcome of the self-regarding actions of the numerous units that compose it. And since market relations are essentially price relations, the study of monopoly capitalism, like that of competitive capitalism, must begin with the workings of the price mechanism.

The crucial difference between the two is well known and can be summed up in the proposition that under competitive capitalism the individual enterprise is a "price taker," while under monopoly capitalism the big corporation is a "price maker."[1] But analysis of the implications of this difference for the functioning of the system as a whole has been surprisingly meager. There is a vast literature, both theoretical and empirical, on the pricing of individual commodities or the products of particular industries but very little on the workings and consequences of a monopoly price *system*.

This lack of connection between the analysis of the parts of the system and the analysis of the whole—between what are nowadays often called micro-economics and macro-economics —did not characterize the older theories of the competitive economy. Whether they approached the matter from the angle of the firm and the industry, like Marshall, or whether, as in the case of Walras, they began with a view of the system as a whole, they sought to demonstrate how a competitive price system tended to produce a state of equilibrium in which resources were allocated, output produced, and income distributed in accordance with clearly defined principles. Further, when this competitive model was "dynamized" by the introduction of capital accumulation (saving and investment), the theory was extended to show how, if the appropriate assumptions were made, the price mechanism (including the rate of interest) would regulate the amount of capital forthcoming to conform to the requirements of a growing population and advancing technology while maintaining full employment of available productive resources.

It was of course obvious that this model of a harmoniously growing system was not a faithful reflection of capitalist reality. There was therefore added a supplementary theory of business cycles which started, and very largely remained, at the macro-economic level. Business cycles and the various phenomena related to them were treated as disturbances in what would otherwise be the normal course of development, these disturbances being due to certain factors which were ab-

[1] This apt terminology was introduced by Tibor Scitovsky, *Welfare and Competition: The Economics of a Fully Employed Economy*, Chicago, 1951, pp. 18, 20.

stracted from in the construction of the smoothly functioning model. The factors most often stressed were the monetary and credit system, the volatility of businessmen's psychology, and the unevenness of technological change. By emphasizing different factors, or combining them in different ways, a number of families of business cycle theories were worked out. From our present point of view, the important thing is that none of these theories involved new assumptions or conclusions about the character and mode of functioning of the price system.

This was the state of affairs when, during the early 1930's, Joan Robinson and E. H. Chamberlin launched the first big attacks on traditional price theory. Not that they denied its validity on its own assumptions, but they did emphatically deny the general relevance of the assumptions, insisting that most industries were neither competitive in the traditional sense nor yet fully monopolistic (a case which in the past had been treated as an interesting exception to the rule but without general significance). The theories of "imperfect competition" and "monopolistic competition" advanced by Robinson and Chamberlin were later elaborated and added to by a host of other writers, and it is now possible to say that a great variety of price patterns affecting individual commodities and industries has been more or less adequately studied.

All of this work, however, remained at the micro-economic level and has had astonishingly little influence on the analysis of the functioning of the system as a whole. In this area, of course, the greatest advances during the last three decades have been associated with the name of Keynes whose magnum opus, *The General Theory of Employment, Interest and Money,* was published in 1936. Though this was several years after Robinson and Chamberlin opened fire on traditional price theory, Keynes showed no trace of influence from the new theories. His work and that of his followers (including, paradoxically enough, that of Mrs. Robinson herself) has remained within the tradition of orthodox business cycle theory, taking the competitive price system for granted and seeking to explore the consequences of certain new, and in many ways more realistic and relevant, assumptions at the macro-economic level.

The reasons for this increasingly pronounced divorce between micro and macro theories are to be sought in the apologetic character of bourgeois economics. As we shall see, the effects of a thoroughgoing reintegration of the two levels of analysis—the substitution of a monopolistic price system for the traditional competitive system, and the analysis of its implications for the whole economy—are nothing short of devastating to capitalism's claims to be considered a rational social order which serves to promote the welfare and happiness of its members. Since a major concern of bourgeois economics has long been to support these claims, economists have naturally shown no enthusiasm for following a course that ends by demonstrating their falsity.

There have of course been exceptions, but as usual in such cases their work has received little of the attention it deserves. The leader in reintegrating micro and macro theories was Michal Kalecki who not only "discovered the *General Theory* [of Keynes] independently"[2] but also was the first to include what he called the "degree of monopoly" in his overall model of the economy.[3] A further long step in the same direction, which owed much to Kalecki's influence, was Josef Steindl's *Maturity and Stagnation in American Capitalism* (1952). And anyone familiar with the work of Kalecki and Steindl will readily recognize that the authors of the present work owe a great deal to them. If we have not quoted them more often or made more direct use of their theoretical formulations, the reason is that for our purposes we have found a different approach and form of presentation more convenient and usable.

[2] Joan Robinson, *Economic Philosophy*, London, 1962, p. 93.
[3] Kalecki's path-breaking works, *Essays in the Theory of Economic Fluctuations* and *Studies in Economic Dynamics*, were published in 1939 and 1943. His *Theory of Economic Dynamics*, London, 1954, is a sort of combined and revised second edition of the two earlier works.

3

When we say that giant corporations are price makers, we mean that they can and do choose what prices to charge for their products. There are of course limits to their freedom of choice: above and below certain prices it would be preferable to discontinue production altogether. But typically the range of choice is wide. What determines which prices will be charged within this range?

The simplest answer is that given by traditional monopoly theory. A monopolist is defined as the only seller of a commodity for which there are no substitutes. As he varies his price from higher to lower, people will buy more of his product but not at the expense of a similar product of a rival seller. Since no other seller will be directly affected by the variation of the monopolist's price, none will have any incentive to react or retaliate. Under these circumstances, the solution to the monopolist's problem is simple: he will lower his price to the point where the addition to his revenue from selling an extra unit (taking account of the fact that the price for all previous units also goes down) exactly equals the addition to his costs involved in producing an extra unit. Up to this point, producing and selling an additional unit brings in more revenue than it adds to costs; beyond this point, the reverse is true. Hence this point defines the price and output which maximize the monopolist's profit.

The typical giant corporation, however, is not a monopolist in this sense. Rather, it is one of several corporations producing commodities which are more or less adequate substitutes for each other. When one of them varies its price, the effect will immediately be felt by the others. If firm A lowers its price, some new demand may be tapped, but the main effect will be to attract customers away from firms B, C, and D. The latter, not willing to give up their business to A, will retaliate by lowering their prices, perhaps even undercutting A. While A's original move was made in the expectation of increasing its profit, the net result may be to leave all the firms in a worse position.

Under these circumstances it is impossible for a single corporation, even if it has the fullest information about the demand for the products of the industry as a whole and about its own costs, to tell what price would maximize its profits. What it can sell depends not only on its own price but also on the prices charged by its rivals, and these it cannot know in advance. A firm may thus make ever so careful an estimate of the profit-maximizing price, but in the absence of knowledge about rivals' reactions it will be right only by accident. A wrong guess about rivals' reactions would throw the whole calculation off and necessitate readjustments which in turn would provoke further moves by rivals, and so on, the whole process quite possibly degenerating into mutually destructive price warfare.

Unstable market situations of this sort were very common in the earlier phases of monopoly capitalism, and still occur from time to time, but they are not typical of present-day monopoly capitalism. And clearly they are anathema to the big corporations with their penchant for looking ahead, planning carefully, and betting only on the sure thing. To avoid such situations therefore becomes the first concern of corporate policy, the *sine qua non* of orderly and profitable business operations.

This objective is achieved by the simple expedient of banning price cutting as a legitimate weapon of economic warfare.[4] Naturally this has not happened all at once or as a con-

[4] Smaller businessmen sometimes blurt out what their more public-relations-conscious big brothers discreetly keep to themselves. The following excerpt from a proceeding of the Federal Trade Commission dealing with the Chain Institute, a trade association of chain manufacturers, provides a classic statement of the all-but-universal attitude of businessmen toward price cutting. The witness, after explaining the usual procedure at meetings of the Institute, proceeded as follows: "But, after we got rid of a lot of this stuff, . . . then we start talking. Maybe somebody will say to you, 'You so-and-so Son of a B, what did you do at Bill Jones'?' And then somebody calls somebody a liar and so forth, and then maybe he would say, 'Well I have got the evidence that you did, and you are a liar,' and then you would get into a fight with this fellow, and first thing

scious decision. Like other powerful taboos, that against price cutting has grown up gradually out of long and often bitter experience, and it derives its strength from the fact that it serves the interests of powerful forces in society. As long as it is accepted and observed, the dangerous uncertainties are removed from the rationalized pursuit of maximum profits.

With price competition banned, sellers of a given commodity or of close substitutes have an interest in seeing that the price or prices established are such as to maximize the profits of the group as a whole. They may fight over the division of these profits—a subject to which we return presently—but none can wish that the total to be fought over should be smaller rather than larger. This is the decisive fact in determining the price policies and strategies of the typical large corporation. And it means that the appropriate general price theory for an economy dominated by such corporations is the traditional monopoly price theory of classical and neo-classical economics. What economists have hitherto treated as a special case turns out to be, under conditions of monopoly capitalism, the general case. This is a view which would probably command fairly

---

you know somebody else would come up and listen to the conversation, and then there would be six of them there, and they would be picking on you—I don't mean picking on me, but picking on these price cutters, you understand. . . . I have a marvellous vocabulary, I can assure you, when it comes to calling names, and it has been tested by every member of the Institute, and when I call a guy a dirty, low kind of so-and-so price cutter, he knows he has been called a price cutter. I will be frank, and if you want to crucify me, I will add this: I would tell him that if he didn't stop these damned price cuttings, I would show him how to cut prices, and many times I did cut them, and when I cut a price, and if it was your price I was cutting, take it from me, brother, you knew your price had been cut. I could go on and on and on—but I want to say that when any two businessmen get together, whether it is a Chain Institute meeting or a Bible class meeting, if they happen to belong to the same industry, just as soon as the prayers have been said, they start talking about the conditions in the industry, and it is bound definitely to gravitate, that talk, to the price structure of the industry. What else is there to talk about?" Federal Trade Commission, *In the Matter of Chain Institute, Inc., et al*, Docket No. 4878, pp. 1096-1098.

wide approval among economists today, though as yet little has been done toward working out its implications.[5]

If maximization of the profits of the group constitutes the content of the pricing process under monopoly capitalism, its form can differ widely according to specific historical and legal conditions. In some countries, sellers are permitted or even encouraged to get together for the purpose of coordinating their policies. Resulting arrangements can vary all the way from tight cartels regulating both prices and outputs (a close approach to the pure monopoly case) to informal agreements to abide by certain price schedules (as exemplified by the famous "Gary dinners" in the American steel industry in the early years of the century). In the United States, where for historical reasons the ideology of competition has remained strong in spite of the facts of monopolization, antitrust laws effectively prevent such open collusion among sellers. Secret collusion is undoubtedly common, but it has its drawbacks and risks, and can hardly be described as the norm toward which a typical oligopolistic industry tends.[6] That norm, it seems clear, is a kind of tacit collusion which reaches its most developed form in what is known as "price leadership."

As defined by Burns, "price leadership exists when the price at which most of the units in an industry offer to sell is determined by adopting the price announced by one of their number."[7] The leader is normally the largest and most powerful firm in the industry—such as U. S. Steel or General Motors[8]

[5] See, for example, the statement of Duesenberry: " . . . the typical relation of prices to costs under oligopolistic conditions is not very different from the relation that would exist under monopolistic conditions." James S. Duesenberry, *Business Cycles and Economic Growth*, New York, 1958, p. 113.

[6] For a description of a recent widely publicized case of collusion, see "The Incredible Electrical Conspiracy," *Fortune*, April, May, 1961.

[7] Arthur R. Burns, *The Decline of Competition: A Study of the Evolution of American Industry*, New York, 1936, p. 76.

[8] See the excellent reports of the Kefauver Subcommittee on Antitrust and Monopoly, Senate Judiciary Committee, 85th Cong., 1st Sess.: *Administered Prices: Steel* (March 1958) and *Administered Prices. Automobiles* (October 1958).

—and the others accept its dominant role not only because it profits them to do so but also because they know that if it should come to price warfare the leader would be able to stand the gaff better than they could.

Price leadership in this strict sense is only the leading species of a much larger genus. In the cigarette industry, for example, the big companies take turns in initiating price changes; and in the petroleum industry different companies take the lead in different regional markets and to a certain extent at different times. So long as some fairly regular pattern is maintained such cases may be described as modified forms of price leadership. But there are many other situations in which no such regularity is discernible: which firm initiates price changes seems to be arbitrary. This does not mean that the essential ingredient of tacit collusion is absent. The initiating firm may simply be announcing to the rest of the industry, "We think the time has come to raise (or lower) price in the interest of all of us." If the others agree, they will follow. If they do not, they will stand pat, and the firm that made the first move will rescind its initial price change.[9] It is this willingness to rescind if an initial change is not followed which distinguishes the tacit-collusion situation from a price-war situation. So long as all firms accept this convention—and it is really nothing but a corollary of the ban on price competition—it becomes relatively easy for the group as a whole to feel its way toward the price which maximizes the industry's profit. What is required is simply that the

[9] We know of no study of this type of price behavior, but reading the business press over a period of years has convinced us that it has been spreading and is now quite common. Items like the following are often encountered: "The Kaiser Aluminum and Chemical Corporation yesterday rescinded its price increase of 1-cent a pound on aluminum ingots announced on Thursday. The action followed an earlier statement by the Aluminum Corporation of America that it would not increase its ingot price at this time. . . . The price of aluminum had been increased by half a cent a pound Oct. 2, by the Reynolds Metal Company, the second largest producer of the metal. This price rise from 22½ cents a pound to 23 cents a pound was quickly met by the entire industry, including foreign suppliers." (*New York Times*, Western Edition, December 7, 1963.)

initiator of change should act with the group interest as well as its own interest in mind and that the others should be ready to signal their agreement or disagreement by following or standing pat. If these conditions are satisfied, we can safely assume that the price established at any time is a reasonable approximation to the theoretical monopoly price.

What differentiates this case from the strict price leadership case is that there all the firms are in effect committed in advance to accept the judgment of one of their number, while here they all make up their minds each time a change is in question. To borrow an analogy from politics, we might say that in the one case we have a "dictatorship" and in the other a "democracy." But the purpose in both cases is the same—to maximize the profits of the group as a whole. The "dictatorships" of course tend to occur in those industries where one firm is much bigger and stronger than the others, like steel and autos; while the "democracies" are likely to be industries in which the dominant firms are more nearly equal in size and strength.

A qualification of the foregoing analysis seems called for. In the "pure" monopoly case, prices move upward or downward with equal ease, in response to changing conditions, depending entirely on whether a hike or a cut will improve the profit position. In oligopoly this is no longer quite the case. If one seller raises his price, this cannot possibly be interpreted as an aggressive move. The worst that can happen to him is that the others will stand pat and he will have to rescind (or accept a smaller share of the market). In the case of a price cut, on the other hand, there is always the possibility that aggression is intended, that the cutter is trying to increase his share of the market by violating the taboo on price competition. If rivals do interpret the initial move in this way, a price war with losses to all may result. Hence everyone concerned is likely to be more circumspect about lowering than raising prices. Under oligopoly, in other words, prices tend to be stickier on the downward side than on the upward side, and this fact introduces a significant upward bias into the general price level in a monopoly capitalist economy. There is truth in *Business Week*'s dictum that in the United States today the price system is one that "works only one way—up."[10]

One further qualification: while price competition is normally taboo in oligopolistic situations, this does not mean that it is totally excluded or that it never plays an important role. Any company or group of companies that believes it can permanently benefit from aggressive price tactics will not hesitate to use them. Such a situation is particularly likely to arise in a new industry where all firms are jockeying for position and no reasonably stable pattern of market sharing has yet taken shape (all industries, of course, have to go through this phase). In these circumstances, lower-cost producers may sacrifice immediately attainable profits to the goal of increasing their share of the market. Higher-cost producers, unable to stand the pace, may be forced into mergers on unfavorable terms or squeezed out of the market altogether. In this fashion, the industry goes through a shake-down process at the end of which a certain number of firms have firmly entrenched themselves and demonstrated their capacity to survive a tough struggle. When this stage is reached, the remaining firms find that aggressive price tactics no longer promise long-run benefits to offset short-term sacrifices. They therefore follow the example of older industries in abandoning price as a competitive weapon and developing a system of tacit collusion that is suited to their new circumstances.

Since at any given time there are likely to be a number of industries in the shake-down phase of development, it is always possible to point to areas of the economy which are far from competitive in the traditional atomistic sense of the term and yet in which price competition is common. Such instances do not, however, disprove the thesis that oligopoly prices are best explained by traditional monopoly price theory; they simply

[10] *Business Week*, June 15, 1957.

serve to remind us that it takes time for a stable oligopoly to emerge and for the corporations which compose it to develop an appropriate pattern of profit-maximizing behavior.

The end of the shake-down period naturally does not mean the end of the struggle for larger market shares; it simply means the end of price competition as a weapon in that struggle. The struggle itself goes on, but with other weapons. And this explains why, though the traditional theory of monopoly price applies with only minor qualifications to the economy of giant corporations, that economy nevertheless does not function as though it were composed of pure monopolies.

4

There are industries, among them very important ones, to which these theoretical considerations do not apply. These include the "natural" monopolies: electric power, telephones, and the other public utilities (railroads used to belong to this group, but they are now subject to severe competition from trucks and airplanes). They also include extractive industries like crude oil production and agriculture. In a sense these two groups stand at opposite poles: the public utilities are such close monopolies and their products so essential that they could easily charge prices that would yield much higher profits than are enjoyed by the typical industrial giant; while the extractive industries tend to be inordinately competitive and unprofitable. Left to themselves, in other words, these industries tend to be either unduly profitable or unprofitable as measured by the norms of Big Business.

Now under monopoly capitalism it is as true as it was in Marx's day that "the executive power of the . . . state is simply a committee for managing the common affairs of the entire bourgeois class."[11] And the common affairs of the entire bourgeois class include a concern that no industries which play an important role in the economy and in which large property

---

[11] *Communist Manifesto*, Part 1, paragraph 12.

interests are involved should be either too profitable or too unprofitable. Extra large profits are gained not only at the expense of consumers but also of other capitalists (electric power and telephone service, for example, are basic costs of all industries), and in addition they may, and at times of political instability do, provoke demands for genuinely effective anti-monopoly action. Abnormally low profits in a major branch of the economy such as agriculture, on the other hand, damage the interests of a large and politically powerful group of property owners who are able through pressure and bargaining with the other capitalists to enlist the necessary support for remedial action. It therefore becomes a state responsibility under monopoly capitalism to insure, as far as possible, that prices and profit margins in the deviant industries are brought within the range prevailing among the general run of giant corporations.

This is the background and explanation of the innumerable regulatory schemes and mechanisms which characterize the American economy today—commission regulation of public utilities, prorationing of oil production, price supports and acreage controls in agriculture, and so on. In each case of course some worthy purpose is supposed to be served—to protect consumers, to conserve natural resources, to save the family-size farm—but only the naive believe that these fine sounding aims have any more to do with the case than the flowers that bloom in the spring. There is in fact a vast literature, based for the most part on official documents and statistics, to prove that regulatory commissions protect investors rather than consumers, that oil prorationing wastes rather than conserves natural resources, that the family-size farm is declining faster than in any previous period of American history.[12] All of this is fully understandable once the basic principle is grasped that under monopoly capitalism the function of the

---

[12] A considerable body of the relevant material is conveniently assembled and summarized in Walter Adams and Horace M. Gray, *Monopoly in America: The Government as Promoter*, New York, 1955.

state is to serve the interests of monopoly capital. As two
champions of free competition have so truthfully said: "With
every advance of monopoly toward greater economic power
and more general social acceptance the federal government
becomes more subservient to it, more dependent on it, more
disposed to favor it with grants of privilege, protection, and
subsidy."[13]

Consequently the effect of government intervention into the
market mechanisms of the economy, whatever its ostensible
purpose, is to make the system work more, not less, like one
made up exclusively of giant corporations acting and interact-
ing in the manner analyzed in this and the preceding chapter.

5

Strengthening monopoly and regularizing its operations is of
course not the only function of the state under monopoly capitalism. Later, especially in Chapters 6 and 7, we shall analyze
at some length how the state, through its taxing and spending
activities and through its policies toward the rest of the world,
plays a decisive role in the way the system operates. The question therefore arises: Would it not be better to adopt from the
outset terminology which calls attention to and emphasizes the
role of the state in this social system? There is ample precedent
for doing so. In *State and Revolution* (1917) Lenin spoke of
"the epoch of the development of monopoly capitalism into
state monopoly capitalism," and it is now the accepted view in
the Communist world that the advanced capitalist countries
have long since passed through this transitional stage and entered that of state monopoly capitalism.

We have chosen not to follow this precedent but rather to
use the terms "monopoly capital" and "monopoly capitalism"
without qualification for two reasons. In the first place, the
state has always played a crucial role in the development of

[13] *Ibid.*, p. 1.

capitalism, and while this role has certainly increased quantitatively we find the evidence of a qualitative change in recent decades unconvincing. Under the circumstances, to lay special emphasis on the role of the state in the present stage of monopoly capitalism may only mislead people into assuming that it was of negligible importance in the earlier history of capitalism. Even more important is the fact that terms like "state capitalism" and "state monopoly capitalism" almost inevitably carry the connotation that the state is somehow an *independent* social force, coordinate with private business, and that the functioning of the system is determined not only by the cooperation of these two forces but also by their antagonisms and conflicts. This seems to us a seriously misleading view—in reality, what appear to be conflicts between business and government are reflections of conflict within the ruling class—and we think it desirable to avoid terminology which tends to give it currency.

6

The abandonment of price competition does not mean the end of all competition: it takes new forms and rages on with ever increasing intensity. Most of these new forms of competition come under the heading of what we call the sales effort, to which the next chapter is devoted. Here we confine attention to those forms of competition which have a direct bearing on costs of production and hence on the magnitude of the surplus.

If it is true, as we have argued, that oligopolies succeed in attaining a close approximation to the theoretical monopoly price and if their never-ceasing efforts to cut costs, so much stressed by James Earley,[14] are generally successful, then it follows with inescapable logic that surplus must have a strong and persistent tendency to rise. But before this conclusion can be accepted, we must ask whether the *system* of oligopolies

[14] Above, pp. 24-26.

generates pressures which force corporate managers to cut costs and improve efficiency. We know that this is the case in the competitive system: as Marx expressed it, "competition makes the immanent laws of capitalist production to be felt by each individual capitalist as external coercive laws."[15] Is this true of the kind of competition that exists among giant corporations? Or must we say about them what Adam Smith said about joint stock companies, which he identified with monopoly: "Monopoly is a great enemy to good management, which can never be universally established but in consequence of that free and universal competition which forces everybody to have recourse to it for the sake of self-defense."[16]

These are extremely important questions for an understanding of monopoly capitalism, and we must be careful in answering them not to take at face value the literature which emanates from the corporate establishment itself. We know that the managers of giant corporations and their spokesmen have every interest in projecting an image of technological progressiveness and organizational efficiency. We also know that such images are often mere rationalizing ideologies. What needs to be determined is not what corporate managements want us to believe but what modes of behavior are imposed upon them by the workings of the system itself.

There are, it seems to us, two aspects of non-price competition which are of decisive importance here. The first has to do with what may be called the dynamics of market sharing. The second has to do with the particular form which the sales effort assumes in the producer goods industries.

To begin with, the firm with lower costs and higher profits enjoys a variety of advantages over higher-cost rivals in the struggle for market shares. (This fact seems to have been largely overlooked by economists,[17] but it is perfectly clear to businessmen.) The firm with the lowest costs holds the

---

[15] *Capital,* Volume 1, Chapter 22, Section 3.

[16] *The Wealth of Nations,* Book 1, Chapter 11, Part 1.

[17] Duesenberry is an exception; see his *Business Cycles and Economic Growth,* especially pp. 124-125.

whip hand; it can afford to be aggressive even to the point of threatening, and in the limiting case precipitating, a price war. It can get away with tactics (special discounts, favorable credit terms, etc.) which if adopted by a weak firm would provoke retaliation. It can afford the advertising, research, development of new product varieties, extra services, and so on, which are the usual means of fighting for market shares and which tend to yield results in proportion to the amounts spent on them. Other less tangible factors are involved which tend to elude the economist's net but which play an important part in the business world. The lower-cost, higher-profit company acquires a special reputation which enables it to attract and hold customers, bid promising executive personnel away from rival firms, and recruit the ablest graduates of engineering and business schools. For all these reasons, there is a strong positive incentive for the large corporation in an oligopolistic industry not only to seek continuously to cut its costs but to do so faster than its rivals.

Here is where the self-defense factor considered so crucial by Adam Smith comes into play. Any company which falls behind in the race to cut costs is soon in trouble. Its power to fight back against attack is undermined, its freedom of maneuver curtailed, its ability to use the normal weapons of the competitive struggle weakened. Playing a more and more passive role, it finds its position progressively deteriorating, and eventually it is faced with some unpleasant but unavoidable alternatives: it can merge, on unfavorable terms of course, with a stronger firm;[18] it can attempt a reorganization and comeback,

[18] The stronger company may be in the same industry, or it may be a successful corporation in an entirely different line which has capital to invest and is therefore on the lookout for opportunities to buy into industries where a well-managed subsidiary could be expected to carve out a profitable niche for itself. Run-down companies which have been ruined by inefficient management, and the securities of which are often grossly undervalued even compared to the liquidation value of their assets, are ideal vehicles for such expansion programs. In recent years many large conglomerate corporate empires, spread-eagling up to a dozen or more industries, have been built up in this fashion.

usually under new management and with new capital; or it can give up the ghost and leave the field to its more successful rivals. This sort of thing happens very often in the business world, and every manager knows of numerous cases and lives in constant fear that a similar fate will overtake him if his company falls behind in the cost race. The stick of failure thus complements the carrot of success in an oligopolistic system no less than in a competitive one.

There is an additional reason, in our judgment as important as it is neglected, why a tendency for costs of production to fall is endemic to the entire monopoly capitalist economy, even including those areas which if left to themselves would stagnate technologically. It stems from the exigencies of non-price competition in the producer goods industries. Here, as in industries producing consumer goods, sellers must be forever seeking to put something new on the market.[19] But they are not dealing with buyers whose primary interest is the latest fashion or keeping up with the Joneses. They are dealing with sophisticated buyers whose concern is to increase profits. Hence the new products offered to the prospective buyers must be designed to help them increase their profits, which in general means to help them reduce their costs. If the manufacturer can convince his customers that his new instrument or material or machine will save them money, the sale will follow almost automatically.

Probably the clearest example of the cost-reducing effects of the innovating activity of manufacturers of producer goods is to be found in agriculture. As Galbraith has pointed out, "there would be little technical development and not much progress in agriculture were it not for government-supported research supplemented by the research of the corporations which devise and sell products to the farmer."[20] No doubt, as this statement implies, government research has been the main factor behind the spectacular reduction in agricultural costs during the last

[19] We discuss the implications of this in the consumer goods field in the next chapter.

[20] J. K. Galbraith, *American Capitalism*, Boston, 1952, pp. 95-96.

two decades, but the sales-hungry manufacturers of farm machinery, fertilizers, pesticides, etc., have also played an important part in the process. Similarly, producers of machine tools, computers and computer systems, business machines, automatic control equipment, loading and transfer machinery, new plastics and metal alloys, and a thousand and one other kinds of producer goods are busy developing new products which will enable their customers—comprising literally the entire business world—to produce more cheaply and hence to make more profits. In a word: producers of producer goods make more profits by helping others to make more profits. The process is self-reinforcing and cumulative, and goes far toward explaining the extraordinarily rapid advance of technology and labor productivity which characterizes the developed monopoly capitalist economy.

We conclude, then, that with regard to the cost discipline which it imposes on its members the monopoly capitalist economy is no less severe than its competitive predecessor, and that in addition it generates new and powerful impulses to innovation. There can therefore be no doubt about the downward trend of production costs under monopoly capitalism.

On the face of it this would seem to be an argument for monopoly capitalism's being considered a rational and progressive system. And if its cost-reducing proclivities could somehow be disentangled from monopoly pricing and a way could be found to utilize the fruits of increasing productivity for the benefit of society as a whole, the argument would indeed be a powerful one. But of course this is just what cannot be done. The whole motivation of cost reduction is to increase profits, and the monopolistic structure of markets enables the corporations to appropriate the lion's share of the fruits of increasing productivity directly in the form of higher profits. This means that under monopoly capitalism, declining costs imply continuously widening profit margins.[21] And continuously widening

[21] What is reported to be true of the country's largest corporation, the American Telephone and Telegraph Company, is really typical of the giant corporations which dominate the economy: "Striking testimony to

profit margins in turn imply aggregate profits which rise not only absolutely but as a share of national product. If we provisionally equate aggregate profits with society's economic surplus, we can formulate as a law of monopoly capitalism that the surplus tends to rise both absolutely and relatively as the system develops.[22]

This law immediately invites comparison, as it should, with the classical-Marxian law of the falling tendency of the rate of profit. Without entering into an analysis of the different versions of the latter, we can say that they all presuppose a competitive system. By substituting the law of rising surplus for the law of falling profit, we are therefore not rejecting or revising a time-honored theorem of political economy: we are simply taking account of the undoubted fact that the structure of the capitalist economy has undergone a fundamental change since that theorem was formulated. What is most essential about the structural change from competitive to monopoly capitalism finds its theoretical expression in this substitution.

But before we explore the implications of the law of rising surplus, we must examine, even if only briefly, some of the arguments which have been or might be used to deny that such a tendency exists.

AT&T's efficiency and surging growth is the fact that rate decreases rather than increases are its present problem. Generally the company no longer asks for higher tariffs; it simply wants the commission [the Federal Communications Commission] to let nature take its course and permit the rate of return to rise. In other words, the Bell System is now so large and efficient that its return on investment will rise almost automatically unless held down by rate reductions." *Business Week,* January 9, 1965, p. 70. For most giant corporations there is no commission to worry about.

[22] As a matter of fact, statistically recorded profits are far from comprising the entire economic surplus. Interest and rent are also forms of surplus; and, as we shall see, under monopoly capitalism still other forms assume decisive importance. Up to this point, however, we have used the term "profits" to mean simply the difference between sales revenue and costs of production, and the aggregate of profits in this sense is a legitimate first approximation to a fully developed concept of the economic surplus.

7

One argument against the theory that surplus has a tendency to rise under monopoly capitalism could be based on Schumpeter's well-known notion of the "perennial gale of creative destruction," which was originally put forward before the First World War but only recently has found widespread favor among the ideologists of monopoly capitalism. The argument holds that in the long run price competition is relatively unimportant and that even in its absence monopoly profits are a transitory phenomenon. In Schumpeter's words:

> But in capitalist reality as distinct from its textbook picture, it is not that kind of competition [price competition] that counts but the competition from the new commodity, the new technology, the new source of supply, the new type of organization (the largest-scale unit of control for instance)—competition which commands a decisive cost or quality advantage and which strikes not at the margins of the profits and the outputs of the existing firms but at their foundations and their very lives. This kind of competition is as much more effective than the other as a bombardment is in comparison with forcing a door, and so much more important that it becomes a matter of comparative indifference whether competition in the ordinary sense functions more or less promptly; the powerful lever that in the long run expands output and brings down prices is in any case made of other stuff.[23]

There was undoubtedly something to be said for this theory when it was first formulated in the early years of the twentieth century. Emergent giant corporations—what Schumpeter calls "the largest-scale unit of control"—were in fact knocking the foundations out from under their smaller competitors and often expanding output and bringing down prices in the process. But in the highly developed monopoly capitalism of today such phenomena are of marginal importance. Once the "largest-scale unit of control" has taken over, "the new commodity, the new technology, the new source of supply, the new type of organization" all tend to be monopolized by a handful of giant

[23] J. A. Schumpeter, *Capitalism, Socialism, and Democracy*, pp. 84-85.

corporations which behave toward each other in the manner
which Schumpeter himself characterized as "corespective."[24]
These corespecters, as he well knew, are not in the habit of
threatening each other's foundations or lives—or even profit
margins. The kinds of non-price competition which they do
engage in are in no sense incompatible with the permanence of
monopoly profits and their steady increase over time.

We are by no means arguing that all, or nearly all, innovation originates in a handful of giant corporations. As was
pointed out in the last chapter, there is good reason to believe
that many of the giants follow a deliberate policy of allowing
smaller firms to experiment with new ideas and new products
and then copy or take over those which prove successful: after
all, it saves money and is in keeping with the principle of betting only on the sure thing. But even if the policy is not deliberate, even if one assumes with T. K. Quinn that small companies are inherently more capable of innovating, the giants
can still move in and buy out and absorb the smaller creators.
Indeed, to be bought out and absorbed is often the ultimate
ambition of the small business.

All this means that Schumpeter's perennial gale of creative
destruction has subsided into an occasional mild breeze which
is no more a threat to the big corporations than is their own
corespective behavior toward each other. One can understand
why Schumpeter clung to his own theory after it had become
obsolete, but the popularity which it has attained in recent
years is another matter. As Galbraith has said, "the present
generation of Americans, if it survives, will buy its steel,
copper, brass, automobiles, tires, soap, shortening, breakfast
food, bacon, cigarettes, whiskey, cash registers and caskets
from one or another of the handful of firms that now supply
these staples. As a moment's reflection will establish, there
hasn't been much change in the firms supplying these products
for several decades."[25] This should be obvious enough, and it

[24] *Ibid.*, p. 90n.
[25] *American Capitalism*, p. 39.

should dispose once and for all of any theory of creative destruction through innovation.

A second objection to the theory of rising surplus is thus stated by Kaldor:

> Marxist economists would probably argue that . . . not only the productivity of labour, but also the degree of concentration of production can be expected to rise steadily with the progress of capitalism. This causes a steady weakening of the forces of competition, as a result of which the share of profit would go on rising beyond the point where it covers investment needs and the consumption of capitalists. Hence, on this argument . . . the system will cease to be capable of generating sufficient purchasing power to keep the mechanism of growth in operation.

The plain answer to this is that so far, at any rate, this has not happened. Though the growing concentration of production in the hands of giant firms proceeded in much the same way as Marx predicted, this was not attended by a corresponding growth in the share of profits. On the contrary, all statistical indications suggest that the share of profits in income in leading capitalist countries such as the United States have shown a falling rather than a rising trend over recent decades, and is appreciably below the level of the late nineteenth century; and despite the extraordinary severity and duration of the depression of the 1930's, the problem of "realising surplus value" appears no more chronic to-day than it was in Marx's day.[26]

In this statement, Kaldor appears to agree that the advance of capitalism has been accompanied by a weakening of the forces of competition and an increase of labor productivity, and he does not deny that these forces should logically lead to a rising share of profit. In other words, he apparently does not reject the theory which he attributes to Marxist economists. But he then asserts, in effect, that no matter how sound the theory, it is refuted by the statistical record. This, we submit, is an unsatisfactory way to leave the matter. There must be something wrong with either the theory or the statistics.

Where Kaldor has gone wrong is, first, in identifying re-

[26] Nicholas Kaldor, "A Model of Economic Growth," *The Economic Journal*, December 1957, p. 621.

corded profits with the theoretical "share of profit." The latter is really what we call surplus, the difference between total output and the socially necessary costs of producing total output. Under certain assumptions this will be equal to aggregate profits; but, as already noted, in the actual economy of monopoly capitalism only part of the difference between output and costs of production appears as profits. In part, therefore, Kaldor's argument results from a conceptual confusion.

But there is a second, even more important, flaw in his argument. The process which he describes as "the share of profit . . . [going] on rising beyond the point where it covers investment needs and the consumption of capitalists" is by its very nature self-limiting and cannot appear in the statistics as an actual continuing increase of profits as a share of total income. Keynes and his followers, including Kaldor himself, have driven home the point that profits which are neither invested nor consumed are no profits at all. It may be legitimate to speak of the potential profits which would be reaped if there were more investment and capitalists' consumption, but such potential profits cannot be traced in the statistical record—or rather they leave their traces in the statistical record in the paradoxical form of unemployment and excess capacity. If Kaldor had looked in the American statistics for such indicators of a rising *tendency* of profits, his search would not have been in vain. After all, the "extraordinary severity and duration of the depression of the 1930's" was hardly an accident, and the persistent rise in the unemployment rate in recent years lends strong support to the view that the problem of realizing surplus value is indeed more chronic today than it was in Marx's time. The truth would seem to be that except in war and periods of war-related prosperity stagnation is now the normal state of the United States economy.[27]

One final objection to the theory of rising surplus can be dealt with more briefly, namely, that labor unions are now

---

[27] These are central themes of the next four chapters.

strong enough to capture for their members increments in profits resulting from the combination of declining costs and monopoly pricing. This is the position taken, for example, by John Strachey in his *Contemporary Capitalism*, and it is of course a common view in the labor movement.

Unions certainly do play an important role in the determination of money wages, and the workers in more strongly organized industries generally do better for themselves than workers in less strongly organized branches of the economy. This does not mean, however, that the working class as a whole is in a position to encroach on surplus or even to capture increments of surplus which, if realized, would benefit the capitalist class relative to the working class.[28] The reason is that under monopoly capitalism employers can and do pass on higher labor costs in the form of higher prices. They are, in other words, able to protect their profit margins in the face of higher wages (and fringe benefits). In many cases in recent years, indeed, they have been able to weave wage increases into their monopolistic pricing policies in such a way as to achieve a prompter and closer approach to the theoretical monopoly price than would otherwise have been possible. For the steel industry, this was convincingly documented by the Kefauver Committee in its hearings and more particularly in its important report on the pricing practices of the big steel corporations;[29] and there is no reason to assume that the experience of steel in the mid-1950's is unique. And, whether or not it is common practice to

[28] If unions have the power which Strachey attributes to them, it is not clear why they should be satisfied to pursue a policy of merely preventing capitalists from appropriating a larger share of total income, which is what Strachey claims they have succeeded in doing in the hundred years or so since Marx formulated his theory of capitalism. One would rather expect them to capture a steadily increasing share for the workers. That they have not done so is surely *prima facie* evidence that they do not in fact have any decisive influence over the class distribution of income but that this is determined by a combination of forces in which the actions and policies of the corporations play a far more important role than those of unions.

[29] *Administered Prices: Steel.*

use wage increases as a pretext to increase profit margins, monopolistic corporations unquestionably have the power to prevent wage increases from lowering them. As Levinson has aptly put it, "While collective economic power may be effective in raising the price of labor, the potentialities of redistribution out of profits are very slight so long as producers remain free to adjust their prices, techniques, and employment so as to protect their profit position."[30]

[30] H. M. Levinson, "Collective Bargaining and Income Distribution," *American Economic Review*, May 1954, p. 316.

4

THE ABSORPTION OF SURPLUS:
CAPITALISTS' CONSUMPTION AND INVESTMENT

In the last chapter it was shown that under monopoly capitalism, owing to the nature of the price and cost policies of the giant corporations, there is a strong and systematic tendency for surplus to rise, both absolutely and as a share of total output. We now come to the problem of the absorption or utilization of the surplus.

In general, surplus can be absorbed in the following ways: (1) it can be consumed, (2) it can be invested, and (3) it can be wasted. In this chapter we confine attention to the capacity of monopoly capitalism to absorb surplus through private consumption and investment.

2

To the extent that surplus is consumed by capitalists, the amount available for investment is correspondingly reduced. It follows that by making appropriate assumptions about capitalists' consumption, it is always possible to arrive at a rate of investment which can be sustained. Given full employment and a certain rate of increase of productivity, total income (or output), including the sum of workers' and capitalists' consumption, can be assumed to rise just fast enough to justify the investment of the part of the surplus not consumed by the capitalists. The problem of surplus absorption can thus be solved—on paper. Whether capitalists' consumption offers any solution in reality is an altogether different question.

Without going into the arithmetic of the matter, one can

79

safely say that no solution can be found along these lines if the amount of surplus not consumed by capitalists (hence requiring investment) rises relatively to total income. We have already seen that surplus does in reality tend to rise relatively to total income. The question therefore reduces itself to this: does capitalists' consumption tend to rise as a share of surplus? If not, the investment-seeking part of surplus must rise relatively to total income, and the possibility that capitalists' consumption might provide a solution to the problem is excluded.

Let us assume that capitalists consume the entire amount of distributed profits. This is not true, of course, but if it can be shown that even in this case capitalists' consumption does not tend to rise as a share of surplus, then the conclusion which follows will hold *a fortiori* for cases in which capitalists save out of their distributed profits.

The problem is now quite simply whether there is in fact a tendency for the distributed share of surplus (dividends) to rise, remain constant, or fall as surplus itself expands. And here the evidence leaves no doubt about the answer.[1] Most large companies have a target dividend payout rate which remains remarkably constant over long periods of time (50 percent seems to be the most common figure). When profits rise, however, they do not immediately adjust dividends to maintain the target rate. For example, if a company has been earning $2 a share for some time and is paying a dividend of $1, and if earnings then rise to $4, the dividend will be raised to $2 not in one year but over a period of several years. In the meantime, the actual payout rate will lag behind the target rate. If this pattern is adhered to—and there is every indication that it is a deeply rooted aspect of corporate behavior—it follows that a continuous rise in earnings would be accompanied by an equally continuous decline in the payout rate.

Under these circumstances, capitalists' consumption would

[1] The propositions which follow are based on John Lintner, "Distribution of Incomes of Corporations Among Dividends, Retained Earnings, and Taxes," *American Economic Review*, May 1956.

increase absolutely, which of course is to be expected, but it would decline as a proportion of surplus and even more as a proportion of total income. Since these conclusions hold *a fortiori* to the extent that capitalists save out of their dividend incomes, it is clear that no solution of the problem of surplus absorption can be expected from this quarter.

3

Not only surplus, then, but also the investment-seeking part of surplus tends to rise as a proportion of total income. Whether this tendency will be realized, however, is another question. In attempting to answer it, we must first determine whether the system normally provides investment outlets large enough to absorb a rising share of a rising surplus.

The logic of the situation is as follows: if total income grows at an accelerating rate, then a larger and larger share has to be devoted to investment; and, conversely, if a larger and larger share is devoted to investment, total income must grow at an accelerating rate.[2] What this implies, however, is nonsensical from an economic standpoint. It means that a larger and larger volume of producer goods would have to be turned out for the sole purpose of producing a still larger and larger volume of producer goods in the future. Consumption would be a diminishing proportion of output, and the growth of the capital stock would have no relation to the actual or potential expansion of consumption.[3]

Quite apart from the fact that such an explosive growth process would sooner or later exceed the physical potentialities of any conceivable economy, there is simply no reason to assume that anything like it has ever occurred or is likely to

[2] See Evsey Domar, *Essays in the Theory of Economic Growth*, New York, 1957, pp. 127-128.

[3] This is essentially the case analyzed by Tugan-Baranowsky in his well-known attempt to refute all underconsumption theories of economic crisis. For the relevant references, as well as a discussion of Tugan's theory, see Paul M. Sweezy, *The Theory of Capitalist Development*, New York, 1942, Chapter 10, Section 2.

occur in the real world. Manufacturers of producer goods do not provide each other with an infinitely expanding market for each others' output, and they know it. In particular, it is sheer fantasy to imagine the cautious, calculating giant corporations of monopoly capitalism planning and carrying out the kind of snowballing expansion programs which this case presupposes.

If accelerating growth is ruled out as totally unrealistic, one is left with the inescapable conclusion that the actual investment of an amount of surplus which rises relatively to income must mean that the economy's capacity to produce grows more rapidly than its output. Such an investment pattern is certainly not impossible; indeed, it has frequently been observed in the history of capitalism. But what is impossible is that it should persist indefinitely. Sooner or later, excess capacity grows so large that it discourages further investment. When investment declines, so do income and employment and hence also surplus itself. In other words, this investment pattern is self-limiting and ends in an economic downturn—the beginning of a recession or depression.

Up to this point, we have been tacitly assuming that the economy is working at or near its full-capacity level. The tendency of surplus to rise which has been the focus of attention is rooted in monopolistic price and cost policies, not in any variation of output in relation to capacity. But as soon as we admit the possibility of less-than-capacity production, certain further points need to be made.

There undoubtedly is a close relationship between profits and operating rate, the latter being defined as the ratio of actual production to capacity production. If we take a corporation's capacity to be that volume of output which, with given costs and prices, yields the maximum profit, it follows that any decline in the operating rate, through either a reduction in output or an increase in capacity or some combination of the two, will result in a decline in profits as well. Moreover, the decline in profits will be more than in proportion to the fall in output, so that profits will disappear altogether at some positive rate of output, which is commonly referred to in business terminology as the "break-even point"—the point at which receipts exactly cover costs leaving neither profit nor loss. The reason for this behavior of profits lies in the existence, especially characteristic of the big corporation, of overhead costs which do not vary with output. Overhead costs per unit fall as output rises. If prices remain the same and if variable costs per unit are constant over the relevant range, profits per unit will rise, as will the profit total as a share of output.

The following arithmetical example, taken from the Kefauver Committee's study of the automobile industry, will help to make the point clear.[4] In 1957, General Motors produced 3.4 million cars and sold them at an average price of $2,213 per car. Variable costs (chiefly hourly-rated labor and materials) amounted to $1,350 per vehicle, leaving $863 for overhead and profit. Total overhead came to $1,870 million which, averaged over 3.4 million units, was $550 per unit. Profit was therefore $313 per unit or an aggregate of $1,068 million. Now if production had declined by 25 percent, profits per unit would have sunk by 58 percent to $130 per unit; while if production had increased by 25 percent, profits would have jumped by 35 percent to $423 per unit. Profits would have disappeared altogether at an output of about 2.2 million units, 65 percent of actual output for that year.[5]

What holds for General Motors holds for other large corporations and for the system as a whole: surplus decreases relatively rapidly whenever production falls below capacity. Moreover, since the rate of dividend payout lags in the downward as well as in the upward direction, the investment-seeking part of

[4] *Administered Prices: Automobiles*, p. 129. The volume of production is given on p. 107.

[5] It should be noted that this is not the break-even point as defined above. Production in 1957 was only 74 percent of the 1955 record, and even in that year the industry was probably not producing at full capacity. The Kefauver Committee concluded that "it seems reasonable to assume . . . that the company's present break-even point lies within the area of 40 to 45 percent of practical capacity." *Ibid.*, p. 112.

Chart 1

Hypothetical Profitability Schedule

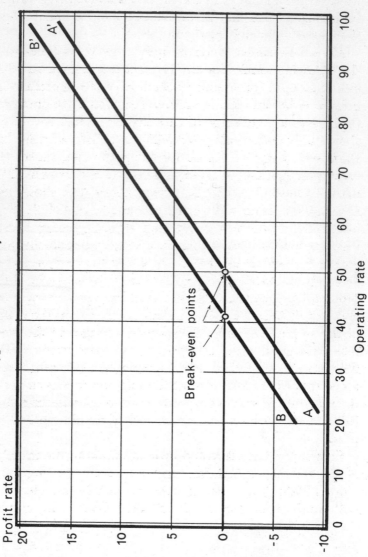

surplus shrinks even faster. On the other hand, if the economy moves up from a position of less-than-capacity production, both surplus and the investment-seeking segment of surplus swell absolutely and relatively.

The relationships which are here at issue can be expressed in the following terms. For any given cost and price structure, we can draw up a "profitability schedule" relating profit rate (calculated either on sales or on invested capital) to operating rate (output as a percentage of capacity). The line AA' in Chart 1 shows a hypothetical profitability schedule of this kind. It starts with negative values for the profit rate, passes through zero at the break-even point, and rises to a maximum at the full capacity level. The line BB', lying above AA', shows how the schedule moves up when prices rise and/or costs fall: the break-even point moves to the left, and at any given operating rate the corresponding profit rate rises. When we spoke in Chapter 3 and at the beginning of this chapter of the tendency of profits (or surplus) to rise, we were referring to a rise of the whole profitability schedule brought about by typical corporate price and cost policies. To these reasons for change in the magnitude of the surplus we now add another: changes in the operating rate with given costs and prices. Any satisfactory analysis of fluctuations of surplus under monopoly capitalism must take account both of shifts of the schedule and of movements along the schedule. The two can be thought of as reflecting the long-run and short-run forces which determine the volume of surplus.

Economists have devoted little attention to the investigation of profitability schedules, but one study dealing with the United States Steel Corporation is available and clearly shows both kinds of movement.[6] Each dot in Chart 2 shows the rela-

---

[6] John M. Blair, "Administered Prices: A Phenomenon in Search of a Theory," *American Economic Review*, May 1959, pp. 442-444. Mr. Blair has kindly provided us with the additional data for 1958-1960. Unfortunately the correlation could not be extended beyond 1960 because in that year the steel industry stopped publishing operating rates, and soon afterwards changes in tax legislation and administration resulted in an unmeasurable understatement of profits compared to earlier years.

Chart 2

U.S. Steel Corporation:
Operating Rate and Rate of Return
on Stockholders' Investment, after Taxes
1920-1940, 1947-1950, and 1953-1960

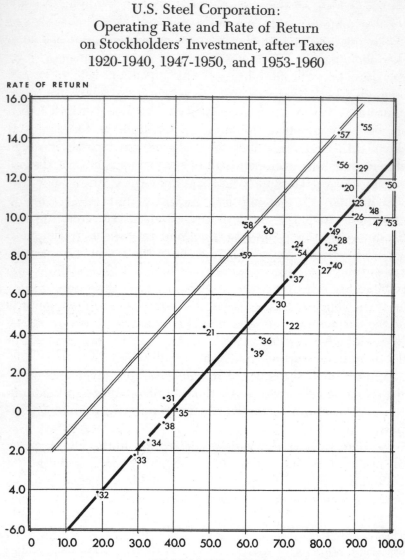

tion for a given year between U.S. Steel's profit rate and its operating rate.[7] Omitting war years, when conditions were untypical, the diagram covers the period from 1920 through 1960. All years through 1954 fall close to a line which shows a break-even point of about 38 percent of capacity and a maximum profit rate of 13 percent at 100 percent of capacity.[8] But from 1955 through 1960, this relationship no longer holds. Instead, all observations fall close to a new line (which we have drawn in by inspection) nearly parallel to the old one and lying some 4 percentage points above it. In 1960, for example, the operating rate was 65 percent. Under the old relationship the expected rate of return would have been a little under 6 percent; the 1960 rate of return was actually 9.4 percent. Thus from 1920 to 1955 the price-cost structure, and hence also the profitability schedule, of U.S. Steel was remarkably stable. Beginning in 1955, changes in prices and costs took place which raised the profitability schedule to a new and much higher level. Two chief factors were probably involved in this development: first, the introduction of new and more automatic steel-making technology; and second, price increases following, but more than proportional to, wage increases. Both are, as we saw in the last chapter, typical products of monopolistic corporate policies.

This example illustrates both aspects of the theory being expounded here: the tendency of the whole profitability schedule to shift upwards over time, and the variability of profits as output moves up or down on a given capacity base.[9] Both are important to an understanding of the dynamics of monopoly

[7] The profit rate here is the rate of return on stockholders' investment after taxes.

[8] The correlation coefficient for the years 1920-1956 is $+0.94$.

[9] Naturally there is no implication that sudden jumps like that of the U.S. Steel schedule in 1955 are typical. Normally the forces at work would produce a more gradual rise of the schedule. The U.S. Steel case is nevertheless highly instructive since the sudden jump does bring out the character and direction of the typical change more clearly than a gradual rise could do.

capitalism. The rise of the schedule shows how surplus swells
when capacity is fully utilized. And the shape of the schedule itself shows how surplus rapidly shrinks when investment outlets
fail and aggregate demand declines. As surplus shrinks, the
investment-seeking part of it shrinks more than in proportion.
On the downswing, in other words, the ratio of consumption to
both surplus and total output rises, and this sooner or later puts
a stop to the contraction. The lower turning point is reached
when the amount of surplus seeking investment is exactly absorbed by available investment outlets. At this point, a temporary equilibrium is reached which is characterized by the
existence of excess productive capacity and unemployed workers. The reverse side of the coin is that an upswing, however
initiated, generates a similar rapid absolute and relative increase of surplus. As soon as the investment-seeking part of
surplus exceeds available investment outlets, the expansion
comes to an end. And it should be remembered that this upper
turning point may be reached long before full utilization of
capacity or full employment of labor is achieved.[10]

4

We have been analyzing what may be called, following
Steindl and others, "endogenous" investment: investment
which is channeled into outlets that arise from the internal
mechanisms of the system. We have seen that these mechanisms tend to generate a steadily rising supply of investment-
seeking surplus, but that in the nature of the case they cannot
generate a corresponding rise in the magnitude of investment
outlets. Hence if endogenous investment outlets were the only
ones available, monopoly capitalism would bog down in a state
of permanent depression. Fluctuations of the kind associated
with expansion and contraction of inventories would occur, but
they would take place within a relatively narrow range, the
upper limit of which would be far below the economy's poten-

---

[10] For a discussion of these relationships in the history of monopoly
capitalism, see Chapter 8, especially pp. 243-244.

tial. The tendency of surplus to rise would be translated in practice into rising unemployment.

But not all investment is endogenous. There is also "exogenous" investment, which may be defined as all investment which takes place independently of the demand factors generated by the normal workings of the system. For example, some new technique of production is invented which will allow a certain commodity to be brought to market more cheaply; investment in plant embodying this technique may then take place even though no change in the demand for the commodity has occurred. Three types of exogenous investment have figured prominently in economic literature: (1) investment to meet the needs of an expanding population; (2) investment in new methods of production and new products; and (3) foreign investment. To what extent can they be expected, singly or in combination, to provide the investment outlets needed to absorb a rising surplus?

(1) *Population.* In recent years economists have put forward diametrically opposed views about the relationship between investment and population growth. According to Hansen, "It is a plain fact that a perfectly enormous amount of capital was absorbed in the nineteenth century for no other reason than the tremendous rate of population growth."[11] Kalecki, on the other hand, argues that

what is important . . . in this context is not an increase in population but an increase in purchasing power. An increase in the number of paupers does not broaden the market. For instance, increased population does not necessarily mean a higher demand for houses; for without an increase in purchasing power the result may well be the crowding of more people into existing dwelling space.[12]

Hansen's argument seems both to put the cart before the horse and to confuse a condition of rapid capital formation with a cause of it. It would be much closer to the truth to say

[11] A. H. Hansen, *Full Recovery or Stagnation?*, New York, 1938, p. 313.
[12] M. Kalecki, *Theory of Economic Dynamics*, London, 1954, p. 161.

that the high rate of investment during the nineteenth century stimulated a high rate of population growth; while the latter, through its effect on the labor force, made possible the continuation of a high rate of investment.

Kalecki, however, seems to go too far in denying any influence of population growth on the demand for investment. In the case of housing which he cites, it is probable that crowding due to population growth will lead people to demand more housing and less of other types of goods; and since housing requires relatively heavy capital investment, this would lead to an expansion in the total amount of investment. Further, speculative builders may be guided by population statistics in making their investment decisions, and the same may be true of certain other types of producers, notably public utilities. But what is relevant in this connection is not overall population growth but rather population growth in particular regions and localities. The latter, in turn, is to a large extent the result of internal migrations which are propelled by the rise of new industries and new modes of transport—in a word, by forces which are related only indirectly, if at all, to the increase in total numbers.

Thus, while there is no reason to deny that population growth per se does create some investment outlets, neither is there any case for assigning great importance to this factor. The experience of the United States during the 1940's and 1950's, when the rate of population growth rose sharply as compared to the depressed rate of the 1930's, strongly supports the theory—which was held by the classical economists—that population growth is a dependent, not an independent, variable. It was war-induced prosperity which boosted the birth rate; the reciprocal influence of the higher birth rate on investment outlets was certainly a factor in the prosperity of the period but hardly the decisive one. As for the future, if (for whatever reason) population growth should continue at a relatively high rate, and if at the same time other investment outlets should dwindle, the consequence would be much more likely to be a rising level of unemployment than a sustained investment boom.

The notion that exogenous investment caused by population growth can make a considerable, let alone decisive, contribution to solving the problem of surplus absorption can be safely rejected as groundless.

(2) *New Methods and New Products.* We are leaving out of account here such epoch-making innovations as the steam engine in the eighteenth century, the railroad in the nineteenth century, and the automobile in the twentieth century. Each of these dominated a whole era of economic history, penetrating into every aspect of social existence and creating, indirectly as well as directly, vast investment outlets. Omitting them from the analysis at this point is not to deny their crucial importance; it is simply to give theoretical expression to the view that each was, so to speak, a unique historical event and must be treated as such. We return to this subject in Chapter 8, where we present a brief historical analysis of the development of United States monopoly capitalism.

Here we are dealing with what may be called "normal" technological innovations, the kind of new methods and new products—often indistinguishable since one producer's new product may be another's new method—which have been forthcoming in a steady stream throughout the capitalist period.[13] A large part of investment over the years has been embodied in improved or altogether new types of producer goods. Does this mean that technological progress automati-

---

[13] "Modern industry never looks upon and treats the existing form of a process as final. The technical basis of that industry is therefore revolutionary, while all earlier modes of production were essentially conservative. By means of machinery, chemical processes and other methods, it is continually causing changes not only in the technical basis of production, but also in the functions of the laborer, and in the social combinations of the labor process. At the same time, it thereby also revolutionizes the division of labor within society, and incessantly launches masses of capital and of work people from one branch of production to another." Marx, *Capital,* Volume 1, Chapter 13, Section 9.

cally provides outlets for investment-seeking surplus and that any shortage of outlets could in principle be overcome by an appropriate increase in the rate of technological progress?

It has long been common among economists to argue as though these were indeed self-evident propositions. Hansen, who in the mid-1930's greatly feared that demographic and geographic factors were having a serious adverse effect on investment outlets, took it for granted that "We are thus rapidly entering a world in which we must fall back upon a more rapid advance of technology than in the past if we are to find private investment opportunities adequate to maintain full employment."[14] And in recent years, with the rise of the Research and Development movement, it is almost as common to assume that the rate of technological change has been, or soon will be, raised to the point where any talk about shortages of investment outlets is strictly anachronistic. A distinguished physicist, concerned with understanding the changing relations between science and industry, finds that the rise of what he calls the "innovation industry" has brought with it an important change in economic and business thought:

> In the *New York Times* or in *Fortune*, you can easily read the new text: the driving force of the economy today is the directed, profitable, institutionalized search for novelty. Here are the endless frontiers, not only of ideas, but of gain. Here is the answer to the "falling rate of profit," the "tendency to underconsumption," the need for new investment outlets. Read Peter Drucker or Sumner Slichter, or even the more technical literature, the burden is the same.[15]

[14] A. H. Hansen, "Economic Progress and Declining Population Growth," *American Economic Review*, March 1939. Reprinted in *Readings in Business Cycle Theory*, selected by a Committee of the American Economic Association, Philadelphia, 1944, where the passage appears at p. 378.

[15] Philip Morrison, "The Innovation Industry," *Monthly Review*, July-August 1959, p. 103. In some cases the gospel of salvation through R and D is preached with extraordinary fervor. Commenting on a McGraw-Hill survey of industry's research spending plans, Sylvia Porter, the financial columnist, fairly gushes with enthusiasm: "This will be the greatest outpouring of new things and services in the entire history of American inventions and innovations. . . . And this will pound home the magnifi-

These views about the favorable effects of more rapid technological change on the functioning of the economy have their
origin in the traditional analysis of a competitive system. What
typically happens under competition, according to the theory,
is that some especially enterprising firms invest in innovations
(in Schumpeter's model they are specifically formed for the
purpose) and for a time enjoy extra profits. Others, wishing to
share in their good fortune, follow suit. Presently supply expands by a significant amount and price begins to fall. Of the
remaining firms, some adopt the new ways in an effort to defend their profit position; others, too slow or too weak to re-
spond to the challenge, are squeezed out, their old equipment
turned into scrap. In the course of this process, which is repeated again and again at a tempo determined by the rate of
technological progress, much new capital is invested and much
old capital is destroyed.[16] A logical corollary is that any speeding up of technological change must open up new investment
outlets and raise the rate of growth of the economy.

Under monopoly capitalism this theory no longer holds.
Here innovations are typically introduced (or soon taken over)
by giant corporations which act not under the compulsion of
competitive pressures but in accordance with careful calculations of the profit-maximizing course. Whereas in the competitive case no one, not even the innovating firms themselves, can
control the rate at which new technologies are generally
adopted, this ceases to be true in the monopolistic case. It is
clear that the giant corporation will be guided not by the

---

cent message that we are now on the threshold of radical changes in our
everyday way of life, we are about to spur our rate of growth far beyond
the sluggish pace of recent years, we are going to pick up speed in the
crucial growth race with the Soviet Union." *San Francisco Chronicle,*
May 1, 1961.
[16] Schumpeter therefore speaks of "The Process of Creative Destruction" the title of Chapter 7 of his *Capitalism, Socialism, and Democracy.* It is worth noting that because capital is destroyed as well as
created, the net addition to the capital stock is never even an approximate
measure of new investment in a competitive economy.

profitability of the new method considered in isolation, but by the net effect of the new method on the overall profitability of the firm. And this means that in general there will be a slower rate of introduction of innovations than under competitive criteria.

To prove this point, let us assume the availability of a new technique of production which, if introduced through a new act of investment, would yield a profit of 12 percent. Under competition the act of investment will be immediately performed, provided only that the rate of interest is less than 12 percent. If the monopolist, however, were to introduce the new method immediately, he would have to follow up either by lowering his price in order to induce the market to absorb the output of both new and old methods or by idling some old equipment so as to avoid putting a larger quantity on the market. Given monopoly capitalism's strong bias against price cutting, it is safe to rule out the first course. The second course—idling old plant to make way for the new—would appeal to the monopolist only if the *difference* between the profit to be made with the new and that actually being made with the old is greater than the profit to be derived from any alternative investment open to him. Suppose that the old method is yielding 10 percent, compared with the 12 percent which the new would yield. In these circumstances, the monopolist would make the investment immediately only if the rate of interest were less than 2 percent (and there were no other possibilities of investing at more than 2 percent). Joan Robinson develops this argument in slightly different terms as follows:

It is sometimes argued that a monopolist presented with the blueprints of a new technique would . . . [install] new plant if average cost per unit of his monopolized commodity with the new technique is less than the prime cost with his existing plant. This argument appears to be fallacious. The monopolist is not obliged to lower his price because a lower-cost technique has been invented. The criterion for him is that the saving of prime cost on a year's output . . . should yield a rate of profit on the new investment as great as he can get in any other way. If he is confined for some reason to producing only this commodity, then he would find it worth while to make the substitution provided that average cost with the new technique, including interest on the finance required, is less than prime cost with the old; but in the normal way a monopolist can keep his old plant going and make any new investment he wants to in something else. Only if cost saving for this commodity is the most attractive investment open to him will he scrap his plant before its physical life is over. For this reason the view that monopoly does not tend to retard the diffusion of innovations seems ill founded.[17]

We conclude that from the monopolist's point of view, the introduction of new techniques in a manner which involves adding to productive capacity (demand being assumed unchanged) will normally be avoided. He will prefer to wait until his existing capital is ready for replacement anyway before installing the new equipment.[18] It is important to recognize what this does and what it does not imply.

It does not mean that there need be any slowing down of the rate of discovery of new techniques. The profit-maximizing big corporation has, as we have already stressed, a strong incentive to discover new, lower-cost techniques; and since its ability to make use of the resources of science and technology is much greater than that of the small competitive firm, we should actually expect monopoly capitalism to speed up the rate of discovery. Nor does it mean that there need be any tendency under monopoly capitalism to suppress new techniques. In any large corporation some equipment will always be reaching the end of its useful life, and it will of course be replaced by new equipment embodying the latest and most profitable techniques available. What the theory does imply is this: under monopoly capitalism the rate at which new techniques will supersede old techniques will be slower than traditional economic theory would lead us to suppose. Paradoxical though it

[17] Joan Robinson, *The Accumulation of Capital*, London, 1956, p. 407.

[18] An exception to this rule, possibly of considerable importance, is discussed below, p. 97.

may seem, we should therefore expect monopoly capitalism to be simultaneously characterized by a rapid rate of technical progress and by the retention in use of a large amount of technologically obsolete equipment. And this is exactly what we do find to be true of the United States today. Members of the McGraw-Hill Department of Economics undertook in 1958 a survey of the extent of obsolescence in existing plant and equipment. They found that it would cost no less than $95 billion to replace all obsolete facilities with the best new plant and equipment. Some of the details turned up are indeed striking:

Our inquiry into the state of American business plant and equipment, in terms of antiquity and degree of obsolescence, also showed that less than one third of it is modern, in the realistic sense of being new since 1950. Yet the years 1950-1958 comprise a period when rapidly changing technology has made older equipment obsolete in many lines of industry. . . .

Something of the significance of the degrees of obsolescence can be gained from these facts: on the average, a 1958 metal working tool is about 54 percent more productive than one that could be purchased in 1948. A combination of new freight cars and modern freight yard equipment can reduce operating costs up to 50 percent. New instruments that automatically direct the flow of chemical (or other raw material) processes, can often reduce costs enough to pay back the cost of the controls in one year. These savings are rarely possible in older plants.[19]

[19] Dexter M. Keezer and others, *New Forces in American Business*, New York, 1958, p. 23. The writers, better as observers than as analysts of the economic scene, interpret these facts to mean that there is a tremendous need for new investment, and they imply that in some unexplained way this need is translatable into demand for investment, what we call investment outlets. Clearly, they are here interpreting monopolistic facts in terms of competitive theory. To avoid misunderstanding, we should add that it is not only in monopolistic industries that obsolete equipment is found. Apart from the fact that even under the most perfectly competitive conditions the process of adjusting to a higher level of technique takes time, there is also the important consideration that competitive industries in a monopolistic economy are likely to be characterized by over-crowding, chronic excess capacity, and low profit rates. In such conditions, old equipment is often obtainable at prices far below

To be sure, some new techniques require little investment in new plant and equipment, and there is no reason why their introduction need be timed in relation to the wearing out of the old. A classic example is the oxygen injection method of steel-making. By inserting oxygen lances into existing furnaces (and relining them for greater heat resistance), the heating time can be drastically reduced and the capacity of the furnaces increased by 50 percent or more. The essence of the innovation here is to speed up the rate of production with existing plant and equipment, a result which, if attainable without large outlays, is naturally as welcome to a monopolist as to a competitor. So far as the adequacy of investment outlets for the system as a whole is concerned, however, innovations of this type are an unmitigated evil. Directly, they absorb little capital. And since they necessarily increase the capacity of existing plant and equipment, they discourage new investment to meet rising demand. To cap the climax, by reducing costs they swell profits and hence the volume of investment-seeking surplus.

The foregoing argument leads to an extremely important conclusion: under monopoly capitalism there is no necessary correlation, as there is in a competitive system, between the rate of technological progress and the volume of investment outlets. Technological progress tends to determine the *form* which investment takes at any given time rather than its amount.[20]

---

costs of production, which constitutes a powerful barrier to the purchase of new and more efficient equipment. In addition, small competitive firms often find it very costly or even impossible to secure financing for new investment. All of which explains why, under monopoly capitalism, the retention in use of demonstrably obsolete equipment can be widespread at the very time that the economy is stagnating for lack of sufficient investment outlets.

[20] It is one of Steindl's great merits to have seen this relationship clearly (*Maturity and Stagnation in American Capitalism*, p. 133), but he made the mistake of formulating it as a general proposition applicable to all stages of capitalism. That it is true under oligopoly is recognized and emphasized by Paolo Sylos Labini in his stimulating work, *Oligopoly and Technical Progress*, Cambridge, Massachusetts, 1962, especially pp. 148-149.

This is not a rigid rule to which there are no exceptions. Particularly in the case of new products, as distinct from new versions of existing products, there may be a rush to get into the market first in order to enjoy for a time an unchallenged monopoly position. A "key feature of new products," says the McGraw-Hill survey, "is that they usually carry very high profit margins. When a company is first in the field, it can set a relatively high price . . . and hope to earn a high return —far higher, in most cases, than on standard products for which markets are intensively competitive. There is, therefore, every incentive to take quick advantage of new product developments by the construction of new plant capacity."[21] The importance of this point should not be exaggerated, however, for the same study, in discussing the lag between scientific discovery and economic application, indicates that there are also factors which work in the opposite direction, inhibiting bursts of investment associated with the introduction of new products:

Capital investment particularly tends to lag because the expenditures required to begin output of a *new product* are usually quite small. Often existing facilities, or a part of them, can be converted to turn out trial quantities of the new product. And the really heavy expenditures required to build a complete new plant are not made until a year or two later. Similarly, expenditures to introduce a *new process* are not usually made until there is a relatively large production volume to justify these outlays. Especially in our heavy industries, new processes tend to be introduced (and, in fact, designed)

[21] *New Forces in American Business*, p. 34. Just how profitable a new product can be is well illustrated by the success story of the Xerox Corporation. In an article devoted to Xerox and its products, *Newsweek* (September 9, 1964) speaks of "the breathtaking profit potential of what has amounted to a monopoly in electrostatic copiers. A 914, for instance, costs something less than $2,500 to manufacture. Yet Xerox leases most of them, recovers even the manufacturing cost through depreciation— and each leased machine is returning an average of at least $4,000 a year. If a customer wants to buy, the price is $29,500. Even Wilson [President of Xerox] has remarked: 'I keep asking myself when I am going to wake up.'" The indicated profit margin of over 1000 percent on sales must be something like a record.

as the low cost way of adding new capacity. [In other words, they merely determine the form of investment which would have been made anyway.] Therefore, capital outlays for both new products and new processes tend to be delayed beyond the time of strictly scientific development, until sales prospects justify the building of large-scale facilities.[22]

To the extent that this argument applies, there is little reason to distinguish between new products and new processes: both tend to be introduced in a controlled fashion and to determine the form which investment takes rather than its magnitude. The new product takes the place of the old, just as the new process takes the place of the old; there is little of that "creative destruction" which Schumpeter saw as the chief dynamic force of the capitalist economy.

One additional reason for doubting the surplus-absorbing capacity of technological innovation is to be found in the depreciation practices of giant corporations. Among the socially necessary costs of production which have to be deducted from the total social product in order to calculate the amount of the surplus, there must of course be included an allowance to make good the wear and tear which the capital stock suffers through use and the passage of time. The proper amount of this allowance, commonly called depreciation, could be known with precision only in an economy from which all technological change was absent. In such an economy the service life of various types of plant and equipment would be established by repeated experience. If it were also a competitive system, the familiar pressures of competition would force producers to include in their long-run cost calculations charges against income which would be just sufficient to replace old equipment as it wears out. Actually, in an economy characterized by both technological change and monopoly there is no way of knowing what the service life of a piece of capital equipment will be, nor are there any competitive pressures tending to force giant corporations to make careful estimates to guide them in establishing

[22] *New Forces in American Business*, p. 62n.

their depreciation charges. There are, on the other hand, strong incentives for corporations to make the depreciation charges as high as the taxing authorities will permit, since the entire segment of gross revenue which can be labeled depreciation escapes the corporate profits tax and at the same time is freely available for corporate purposes in the same way that retained earnings are available. Quite naturally, businessmen are always pressing for legislative and administrative action to liberalize rules governing depreciation allowances. In recent years, they have been notably successful in getting what they wanted.

This, combined with the fact that the total depreciable capital stock of the advanced capitalist countries has by now reached enormous proportions, means that in present-day monopoly capitalism vast (and growing) sums of money flow into corporate coffers in the form of depreciation allowances. In theory, of course, part of this stream should be considered as legitimate cost of production and part as disguised profit; but since no one knows, and no one can know, where the one stops and the other begins, there is no way of making an accurate quantitative separation. One is almost forced to accept the prevalent convention that profits (and hence also surplus in our sense) are to be reckoned net of depreciation as it acually appears in the corporate books and is reported to the tax-gatherer.[23]

[23] An idea of the orders of magnitude involved here is afforded by a recent Department of Commerce study of postwar profits. Treasury rules governing depreciation for tax purposes were considerably liberalized in 1962. "This latest change in procedure, together with the accelerated amortization authorized in World War II and again in the Korean War crisis, and the larger depreciation allowances stemming from the Internal Revenue Act of 1954, will yield a corporate profits total in 1962 about $6-7 billion lower than would have been the case had these legal changes not occurred." Robert E. Graham, Jr., and Jacquelin Bauman, "Corporate Profits and National Output," *Survey of Current Business,* November 1962, p. 19. In percentage terms, this means that corporate profits in 1962 were about 15 percent lower than they would have been if the depreciation practices of the period before the Second World War had still been in use. On this subject, see also the Appendix below, pp. 372-378.

What cannot be accepted, however, is that the implications of these facts and relations should be either misrepresented or ignored. At any given level of income, total investment outlets must be sufficient to absorb not only the part of surplus that is not consumed but also the entire sum of depreciation allowances. This does not mean that corporate managements are obliged to invest the particular depreciation allowances that happen to come under their control: they can use them for any corporate purpose. But it does mean that, for the system as a whole, investment must be at least as large as depreciation before we can even begin to speak of the absorption of surplus.

Because of the deep-rooted connotations of the term "depreciation," one is likely to fall into the trap of assuming that the need to replace worn-out plant and equipment will automatically provide an outlet for depreciation allowances, leaving surplus to cover requirements for "new" investment. Actually, this would be the case only in an economy in which methods of production and consumers' tastes remained unchanged and outlets for new investment were related entirely to growing population and/or rising per capita income. In the actual capitalist economy, these conditions are far from being realized. Techniques of production and consumers' tastes are both continuously changing (or being changed), and under these conditions the distinction between "replacement" and "new" investment becomes quite meaningless. Old capital is always wearing out and new capital is always being invested, but there is no necessary relation between the two processes. If a machine making some product for which consumers are losing their taste wears out, it will not be replaced at all. If equipment embodying an obsolete method wears out, it will be replaced by equipment embodying a new method—provided future demand is expected to be high enough to warrant continuation of production. From the point of view of rational corporate management, all investment is new investment to be directed into this or that channel strictly according to future profit prospects and not at all according to established patterns. We can only say, as of any given time, that there is a definite total amount of investment which must find outlets if the existing level of output and employment is to be maintained, and that this total is equal to all of depreciation plus the amount of surplus forthcoming at that level of output minus the portion of surplus that is being consumed.

Now, the point we want to drive home is simply this: where the amount of depreciation is very large, as in present-day monopoly capitalism, it is quite possible that business can finance from this source alone all the investment it considers profitable to make in innovations (both new products and new processes), leaving no "innovational" outlets to help absorb investment-seeking surplus. Technological progress may, in other words, do little more than shape the most profitable uses for funds made available to corporate managements through their own "generous" depreciation policies. To the extent that this is so, technological progress makes no contribution at all to solving the problem of outlets for the "visible" part of investment-seeking surplus: whatever investment may be required to embody available innovations may well be less than enough to absorb the rising tide of depreciation allowances.

To attempt to prove this statistically is beyond the aim of the present work. And yet the view that technological progress is largely irrelevant to the problem of investment outlets is so likely to meet with resistance and at the same time so important to the general theory of monopoly capitalism that it seems desirable to present in support a few summary data.

The decade 1953-1962 was one of rapid and probably accelerating technological progress. The spectacular increase in Research and Development expenditures, shown in the first column of Table 1, may be taken as a rough indicator of the rate of advance of technology. If this had entailed the opening up of vast new investment outlets, this should certainly show up in outlays on plant and equipment (second column). Instead what we find is that the entire increase in outlays on plant and equipment for the decade as a whole took place between 1953 and 1957. From 1957 to 1962, while R and D continued to soar, outlays on plant and equipment fluctuated around an average some 8 percent below the 1957 level. Alongside these developments there occurred a sustained rise in the tide of depreciation allowances (third column) with a resultant increase in the proportion of plant and equipment outlays covered by depreciation from under 50 percent in 1953 to over 80 percent in 1962.

Table 1

Selected Financial Data for
Non-Financial Corporations, 1953-1962
(Billions of dollars)

	Research and Development Expenditures (R & D)	Outlays on Plant and Equipment (P & E)	Depreciation Allowances (D)	D as Percent of P & E
1953	3.5	23.9	11.8	49.4
1954	4.0	22.4	13.5	60.2
1955	4.8	24.2	15.7	65.7
1956	6.1	29.9	17.7	59.2
1957	7.3	32.7	19.7	60.2
1958	8.2	26.4	20.3	76.9
1959	9.0	27.7	21.6	78.0
1960	10.5	30.8	23.1	75.0
1961	11.0	29.6	24.8	85.2
1962	12.0	32.0	26.2	81.9

Sources: For R & D: McGraw-Hill Publishing Co., *Keys to Prosperity*, New York, n. d.; *Business Week*, April 29, 1961; and McGraw-Hill Press Release, April 26, 1963. For P & E and D: *Survey of Current Business*, annual review articles on sources and uses of corporate funds.

Without claiming that these data constitute proof, we nevertheless do believe that they provide strong support for the view that there is little if any correlation between innovation and investment outlets, and that monopoly capitalism is increasingly able to take care of its investment needs from depreciation allowances.

It could still be argued that with R and D expenditures running at more than a third of investment in plant and equipment, the R and D movement per se constitutes a highly significant investment outlet.[24] This would unquestionably be so if R and D were financed out of gross profits (depreciation plus net profits): if such were the case, these outlays would be on the same footing as investment in plant and equipment. In actual business practice, however, R and D expenditures are treated as costs of production and are recovered from sales revenue before gross profits are calculated. It is therefore obvious that the R and D movement does not create any outlets for the investment of gross profits.

This is not to say that R and D expenditures are really costs of production. Obviously they are not. From a social point of view, they constitute a form of surplus utilization comparable, say, to expenditures on education. In a formal sense, the best analogy is with selling costs, the analysis of which will be developed in the next chapter. (As a matter of fact, much that goes under the heading of R and D is little more than a glorified form of salesmanship so that the affinity between the two is substantively as well as conceptually close.)

Finally, our conclusion is that technological progress is no more likely than population growth to make a significant contribution to solving the problem of surplus absorption.

(3) *Foreign Investment.* For an understanding of the state of the world today—in particular its division into economically advanced and underdeveloped areas and the dialectics of their interaction—there are few subjects more important than foreign investment. For the moment, however, this range of prob-

---

[24] If we include R and D expenditures by non-business entities (governments, universities, foundations) total expenditures, according to the National Science Foundation, amounted to $12.4 billion in 1959, some 45 percent of outlays on plant and equipment in that year. National Science Foundation, *Review of Data on Research and Development*, NSF 61-9, Washington, February 1961, p. 1.

lems does not concern us: we are only interested in foreign investment as an outlet for investment-seeking surplus generated in the corporate sector of the monopoly capitalist system. And in this respect it neither does nor can be expected to play an important role. Indeed, except possibly for brief periods of abnormally high capital exports from the advanced countries, foreign investment must be looked upon as a method of pumping surplus out of underdeveloped areas, not as a channel through which surplus is directed into them.

The classic case is Britain in the heyday of its imperial power. It may be true that before about 1870, when the British economy was still in its competitive phase, a substantial net export of capital—thus a drain on Britain's domestically produced surplus—did take place. But in the years between 1870 and the First World War, Britain's income from overseas investment far exceeded capital exports. According to Cairncross's estimates, in the years 1870-1913, net export of capital totaled £2.4 billion, while income received from foreign investments came to £4.1 billion: capital export was thus only three-fifths of income received.[25] (These figures of course do not include the huge sums extracted from the empire in the form of salaries and pensions to the colonial bureaucracy.) Out of this tribute, Britain was able to maintain the world's largest leisure class and to pay for a military establishment which played the role of global policeman.

American experience has not been essentially different. In 1963, United States corporations (nearly all giants) had foreign direct investments amounting to $40.6 billion. But a large proportion of this—probably the majority—was acquired without any outflow of capital from the United States. A typical example is described by Cleona Lewis:

In many cases patent rights represent the larger part of a company's contribution toward the establishment of a foreign subsidiary or affiliate. Thus, when the Ford Motor Company of Canada was founded by a Canadian, Gordon MacGregor, in 1904, a 51 percent

[25] A. K. Cairncross, *Home and Foreign Investment, 1880-1913*, Cambridge, England, 1953, p. 180.

equity was turned over to the Detroit company in exchange for all Ford rights and processes in perpetuity in Canada, New Zealand, Australia, India, South Africa, and British Malaya. The years that followed were highly successful, and though large dividends were paid, re-invested earnings were also large. In 1912, a stock dividend increased the company's outstanding stock from $125,000 to 1 million dollars; and in October 1915, a 600 percent stock dividend was voted, increasing the company's outstanding stock to 7 million dollars. By the close of 1925, the company's capital and surplus stood on the balance sheet at more than 31 million dollars. It was estimated that by 1927 stock purchases had increased the American share in the company to around 85 percent. In the meantime, the company had paid out about 15 million dollars in cash dividends. Thus the cost to the American economy of this large investment in Canada would seem to have been the patent rights involved, plus something less than the re-investment of dividends received.[26]

Even in cases where substantial sums of capital are exported, subsequent expansion commonly takes place through plowing back of profits; and the return flow of interest and dividends (not to mention remittances disguised in the form of payment for services and the like) soon repays the original investment many times over—and still continues to pour capital into the coffers of the parent corporation in the United States. It is not surprising, therefore, that while capital does flow out of the country every year, the return flow of investment income is invariably much larger. The two series, which can be constructed from official government statistics for the years 1950 and after, are shown in Table 2.

In interpreting these figures—which it should be remembered do not include management fees, royalties, and various forms of hidden remittances[27]—it is important to bear in mind that according to the same sources total direct foreign invest-

---

[26] Cleona Lewis, *America's Stake in International Investment*, Washington, 1938, pp. 300-301.

[27] "In addition to receipts in the form of dividends, interest, and branch profits, U. S. parent companies are receiving from their foreign affiliates substantial amounts in payment for management services of various kinds or for the use of patents, copyrights, and similar intangible property. By 1961, this flow was approaching $0.4 billion annually, and

Table 2

Investment Outflow and Income, 1950-1963
(Millions of dollars)

	Net Direct Investment Capital Outflow	Direct Investment Income
1950	621	1,294
1951	528	1,492
1952	850	1,419
1953	722	1,442
1954	664	1,725
1955	779	1,975
1956	1,859	2,120
1957	2,058	2,313
1958	1,094	2,198
1959	1,372	2,206
1960	1,694	2,355
1961	1,599	2,768
1962	1,654	3,050
1963	1,888	3,059
Totals	17,382	29,416

Sources: United States Department of Commerce, *Survey of Current Business*, November, 1954; thereafter annual survey article in August of each year.

ment expanded from $11.8 billion in 1950 to $40.6 billion in 1963, an increase of $28.8 billion. It thus appears that during this period American corporations were able to take in as income $12 billion more than they sent out as capital, while at the same time expanding their foreign holdings (through reinvesting profits earned abroad, borrowing from foreign banks and investors, etc.) by $28.8 billion.

One can only conclude that foreign investment, far from

was continuing to rise more rapidly than amounts labelled 'income.'" Samuel Pizer and Frederick Cutler, "Expansion in U. S. Investments Abroad," *Survey of Current Business*, August, 1962, p. 24.

There are of course no data on the amounts extracted from foreign subsidiaries by such devices as false invoicing, rigging prices of imports from and exports to the parent company, and so on.

being an outlet for domestically generated surplus, is a most efficient device for transferring surplus generated abroad to the investing country. Under these circumstances, it is of course obvious that foreign investment aggravates rather than helps to solve the surplus absorption problem.

5

Twist and turn as one will, there is no way to avoid the conclusion that monopoly capitalism is a self-contradictory system. It tends to generate ever more surplus, yet it fails to provide the consumption and investment outlets required for the absorption of a rising surplus and hence for the smooth working of the system. Since surplus which cannot be absorbed will not be produced, it follows that the *normal* state of the monopoly capitalist economy is stagnation. With a given stock of capital and a given cost and price structure, the system's operating rate cannot rise above the point at which the amount of surplus produced can find the necessary outlets. And this means chronic underutilization of available human and material resources. Or, to put the point in slightly different terms, the system must operate at a point low enough on its profitability schedule not to generate more surplus than can be absorbed. Since the profitability schedule is always moving upward, there is a corresponding downdrift of the "equilibrium" operating rate. Left to itself—that is to say, in the absence of counteracting forces which are no part of what may be called the "elementary logic" of the system—monopoly capitalism would sink deeper and deeper into a bog of chronic depression.

Counteracting forces do exist. If they did not, the system would indeed long since have fallen of its own weight. It therefore becomes a matter of the greatest importance to understand the nature and implications of these counteracting forces, and it is to this task that the next three chapters are devoted. Here we confine ourselves to a few preliminary remarks.

The self-contradictory character of monopoly capitalism—its

chronic inability to absorb as much surplus as it is capable of producing—impresses itself on the ordinary citizen in a characteristic way. To him, the economic problem appears to be the very opposite of what the textbooks say it is: not how best to utilize scarce resources but how to dispose of the products of superabundant resources. And this holds regardless of his wealth or position in society. If he is a worker, the ubiquitous fact of unemployment teaches him that the supply of labor is always greater than the demand. If he is a farmer, he struggles to stay afloat in a sea of surpluses. If he is a businessman, his sales persistently fall short of what he could profitably produce. Always too much, never too little.

This condition of affairs is peculiar to monopoly capitalism. The very notion of "too much" would have been inconceivable to all pre-capitalist forms of society; and even in the competitive stage of capitalism, it described a temporary derangement, not a normal condition. In a rationally ordered socialist society, no matter how richly endowed it might be with natural resources and technology and human skills, "too much" could only be a welcome signal to shift attention to an area of "too little." Only under monopoly capitalism does "too much" appear as a pervasive problem affecting everyone at all times.

From this source stem a whole series of attitudes and interests of crucial importance for the character and functioning of monopoly capitalist society. On the one hand, there is a stubborn spirit of restrictionism which pervades the institutional structure.[28] Union featherbedding and Henry Wallace's plowing under of little pigs are only the best publicized examples of practices which are all but universal in business and government: the most primitive reaction to an excess of supply is simply to cut back. During the 1930's, when "too much" took on the dimensions of a universal disaster, primitive restrictionism acquired, in the National Industrial Recovery Act and the

[28] This is what the French, by a somewhat attenuated logic, call Malthusianism.

National Recovery Administration, the dignity and sanction of official national policy.

But cutting back as a remedy for "too much," even if beneficial to particular groups or individuals, only aggravates the situation as a whole. A secondary and more sophisticated set of attitudes and policies therefore emerges, gropingly and slowly at first but with increasing purposefulness and momentum as monopoly capitalism develops. Their rationale derives from the simple fact that the obverse of "too much" on the supply side is "too little" on the demand side; instead of cutting back supply they aim at stimulating demand.

The stimulation of demand—the creation and expansion of markets—thus becomes to an ever greater degree the leitmotif of business and government policies under monopoly capitalism. But this statement, true as it is, can easily be misleading. There are many conceivable ways of stimulating demand. If a socialist society, for example, should find that through some planning error more consumer goods were being produced than could be sold, given the existing structure of prices and incomes, the simplest and most direct remedy would clearly be to cut prices.[29] This would reduce the amount of surplus at the disposal of the planning authorities and correspondingly raise the purchasing power of consumers. The threatened glut could be quickly and painlessly averted: everyone would be better off, no one worse off. Such a course of action is obviously not open to a monopoly capitalist society, in which the determination of prices is the jealously guarded prerogative of the giant corporations. Each makes its own decisions with a view to maximizing its own private profit. Except for short periods of all-out war, when inflationary pressures threaten the entire economic and social fabric, there is no agency charged with controlling prices. Moreover, every attempt to maintain or establish such an agency in peacetime has resulted either in ignominious failure (witness the fiasco of price control after the

---

[29] See Kalecki, *Theory of Economic Dynamics*, pp. 62-63.

Second World War) or in the thinly disguised legalization of monopoly pricing practices in "regulated" industries. The plain fact is that the pricing process is controlled by the most powerful vested interests in monopoly capitalist society. To imagine that it could possibly be regulated in the public interest would be to imagine away the very characteristics of that society which make it what it is.

If stimulation of demand through price reduction is impossible within the framework of monopoly capitalism, this cannot be said of other possible methods. Take, for example, advertising and related forms of salesmanship, which will be analyzed at length in the next chapter. Every giant corporation is driven by the logic of its situation to devote more and more attention and resources to the sales effort. And monopoly capitalist society as a whole has every interest in promoting rather than restricting and controlling this method of creating new markets and expanding old ones.

Just as with price cutting and salesmanship, other forms of stimulating demand either are or are not compatible with the pattern of interests, the structure of power, the web of ideology that constitute the essence of monopoly capitalist society. Those which are compatible will be fostered and promoted; those which are incompatible will be ignored or inhibited. The question for monopoly capitalism is not whether to stimulate demand. It must, on pain of death.

The question is how to stimulate demand. And here, as we shall try to show, the system has its own built-in selective mechanisms which have the most far-reaching consequences for every aspect of life in monopoly capitalist society.

5

THE ABSORPTION OF SURPLUS:
THE SALES EFFORT

In analyzing the utilization of society's economic surplus—the difference between total social output and the socially necessary costs of producing it—economic theory has traditionally centered attention on capitalists' consumption and private investment, the subject dealt with in the preceding chapter. Not that other modes of utilization have been completely ignored. State and church have always been recognized as co-consumers of surplus, and both the classics and Marx considered that in addition to public officials and the clergy there was an important category of "unproductive" workers, typified by domestic servants, who received a large part or all of their incomes from capitalists and landlords. Further, Marx added to the charges on surplus what he called the expenses of circulation:

> The general law is that *all expenses of circulation, which arise only from changes of form, do not add any value to the commodities.* They are merely expenses required for the realization of value, or for its conversion from one form into another. The capital invested in those expenses (including the labor employed by it) belongs to the dead expenses of capitalist production. They must be made up out of the surplus product and are, from the point of view of the entire capitalist class, a deduction from the surplus value or surplus product.[1]

In principle there has thus never been any question about the existence of modes of surplus utilization other than capitalists' consumption and accumulation. However, these alterna-

[1] *Capital*, Volume 2, Chapter 6, Section 3.

tive modes have generally been treated as a subject of secondary interest. They were thought of as involving a redistribution of the consumption outlays of the capitalist class or as reducing somewhat the rate of accumulation, never as a decisive factor in determining the way the whole economic system works and the character of the society resting on this economic base.

It is easy to understand why, under competitive capitalism, these views prevailed. The dominant bourgeoisie of the eighteenth and nineteenth centuries was interested in reducing taxes and tithes to a minimum, with the result that the proportion of surplus consumed by church and state was much smaller than it had been in feudal times and could reasonably be thought of as continuing to decline as capitalist society grew richer. Likewise the expenses of circulation were greatly reduced compared to the mercantile period when merchant capital still held the upper hand over industrial capital, and this too seemed to point to a future in which capitalists' consumption and accumulation would increasingly pre-empt society's surplus product.

Whether these two modes of utilization would be sufficient to absorb all the surplus the economy was capable of producing, a question which made an early appearance in economic literature, was earnestly debated by Malthus and Ricardo, and dominated the writings of Sismondi and a long line of heretical "underconsumptionists." The theme also appears, though in a distinctly subordinate place, in the writings of Marx and his followers. What prevented both the classics and Marx from being more concerned with the problem of the adequacy of modes of surplus absorption was perhaps their profound conviction that the central dilemma of capitalism was summed up in what Marx called "the falling tendency of the rate of profit." Looked at from this angle, the barriers to capitalist expansion appeared to lie more in a shortage of surplus to maintain the momentum of accumulation than in any insufficiency in the characteristic modes of surplus utilization. And of course in the theories of the neo-classical economists, focused as they were on the equilibrating mechanisms of the market, the whole problem of capitalism's long-run tendencies virtually dropped out of sight for a half century or more.

When we pass from the analysis of a competitive system to that of a monopolistic system, a radical change in thinking is called for. With the law of rising surplus replacing the law of the falling tendency of the rate of profit, and with normal modes of surplus utilization patently unable to absorb a rising surplus, the question of other modes of surplus utilization assumes crucial importance. That they should be there in large and growing volume becomes a life-and-death issue for the system. And as they grow relative to capitalists' consumption and accumulation, they increasingly dominate the composition of social output, the rate of economic growth, and the quality of society itself.

One of these alternative modes of utilization we call the sales effort. Conceptually, it is identical with Marx's expenses of circulation. But in the epoch of monopoly capitalism, it has come to play a role, both quantitatively and qualitatively, beyond anything Marx ever dreamed of.

2

The sales effort made its appearance long before capitalism's latest, monopolistic phase. There is hardly any phenomenon in the economic and social universe which springs up without prior notice, like a *deus ex machina*. It is usual for tendencies to make a tentative appearance and to remain weak and insignificant for a longer or shorter period of time. Some never outgrow the stage of being tiny shoots, and are overpowered and smothered by countervailing processes. Others grow to be mighty trees which ultimately turn into prominent features of the social landscape.[2] Thus the sales effort is much older than

---

[2] It is the ability to distinguish between the former and the latter which constitutes the essential difference between comprehension of the historical process and the empiricist's accumulation of historical "facts."

capitalism as an economic and social order. It appears in various forms in antiquity, becomes quite pronounced in the Middle Ages, and grows in scope and intensity in the capitalist age. Its essence is succinctly described by Sombart:

> To excite interest, to evoke confidence, to awaken the urge to buy—this is the climax of the fortunate trader's endeavor. The means by which it is attained make no difference. It suffices that it is achieved by internal rather than external compulsion, that the other parties to their transaction enter the deal not against their will but by their own resolve. Suggestion must be the aim of the trader. Of the means of inner compulsion there are many.[3]

Yet large and variegated as the arsenal of these "means of inner compulsion" may have been in earlier times, it is only under monopoly capitalism in its most advanced stage—in the United States today—that they have assumed gigantic dimensions. This expansion has profoundly affected the sales effort's role in the capitalist system as a whole: from being a relatively unimportant feature of the system, it has advanced to the status of one of its decisive nerve centers. In its impact on the economy, it is outranked only by militarism. In all other aspects of social existence, its all-pervasive influence is second to none.

The tremendous growth of the sales effort and the spectacular intensification of its sway stem from its having undergone a far-reaching qualitative change. Price competition has largely receded as a means of attracting the public's custom, and has yielded to new ways of sales promotion: advertising, variation of the products' appearance and packaging, "planned obsolescence," model changes, credit schemes, and the like.

3

In an economic system in which competition is fierce and relentless and in which the fewness of the rivals rules out price cutting, advertising becomes to an ever increasing extent the

---

[3] *Der Bourgeois: Zur Geistesgeschichte des Modernen Wirtschaftsmenschen,* Munich and Leipzig, 1913, p. 74.

principal weapon of the competitive struggle. The immediate commercial purposes and effects of advertising have been thoroughly analyzed in economic literature and are readily grasped. Under conditions of atomistic competition, when an industry comprises a multitude of sellers each supplying only a small fraction of a homogeneous output, there is little room for advertising by the individual firm. It can sell at the going market price whatever it produces; if it expands its output, a small reduction of price will enable it to sell the increment, and even a small increase of price would put it out of business by inducing buyers to turn to its competitors who continue to offer the identical product at an unchanged price. To be sure, even under such circumstances there can still be advertising by producers' associations, urging consumers to expand their purchases of some generic product. But appeals of this kind ("Drink More Whiskey" or "Smoke More Cigarettes") have never played a major role in the history of advertising.

The situation is quite different when the number of sellers is small and each accounts for a large proportion of an industry's output and sales. Such relatively large firms are in a position to exercise a powerful influence upon the market for their output by establishing and maintaining a pronounced difference between their products and those of their competitors. This differentiation is sought chiefly by means of advertising, trademarks, brand names, distinctive packaging, and product variation; if successful, it leads to a condition in which the differentiated products cease, in the view of consumers, to serve as close substitutes for each other. The more telling the effort at product differentiation, the closer is the seller of the differentiated product to the position of a monopolist. And the stronger the attachment of the public to his particular brand, the less elastic becomes the demand with which he has to reckon and the more able he is to raise his price without suffering a commensurate loss of revenue.

All this applies in the first instance to consumer goods, but it is of considerable and growing relevance in the area of producer goods as well. It is enough to look at any of the innumerable general and specialized magazines addressed to businessmen to become convinced that even highly informed, technically competent buyers are by no means impervious to the appeal of advertising.

Just as advertising and related policies can create an attachment in buyers to a given product, it is also possible to generate demand for a new, or apparently new, product. In the words of E. H. Chamberlin in his pathbreaking work on the subject:

> Advertising affects demands . . . by altering the wants themselves. The distinction between this and altering the channel through which existing wants are satisfied, although obscured in practical application by the fact that the two are often mingled, is perfectly clear analytically. An advertisement which merely displays the *name* of a particular trademark or manufacturer may convey no information; yet if this name is made more familiar to buyers they are led to ask for it in preference to unadvertised, unfamiliar brands. Similarly, selling methods which play upon the buyer's susceptibilities, which use against him laws of psychology with which he is unfamiliar and therefore against which he cannot defend himself, which frighten or flatter or disarm him—all of these have nothing to do with his knowledge. They are not informative; they are manipulative. They create a new scheme of wants by rearranging his motives.[4]

And, obviously, the more intense the newly created wants are, the higher can be the price of the products and the larger the profits of the firm which caters to these wants. Accordingly, as noted by Scitovsky, "the secular rise in advertising expenditures is a sign of a secular rise of profit margins and decline of price competition."[5]

4

Ambiguous as statistical time series often are in the area of economic and social developments, the fact that advertising

---

[4] *The Theory of Monopolistic Competition*, Cambridge, Massachusetts, 1931, p. 119.

[5] Tibor Scitovsky, *Welfare and Competition*, p. 401n.

expenditures in the American economy have experienced a truly spectacular secular rise is unquestionable. A century ago, before the wave of concentration and trustification which ushered in the monopolistic phase of capitalism, advertising played very little part in the process of distribution of products and the influencing of consumer attitudes and habits. Such advertising as did exist was carried on mainly by retailers, and even they did not attempt to promote distinctive brands or labeled articles. The manufacturers themselves had not yet begun to exploit advertising as a means of securing ultimate consumer demand for their products. By the 1890's, however, both the volume and the tone of advertising changed. Expenditures upon advertising in 1890 amounted to $360 million, some seven times more than in 1867. By 1929, this figure had been multiplied by nearly 10, reaching $3,426 million.[6]

Thus as monopoly capitalism reached maturity, advertising entered "the state of persuasion, as distinct from proclamation or iteration."[7] This new phase in the work of the advertiser was already fully described as early as 1905 in *Printer's Ink:*

This is a golden age in trademarks—a time when almost any maker of a worthy product can lay down the lines of a demand that will not only grow with years beyond anything that has ever been known before, but will become to some degree a monopoly. . . . Everywhere . . . there are opportunities to take the lead in advertising—to replace dozens of mongrel, unknown, unacknowledged makes of a fabric, a dress essential, a food with a standard trademarked brand, backed by the national advertising that in itself has come to be a guarantee of worth with the public.[8]

Accordingly, the advertising business has grown astronomically, with its expansion and success being continually promoted by the growing monopolization of the economy and by

---

[6] *Historical Statistics of the United States: Colonial Times to 1957,* Washington, 1960, p. 526.

[7] E. S. Turner, *The Shocking History of Advertising,* New York, 1953, p. 36.

[8] Quoted in David M. Potter, *People of Plenty,* Chicago, 1954, pp. 170-171.

the effectiveness of the media which have been pressed into its
service—especially radio, and now above all television. Total
spending on advertising media rose to $10.3 billion in 1957,
and amounted to over $12 billion in 1962.[9] Together with out-
lays on market research, public relations, commercial design,
and similar services carried out by advertising agencies and
other specialized firms, the amount now probably exceeds $20
billion. And this does not include the costs of market research,
advertising work, designing, etc., carried on within the producing corporations themselves.

This truly fantastic outpouring of resources does not reflect
some frivolous irrationality in corporate managements or some
peculiar predilection of the American people for singing com-
mercials, garish billboards, and magazines and newspapers
flooded with advertising copy. What has actually happened
is that advertising has turned into an indispensable tool
for a large sector of corporate business. Competitively employed, it has become an integral part of the corporations'
profit maximization policy and serves at the same time as a
formidable wall protecting monopolistic positions. Although
advertising at first appeared to corporate managements as a
deplorable cost to be held down as much as possible, before
long it turned into what one advertising agency has rightly
called "a must for survival" for many a corporate enterprise.[10]

---

[9] *Statistical Abstract of the United States: 1963*, Washington, p. 846.

[10] An extreme case of this "must for survival" principle is presented
by a proprietary drug called Contac recently launched by one of the
country's largest pharmaceutical firms. This drug's advertising budget is
estimated at a "breathtaking $13 million, spent in probably one of the
most elaborate drug product campaigns ever devised. Most of the budget
is in television." For this outlay, the pharmaceutical firm "is said to be
deriving about $16 million in drug store sales, expressed in wholesale
prices." (*New York Times*, January 9, 1964.) Allowing for a handsome
profit margin, which of course is added to selling as well as production
cost, it seems clear that the cost of production can hardly be more than a
minute proportion of even the wholesale price. And when the retailer's
margin is added, the fraction of the price to the consumer must be
virtually invisible.

5

As mentioned earlier, the phenomenon of advertising has not escaped the attention of academic economics. Already Alfred Marshall distinguished between "constructive" and "combative" advertisements—commending the former as designed "to draw the attention of people to opportunities for buying or selling of which they may be willing to avail themselves," and condemning the latter as being mainly tools of persuasion and manipulation.[11] Later, Pigou went further, suggesting that "the evil might be attacked by the state through the taxation, or prohibition, of competitive advertisements—if these could be distinguished from advertisements which are not strictly competitive."[12] And this method of dealing with the matter— sorting out "good" and "bad" aspects of advertising, defending the one and inveighing against the other—has dominated most subsequent writing by professional economists, has indeed become a characteristic feature of a prominent branch of economics, the so-called economics of welfare.

Work by these economists, and even more the voluminous publications of a large number of commentators on social problems who have adopted a similar approach, have made a significant contribution to our knowledge about advertising. With this information on hand, it can hardly be seriously claimed that advertising performs to any appreciable extent what Marshall and Pigou considered to be a "constructive" function or leads to what other economists have called a "more informed and more perfect market." Indeed, few would question today the statement of Louis Cheskin, a veteran expert in marketing techniques, that "because consumers know little about most products, they look for labels, trademarks, and brand names," or his observation that "a superior product means superior in the eyes of the consumers. It does not necessarily mean superior in terms of objective value or according to laboratory

[11] *Industry and Trade,* London, 1920, p. 305.
[12] *Economics of Welfare,* 4th ed., London, 1938, p. 199.

standards." The preferences of the consumer, in other words,
are not generated by confronting him with a choice between
genuinely different products but rather by the employment
of increasingly refined and elaborate techniques of suggestion
and "brainwashing": this too has become a matter of common
knowledge. To quote Cheskin again, "studies that have been
conducted in the last twelve years show conclusively that
individuals are influenced by advertising without being aware
of that influence. An individual is motivated to buy something by an ad, but he often does not know what motivated
him."[13] Equally convincing are the numerous studies which
show that advertising induces the consumer to pay prices
markedly higher than those charged for physically identical
products which are not backed by suitable advertising techniques.[14]

Finally, the argument sometimes advanced in favor of advertising, that it enables the media to finance the production of
high-quality musical and literary programs, is on a level with
burning down the house in order to roast the pig. There is not
only serious question as to the value of artistic offerings carried
by the mass communication media and serving directly or indirectly as vehicles of advertising; it is beyond dispute that all
of them could be provided at a cost to consumers incomparably
lower than they are forced to pay through commercial advertising.

6

The kind of reasoning that seeks to weigh the "good" and the
"bad" sides of advertising has led traditional welfare economics
to a nearly unanimous condemnation of advertising as involv-

[13] Louis Cheskin, *Why People Buy*, New York, 1959, pp. 65, 54, 61.
Clearly, to condemn so-called subliminal advertising as particularly ob-
noxious is hardly justified: all advertising is in essence subliminal.

[14] We discuss later the related yet separate function of advertising, of
frequently defrauding the consumer either by making him like what he
gets regardless of price and quality or by inducing him to buy a product
which differs substantially from its advertised description.

ing a massive waste of resources, a continual drain on the consumer's income, and a systematic destruction of his freedom of choice between genuine alternatives.[15] Yet this approach has consistently failed to encompass the two issues which are really most important. One is that advertising in all of its aspects cannot be meaningfully dealt with as some undesirable excrescence on the economic system which could be removed if "we" would only make up our minds to get rid of it. The very offspring of monopoly capitalism, the inevitable by-product of the decline of price competition, advertising constitutes as much an integral part of the system as the giant corporation itself. As Pigou casually observed—without further pursuing the theme—"it could be removed altogether if conditions of monopolistic competition were destroyed."[16] But obviously overcoming capitalism—for this is what destruction of monopolistic competition would mean today—has not been within the purview of welfare economics, the concern of which is to remove or rather to mitigate the most calamitous results of capitalism in order to fortify the very system that necessarily produces and reproduces these calamitous results.

The second and even greater weakness of the welfare-

[15] This does not apply to the "new" welfare economics which reflects perhaps more than any other field of economics the eclipse of reason in bourgeois thought in the age of monopoly capitalism. Taking as its point of departure the consumer's "revealed preference," this fashionable doctrine refrains from expressing any "value judgments." Thus one of its most eminent spokesmen, Paul A. Samuelson, washes his hands of the whole matter: "Defenders of advertising claim many economic advantages for it. Useful information can be brought to the public; mass production markets are created; and as a by-product of advertising expense we have a private press, a choice of many radio and television programs, and thick magazines. So the argument goes. On the other side, it is claimed that much advertising is self-canceling and adds little to the consumer's valid information; that for each minute of symphonic music, there is half an hour of melodrama. The situation would be the more debatable were it not for the surprising fact, turned up by the Gallup poll, that many people seem to like advertising. They do not believe all they hear, but they cannot help remembering it just the same." *Economics,* 5th ed., New York, 1961, p. 138.

[16] *Economics of Welfare,* p. 199.

economics approach to advertising derives from the explicit or implicit assumption of full employment of resources which underlies all of its reasoning. With Say's Law as the point of departure, advertising (and the sales effort in general) is seen as creating certain "distortions" in the economy. For one thing, since it is agreed that the costs of advertising and selling are borne by the consumer,[17] it is held that the proliferation of advertising causes a redistribution of income: the income of consumers is reduced while that of the advertisers and of the advertising media is increased by the same amount. Furthermore, since advertising admittedly diverts consumers' purchases from one commodity to another, causes them to make their buying decisions on irrational grounds, and induces them to spend some of their income on worthless or adulterated products, it is blamed for falsifying the outcome of free consumers' choice and thus interfering with the maximization of consumers' satisfaction. But within this frame of reference advertising is not seen as altering the total volume of consumers' purchases, and therefore hardly calls for much attention in an analysis of the working principles of the capitalist system as a whole.

This treatment systematically obscures the central function of advertising and of all that goes with it in the economy of monopoly capitalism—a function much more clearly understood by businessmen and business analysts dealing with the realities of the American economy. Thus the McGraw-Hill Department of Economics writes: "In fact, broadly defined, as it properly can be, to include the whole range of marketing operations from product design through pricing and advertising right on to doorbell pushing and the final sale, selling or marketing not only is a symbol of a free society but is in ever-increasing measure a working necessity in our particular free

---

[17] "In the last analysis, these costs, borne by the consumer, must be counted as selling costs—costs of *altering* his demands, rather than as production costs—costs of satisfying them." Chamberlin, *The Theory of Monopolistic Competition*, p. 123.

society."[18] And the predicament that would overcome "our particular free society" in the absence of this whole range of marketing operations is outlined in the grim words of a prominent New York investment banker: "Clothing would be purchased for its utility value; food would be bought on the basis of economy and nutritional value; automobiles would be stripped to essentials and held by the same owners for the full ten to fifteen years of their useful lives; homes would be built and maintained for their characteristics of shelter, without regard to style, or neighborhood. And what would happen to a market dependent upon new models, new styles, new ideas?"[19]

This in truth is the nub of the matter. What indeed would happen to a market continually plagued by insufficient demand? And what would happen to an economic system suffering from chronic underconsumption, underinvestment, and underemployment? For the economic importance of advertising lies not primarily in its causing a reallocation of consumers' expenditures among different commodities but in its effect on the magnitude of aggregate effective demand and thus on the level of income and employment. This has been readily grasped by professors of marketing and advertising as well as by business journalists, but with few exceptions it has been ignored by economic theorists.[20]

This neglect is due to not recognizing that monopoly capital-

[18] Dexter M. Keezer and associates, *New Forces in American Business*, p. 90.

[19] Paul Mazur, *The Standards We Raise*, New York, 1953, p. 32. It does not seem to have occurred to Mr. Mazur that in the selection of clothing and food, esthetic considerations and taste could play their part; that houses could be built, and built well, without regard to Madison-Avenue imposed "style" but with full regard to the art of achitecture; that neighborhoods could be neither "exclusive" nor "restricted" nor dreary tracts nor slums but parts of residential areas well planned with regard to natural location, proximity to places of work, parks, playgrounds, and transportation facilities.

[20] The most notable exception, and we believe the first, was K. W. Rothschild. See his unfortunately little noticed paper "A Note on Advertising," *Economic Journal*, April 1942.

ism is characterized by a tendency to chronic stagnation as
well as to the complex nature of the way in which advertising
operates to counteract it. For while it is essential to understand
that the entire advertising effort constitutes one mode of utilization of the economic surplus, the manner in which it is treated
in business accounting tends to obscure this basic point. The
difficulty arises from the fact that advertising expenses, being
counted as costs, appear to be on the same footing as production costs and of course do not enter into profits. Yet since they
are manifestly unrelated to necessary costs of production and
distribution—however broadly defined—they can only be
counted as a part of aggregate surplus.

This segment of surplus is marked by certain peculiarities.
For one thing, it is a composite of two heterogeneous elements.
The first element is that part of society's aggregate advertising
and other selling expenses which is paid for by an increase of
the prices of consumer goods bought by productive workers.
Their real wages are reduced by this amount, and the surplus,
which is the difference between the aggregate net output and
the aggregate real wages of productive workers, is correspondingly increased. The other element is more complicated. It is
the remainder of the advertising and selling expenses which are
borne by the capitalists themselves and by unproductive workers via increased prices of the goods which they purchase. This
component of the outlays on advertising and the sales effort,
not being borne by productive workers, does not constitute an
increase of the surplus but does cause its redistribution: some
individuals living off the surplus are deprived of a fraction of
their incomes in order to support other individuals living off
the surplus, namely, those who derive their incomes from
wages, salaries, and profits generated by the selling "industry"
itself.

An even more significant characteristic of the segment of the
total surplus which nourishes the sales effort is what might be
called its "self-absorbing" nature. For at the same time that
some of this surplus is being extracted from productive workers

and an additional amount is being withdrawn from unproductive workers, the whole amount involved is utilized for the maintenance of the sales effort. Unlike the component of surplus which takes the form of net profits, the fraction which takes the form of selling costs calls for no counterpart in capitalists' consumption, no investment outlets. It provides, as it were, its own offsets and outlets. (There is just one qualification to this statement: the profits of advertising agencies and other enterprises engaged in the sales effort obviously enter the general pool of profits and must be offset by capitalists' consumption or investment or both.)

The direct impact of the sales effort on the income and output structure of the economy is therefore similar to that of government spending financed by tax revenue. This impact, measured by what has come to be called in economic literature the "balanced budget multiplier," is to expand aggregate income and output by an amount as large as the original revenue (and outlay).[21] And of course the expansion of aggregate income is associated with higher employment of unproductive workers in advertising agencies, advertising media, and the like.

So far we have directed attention to the direct relation of advertising to income generation and surplus absorption. The indirect effects are perhaps no less important and operate in the same direction. Generally speaking, they are of two kinds: those which affect the availability and nature of investment opportunities, and those which affect the division of total social income between consumption and saving (what Keynesians call the propensity to consume).

With regard to investment opportunities, advertising plays a role similar to that which has traditionally been assigned to innovations. By making it possible to *create* the demand for a product, advertising encourages investment in plant and equipment which otherwise would not take place. It makes no differ-

[21] The balanced budget theorem is discussed at greater length below, pp. 144-145.

ence whether the advertised product is really new or not: a
new brand of an old product will do as well. There is of course
a waste of resources in such cases; but in the presence of unemployment and idle capacity, these resources would have
otherwise remained unutilized: advertising calls into being a
net addition to investment and income.

With regard to the division of total income between consumption and saving, the effect of advertising is unambiguous
and, though unmeasurable, probably very large. In this connection it is essential to keep in mind that the monopoly capitalist period has witnessed a large growth of national income
and an even larger growth of the economic surplus. These developments, taken together with the technological advances to
which they have been related as both cause and effect, have
led to important changes in the occupational distribution of
the labor force. The stratification within the working class narrowly defined has increased, with many categories of skilled
and white collar workers achieving incomes and social status
which not so long ago were enjoyed only by members of the
middle classes. At the same time, old strata of "surplus eaters"
have grown and new ones have been added: corporate and
government bureaucrats, bankers and lawyers, advertising copy
writers and public relations experts, stockbrokers and insurance
agents, realtors and morticians, and so on and on seemingly
without limit. All of these groups, and of course also what C.
Wright Mills called the corporate rich and the very rich, have
incomes large enough to live not only in comfort but in varying
degrees of luxury. A large proportion of them customarily save
some of their incomes, and when their incomes rise all are
faced with a choice between consuming or saving the increment. On the other hand, it is also true that these groups are
eminently credit-worthy and, given the proliferation of lending
institutions which is characteristic of monopoly capitalism, find
it easy to borrow money to purchase a house, an automobile, a
boat, or whatever strikes their fancy. In these circumstances,
the amount of what is often called discretionary spending—the

sum of income which might either be saved or spent plus credit
available to consumers—is enormous, running to tens of billions of dollars a year. The function of advertising, perhaps its
dominant function today, thus becomes that of waging, on
behalf of the producers and sellers of consumer goods, a relentless war against saving and in favor of consumption.[22] And the
principal means of carrying out this task are to induce changes
in fashion, create new wants, set new standards of status, en-
force new norms of propriety. The unquestioned success of
advertising in achieving these aims has greatly strengthened its
role as a force counteracting monopoly capitalism's tendency
to stagnation and at the same time marked it as the chief archi-
tect of the famous "American Way of Life."

7

The strategy of the advertiser is to hammer into the heads of
people the unquestioned desirability, indeed the imperative
necessity, of owning the newest product that comes on the
market.[23] For this strategy to work, however, producers have
to pour on the market a steady stream of "new" products, with
none daring to lag behind for fear his customers will turn to his
rivals for their newness.

Genuinely new or different products, however, are not easy
to come by, even in our age of rapid scientific and technologi-

---

[22] Some advertising—that of savings banks, savings and loan associations, life insurance companies, and the like—of course works in the
opposite direction, but quantitatively this is small compared with the
efforts of the purveyors of goods and services.

[23] Vance Packard quotes the research and marketing director of the
Chicago Tribune (which styles itself "The World's Greatest Newspaper")
as saying that "tradition bores us now. Instead of being an asset, it is
virtually a liability to a people looking for the newest—the newest—
always the newest!" *The Waste Makers*, New York, 1960, p. 165. Packard's works, like those of many other latter-day muckrakers, provide a
great deal of useful information and at the same time show, in Marx's
words, "the strength and the weakness of that kind of criticism which
knows how to judge and condemn the present, but not how to comprehend it." *Capital*, Volume 1, Chapter 15, Section 8e.

cal advance. Hence much of the newness with which the consumer is systematically bombarded is either fraudulent or related trivially and in many cases even negatively to the function and serviceability of the product. Good examples of fraudulent newness are admiringly described by Rosser Reeves, head of the Ted Bates advertising agency, one of the country's largest:

Claude Hopkins, whose genius for writing copy made him one of the advertising immortals, tells the story of one of his great beer campaigns. In a tour through the brewery, he nodded politely at the wonders of malt and hops, but came alive when he saw that the empty bottles were being sterilized with live steam. His client protested that every brewery did the same. Hopkins patiently explained that it was not *what* they did, but what they *advertised* they did that mattered. He wrote a classic campaign which proclaimed "OUR BOTTLES ARE WASHED WITH LIVE STEAM!" George Washington Hill, the great tobacco manufacturer, once ran a cigarette campaign with the now-famous claim: "IT'S TOASTED!" So, indeed, is every other cigarette, but no other manufacturer has been shrewd enough to see the enormous possibilities of such a simple story. Hopkins, again, scored a great advertising coup when he wrote: "GETS RID OF FILM ON YOUR TEETH!" So, indeed, does every toothpaste.[24]

These examples could of course be endlessly multiplied. But from our present point of view the important thing to stress is not the ubiquity of this phenomenon but that it is confined entirely to the marketing sphere and does not reach back into the production process itself.

It is entirely different with the second kind of newness. Here we have to do with products which are indeed new in design and appearance but which serve essentially the same purposes as old products they are intended to replace. The extent of the difference can vary all the way from a simple change in packaging to the far-reaching and enormously expensive annual changes in automobile models. What all these product varia-

---

[24] Rosser Reeves, *Reality in Advertising*, New York, 1961, pp. 55-56. This book is reputed to be the most sophisticated guide to successful advertising.

tions have in common is that they do reach back into the process of production: the sales effort which used to be a mere adjunct of production, helping the manufacturer to dispose profitably of goods designed to satisfy recognized consumer needs, increasingly invades factory and shop, dictating what is to be produced according to criteria laid down by the sales department and its consultants and advisers in the advertising industry. The situation is well summed up by the McGraw-Hill Department of Economics:

> Today, the orientation of manufacturing companies is increasingly toward the market and away from production. In fact, this change has gone so far in some cases that the General Electric Company, as one striking example, now conceives itself to be essentially a marketing rather than a production organization. This thinking flows back through the structure of the company, to the point that marketing needs reach back and dictate the arrangement and grouping of production facilities.[25]

Vance Packard adds the information that "whenever engineers in the appliance industry assembled at conferences in the late fifties, they frequently voiced the lament that they had become little more than pushbuttons for the sales department," and he quotes Consumers Union to the effect that "a good deal of what is called product research today actually is a sales promotion expenditure undertaken to provide what the trade calls a profitable 'product mix.' "[26] And even this is not all. Researchers for *Fortune* magazine, that faithful chronicler of the mores and virtues of Big Business, looking into the Research and Development programs of large American corporations, found that this multi-billion-dollar effort is much more closely related to the production of salable goods than to its much touted mission of advancing science and technology.[27]

[25] Dexter M. Keezer and associates, *New Forces in American Business*, p. 97.

[26] *The Waste Makers*, p. 14.

[27] Eric Hodgins, "The Strange State of American Research," *Fortune*, April 1955. A similar conclusion is suggested by D. Hamberg, "Invention in the Industrial Research Laboratory," *Journal of Political Economy*, April, 1963.

As far as the consumer is concerned, the effect of this shift in the center of economic gravity from production to sales is entirely negative. In the words of Dexter Masters, former director of Consumers Union, the largest and most experienced organization devoted to testing and evaluating consumers goods:

> When design is tied to sales rather than to product function, as it is increasingly, and when marketing strategy is based on frequent style changes, there are certain almost inevitable results: a tendency to the use of inferior materials; short cuts in the time necessary for sound product development; and a neglect of quality and adequate inspection. The effect of such built-in obsolescence is a disguised price increase to the consumer in the form of shorter product life, and, often, heavier repair bills.[28]

But for the economy as a whole, the effect is just as surely positive. In a society with a large stock of consumer durable goods like the United States, an important component of the total demand for goods and services rests on the need to replace a part of this stock as it wears out or is discarded. Built-in obsolescence increases the rate of wearing out, and frequent style changes increase the rate of discarding. (In practice, as Masters points out, the two are inextricably linked together.) The net result is a stepping up in the rate of replacement demand and a general boost to income and employment. In this respect, as in others, the sales effort turns out to be a powerful antidote to monopoly capitalism's tendency to sink into a state of chronic depression.

8

The emergence of a condition in which the sales and production efforts interpenetrate to such an extent as to become virtually indistinguishable entails a profound change in what constitutes socially necessary costs of production as well as in the nature of the social product itself. In the competitive model, given all the assumptions upon which it rests, only the minimum costs of production (as determined by prevailing tech-

---

[28] Quoted by Vance Packard, *The Waste Makers*, p. 127.

nology), combined with the minimum costs of packaging, transportation, and distribution (as called for by existing customs), could be recognized by the market—and by economic theory—as socially necessary costs of purveying a product to its buyer. That product itself, although under capitalism not produced with a view to its use value but as a commodity with a view to its exchange value, could be legitimately considered an object of utility satisfying a genuine human need. To be sure, even during capitalism's competitive phase, to which this model approximately applies, socially necessary costs exceeded what they would have been in a less anarchic system of production, but there was no real problem of selling costs and certainly no interpenetration of the production and sales efforts. Socially necessary costs could be unambiguously defined, and at least in principle measured, as those outlays indispensable to the production and delivery of a useful output—given the attained state of development of the forces of production and the corresponding productivity of labor. And once costs had been defined, the social surplus was easily identifiable as the difference between total output and costs.[29]

Matters are very different under the reign of oligopoly and monopoly. Veblen, who was the first economist to recognize and analyze many aspects of monopoly capitalism, put his finger on the crucial point at a relatively early stage:

> The producers have been giving continually more attention to the salability of their product, so that much of what appears on the books as production-cost should properly be charged to the production of salable appearances. The distinction between workmanship and salesmanship has been blurred in this way, until it will doubtless hold true now that the shop-cost of many articles produced for

[29] Capitalist accounting methods treat rent and interest as costs for the individual firm. If the total costs of social output are calculated by adding up the costs of the individual producers, rent and interest will be included as costs and excluded from the surplus. Both classical and Marxian economics, however, had no difficulty in seeing through this appearance to the reality that rent and interest are as much components of the social surplus as profits.

the market is mainly chargeable to the production of salable appearances, ordinarily meretricious.[30]

Whether this phenomenon was really as widespread in the early 1920's as Veblen's statement might seem to imply is questionable. What is not open to dispute is that as a description of the situation in the 1950's and 1960's it is one hundred percent on target. And it raises a question which is as important as it is difficult for any theory which has socially necessary costs and surplus among its fundamental concepts.

The question is: what are socially necessary costs when, in Veblen's words, the distinction between workmanship and salesmanship has been blurred? This question does not arise from the mere existence of selling costs. As long as the selling "industry" and the sales departments of producing enterprises are separate and do not impinge upon the production departments, everything is plain sailing. In that case, selling costs, like rent and interest, can be readily recognized as a form of surplus to be subtracted from aggregate costs in order to arrive at the true socially necessary costs of production. But how should we proceed when selling costs are literally indistinguishable from production costs, as is the case, for example, in the automobile industry? No one doubts that a large part of the actual labor which goes into producing an automobile—how much we shall examine presently—has the purpose not of making a more serviceable product but of making a more salable product. But the automobile, once designed, is a unit which is turned out by the combined efforts of all the workers in the shop and on the assembly line. How can the productive workers be distinguished from the unproductive? How can selling costs and production costs be separated?

The answer is that they cannot be distinguished and separated on the basis of any data entering into the books of the automobile companies. The only meaningful procedure is to

[30] Thorstein Veblen, *Absentee Ownership and Business Enterprise in Recent Times*, New York, 1923, p. 300.

compare the actual costs of automobiles as they are, including all their built-in sales features, with what would be the costs of automobiles designed to perform the same functions but in the safest and most efficient manner. The costs of the latter would then be the socially necessary costs of automobiles, and the difference between these hypothetical costs and the actual costs of automobiles would be labeled selling costs. If we generalize from this example, it will be seen that on a social scale the identification of that part of the social product which represents sales costs, and should therefore be included in surplus, necessarily involves a comparison of the hypothetical costs of a hypothetical product mix with the actual costs of the actual product mix.

It is salutary to remember that comparisons of this kind, while for obvious reasons not undertaken in quantitative terms, were in principle fully acceptable to classical political economy. Its proponents had no hesitation about contrasting the structure and costs of output that would be forthcoming under the regime of laissez faire with the structure and costs of the output which was actually being produced by the hybrid feudal-mercantilist-capitalist system against which they fought their ideological and political battles. Their object was to confront reality with reason and to draw the necessary conclusions for conscious action designed to bring about desirable change. And this confrontation inevitably involved comparisons of what was with what would be reasonable.

Modern economics of course sees matters quite differently. For it, whatever is produced and "freely" chosen by consumers is the only relevant output; all costs incurred in the process are on a par and all are by definition necessary. From this starting point, it is only logical to reject as unscientific any distinction between useful and useless output, between productive and unproductive labor, between socially necessary costs and surplus. Modern economics has made its peace with things as they are, has no ideological or political battles to fight, wants no confrontations of reality with reason.

Not the least deplorable result of this attitude is that the energies of economists and statisticians have been directed away from the subjects here under consideration, though their elucidation is clearly of crucial importance to an understanding of the working principles of monopoly capitalism. To be sure, the required research work is beset with formidable conceptual and practical difficulties. Drawing up specifications of a hypothetical product mix and estimating its cost call for much ingenuity and good judgment; information on the cost of actual output is often shrouded in secrecy and at best can be obtained only by piecing together scattered and incomplete bits of evidence. Nevertheless, that much can be accomplished in this area has been proved beyond any doubt by a brilliant and methodologically path-breaking study of the costs of automobile model changes by Franklin M. Fisher, Zvi Grilliches, and Carl Kaysen.[31] A brief summary of this study will serve to define more sharply the nature of the questions with which we are concerned, to give some idea of the orders of magnitude involved, and to suggest lines along which further research is urgently needed.

The principal problem—the necessity of comparing the cost and quality of actual output with the cost and quality of a hypothetical output—is solved by Fisher, Grilliches, and Kaysen by taking 1949 as their point of departure and using the model of that year as the standard of quality and cost. The authors emphasize that the 1949 model was chosen as a standard not because of any particular merits but simply because that was the earliest year for which all necessary data were available. Conceptually, it would clearly have been possible to adopt as the standard a more rationally conceived and constructed model than that of 1949—safer, more durable, more

---

[31] "The Costs of Automobile Model Changes Since 1949," *Journal of Political Economy*, October 1962. An abstract, omitting details of estimating procedures, was presented at the 1961 annual meeting of the American Economic Association and appears in the *American Economic Review*, May 1962, beginning at page 259. Our quotations are from the latter version.

efficient, more economical to operate. Perhaps such an automobile actually exists somewhere in the world, perhaps it
would be necessary to have a team of experts blueprint one.
From a methodological point of view, either could be substituted for the 1949 model, and such a substitution would undoubtedly result in much higher estimates of the costs of model
changes. But even taking the imperfect product of 1949 as its
yardstick, the investigation leads to an estimate of costs which
the authors themselves consider to be "staggeringly high."

They "concentrate on the cost of the resources that would
have been saved had cars with the 1949 model lengths,
weights, horsepowers, transmissions, etc., been produced in
every year. As there was technological change in the industry,
[they] were thus assessing not the resource expenditure that
would have been saved had the 1949 models themselves been
continued but rather the resource expenditures that would
have been saved had cars with 1949 specifications been continued but been built with the developing technology as estimated from actual car construction cost and performance
data." These calculations showed that the cost of model
changes "came to about $700 per car (more than 25 percent of
purchase price) or about $3.9 billion per year over the 1956-
1960 period."

And this is by no means the whole story, since "there are
other costs of model changes which are not exhausted with the
construction of the car but are expended over its life." Among
these are costs resulting from accelerated obsolescence of repair parts, higher repair costs stemming from certain changes
in car design and construction, and additional gasoline consumption. Confining themselves to estimating the last of these
items, the authors found that

whereas actual gasoline mileage fell from 16.4 miles per gallon in
1949 to 14.3 miles per gallon ten years later, then rising to about 15.3
in 1960 and 1961, the gasoline mileage of the average 1949 car
would have *risen* to 18.0 miles per gallon in 1959 and 18.5 in 1961.
This meant that the owner of the average 1956-1960 car was paying

about $40 more per 10,000 miles of driving (about 20 percent of his total gasoline costs) than would have been the case had 1949 models been continued.

The additional gasoline consumption due to model changes was estimated to average about $968 million per year over the 1956-1960 period. And in addition, the authors estimated that "since such additional expenditure continues over the life of the car, . . . even if 1962 and all later model years were to see a return to 1949 specifications, the 1961 present value (in 1960 prices) of additional gasoline consumption by cars already built through 1961 discounted at 10 percent would be about $7.1 billion."

Summing up the costs of model changes proper and of additional gasoline costs caused by model changes, the authors concluded: "We thus estimated costs of model changes since 1949 to run about $5 billion per year over the 1956-1960 period with a present value of future gasoline costs of $7.1 billion. If anything, these figures are underestimates because of items not included."

All these calculations take for granted that the costs of automobiles include the enormous monopoly profits of the giant automobile manufacturing corporations (among the highest in the economy) and dealers' markups of from 30 to 40 percent of the final price to the purchaser. If these were omitted from costs, it appears that the real cost of production of a 1949 automobile built with the technology of 1956-1960 would have been less than $700. If we assume further that a rationally designed car could have been turned out at a cost of, say, $200 less than the 1949 model, and assume further the existence of an economical and efficient distributive system, we would have to conclude that the final price to consumers of an automobile would not need to exceed something like $700 or $800. The total saving of resources would then be well above $11 billion a year. On this calculation, automobile model changes in the late 1950's were costing the country about 2.5 percent of its Gross National Product!

It comes as a surprise that such a crucial component of the sales effort as advertising amounted to no more than $14 per car, about 2 percent of the cost of model changes. While automobiles are unquestionably an extreme case, this nevertheless may be taken as an indication of the scope and intensity of the interpenetration of sales and production activities, of the vast amount of selling costs that do not appear as such but are merged into the costs of production. In the case of the automobile industry, and doubtless there are many others that are similar in this respect, by far the greater part of the sales effort is carried out not by obviously unproductive workers such as salesmen and advertising copy writers but by seemingly productive workers: tool and die makers, draftsmen, mechanics, assembly line workers.

But what we would like to stress above all is that the Fisher-Grilliches-Kaysen study definitively establishes the feasibility in principle of a meaningful comparison between an actual and a hypothetical output, and between the costs incurred in producing the actual output and those that would be incurred in producing a more rational output. If carried out for the economy as a whole, such a comparison would provide us with an estimate of the amount of surplus which is now hidden by the interpenetration of the sales and production efforts.

9

This is not to suggest that a full-scale computation of this kind could be adequately carried out at the present time. No group of economists, no matter how imaginative, and no group of statisticians, however ingenious, could, or for that matter should, attempt to specify the structure of output that could be produced under a more rational economic order. It would certainly be very different from the structure with which we are familiar today; but, as so often, it is possible to see clearly what is irrational without necessarily being able to present the details of a more rational alternative. One need not have a specific idea of a reasonably constructed automobile, a well planned neighborhood, a beautiful musical composition, to recognize that the model changes that are incessantly imposed upon us, the slums that surround us, and the rock-and-roll that blares at us exemplify a pattern of utilization of human and material resources which is inimical to human welfare. One need not have an elaborate plan for international cooperation and coexistence to perceive the horror and destructiveness of war. What is certain is the negative statement which, notwithstanding its negativity, constitutes one of the most important insights to be gained from political economy: an output the volume and composition of which are determined by the profit maximization policies of oligopolistic corporations neither corresponds to human needs nor costs the minimum possible amount of human toil and human suffering.[32] The concrete structure of a rational social output and the optimal conditions for its production can only be established in the fullness of time—by a process of groping, of trial and error—in a socialist society where economic activity is no longer dominated by profits and sales but instead is directed to the creation of the abundance which is indispensable to the welfare and all-round development of man.

10

On an equal footing with the sales effort—or at least that part of it which is separable from production—as a mode of utilizing surplus is the diversion of a vast volume of resources

[32] That products designed according to the dictates of profit maximization can be in the most literal sense inimical to the elementary need for survival is illustrated by a report in the *New York Times* (March 3, 1964), according to which the American Automobile Association finds the automobile manufacturers guilty of grossly neglecting safety considerations for the sake of body glamor. Recommendations of competent engineers, said Robert S. Kretschmar, a national director of the AAA and head of its Massachusetts branch, "have been over-ridden by the body stylists and the merchandising people." And he continued: "The manufacturers look upon an automobile as 'glamor merchandise,' not as a mechanism that should be made as safe as possible." Among safety shortcomings were listed "a lack of fail-safe brakes, faulty tires, poor interior design, poor steering design, and weak and thin construction." And yet the automobile industry spends many millions of dollars every year on research and development!

into what is booked in national income accounts under the rubric "Finance, Insurance, and Real Estate."[33] Since no new questions of principle are involved, there is no need for lengthy discussion of these activities and their economic significance. What does require emphasis, however, is their sheer magnitude.

In 1960 this sector of the economy accounted for income totaling $42.3 billion, equal to 10.2 percent of aggregate national income for that year.[34] This was almost as much as the combined income generated in agriculture, mining, and contract construction. That some of the resource utilization of the finance, insurance, and real estate sector should be counted as necessary costs of producing the social output no one would deny. Any society based on division of labor and the purchase and sale of commodities requires some sort of banking system, though its functions could be much simpler and hence its costs much lower than they are now. If all sorts of insurance were automatically provided to everyone as part of a comprehensive social security system, all the footless trappings of agents and salesmen and collectors and accountants and actuaries and huge buildings to house them could be dispensed with. And as for real estate—which in dollar volume accounts for well over half the total income of the sector ($25.8 billion in 1960)—a staff of supervisory and service workers is clearly necessary, but the entire parasitic business of buying and selling and speculating in real estate, where the big money is made under capitalism, would have no reason for existence in a rational social order. Most of what our society lays out for finance,

[33] "The finance, insurance, and real estate division includes private establishments in the field of finance (banks and trust companies; credit agencies other than banks; holding companies; other investment companies; brokers and dealers in securities and commodity contracts), insurance (carriers of insurance, and insurance agents and brokers), and real estate (owners, lessors, lessees, buyers, sellers, agents, and real estate developers)." United States Department of Commerce, *Business Statistics 1963, a Supplement to the Survey of Current Business*, p. 235.

[34] *Statistical Abstract of the United States: 1962*, p. 317.

insurance, and real estate is merely a form of surplus absorption, characteristic of capitalism in general, and, in its present greatly expanded magnitude, of monopoly capitalism in particular. To a large extent it is rooted in the very nature of the corporate system, never better described than by Marx at a time when the corporation was only beginning its climb to dominance: "It reproduces a new financial aristocracy, a new variety of parasites in the shape of promoters, speculators, and merely nominal directors; a whole system of swindling and cheating by means of corporate promotion, stock issuance, and stock speculation."[35] And yet the entire expenditure of resources needed to maintain this gigantic system of speculating, swindling, and cheating, just like the expenditures on advertising and model changes, figures in the capitalist mode of reckoning as necessary costs of production.

Perhaps this is as it should be. Just as advertising, product differentiation, artificial obsolescence, model changing, and all the other devices of the sales effort do in fact promote and increase sales, and thus act as indispensable props to the level of income and employment, so the entire apparatus of "finance, insurance, and real estate" is essential to the normal functioning of the corporate system and another no less indispensable prop to the level of income and employment. The prodigious volume of resources absorbed in all these activities does in fact constitute necessary costs of capitalist production. What should be crystal clear is that an economic system in which *such* costs are socially necessary has long ceased to be a socially necessary economic system.

[35] *Capital*, Volume 3, Chapter 27.

6

THE ABSORPTION OF SURPLUS:
CIVILIAN GOVERNMENT

In the preceding chapter it was shown that the sales effort absorbs, directly and indirectly, a large amount of surplus which otherwise would not have been produced. The purpose of this and the following chapters is twofold: to demonstrate, first, that government plays a similar role but on a larger scale; and second, that the uses to which government puts the surplus which it absorbs are narrowly circumscribed by the nature of monopoly capitalist society and as time goes on become more and more irrational and destructive.

In the older theories—and here we include Marxian as well as classical and neoclassical economics—it was normally taken for granted that the economy was operating its plant and equipment at full capacity so that anything government might take from total output of society would necessarily be at the expense of some or all of its members.[1] When to this was added the assumption that real wages are fixed at a conventional subsistence minimum and are hence for all practical purposes irreducible, it followed that the burden of financing government must fall on the surplus-receiving classes: part of what they would otherwise consume or add to their capital goes to the state through taxation for the support of officials,

[1] In the Marxian theory, unemployment (the "industrial reserve army" or "relative surplus population") was assumed to be normal and to play a key role in regulating the wage rate. In the absence of idle plant and equipment, however, the unemployed could not be put to work to produce additional surplus.

police, armed forces, poor relief, etc. This was the core of the classical theory of public finance, and for obvious reasons it acted as a powerful bulwark of the principle that the best government is that which governs least. The interests of the rich and powerful, it seemed clear, were best served by limiting government, as nearly as possible, to the role of policeman—a limitation which was likewise justified, ostensibly for the good of society as a whole, by the theory of self-adjusting competitive markets.

Under monopoly capitalism, matters are very different. Here the normal condition is less than capacity production. The system simply does not generate enough "effective demand" (to use the Keynesian term) to insure full utilization of either labor or productive facilities. If these idle resources can be put to work, they can produce not only necessary means of subsistence for the producers but also additional amounts of surplus. Hence if government creates more effective demand, it can increase its command over goods and services without encroaching on the incomes of its citizens. This creation of effective demand can take the form of direct government purchases of goods and services, or of "transfer payments" to groups which can somehow make good their claims for special treatment (subsidies to businessmen and farmers, doles to the unemployed, pensions to the aged, and so on).

Thanks largely to the work of Keynes and his followers, these possibilities first began to be understood during the depression of the 1930's. For some time it was widely believed, however, even among economists, that government could create additional demand only if it spent more than it took in and made up the difference by such forms of "deficit financing" as printing more money or borrowing from the banks. The theory held that the total increment in demand (government plus private) would be some multiple of the government deficit. The strength of the government stimulus was therefore believed to be proportional not to the level of government spending as such but to the magnitude of the deficit. Thus no amount of government spending could exercise an expansionary effect on total demand if it was matched by an equivalent amount of taxation.

This view is now generally recognized to be wrong. Where there is unemployed labor and unutilized plant, government can create additional demand even with a balanced budget. A simple numerical example will illustrate the point, without omitting any of the essential factors. Suppose that total demand (= Gross National Product, GNP) is represented by the figure 100. Suppose that the government share of this is 10, which is exactly matched by taxation of 10. Government now decides to increase its purchases of goods and services—say, for a larger army and more munitions—by another 10 and to collect additional taxes of the same amount. The increased spending will add 10 to total demand and (since there is idle labor and plant available) to total output as well. The other side of the coin is an increase of income by 10, the equivalent of which can be drained into the public treasury through taxation without affecting the level of private spending. The net result is an expansion of GNP by 10, the exact amount of the increase in the government's balanced budget. In this case the "multiplier" is equal to 1: the increased taxation cuts off any secondary expansion of private demand.

Suppose now that a further expansion of government spending by 2 is decided upon but that this time no additional taxes are to be collected, the entire amount thus representing a deficit.[2] As government pays out this new money, private incomes are raised and part of the increase is spent, and so on. Since the increments to private spending become negligibly small after a few rounds, the amount of the aggregate addition to private spending can be calculated if the proportion of each increment spent is known. Assume, for example, that this aggregate addition is 3. Then the overall expansion of demand attributable to the deficit comes to 5 (2 government and 3 private). In this case, therefore, the multiplier is 2.5.

[2] For this result, some reduction in tax rates would of course be necessary.

Looking now at the whole economy we see that, compared to the initial state, GNP has risen from 100 to 115, private spending from 90 to 93, government spending from 10 to 22, and the government is running a deficit of 2. Clearly this situation will last only as long as the government continues to run the deficit. Assume that a decision is made to balance the budget again. If spending were reduced by 2 to wipe out the deficit, the multiplier would work in reverse and GNP would sink to 110. If instead spending were maintained and taxes raised by 2, the private increment would be cut off and GNP would stabilize at 112.

These highly simplified examples could be qualified and refined.[3] The main principles, however, would not be affected. They can be summarized as follows: (1) The influence of government on the level of effective demand is a function of both the size of the deficit and the absolute level of government spending. (2) A temporary deficit has temporary effects. (3) Even a persistent deficit, unless it grows steadily larger, will not cumulatively raise effective demand.

Since the focus of our attention is the economy of the United States, and since American fiscal history has not been characterized by persistent and steadily mounting deficits, we can concentrate on changes in the level of government spending. It has been through changes in the overall total of spending that government has exercised its greatest influence on the magnitude of effective demand and hence on the process of surplus absorption.

2

What has actually happened to government spending during the monopoly capitalist period?[4] Official statistics for both

[3] See, for example, Daniel Hamberg, *Principles of a Growing Economy*, New York, 1961, Chapters 12 and 17.

[4] The relevant figure here is total government spending including transfer payments, not only "government purchases of goods and services" which constitute the government component of GNP in the official statistics. As seen above, government generates effective demand by transferring purchasing power to individuals and business firms as well as

government spending (state and local as well as federal) and
GNP go back only as far as 1929, and available data for earlier
years are neither strictly comparable nor very accurate. Nevertheless enough is known to leave no doubt about the orders of
magnitude involved and hence about the overall trend. Table 3
presents figures for selected non-war years going back to the
beginning of the century.

Table 3
Government Spending, 1903-1959
(Billions of dollars)

	Gross National Product (GNP)	Total Government Spending (GS)	GS as Percent of GNP
1903	23.0	1.7	7.4
1913	40.0	3.1	7.7
1929	104.4	10.2	9.8
1939	91.1	17.5	19.2
1949	258.1	59.5	23.1
1959	482.1	131.6	27.3
1961	518.7	149.3	28.8

Sources: For 1903 and 1913, Paolo Sylos Labini, *Oligopoly and Technical
Progress,* Cambridge, Massachusetts, 1962, p. 181. For later years, Council of
Economic Advisers, *1962 Supplement to Economic Indicators,* Washington,
1962, p. 3.

The trend of government spending, both absolutely and as a
percentage of GNP, has been uninterruptedly upward throughout the present century. Until 1929 the rise was slow—from 7.4
percent of GNP in 1903 to 9.8 percent in 1929. Since 1929 it
has been much faster, the ratio now being well over one quarter. The rise in this ratio can be considered an approximate
index of the extent to which government's role as a creator of

by direct purchases of goods and services. In the official GNP estimates,
however, transfer payments are excluded from the government component and go to swell the personal and business components. This procedure, statistically necessary to avoid double counting, should not be allowed to obscure the true magnitude of government's role as a creator of
effective demand.

effective demand and absorber of surplus has grown during the monopoly capitalist era.[5]

This trend to more and more government spending of course tells us nothing whatever about the desirability or undesirability of the developments that underlie it. Such judgments can be formed only when due account is taken of the forms assumed by government-absorbed surplus—a subject we have not yet reached. In the meantime it should be noted that the trend toward larger government absorption of surplus, both absolutely and relative to society's total output, is not peculiar to monopoly capitalism. It is apparently a feature of most expanding economic systems. In a rationally ordered socialist society with productive potential comparable to that of the United States, the amount and proportion of surplus absorbed by the state for the satisfaction of the collective wants and needs of the people would certainly be larger, not smaller, than the amount and proportion absorbed by government in this country today.

To return to our main theme: the vast and growing amounts of surplus absorbed by government in recent decades are not, we repeat, deductions from what would otherwise be available to corporations and individuals for their private purposes. The structure of the monopoly capitalist economy is such that a continually mounting volume of surplus simply could not be absorbed through private channels; if no other outlets were available, it would not be produced at all. What government absorbs is in addition to, not subtracted from, private surplus. Even more: since a larger volume of government spending pushes the economy nearer to capacity operation, and since up

[5] The United States is by no means an extreme case in respect to the role of government as a creator of effective demand. Here are figures showing the percentage of total government spending to GNP in selected recent years for six advanced capitalist countries: United Kingdom (1953), 35.7 percent; Belgium (1952), 31.2 percent; West Germany (1953), 30.8 percent; Canada (1953), 26.6 percent; Sweden (1952), 25.9 percent; United States (1957), 25.5 percent. F. M. Bator, *The Question of Government Spending*, New York, 1960, p. 157.

to this point surplus grows more rapidly than effective demand as a whole, it follows that both the government and the private segments of surplus can and indeed typically do grow simultaneously. It is only when government absorption continues to expand even after full utilization has been reached, as during the later years of the Second World War, that private surplus is encroached upon.

These relationships can be illustrated by what has happened to corporate profits before and after taxes in recent decades. Before the Second World War, taxation of corporate incomes was rather low. During the war, rates were sharply increased, were raised again during the Korean War, and have remained high ever since. This change in the level of corporate taxation, however, has not meant any reduction in profits after taxes. On the contrary, the amount of profits after taxes increased as the economy expanded, and remained at about the same proportion of national income during the 1950's as during the 1920's.

Table 4
Share of Corporate Profits in National Income
(Percent)

	Before Taxes	After Taxes
1919-1928	8.4	6.7
1929-1938	4.3	2.8
1939-1948	11.9	6.0
1949-1957	12.8	6.3

Source: Irving B. Kravis, "Relative Income Shares in Fact and Theory," *American Economic Review*, December 1959, p. 931. The figures after 1929 are official Department of Commerce data; those for 1919-1928 are Kuznets's data adjusted by Kravis.

Table 4 shows clearly that what impairs the after-tax profitability of corporations, absolutely and relative to the rest of the economy, is not high taxation, and certainly not high government spending, but depression.[6] What the government takes in

---

[6] One other injurious factor should be mentioned: price controls. The poorer showing of the 40's as compared with either the 20's or the 50's is most plausibly explained by wartime controls. This factor was also

taxes is in addition to, not a subtraction from, private surplus. Moreover, since large-scale government spending enables the economy to operate much closer to capacity, the net effect on the magnitude of private surplus is both positive and large.

The American ruling class, at any rate its leading echelon of managers of giant corporations, has learned these lessons through the rich experience of three decades of depression, war, and Cold War. And its attitude toward taxation and government spending has undergone a fundamental change. The older hostility to any expansion of government activities has not of course disappeared. In the realm of ideology, deeply rooted attitudes never disappear quickly. Moreover, in some sections of the ruling class—especially rentiers and smaller businessmen—hatred of the tax collector dominates feelings about the role of government. But the modern Big Businessman, though he sometimes speaks the traditional language, no longer takes it so seriously as his ancestors. To him, government spending means more effective demand, and he senses that he can shift most of the associated taxes forward onto consumers or backward onto workers.[7] In addition—and this point is of great importance in understanding the subjective attitudes of Big Businessmen—the intricacies of the tax system, specially tailored to fit the needs of all sorts of special interests, open up endless opportunities for speculative and windfall gains.[8] All in all, the decisive sector of the American ruling

---

present, to a lesser extent, during the Korean War and hence affected the record of the 50's. In addition, the creeping stagnation of the 50's was of course reflected in a downdrift of the corporate profit share both before and after taxes.

[7] As Professor Boulding says, "the relative stability of profits after taxes is evidence that the corporation profits tax is in effect almost entirely shifted; the government simply uses the corporation as a tax collector." K. E. Boulding, *The Organizational Revolution*, New York, 1953, p. 277.

[8] An article in the *Harvard Law Review* begins as follows: "The genesis of this paper is the casual remark of a Washington lawyer who asked, 'What is the point of litigating a tax case when we can have the statute amended for the same outlay of time and money?' Probably his

class is well on the way to becoming a convinced believer in the beneficent nature of government spending.

What about workers and other lower-income groups? Since the big corporations shift their tax burdens, is not the increased absorption of surplus by government in the last analysis squeezed out of what Veblen called the underlying population? This question has already been answered, at least by implication. If what government takes would otherwise not have been produced at all, it cannot be said to have been squeezed out of anybody. Government spending and taxing, which used to be primarily a mechanism for transferring income, have become in large measure a mechanism for creating income by bringing idle capital and labor into production. This is not to say that no one gets hurt in the process. Those with relatively fixed incomes (rentiers, pensioners, some groups of unorganized workers) certainly do suffer as taxes rise and are shifted by the corporate sector. But the losses of these groups are of secondary magnitude and importance compared to the gains of that large proportion of the workers which owes its employment, directly or indirectly, to government spending. Furthermore, the bargaining power of the working class as a whole, hence its ability to defend or improve its standard of living, is of course greater the lower the level of unemployment. Thus, within the framework of monopoly capitalism, the lower-income classes taken as a whole are better off with higher government spending and higher taxes. This explains why, despite the wails of some traditionalists, there has never been any really effective political opposition to the steady rise of gov-

---

statement was inaccurate, and certainly it was extreme, but it comes as no surprise to sophisticated counsel daily studying the tax services to identify new patchwork stitched upon the internal revenue quilt. Whether their efforts take the form of new sections, or euphemistically called 'technical changes,' there is today an accelerating tendency away from uniformity and toward preferential treatment." William L. Cary, "Pressure Groups and the Revenue Code: A Requiem in Honor of the Departing Uniformity of the Tax Laws," *Harvard Law Review*, March 1955.

ernment spending and taxing which has characterized recent decades. Given the inability of monopoly capitalism to provide private uses for the surplus which it can easily generate, there can be no doubt that it is to the interest of all classes—though not of all elements within them—that government should steadily increase its spending and its taxing.

We must therefore reject decisively the widely accepted notion that massive private interests are opposed to this trend. Not only is the viability of the system as a whole dependent on its continuation but likewise the individual welfare of a great majority of its members. The big question, therefore, is not whether there will be more and more government spending, but on what. And here private interests come into their own as the controlling factor.

3

The main facts about the changing composition of government spending in the period of its most rapid growth (since 1929) are well known. Table 5, comparing 1929 with 1957, shows government spending, broken down into three major components, as percentages of GNP.[9] "Non-defense purchases" includes all purchases of goods and services for civilian purposes by federal, state, and local governments. "Transfer payments" includes unemployment benefits, old age pensions, veterans' allowances, etc.; interest on government debt; and subsidies less surpluses of government enterprises.[10] "Defense purchases" include all purchases (almost exclusively by the federal government) of goods and services for military purposes less sales of military items.

During the interval 1929-1957, total government spending increased from roughly one tenth to one quarter of GNP, most

[9] We have taken the year 1957 as the latest in order to make use of Bator's estimates, which are refinements of official Department of Commerce figures.

[10] "Transfer payments" does not include grants-in-aid from federal to state and local governments which are included under expenditures by state and local governments.

Table 5
Government Spending, 1929-1957
(Percent of GNP)

	1929	1957
Non-defense purchases	7.5	9.2
Transfer payments	1.6	5.9
Defense purchases	0.7	10.3
Total	9.8	25.4

Source: F. M. Bator, *The Question of Government Spending*, 1960, Tables 1 and 2.

of the difference representing absorption of surplus which would otherwise not have been produced. Of this proportionate increase in the ratio of government spending to GNP, almost nine tenths was transfer payments and defense purchases, little more than one tenth non-defense purchases. How are we to interpret these figures?

In the first place, government's direct contribution to the functioning and welfare of society is almost entirely subsumed under non-defense purchases. Here we have public education, roads and highways, health and sanitation, conservation and recreation, commerce and housing, police and fire protection, courts and prisons, legislatures and executives. And here, despite an enormous increase in outlays on highways, associated with a more than doubling of the number of automobiles in use since 1929, there has been very little expansion relative to the size of the economy as a whole. Increased non-defense purchases of goods and services have thus made almost no contribution to the solution of the surplus absorption problem.

Transfer payments, on the other hand, have grown significantly, expanding from less than 2 percent to nearly 6 percent of GNP. While an appreciable fraction of this increase (12 percent) represents expanded interest payments (which go largely to banks, corporations, and upper-income individuals), by far the larger part is accounted for by various forms of

~~social security~~ payments (unemployment, old age and sur-vivors, veterans) which certainly do enhance the welfare of large groups of needy citizens. This is the only substantial ele-ment of truth in the common assertion that since 1929 this country has become a "welfare state." In other respects expen-ditures affecting the welfare of the people have grown only about as fast as the economy as a whole. As to surplus absorp-tion, the growth of transfer payments has undoubtedly made a significant contribution.[11]

It is of course in the area of defense purchases that most of the expansion has taken place—from less than 1 percent of GNP to more than 10 percent, accounting for about two thirds of the total expansion of government spending relative to GNP since the 1920's.[12] This massive absorption of surplus in mili-tary preparations has been the key fact of postwar American economic history. Some six or seven million workers, more than 9 percent of the labor force, are now dependent for jobs on the arms budget. If military spending were reduced once again to pre-Second World War proportions, the nation's economy would return to a state of profound depression, characterized by unemployment rates of 15 percent and up, such as prevailed during the 1930's.

[11] The contribution would be greater but for the fact that the financ-ing of the social security system is closely tied to the regressive payroll tax. This is but one of many complications which we cannot analyze in a brief survey.

[12] It should be remembered that both 1929 and 1957 were peacetime years. The ratio of defense spending to GNP reached a maximum of 41 percent in 1943 and 1944. At that level there was considerable encroach-ment on private surplus, evidenced by the fact that corporate profits after taxes as a percentage of GNP declined steadily during the war years (from 7.5 percent in 1941 to 3.9 percent in 1945). But even the enor-mous amounts of surplus absorbed by government during the war were for the most part produced by a fuller and more rational utilization of resources, not by subtraction from private surplus or from the real in-comes of workers. The latter, in fact, attained a peak during the war which was not equaled until the mid-1950's. See Paul M. Sweezy, "The Condition of the Working Class," *Monthly Review*, July-August 1958, pp. 120-121.

This is of course widely denied, the dissenters falling into two main categories. First, there are those who claim that if taxes were cut simultaneously with a reduction in arms spending, private spending would increase to a compensating extent. Much of this book up to this point has been devoted to showing why the system does not and cannot work this way, and there is no need to repeat the argument here. The second group recognizes that arms spending is now acting as a prop to the economy (though generally tending to underestimate its importance) and that its removal would have serious consequences. These consequences, they argue, can be avoided by substituting other kinds of government spending for arms spending. In place of the warfare state, they say, we can and eventually should build a genuine welfare state.[13] And they have no difficulty in enumerating useful and needed projects which would require government outlays as large as, or even larger than, the present arms budget.[14]

The argument that non-defense spending is as effective in sustaining the economy as defense spending, and that "we" therefore should substitute the one for the other is no doubt valid enough as a statement of what is desirable. Whether it is also valid as a statement of what is possible, within the framework of monopoly capitalist society, is a different question, one which advocates of the change-over too often ignore. Yet this is clearly the crux of the matter for anyone who is interested in understanding how the system really works.

To answer this question, it is necessary to take into account

[13] For a succinct statement of this position, see J. K. Galbraith, "We Can Prosper Without Arms Orders," *The New York Times Magazine*, June 22, 1952.

[14] For example, Reginald Isaacs, chairman of the Department of City and Regional Planning at Harvard University, after extensive research for the American Council to Improve Our Neighborhoods (ACTION), concluded (in 1958) that required outlays for urban renewal would total just under two trillion dollars by 1970 and that the "necessary federal participation expenditures alone will rival those for national security." Reginald R. Isaacs, in Committee for Economic Development, *Problems of United States Economic Development*, New York, 1958, Volume 1, p. 339.

the modalities of political power in a monopoly capitalist society, and more specifically in its particular American version.
Since this is a large subject which cannot be dealt with at
length in the present study, we shall have to confine ourselves
to a few observations and suggestions.

4

Except in times of crisis, the normal political system of capitalism, whether competitive or monopolistic, is bourgeois democracy. Votes are the nominal source of political power, and
money is the real source: the system, in other words, is democratic in form and plutocratic in content. This is by now so well
recognized that it hardly seems necessary to argue the case.
Suffice it to say that all the political activities and functions
which may be said to constitute the essential characteristics of
the system—indoctrinating and propagandizing the voting
public, organizing and maintaining political parties, running
electoral campaigns—can be carried out only by means of
money, lots of money. And since in monopoly capitalism the
big corporations are the source of big money, they are also the
main sources of political power.

It is true that there is a latent contradiction in this system.[15]
The non-property-owning voters, who constitute the overwhelming majority, may form their own mass organizations
(trade unions, political parties), raise necessary funds through
dues, and thereby become an effective political force. If they
succeed in winning formal political power and then attempt to
use it in a way which threatens the economic power and privi-

[15] Marx wrote of the democratic French constitution adopted in
1848: "The most comprehensive contradiction of this constitution consisted in the following: the classes whose social slavery the constitution is
to perpetuate, proletariat, peasants, petty bourgeois, it puts in possession
of political power through universal suffrage. And from the class whose
old social power it sanctions, the bourgeoisie, it withdraws the political
guarantees of this power. It forces its rule into democratic conditions,
which at every point help the hostile classes to victory and jeopardize the
very foundations of bourgeois society." Karl Marx, *The Class Struggles in
France: 1848-1850*, International Publishers edition, New York, 1934, pp.
69-70.

leges of the moneyed oligarchy, the system is confronted by a crisis which can be resolved according to its own rules only if the oligarchy is prepared to give up without a fight. Since to the best of our knowledge there is no case in history of a privileged oligarchy's behaving this way, we can safely dismiss the possibility. What happens instead is that the oligarchy, which controls either directly or through trusted agents all the instrumentalities of coercion (armed forces, police, courts, etc.), abandons the democratic forms and resorts to some form of direct authoritarian rule. Such a breakdown of bourgeois democracy and resort to authoritarian rule may also occur for other reasons—such as, for example, a prolonged inability to form a stable parliamentary majority, or successful resistance by certain vested interests to reforms necessary for the proper functioning of the economy. The history of recent decades is particularly rich in examples of the substitution of authoritarian for democratic government in capitalist countries: Italy in the early 1920's, Germany in 1933, Spain in the later 1930's, France in 1958, and many more.

In general, however, moneyed oligarchies prefer democratic to authoritarian government. The stability of the system is enhanced by periodic popular ratifications of oligarchic rule—this is what parliamentary and presidential elections normally amount to—and certain very real dangers to the oligarchy itself of personal or military dictatorship are avoided. Hence in developed capitalist countries, especially those with a long history of democratic government, oligarchies are reluctant to resort to authoritarian methods of dealing with opposition movements or solving difficult problems, and instead devise more indirect and subtle means for accomplishing their ends. Concessions are made to pull the teeth of trade-union and labor political movements professing radical aims. Their leaders are bought off—with money, flattery, and honors. As a result, when they acquire power they stay within the confines of the system, merely trying to win a few more concessions here and there to keep the rank and file satisfied, yet never challenging the real bastions of oligarchic power in the economy and in the coercive branches of the state apparatus. Similarly, the oligarchy alters the machinery of government to the extent necessary to prevent any stalemates and deadlocks which might involve the breakdown of democratic procedures (for example, the number of political parties is deliberately limited to prevent the emergence of government by unstable parliamentary coalitions). By these methods, and many others, democracy is made to serve the interests of the oligarchy far more effectively and durably than authoritarian rule. The possibility of authoritarian rule is never renounced—indeed, most democratic constitutions make specific provision for it in times of emergency—but it is decidedly not the preferred form of government for normally functioning capitalist societies.

The United States system of government is of course one of bourgeois democracy in the sense just discussed. In constitutional theory, the people exercise sovereign power; in actual practice, a relatively small moneyed oligarchy rules supreme. But democratic institutions are not merely a smoke screen behind which sit a handful of industrialists and bankers making policies and issuing orders. Reality is more complicated than that.

The nation's Founding Fathers were acutely aware of the latent contradiction in the democratic form of government, as indeed were most political thinkers in the late eighteenth and early nineteenth centuries. They recognized the possibility that the propertyless majority might, once it had the vote, attempt to turn its nominal sovereignty into real power and thereby jeopardize the security of property, which they regarded as the very foundation of civilized society. They therefore devised the famous system of checks and balances, the purpose of which was to make it as difficult as possible for the existing system of property relations to be subverted. American capitalism later developed in a context of numerous and often bitter struggles among various groups and segments of the moneyed classes—which had never been united, as in Europe, by a common struggle against feudal power. For these and other reasons, the governmental institutions which have taken shape in the United States have been heavily weighted on the side of protecting the rights and privileges of minorities: the property-owning minority as a whole against the people, and various groups of property-owners against each other. We cannot detail the story here—how the separation of powers was written into the Constitution, how states' rights and local autonomy became fortresses for vested interests, how political parties evolved into vote-gathering and patronage-dispensing machines without program or discipline. What interests us is the outcome, which was already shaped before the end of the nineteenth century. The United States became a sort of utopia for the private sovereignties of property and business. The very structure of government prevented effective action in many areas of the economy or social life (city planning, for example, to cite a need which has become increasingly acute in recent years[16]). And even where this was not so, the system of political representation, together with the absence of responsible political parties, gave an effective veto power to temporary or permanent coalitions of vested interests. The positive role of government has tended to be narrowly confined to a few functions which could command the approval of substantially all elements of the moneyed classes: extending the national territory and protecting the interests of American businessmen and investors abroad, activities which throughout the nation's history have been the first concern of the federal government;[17]

---

[16] *1400 Governments,* a recently published book by Robert C. Wood of the Massachusetts Institute of Technology, refers in its title to the number of separate governmental authorities operating within the New York metropolitan area. Each of these authorities is the repository and representative of vested interests; there is no overall authority to control and coordinate their policies. To speak of "planning" in these circumstances is of course ridiculous.

[17] Failure to understand this is one of the greatest weaknesses of most American historical writing. There are exceptions, however. See, for example, R. W. Van Alstyne, *The Rising American Empire,* New York, 1960, where the decisive character of foreign relations in shaping the nation's development from earliest times is correctly appreciated.

perfecting and protecting property rights at home; carving up
the public domain among the most powerful and insistent
claimants; providing a minimum infrastructure for the profitable operation of private business; passing out favors and subsidies in accordance with the well-known principles of the log-
roll and the pork barrel. Until the New Deal period of the
1930's, there was not even any pretense that promoting the
welfare of the lower classes was a responsibility of government: the dominant ideology held that any reliance on government for income or services was demoralizing to the individual,
contrary to the laws of nature, and ruinous to the system of
private enterprise.

This was the situation which prevailed at the time of the
collapse of the boom of the 1920's. We have already seen that
only a small increase in the relative importance of government
spending had taken place since the turn of the century (mostly
caused by the building of roads and highways to accommodate
the rapidly growing number of automobiles), and in Chapter 8
we shall see why this was nevertheless on the whole a period of
capitalist prosperity. But with the coming of the Great Depression, the need for government to play a larger role suddenly
became acute. How was this need met in the liberal New Deal
period? In order to answer this question we have constructed
Table 5a, which is the same as Table 5 except that it compares
1929 with 1939 instead of with 1957:

Table 5a

Government Spending, 1929-1939

(Percent of GNP)

	1929	1939
Non-defense purchases	7.5	13.3
Transfer payments	1.6	4.6
Defense purchases	0.7	1.4
Total	9.8	19.3

The changes which took place between 1929 and 1939 are in
sharp contrast to those which took place between 1929 and
1957. Even though the Second World War had already begun

before the end of 1939 and American involvement was clearly a possibility, defense purchases were still of quite minor importance. On the other hand, both categories of civilian spending —non-defense purchases and transfers—increased sharply relative to GNP. Of the total increase in government spending relative to GNP during the decade of the 1930's, more than 60 percent was in non-defense purchases and more than 30 percent in transfers, less than 10 percent in defense purchases.

Here, it might seem, is evidence that the problem of inadequate surplus absorption can be solved, as some liberals claim, by increased government spending for welfare purposes. In actual fact, it is no such thing. Not that we wish to call in question the welfare goals which the New Deal increases in government spending were intended to serve. True, a large part of these outlays were in the nature of salvage operations for depression-threatened property owners of various sizes and descriptions,[18] but also much of genuine value for the non-owning classes was accomplished or at least initiated. But this is essentially beside the point. What was wrong with the government spending of the 1930's was not its direction but its magnitude: there was just not enough of it to come anywhere near offsetting the powerful depressive forces at work in the private sector of the economy. Measured in current dollars, government spending increased from $10.2 billion in 1929 to $17.5 billion in 1939, more than 70 percent. At the same time, however, GNP itself declined from $104.4 billion to $91.1 billion (a fall of 12.7 percent) and unemployment as a percentage of the labor force rose from 3.2 percent to 17.2 percent.[19]

Regarded as a salvage operation for the United States economy as a whole, the New Deal was thus a clear failure. Even Galbraith, the prophet of prosperity without war orders, has

[18] This often neglected aspect of the New Deal is ably dealt with by A. H. Hansen in his *Fiscal Policy and Business Cycles*, New York, 1941, Chapter 4.

[19] Even measured in constant (1957) dollars, GNP grew only from $193.5 billion in 1929 to $201.4 billion in 1939, which was not enough to keep real per capita GNP from slightly declining.

recognized that the goal was not even approached during the 1930's. "The Great Depression of the thirties," in his words, "never came to an end. It merely disappeared in the great mobilization of the forties."[20]

War spending accomplished what welfare spending had failed to accomplish. From 17.2 percent of the labor force, unemployment declined to a minimum of 1.2 percent in 1944. The other side of the coin was an increase of government spending from $17.5 billion in 1939 to a maximum of $103.1 billion in 1944. This is not to suggest that in peacetime an increase in spending of this magnitude would have been required to produce the virtual disappearance of unemployment. If it had not been for the fact that during the war civilian spending had to be restrained in various ways, near-full employment would have been reached at a considerably lower level of government spending. But a very large increase over the 1939 level—probably of the order of a doubling or tripling —would surely have been necessary. Why was such an increase not forthcoming during the whole depressed decade? Why did the New Deal fail to attain what the war proved to be within easy reach?

5

The answer to these questions is that, *given the power structure of United States monopoly capitalism*, the increase of civilian spending had about reached its outer limits by 1939. The forces opposing further expansion were too strong to be overcome.

In analyzing these forces and the limits they place on the expansion of civilian spending, it is relevant to point out first of all that spending originating at the state and local levels is much less flexible than spending originating at the federal level. Property taxes play the dominant role in state and local finance. They are harder to shift or evade than the taxes which provide the bulk of federal revenues (corporate and personal

[20] *American Capitalism*, p. 69.

income taxes, payroll taxes, excise taxes, customs duties), and indeed to the extent that they fall on the personal property of individuals they cannot be shifted at all. Furthermore, high property tax rates do not open up avenues of rapid enrichment to the moneyed elite as do high rates of income tax when combined with low rates of capital gains tax. For the wealthy individuals and groups who dominate local politics, more spending at the state and municipal levels means bigger tax bills; and since the amounts spent by any one city or state are likely to be small relative to the economy as a whole, there is no reason to expect a compensating rise in incomes. State and local expenditures are therefore generally held close to the minimum required to maintain various indispensable functions and services. What Hollingshead says of Elmtown applies quite generally to cities and towns throughout the country:

Large tax bills accompany extensive ownership; consequently these families [belonging to class I, at the top of the socioeconomic hierarchy] have a direct interest in keeping assessments and tax rates low. They accomplish this effectively, within the community and the county, through the control of the two major political party organizations on the township and county levels. The candidates for public office, except the district attorney and the judge, are generally not members of class I, but this does not mean they are free from controls exerted by class I interests. Money, legal talent, and political office are instruments used to translate interests into effective power. They are relied upon to implement decisions in contests which involve raising tax bills through public improvements, such as new public buildings, schools, roads, or welfare programs. This behind-the-scenes control results in the formulation of conservative policies and the election of officials who act in the capacity of agents for class I interests.[21]

With this background, it is hardly surprising that there has been little change in the relative importance of state and local outlays during the last three decades when the role of govern-

[21] August B. Hollingshead, *Elmtown's Youth: The Impact of Social Classes on Adolescents,* New York, 1949, p. 86. Professor of sociology at Yale, Hollingshead is one of the leading students of social classes in contemporary American society.

ment spending as a whole has undergone such a radical transformation. State and local expenditures constituted 7.4 percent
of GNP in 1929, and 8.7 percent in 1957.[22] It is true that the
proportion rose to nearly 13 percent at the bottom of the Great
Depression, and fell to less than 4 percent during the war. The
explanation in both cases, however, is clear: it was impossible
to curtail the functions of state and local governments in line
with the precipitous drop in GNP which marked the Great
Depression; and during the war, controls prevented state and
local spending from rising in step with GNP. What is important is that, with the return to "normalcy" after the war, the
percentage reverted to approximately the level of the 1920's.

Given the structure of United States government and politics, then, any further variations in the role of government in
the functioning of the economy will in all likelihood be initiated at the federal level. What follows must therefore be understood as applying largely to the forces which determine the
amount of federal spending.

Here, as we have seen, the size of the tax bill, though not
without influence, is far from being a decisive factor in determining the amount of government spending. With productive
resources idle—the normal situation for monopoly capitalism
—more spending means higher incomes out of which increased
taxes can be paid. Some people will get hurt, but few of them
are likely to belong to the moneyed oligarchy which holds political power. The oligarchy as a whole stands to gain and
hence has a strong incentive to keep pushing up the level of
government spending.

If taxes are not the decisive factor, what does determine the
limits on the expansion of civilian spending? The answer is the
particular interests of the individuals and groups which comprise the oligarchy and the way these interests are affected by
the various types of spending.

We can postulate that for every item in the budget there is

---

[22] F. M. Bator, *The Question of Government Spending,* p. 127.

some minimum amount which has general approval and which evokes no appreciable opposition. As this amount is exceeded, approval for further increments gradually declines and opposition builds up until an equilibrium is reached and further expansion stops. Starting from this schema, we might attempt to determine the equilibrium points for the major budget items, hoping in this way to discover the individual spending limits and, by aggregation, the overall limit. This procedure, however, would be wrong. It ignores the existence of what may be called an "interdependence effect," which rules out simple aggregation of individual limits.

The point can be elucidated by considering two budget items simultaneously, say housing and health. Very few people nowadays are opposed to a modest public housing program, and of course everyone is in favor of at least enough spending on health to control epidemic diseases. But beyond a certain point, opposition begins to build up in each case, at first from real estate interests to housing and from the medical profession to public programs of medical care. But real estate interests presumably have no special reasons to oppose medical care, and doctors no special reasons to oppose housing. Still, once they have each gone into opposition to further increases in their own spheres, they may soon find it to their joint interest to combine forces in opposing both more housing and more public health. The opposition to each individual item thus builds up faster when two items are under consideration, and fastest of all for across-the-board increases in the whole budget. We might say figuratively that if one item is being considered, opposition grows in proportion to the amount of the increase; while if all items are being considered, opposition grows in proportion to the square of the increase.[23]

[23] The following observation from a letter to the *New York Times* (August 5, 1962) by James MacGregor Burns, professor of political science at Williams College, is apropos: "The gap between President and Congress today is too wide to be bridged by the usual techniques of

In practice, of course, no such simple quantitative relationships can be postulated, still less demonstrated. We need only keep in mind that resistance from the moneyed oligarchy as a whole to each item in a proposed general increase of civilian government spending will be much more intense than if the same items were being considered in isolation.[24] This is of great importance for our problem, because what we are concerned with is situations where the need is for a large expansion of total government spending, something which could hardly be achieved unless many budget items were increased at the same time.

In the case of almost every major item in the civilian budget, powerful vested interests are soon aroused to opposition as expansion proceeds beyond the necessary minimum. This occurs whenever a significant element of competition with private enterprise is involved, but it is also true of other items where competition with private enterprise is largely or even wholly absent.

There are many urgent social needs which government can satisfy only by entering into some form of competition with private interests. River valley development, for example, an area in which private enterprise could never hope to operate effectively, is essential for flood control, water conservation, rebuilding eroded soils, etc. But it also produces electric power which competes with private power and thus provides a yardstick by which the performance of the private power monopolies can be measured. For this reason, river valley development is bitterly opposed not only by the utilities themselves but also by the entire Big Business community. The history of the Tennessee Valley Authority affords eloquent testimony to the effectiveness of this opposition. TVA had its origin in the gov-

---

pressure and bargain. The opposing elements are so strong and interlocked that he cannot push one policy as much as might seem feasible to the outsider without activating the whole machinery of opposition."

[24] This rule does not apply to increases in military spending; see below, pp. 207-213.

ernment's need for nitrates during the First World War. A dam, hydro-electric generating facilities, and a nitrate plant were built at Muscle Shoals, Alabama, to satisfy strictly military requirements. During the 1920's, a campaign to turn Muscle Shoals into a broad river valley development scheme was led by Senator Norris of Nebraska; but, in this period of capitalist prosperity, nothing came of it, and even the original investment was allowed to deteriorate in idleness. It was only during the "Hundred Days" after Roosevelt's inauguration in 1933—a period of near-panic for the moneyed oligarchy—that Norris's determined efforts were crowned with success. And the oligarchs have been regretting their moment of weakness ever since. From their point of view, the trouble with TVA was that it was a tremendous success. It gave the American people their first glimpse of what can be achieved by intelligent planning under a governmental authority equipped with the powers necessary to carry out a rational program. To cite only one of its achievements, by the later 1950's a typical household in the TVA area was paying only half as much for its electricity and consuming twice as much as the national average. And on a world-wide scale, TVA had become a symbol of the New Deal, a light showing others the way to democratic progress. Under these circumstances, the oligarchy did not dare destroy TVA outright. Instead, it organized a long-range campaign of unremitting criticism and harassment destined to hedge TVA in, curtail its functions, force it to conform to the norms of capitalist enterprise. And this campaign has achieved considerable successes: TVA has never been allowed to realize anything like its full potential. Nevertheless, its popularity with the people of the seven-state area in which it operates has protected it from being gutted and perverted from its original aims. The greatest triumph of the anti-TVA campaign, therefore, has been its total success in keeping the principle of the multi-purpose river valley authority from being applied to any of the other numerous river valleys of the United States where it could so richly further the people's welfare. The need for more TVA's is easily demonstrable to any rational person; during the 1930's and later, expanded government outlays on river valley development would frequently have made excellent sense as a partial solution to the problem of inadequate surplus absorption. But what Marx called the Furies of private interest, having been thoroughly aroused, easily repelled any further encroachment on their sacred domain.[25]

Public housing, potentially a vast field for welfare spending, is another activity which encroaches upon the realm of private enterprise. A really effective low-cost housing program would necessarily call for extensive building in open spaces, which abound in most cities in the United States. But this is precisely what the powerful urban real estate interests are against. On the rock of this opposition, all attempts to launch a serious attack on the twin problems of insufficient and inadequate housing have foundered. Instead we have had fine-sounding "slum clearance" or "urban renewal" programs, which, while liberally rewarding the owners of run-down property, typically throw more people on the streets than they house.[26] Moreover, the mausoleum-like "project" which is the usual embodiment of

[25] In the light of this record, there is something peculiarly repulsive about the way the oligarchy repeatedly cites TVA as proof of the United States' devotion to progressive goals in the underdeveloped countries of the world. Secretary of State Rusk, seeking to persuade Latin American governments to join in destroying the historic achievements of the Cuban Revolution, told the Punta del Este meeting of Foreign Ministers in January 1962: "Years of thought and work and debate were required to prepare America for the necessary steps of self-help and social reform. I remember well the bitter resistance before Franklin D. Roosevelt was able to win support for the Tennessee Valley Authority, that immense network of dams and power stations and fertilizer factories and agricultural extension offices which has wrought such miraculous changes in our South. But a succession of progressive leaders, determined to bring about social change within a framework of political consent, carried through an 'alliance for progress' within the United States." (*New York Times*, January 26, 1962.) If TVA has wrought such miracles, why has this great "succession of progressive leaders" never succeeded in getting even one more river valley authority established? (It is interesting that the Secretary of State, in this meeting of North, Central, and South American countries, apparently saw nothing inappropriate in referring to the United States simply as "America.")

[26] For a fuller analysis of "urban renewal," see below, pp. 294-298.

public housing is no kind of environment in which a viable
community could take root and grow. "Slum clearance" is thus
in reality slum creation, both off-site and on-site; and "urban
renewal" is a system of outdoor relief for landlords in the decaying "gray belts" which are inexorably creeping out from the
centers of our big cities. So grim indeed has been the American
experience with public housing since it first became a political
issue during the 1930's that today it no longer commands even
a modicum of popular support. "Back in the 30's," writes
Daniel Seligman, an editor of *Fortune* magazine, "proponents of
public housing were possessed of a missionary fervor. New
housing, they believed, would by itself exorcise crime and vice
and disease. But public housing didn't do what its proponents
expected. Today, public-housing people are searching for a
new rationale and their fervor is gone; the movement today is
so weak that most real estate groups hardly bother to attack it
any more."[27] A deliberate plot to sabotage public housing
could hardly have succeeded more brilliantly: the private interests don't have to oppose any more—the public does it for
them.

River valley development and public housing are but two
examples of government activities which trespass upon the territory of private interests. In all such cases, since private interests wield political power, the limits of government spending
are narrowly set and have nothing to do with social needs—no
matter how shamefully obvious. But it is not only where there
is competition with commercial enterprise that such limits are
imposed: the same thing happens in areas like education and
health where direct competition is either non-existent or of
relatively minor importance. Here too the opposition of private
interests to increased government spending is soon aroused;
and here too the amounts actually spent bear no relation to
demonstrable social need.

The reason for this is by no means obvious. It is no explana-

[27] William H. Whyte, Jr., and others, *The Exploding Metropolis*,
New York, 1958, p. 93.

tion to say that by far the greater part of these non-competitive government activities fall within the sphere of state and local governments. True, no significant increases in government spending are likely to be initiated at the state and local levels, but this is essentially beside the point. The federal government can play a larger role in these matters, both directly and via grants-in-aid to state and local units; and in fact it has been doing so in recent years, though on a very modest scale. The problem here is to explain why, in a period when the health of the economy urgently demanded a steadily rising volume of federal spending, so small a proportion of the increases has been devoted to satisfying society's communal consumption requirements. Why does the moneyed oligarchy, for example, so consistently and effectively oppose the proposals for increased federal aid to education which are put before the Congress year after year by Presidents who are themselves anything but radical crusaders? The need—for more schools and classrooms, for more teachers, for higher teachers' salaries, for more scholarships, for higher standards at all levels—is obvious to any citizen who keeps his eyes open; it has been proved time and again in government reports, scholarly treatises, popular tracts. The specter of being outclassed by the Soviet Union has been held up to the country with frantic urgency ever since the first Sputnik went into orbit in 1957: the race between the systems, we are told, will eventually be won by the side not with the greatest firepower but with the greatest brainpower. And, despite all this, President Kennedy began a news conference on January 15, 1962, more than four years after Sputnik I, with these ominous figures:

In 1951 our universities graduated 19,600 students in the physical sciences. In 1960, in spite of the substantial increase in our population during the last ten years and in spite of the fact that the demand for people of skill in this field has tremendously increased with our efforts in defense and space, industrial research, and all the rest, in 1960 the number had fallen from 19,600 to 17,100.

In 1951 there were 22,500 studying in the biological sciences. In 1960 there were only 16,700.

In the field of engineering, enrollment rose from 232,000 to 269,-000 in the period 1951 to 1957. Since 1957, there has been a continual decline in enrollments. Last year the figure was down to 240,-000.[28]

How are such things possible with the national interest at stake—in the simplest and crudest sense of the term, one that should be easily understandable to the dullest member of the oligarchy? How can it happen that even modest increases in federal aid to education are so often turned down?

The answer, in a nutshell, is that the educational system, as at present constituted, is a crucial element in the constellation of privileges and prerogatives of which the moneyed oligarchy is the chief beneficiary. This is true in a triple sense.

First, the educational system provides the oligarchy with the quality and quantity of educational services which its members want for themselves and their offspring.[29] There is no shortage of expensive private schools and colleges for the sons and daughters of the well-to-do. Nor are the public schools of the exclusive suburbs and exurbs starved of funds, like the schools which serve the lower-middle and working classes in the cities and the countryside. The educational system, in other words, is not a homogeneous whole. It consists of two parts, one for the oligarchy and one for the rest of the population. The part which caters to the oligarchy is amply financed. It is a privilege and a badge of social position to go through it. And the very fact that it serves only a small part of the population is precisely its most precious and jealously guarded feature. This is why any attempt to generalize its benefits is bound to be stubbornly fought by the oligarchy. This is also perhaps the most basic reason for the strength of the opposition to expanded programs of federal aid to education.

[28] *New York Times,* January 16, 1962.

[29] This does not mean that it provides them with a good education. On this and other aspects of the class character of the United States educational system, see below, pp. 305-335.

Second—the other side of the same coin—that part of the educational system which is designed for the vast majority of young people must be inferior and must turn out human material fitted for the lowly work and social positions which society reserves for them. This aim of course cannot be achieved directly. The egalitarianism of capitalist ideology is one of its strengths, not to be lightly discarded. People are taught from earliest childhood and by all conceivable means that everyone has an equal opportunity, and that the inequalities which stare them in the face are the result not of unjust institutions but of their own superior or inferior natural endowments. It would contradict this teaching to set up, in the manner of European class-divided societies, two distinct educational systems, one for the oligarchy and one for the masses. The desired result must be sought indirectly, by providing amply for that part of the educational system which serves the oligarchy while financially starving that part which serves the lower-middle and working classes. This ensures the inequality of education so vitally necessary to buttress the general inequality which is the heart and core of the whole system. No special arrangements are needed, however, to achieve this force-feeding of one part of the educational system and starving of the other. The private schools and colleges are in any case well provided for, and the established system of local control and financing for public schools automatically results in extremely unequal treatment for the suburban and exurban public schools in contrast to the urban and rural schools. What is crucial is to prevent this delicate balance from being upset by massive federal invasion, with the enormous taxing and spending powers of the national government being used to implement the educational reformers' age-old ideal of equal and excellent educational opportunity for all. Here we have a second compelling reason for the oligarchy to keep government spending to a minimum in an area which reason tells us could beneficially absorb a large proportion of society's surplus product.

The third sense in which the educational system supports

the existing class structure is complementary to the first two. Every viable class society must provide a method by which brains and talent from the lower classes can be selected, used by, and integrated into the upper classes. In Western feudal society, the Catholic Church provided the necessary mechanism. Competitive capitalism made it possible for able and aggressive lower-class boys to ascend a purely economic ladder into the oligarchy. Monopoly capitalism has effectively blocked this channel of upward mobility: it is now rarely possible to start a small business and build it up into a big one. A substitute mechanism has been found in the educational system. Through low-tuition state universities, scholarships, loans and the like, boys and girls who are really able and ambitious (desirous of success, as society defines it) can move up from the inferior part of the educational system. Accepted into the better preparatory schools, colleges, and universities, they are given the same training and conditioning as upper-class young people. From there the road leads through the corporate apparatus or the professions into integration in the upper-middle, and occasionally the higher, strata of society. The superficial observer, having heard the slogans about equal opportunity, may see evidence here that the educational system works to undermine the class structure. Nothing could be further from the truth. The ideal of equal opportunity for all could be realized only by abolition of the special privileges of the upper classes, not by making these privileges available to a select group from the lower classes. This simply strengthens the class structure by infusing new blood into the upper classes and depriving the lower classes of their natural leaders.[30] And these are the objectives that are actually served by currently fashionable educational reforms, including such modest increases in federal aid as the oligarchy is prepared to put up with. Any serious attempt to meet the real educational needs of

[30] "The more a ruling class is able to assimilate the most prominent men of a ruled class," Marx wrote, "the more solid and dangerous is its rule." *Capital*, Volume 3, Chapter 36.

a modern technologically and scientifically advanced society would necessitate a totally different approach—including a commitment of resources on a scale that no dominant oligarchy intent on preserving its own narrow privileges would even dream of.[31]

It would be possible to run through the gamut of civilian spending objects and show how in case after case the private interests of the oligarchy stand in stark opposition to the satisfaction of social needs. Real competition with private enterprise cannot be tolerated, no matter how incompetent and inadequate its performance may be; undermining of class privileges or of the stability of the class structure must be resisted at any cost. And almost all types of civilian spending involve one or both of these threats. There is just one major exception to this generalization in the United States today, and it is very much the type of exception which proves the rule: government spending on highways.

There is no need here to detail the importance of the automobile to the American economy.[32] We need only say that the main business of several of the largest and most profitable corporations is the production of motor vehicles; the petroleum industry, with some ten corporations having assets of more than a billion dollars, makes most of its profits from the sale of gasoline for use in motor vehicles; several other major monopolistic industries (rubber, steel, glass) are crucially dependent on sales to automobile makers or users; more than a quarter of a million persons are employed in the repair and servicing of automobiles; and countless other businesses and jobs (trucking, motels, resorts, etc.) owe their existence, directly or indirectly, to the motor vehicle. This complex of private interests clustering around one product has no equal elsewhere in the economy—or in the world. And the whole complex, of course, is completely dependent on the public provision of roads and

---

[31] For a discussion of the results actually achieved by the present class educational system, see below, pp. 318-335.

[32] The subject is treated more fully in Chapter 8.

highways. It is thus only natural that there should be tremendous pressure for continuous expansion of government spending on highways. Counter-pressures from private interests do exist—notably from the railroads, hard hit by the growth of highway transportation, but the railroads have been no match for the automobile complex. Government spending on highways has soared; limitations posed by state and local finances have been overcome by increasingly liberal federal grants-in-aid. And today highways are second only to education as an object of civilian government spending.[33]

This fact does not in itself prove that spending on highways has gone beyond any rational conception of social need. What does prove it—dramatically and overwhelmingly—is the frightful havoc which has been wreaked on American society by the cancerous growth of the automobile complex, a growth which would have been impossible if government spending for the required highways had been limited and curtailed as the oligarchy has limited and curtailed spending for other civilian purposes. Cities have been transformed into nightmares of congestion; their atmosphere is fouled by disease-bearing pollutants; vast areas of good urban and rural land are turned into concrete strips and asphalt fields; peaceful communities and neighborhoods are desecrated by the roar and stench of cars and trucks hurtling past; railroads, which can move goods and passengers efficiently and unobtrusively, lose traffic and correspondingly raise rates in a vicious circle which threatens the very existence of commuter service for our biggest cities; urban rapid transit systems are at once starved and choked, so that getting around the downtown area of New York, Chicago, and dozens of other metropolises becomes an ordeal to which only the necessitous or the foolhardy will submit. And the usual

---

[33] In 1957, total government purchases of goods and services for civilian purposes came to $40.4 billion. Of this, $13.6 or 33.7 percent went for education and $7.2 billion or 17.8 percent for highways—the two items together accounting for more than half of civilian government spending. See F. M. Bator, *The Question of Government Spending*, pp. 26-29.

remedy for this increasingly frightful and frightening state of
affairs? More highways, more streets, more garages, more parking areas—more of the same poison that is already threatening
the very life of an increasingly urbanized civilization. And all
this is made possible by lavish grants of public funds, eagerly
sought and approved by an oligarchy of wealth which fights
tooth and nail against every extension of those public services
which would benefit the great body of their fellow citizens.
Nowhere is the madness of American monopoly capitalism
more manifest, or more hopelessly incurable.

6

The New Deal managed to push government spending up by
more than 70 percent, but this was nowhere near enough to
bring the economy to a level at which human and material
resources were fully employed. Resistance of the oligarchy to
further expansion in civilian spending hardened and held with
unemployment still well above 15 percent of the labor force.
By 1939 it was becoming increasingly clear that liberal reform
had sadly failed to rescue United States monopoly capitalism
from its own self-destructive tendencies. As Roosevelt's second
term approached its end, a profound sense of frustration and
uneasiness crept over the country.

Then came the war, and with it salvation. Government
spending soared and unemployment plummeted. At the end of
the war, to be sure, arms spending was cut back sharply; but
owing to the backlog of civilian demand built up during the
war (compounded of supply shortages and a massive accumulation of liquid savings), the downturn associated with this
cutback was relatively mild and brief and soon gave way to an
inflationary reconversion boom. And the boom was still going
strong when the Cold War began in earnest. Military spending
reached its postwar low in 1947, turned up in 1948, received a
tremendous boost from the Korean War (1950-1953), declined
moderately during the next two years, and then in 1956 began
the slow climb which continued, with a slight interruption in

1960, into the 1960's. As a percentage of GNP, the variations of military spending have followed a similar pattern, except that there was very little change from 1955 to 1961.[34]

In Chapter 8, we have more to say about the performance of the economy in the postwar period. Here we need only note that the difference between the deep stagnation of the 1930's and the relative prosperity of the 1950's is fully accounted for by the vast military outlays of the 50's. In 1939, for example, 17.2 percent of the labor force was unemployed and about 1.4 percent of the remainder may be presumed to have been employed producing goods and services for the military.[35] A good 18 percent of the labor force, in other words, was either unemployed or dependent for jobs on military spending. In 1961 (like 1939, a year of recovery from a cyclical recession), the comparable figures were 6.7 percent unemployed and 9.4 percent dependent on military spending, a total of some 16 percent. It would be possible to elaborate and refine these calculations, but there is no reason to think that doing so would affect the general conclusion: the percentage of the labor force either unemployed or dependent on military spending was much the same in 1961 as in 1939. From which it follows that if the military budget were reduced to 1939 proportions, unemployment would also revert to 1939 proportions.[36]

[34] Here are the percentages of GNP, 1946-1961:

1946—8.9	1950— 5.0	1954—11.0	1958—10.1
1947—4.9	1951—10.3	1955— 9.8	1959— 9.6
1948—4.5	1952—13.4	1956— 9.9	1960— 9.0
1949—5.2	1953—11.0	1957—10.0	1961— 9.4

Source: *Economic Report of the President*, January 1962, p. 207. The figures are slightly different from those cited earlier from Bator for 1957 and earlier years (pp. 152, 159).

[35] This was the ratio of "national defense" purchases of goods and services to total GNP.

[36] Obviously this conclusion does not follow in the prevailing liberal logic of today. One group of liberals, having apparently forgotten all about Keynes and never having understood the relation of monopoly to the functioning of the economy, asserts that if there were less military

Why has the oligarchy, which keeps such a tight rein on civilian spending, become in the last two decades so open-handed with the military?

---

spending there would be more private investment and consumption. They do not explain why it failed to work out that way during the 30's, when there was in fact less military spending, nor do they explain why unemployment has crept up during the 50's and 60's, when military spending as a proportion of GNP has remained generally stable. Until they can offer a rational explanation of these phenomena—which we believe can be done only along the lines sketched out in this book—their pronouncements on the probable effects of military cutbacks are not entitled to be taken seriously. Another group of liberals, who at least have not altogether forgotten the Great Depression, postulate with equal fluency a substitution of welfare spending for military spending. But they neglect to reveal their magic formula for converting the oligarchy to their way of thinking. We must say of such liberals what Marx said of the bourgeois reformers of his day: "They all want the impossible, namely, the conditions of bourgeois existence without the necessary consequences of those conditions." Karl Marx and Friedrich Engels, *Selected Correspondence*, New York, 1935, p. 15.

7

THE ABSORPTION OF SURPLUS:
MILITARISM AND IMPERIALISM

The question posed at the end of the last chapter can be reformulated: Why does the United States oligarchy need and maintain such a huge military machine nowadays when it used to get along with such a little one? In order to answer this question, we must first consider the role of armed force in capitalist society.

From its earliest beginnings in the Middle Ages capitalism has always been an international system. And it has always been a hierarchical system with one or more leading metropolises at the top, completely dependent colonies at the bottom, and many degrees of superordination and subordination in between. These features are of crucial importance to the functioning of both the system as a whole and its individual components, though this is a fact the importance of which bourgeois economists have consistently ignored or denied and even Marxists have often underestimated.[1] In particular, it would be quite impossible to understand the role of armed force in capitalist society without placing the international character of the system at the very center of the analytic focus.

[1] Marx himself understood the crucial importance of the international structure of capitalism, but the plan of *Capital* and, perhaps even more important, the fact that he did not live to complete his work have given rise to what appears to be a widespread impression that Marx considered the international character of the capitalist system to be of secondary significance. This could not be said of Lenin of course, but even today there are many Marxists who seem to think that capitalism as an international system can be understood as merely a collection of national capitalisms. There is therefore justification for the criticisms expressed by Oliver Cox in his *Capitalism as a System* (New York, 1964, Chapter 14)

It is not that armed force under capitalism is used only in the international sphere. In every capitalist country, it is used to dispossess, repress, and otherwise control the domestic labor force. But in relation to the problem which concerns us—the absorption of surplus by the military machine in the United States today—this aspect is of negligible importance and can be abstracted from.[2] We can concentrate on the international uses of armed force.

The hierarchy of nations which make up the capitalist system is characterized by a complex set of exploitative relations. Those at the top exploit in varying degrees all the lower layers, and similarly those at any given level exploit those below them until we reach the very lowest layer which has no one to exploit. At the same time, each unit at a given level strives to be the sole exploiter of as large a number as possible of the units beneath it. Thus we have a network of antagonistic relations pitting exploiters against exploited and rival exploiters against each other. Disregarding juridical categories, we can call those at or near the top of the hierarchy "metropolises" and those at or near the bottom "colonies." The sphere of exploitation of a

---

and value in his reiterated insistence that the international character of capitalism has always had a decisive effect on the nature and functioning of the national units which compose it.

[2] Our angle of vision also excludes from view another aspect of the matter which, in a different context, would have to be rated extremely important. The technology of warfare and the organization and provisioning of armed forces have always—and not only under capitalism—exercised a profound influence on economic development. "In general, the army is important for economic development. For instance, it was in the army that the ancients first developed a complete wages system. Similarly among the Romans the *peculium castrense* was the first legal form in which the right of others than fathers of families to movable property was recognized. So also the guild system among the corporation of *fabri*. Here too the first use of machinery on a large scale. Even the special value of metals and their use as money appears to have been originally based . . . on their military significance. The division of labor *within* one branch was also first carried out in the armies. The whole history of the forms of bourgeois society is very strikingly epitomized here." Marx to Engels, September 25, 1857. *Selected Correspondence*, pp. 98-99.

given metropolis, from which rivals are more or less effectively excluded, is its "empire." Some in the intermediate layers may become incorporated into an empire, with one occasionally even bringing an empire of its own along with it (for example, Portugal and the Portuguese empire as subordinate units within the larger British empire); others in the intermediate layers may succeed in retaining a relative independence, as the United States did during roughly its first century and a half of nationhood.

Now it is obvious that all nations—except the dependent and defenseless ones at the bottom—have a need for armed force to maintain and if possible improve their positions in the exploitative hierarchy. How much a given nation needs at a given time depends on its position in the hierarchy and on the pattern of relations in the hierarchy as a whole at that particular time. Leading nations will always require most, and the magnitude of their needs will vary according to whether there is or is not an active struggle going on among them for the top position. The needs of secondary nations will also vary from time to time in function of several variables, especially their ability to make a protective alliance with one or more of the contenders for leadership.

This schema, being distilled from capitalist history, can naturally be illustrated from the same source. Thus the seventeenth and eighteenth centuries, which saw almost continuous struggles for empire and leadership among the Spanish, Dutch, British, and French—finally narrowing down to a prolonged duel between the last two—were highly "militarized" centuries. The year 1815 marked a decisive British victory, followed by more than half a century of *Pax Britannica*. With one unchallenged leader sitting on top and stabilizing the whole system through its own strength and a flexible system of alliances, the emphasis on militarism and the need for armed force declined markedly throughout the capitalist world.[3] The German

---

[3] Not unnaturally, bourgeois thought came to regard this situation as normal rather than exceptional, a conclusion which appeared all the more plausible since this was also the period when Britain moved indus-

and Japanese challenges, beginning respectively with the unifi-
cation of the Reich under Prussian hegemony and the Meiji
Restoration, of course upset this relative equilibrium and led
directly to the new upsurge of militarism which culminated in
the First and Second World Wars.

With so much by way of theoretical introduction, we can
give a sketch of the development of American capitalism's need
for military strength. The United States was expansionist and
empire-minded long before it achieved independence and nationhood, but the country's early leaders were under no illusion
that they could successfully challenge the older imperialist
powers for a top leadership role.[4] They therefore pursued a

---

trially so far ahead of its chief rivals that it could espouse the doctrine of
free trade and safely dismantle much of the apparatus of monopoly and
protection with which all the older empires had surrounded themselves.
Political economy now saw in imperialism and war not the means to the
nation's enrichment, which had been the mercantilist view, but unjustifia-
ble encroachments by the state on capital accumulation. Bourgeois ideology went so far as to proclaim, in the words of Schumpeter, that "Modern pacifism and modern international morality are . . . products of
capitalism. . . . As a matter of fact, the more completely capitalist the
structure and attitude of a nation, the more pacifist—and the more prone
to count the costs of war—we observe it to be." *Capitalism, Socialism,
and Democracy,* p. 128.

It is important to understand that a hundred years ago there was an
important kernel of truth in this position. Under conditions of competition and with full employment implicitly assumed, it was correct to
regard wasteful government expenditures as a brake on capital accumulation and hence to oppose them. Nowadays, however, such ideas—and
one occasionally meets them in the *Wall Street Journal* and similar
bastions of old-fashioned conservatism—are strictly anachronistic. With
idle men and idle machines as normal features of monopoly capitalism,
advanced bourgeois thought, thoroughly steeped in Keynesian doctrine,
knows perfectly well that additional government spending, no matter how
wasteful the result, raises income and profits. Moreover, the biggest and
most powerful corporations get the lion's share of armament contracts
and shift whatever additional taxes may go with them onto their customers (to a large extent the government itself). Under these conditions,
there is certainly no longer any reason for bourgeois ideology to boast of
its pacifism and its propensity to count the costs of militarism.

[4] See the excellent study of R. W. Van Alstyne, *The Rising American
Empire.* Van Alstyne demonstrates that "The concept of an American

policy of alliances and deals designed to take maximum advantage of the needs and conflicts of the leaders. Independence itself was made possible by an alliance with France against Britain; and Napoleon agreed to what was from the American point of view the extremely advantageous Louisiana Purchase because he hoped in this way to strengthen the United States in its resistance to British domination of the Atlantic. After 1815, during the period of unchallenged British leadership, the United States on the whole played the part of a British ally, always however extracting the maximum price for its support. By such means, during the nineteenth century, Washington built up a large, if still secondary, empire and staked out a claim to a still larger one (especially in the Monroe Doctrine) without ever experiencing the need for a commensurately large military machine.

Having already achieved the status of a "have" power by the time the Germans and Japanese were ready to launch their leadership bids, the United States was constrained to make common cause with the other "have" powers in the First and Second World Wars. This, however, did not prevent the United States from pressing its own leadership claims. In fact during the entire period from 1914 to 1945, the relative strength of the United States grew more or less continuously at the expense of both allies and enemies; and at the end of the Second World War the United States emerged as the undisputed leader nation, its position in the capitalist world fully as commanding as that of Britain had been after 1815.

This alone would be enough to explain why United States military needs, enormously inflated during the two wars, remained huge by any peacetime standards after the second war. The undisputed leader must maintain a clear military superiority either through its own armed forces or through the manipulation of alliances, or both. The United States chose both. At

---

empire and the main outlines of its future growth were complete by 1800." (P. 100.)

the same time, as the old colonial empires increasingly broke
up—for a complex of reasons which we cannot analyze here—
the United States used its military and financial power to attract large segments of them into its own neo-colonial empire.[5]
In this fashion, a vast world-wide American empire has come
into being, control and policing of which have added greatly to
United States military needs.[6]

It is thus easy to account for the fact that United States
military needs remained high after the Second World War. But
Britain had a similar experience in the nineteenth century
without feeling a steadily *mounting* need for military strength.
In fact, British experience would seem to support the view that
the very existence of an undisputed leader would have the
effect of stabilizing the needs of all the units in the capitalist
hierarchy, including those of the leader itself.

2

To explain why United States military needs expanded rapidly during the postwar period, we have to go beyond a theory
based on past capitalist experience and take account of a new
historical phenomenon, the rise of a world socialist system as a
rival and alternative to the world capitalist system. Why
should the rise of a socialist rival generate steadily mounting
military needs on the part of the capitalist leader nation?

[5] Largely because of its own history as an ex-colony which had had to
struggle for independence, United States expansionism has rarely taken
the form of colonialism. The country was therefore the pioneer in developing, especially in Latin America, the forms of rule and exploitation
which it is customary nowadays to call neo-colonialism. This long experience has greatly facilitated the process of turning ex-colonies of Britain
and the other older imperialist powers into neo-colonies of the United
States.

[6] Legitimate differences of opinion will of course exist as to whether
this or that country should be counted as belonging to the American
empire. We offer the following list as being on the conservative side: The
United States itself and a few colonial possessions (notably Puerto Rico
and the Pacific islands); all Latin American countries except Cuba; Canada; four countries in the Near and Middle East (Turkey, Jordan, Saudi
Arabia, and Iran); four countries in South and Southeast Asia (Paki-

Official and unofficial molders of public opinion—from Presidents and Secretaries of States to small-town editorial writers —have a ready answer: the United States must protect the "free world" against the threat of Soviet (or Chinese) aggression. The reality and seriousness of the threat are either taken for granted or "proved" by two lines of argumentation. A series of real or alleged Communist actions going back to the period immediately preceding the Second World War (most notably the Soviet-Finnish War) and coming right down to the drawn-out guerrilla war in South Vietnam are pointed to as "obvious" examples of Communist aggressiveness. In addition, a theoretical explanation for this supposedly aggressive behavior is offered in the form of a syllogism: totalitarian states are aggressive, witness Nazi Germany and imperial Japan; the Soviet Union is a totalitarian state; hence the Soviet Union must be aggressive. *this may be true though*

The theme of Soviet aggressiveness has been repeated so often and so loudly during the last quarter century that it is now accepted by most Americans as a fact—as little to be

---

stan, Thailand, the Philippines, and South Vietnam); two countries in East Asia (South Korea and Formosa); two countries in Africa (Liberia and Libya); and one country in Europe (Greece). On this count the American empire, as of 1960, had the following dimensions:

	Area (Thousands of square miles)	Population (Millions)
United States and possessions	3,682	183.3
Nineteen Latin American countries	7,680	196.5
Canada	3,852	17.9
Four Near and Middle Eastern countries	1,693	55.5
Four South and Southeast Asian countries	735	161.3
Two East Asian countries	52	35.3
Two African countries	722	2.5
One European country	51	8.3
Totals	18,467	660.6

Source: *Statistical Abstract of the United States, 1962,* pp. 7, 911-912. For South Vietnam, *The World Almanac,* 1962, p. 387.

questioned as that night follows day. And yet, paradoxical
though it may seem, we know of no serious analyst of Soviet
society and Soviet policy who really believes it. Even the ideological formulator of the famous "containment" doctrine,
George F. Kennan, then chief of the State Department's policy
planning staff, flatly rejected the idea that the USSR is an aggressive power in the sense that Hitler Germany was.[7] And the
various columnists, historians, and political scientists who have
upheld the thesis that Soviet policy has always been essentially
defensive include many of the outstanding leaders of American
intellectual life. In truth it would be hard to name any thesis
which has been more thoroughly investigated or more solidly
supported.[8] In addition, the more thoughtful politicians, men
like Chester Bowles and Senator Fulbright, are often at pains
to emphasize the theme that the Soviet threat—the existence of
which they do not doubt—is not military but economic, political, and ideological. Even those, or perhaps especially those,
who are most belligerent in their attitudes toward the USSR do
not believe in the aggressive character of Soviet policy. As
Walter Lippmann has written:

[7] See the celebrated article, "The Sources of Soviet Conduct," by X
[Kennan], *Foreign Affairs,* July 1947. This article was written at the
very time when President Truman was whipping up hysterical fear of the
Soviet Union in order to secure adoption by the Congress of the Truman
Doctrine.

An excellent statement by Professor Neal D. Houghton of the Government Department of the University of Arizona deserves quotation
here. Referring to "the assumption that Russia means to 'attack' the
United States and the West," he writes: "In all the ranks of folk who
have based our defense and Cold War policies on this psychotic fear,
apparently, not one single person has ever taken the trouble to *justify* this
fear *rationally.* Nobody has bothered to explain unemotionally *why* Russia should have such designs. . . . On the other hand every rational
inquirer into the matter of whom I know, has come out with a conviction
that neither the Russian people nor the Soviet leaders have, or ever have
had, any such desire or design." Neal D. Houghton, "The Challenge to
International Leadership in Recent American Foreign Policy," *Social
Science,* June 1961, p. 174.

[8] See the monumental work of D. F. Fleming, *The Cold War and Its
Origins, 1917-1960,* 2 vols., New York and London, 1961. This elabo-

A war party consists of people conspiring and agitating to start a war from which the country will win, they think, profit and glory. It would be hard to find an American who thinks that in any great war today there would be much profit or glory. The war whoop party consists of people who suppose that no matter what we do the Russians will not go to war.[9]

And William S. Schlamm, the former editor of *Fortune* magazine who advocates nuclear ultimatums as a method of getting the Russians out of Eastern Europe, is most emphatic that "Communism *thrives* on peace, *wants* peace, *triumphs* in peace."[10]

Any rounded discussion of this subject would of course have to analyze the basic differences between Nazism (or other forms of fascism) and socialism, to show that far from being similar they are polar opposites. Militarism and conquest are completely foreign to Marxian theory, and a socialist society contains no class or group which, like the big capitalists of the imperialist countries, stands to gain from a policy of subjugating other nations and peoples. Such a discussion would, however, be out of place here and in any case would only reinforce the conclusion already obvious to well-informed people: Soviet foreign policy is essentially defensive and bears no resemblance to the aggressive war policies of Nazi Germany and its Axis partners.

3

above is used as reasoning not true

The American oligarchy's need for a huge military machine must be sought elsewhere than in a non-existent threat of Soviet aggression. Once we recognize this and free our minds of the cant and confusion generated by the oligarchy's ideological and propagandistic distortions, we shall soon discover what we

---

rately documented study has been called "one of the great works of our time" by Frederick L. Schuman, himself one of the country's leading authorities on international relations. (*The Nation,* January 13, 1963.)

[9] *The Washington Post,* March 5, 1963.

[10] Quoted in Fleming, *The Cold War and Its Origins,* Volume 2, p. 1096.

are looking for: the same implacable hatred of socialism, the same determination to destroy it, that has dominated the leading nations of the capitalist world from the time the Bolsheviks seized power in November 1917. The central purpose has always been the same: to prevent the expansion of socialism, to compress it into as small an area as possible, and ultimately to wipe it off the face of the earth. What has changed with changing conditions are the methods and strategies used to achieve these unchanging goals.

When the Soviet regime was young and weak, there seemed real promise in financing and supplying its counter-revolutionary opponents and invading its territory. When these efforts failed—owing in considerable measure to the resistance of the war-weary workers of the capitalist countries—a *cordon sanitaire* of reactionary client states was erected on the USSR's western boundaries, and a period of uneasy stalemate had to be accepted. A decade later came the policy of building up the German and Japanese military machines and pushing them toward an eventual attack on the Soviet Union. This strategy backfired—so badly, indeed, as to force the Western powers into an alliance with their intended victim. When the smoke had cleared from the battlefields, the Soviet Union was still there—and the *cordon sanitaire* had been replaced by a protective belt of socialist countries reaching into the heart of Europe. Thus, beginning in a handful of Czarist Russia's industrial cities, socialist power had spread out to embrace the vast area from the Elbe to the Pacific. The traditional centers of capitalism in Europe and Asia now either lay in ruins or were staggering along, barely able to stave off economic collapse. Furthermore, most of the colonial and semi-colonial countries were in ferment, with socialist forces for the first time presenting a serious challenge to long-established regimes. Clearly, world capitalism was facing an unprecedented crisis.

In this crisis the United States stepped forward and assumed full leadership of a great capitalist counter-offensive. The idea took shape in President Truman's mind at least as early as the autumn of 1945,[11] but American public opinion was not yet prepared for it. It took more than a year of intense anti-Communist propaganda—of which Winston Churchill's famous "Iron Curtain" speech, delivered at Fulton, Missouri, on March 5, 1946, was perhaps the highlight—before Truman and his advisers judged that the people and their representatives in Congress were ready to underwrite a world-wide anti-socialist crusade.

On February 24, 1947, the British, struggling to overcome an acute economic crisis, announced that they were withdrawing their support from the right-wing government then in power in Greece, which was fighting for its life against a revolutionary guerrilla movement. The immediate United States response was the Truman Doctrine. This in effect proclaimed an American protectorate over Greece and Turkey and announced that "it must be the policy of the United States to support free peoples who are resisting attempted subjugation by armed minorities or by outside pressure." In Fleming's words:

> No pronouncement could have been more sweeping. Wherever a Communist rebellion developed the United States would suppress it. Wherever the Soviet Union attempted to push outward, at any point around its vast circumference, the United States would resist. The United States would become the world's anti-Communist, anti-Russian policeman.[12]

Sweeping as it was, the Truman Doctrine by no means defined the full scope of Washington's new global policy. It expressed what may be called the negative side of that policy—the determination to prevent any further spread of socialism. The positive side, comprising a set of long-range goals, was concisely and clearly set forth in two major speeches of Secretary of State Dean Acheson in March 1950, several months before the outbreak of the Korean War.

In the first speech, Acheson defined the aim of United States

---

[11] This is conclusively demonstrated by Fleming, *ibid.*, Volume 1, especially pp. 441-442.
[12] *Ibid.*, p. 446.

policy as the establishment of "situations of strength." Now, situations of strength might simply be strong points from which to defend the status quo. Or they might be staging areas from which to conquer new ground. And Acheson quickly made clear what he meant. On March 16 in Berkeley, California, he stated that if the two systems were to co-exist, certain points of difference would sooner or later have to be settled. He listed seven of these points; they may be summarized as follows:

First Point: The German, Austrian, and Japanese peace treaties must make those countries "free"—in other words, capitalist countries allied with the United States against the Soviet Union.

Second Point: "Orderly representative processes" must be introduced into "the whole group of countries we are accustomed to think of as the satellite area"—in other words, the Soviet Union must stand aside while the United States organizes counter-revolutions in Eastern Europe.

Third Point: "The Soviet leaders could drop their policy of obstruction in the United Nations"—in other words, the Soviet Union must acquiesce in the UN's becoming an instrument of American policy.

Fourth Point: The Soviet Union must accept "realistic and effective arrangements for the control of atomic energy and the limitations of armaments in general"—in other words, the Soviet Union must place her work in the field of atomic energy under the control of an American-dominated agency and submit her military apparatus to outside inspection.

Fifth Point: The Soviet Union must "desist from, and cooperate in efforts to prevent, indirect aggression across national frontiers"—in other words, since "indirect aggression" is the usual pseudonym for social revolution, the Soviet Union must not only agree to United States counter-revolutionary actions but actually aid and abet them.

Sixth Point: The Soviet Union and its allies (as long as it has any) must give American official representatives the run of their countries.

Seventh Point: The Soviet leaders must stop criticizing the United States and its allies.

Professor Frederick L. Schuman of Williams College immediately commented on the "seven points" as follows: "By coincidence, they embrace the 'five points' in James Burnham's *The Coming Defeat of Communism* which is dedicated to the proposition that 'there is only one possible objective of United States foreign policy: the destruction of Communist power.' "[13] This indeed had been the guiding star of United States policy ever since 1917, and it remains so today.

4

The implementation of this global policy of anti-Communism required, among other things, the following:

(1) The speediest rehabilitation and strengthening of the traditional centers of capitalist power and their integration into a military alliance dominated by the United States. These objectives were accomplished through the Marshall Plan, announced in June 1947, just three months after the Truman Doctrine; and through the North Atlantic Treaty Organization, negotiated during the next year and signed in April 1949. A similar turn in policy soon occurred in Japan, culminating in the signing of a separate peace treaty in 1951. The underlying conditions for the revival of capitalism in Western Europe and Japan were much more favorable than they appeared. Fixed capital and trained manpower were amply available; needed were large infusions of working capital, and these the United States was able to supply. In solving this problem, Washington may be said to have scored its one really large-scale, solid foreign policy success of the postwar period.

(2) The weaving of a network of military pacts and bases around the entire perimeter of the socialist bloc. This operation

---

[13] *The Daily Compass*, March 24, 1950.

began with NATO and has been going on ever since. The network now includes, in addition to NATO, the Southeast Asia Treaty Organization, the Central Treaty Organization (originally known as the Baghdad Pact), and bilateral treaties or "mutual assistance" agreements with dozens of countries everywhere: Spain, Turkey, Pakistan, the Philippines, Formosa, Japan, and many others. By 1959, the United States had, according to Fleming, a total of 275 major base complexes in 31 countries and more than 1,400 foreign bases, counting all sites where Americans were then stationed and sites designed for emergency occupation. These bases cost nearly $4 billion and were manned by approximately a million American troops.

(3) Above all, United States policy required arms of all kinds and descriptions and the men to use them, to lend muscle and sinew to this world-wide skeleton of alliances, thus establishing the "positions of strength" from which the expansion of socialism could be stemmed and enough counter-pressure could in due course be brought to bear to force its retreat. Failing these objectives, the military establishment would be designed to be powerful enough to wage and win a war against the Soviet Union, thus clearing the way for the final liquidation of socialism by purely military means.

To sum up: the need of the American oligarchy for a large and growing military machine is a logical corollary of its purpose to contain, compress, and eventually destroy the rival world socialist system.

5

We cannot leave this subject of the need for military strength without inquiring into the causes of capitalist hostility to the existence of a rival world socialist system. If, as some people seem to think, this hostility is based largely on irrational prejudices and fears, like the sedulously cultivated belief in Soviet aggressiveness, then there would seem to be at least a chance that in time more rational views might come to prevail. In that case, peaceful coexistence and disarmament could be looked upon not as propaganda slogans in the struggle between the two systems but as realizable goals. On the other hand, if the prejudices and fears are, as so often happens, simply masks for deep-rooted interests, then we would have to assess the outlook differently.

First, we must dispose of one very common argument purporting to prove that the spread of socialism is a mortal threat to the existence of the capitalist system. It is often said that capitalism cannot exist without foreign trade and that every advance of socialism means a constriction of capitalism's trading area. Hence, the argument continues, for the leading capitalist countries, even if they are not threatened by powerful internal socialist movements, the struggle against socialism is quite literally a struggle for survival. Put in this form, the reasoning from capitalist interests involves a *non sequitur*. It is true that capitalism is inconceivable without foreign trade, but it is not true that socialist countries are unwilling or unable to trade with capitalist countries. Hence the spread of socialism, taken by itself, does not imply any reduction of the trading area open to the capitalist countries. One can even go further. Bourgeois economists never tire of repeating that the more industrially developed a country is, the greater its potential as a trading partner. Since underdeveloped countries industrialize more rapidly under socialism than under capitalism, the leading capitalist countries, on this argument, should welcome the spread of socialism in the underdeveloped parts of the capitalist world. That they do not but instead resist it tooth and nail must be explained on other grounds.

The problem is in reality much more complex and can only be fruitfully posed in quite different terms. Capitalist governments do not, in general, trade with each other. Most trade in the capitalist world is carried on by private enterprises, mainly by large corporations. What these corporations are interested in is not trade as such but profits: the reason they and the governments they control are opposed to the spread of socialism is not that it necessarily reduces their chances of importing

or exporting (though of course it may), but that it does necessarily reduce their opportunities to profit from doing business
with and in the newly socialized area. And when account is
taken of the fact that for corporations in the leading capitalist
countries, profit rates from doing business with and in the less
developed and underdeveloped countries are generally higher
than domestic profit rates, the reason for the vehemence of
opposition to the spread of socialism in precisely those areas
will be appreciated.

We advisedly use the general term "doing business with and
in" rather than the more limited "buying from and selling to."
The international relationships and interests of the typical
giant corporation today are likely to be diverse and extremely
complex, much more so than mere exporting or importing.
There is perhaps no better way to make this clear than by
summarizing the world-wide scope and character of what is
unquestionably the leading United States "multinational corporation"—Standard Oil of New Jersey.[14] The facts and figures which follow are taken from official publications of the
company.[15]

In terms of dollar assets, Jersey Standard is the largest industrial corporation in the United States, the total at the end of
1962 amounting to $11,488 million. Aggregate revenues for the
same year were $10,567 million and net income (profit) $841

[14] The term "multinational corporation" seems to have originated
with David E. Lilienthal, Director of the Tennessee Valley Authority
under Roosevelt and of the Atomic Energy Commission under Truman,
and now Chairman of the Development and Resources Corporation
which is backed and controlled by the international banking house of
Lazard Frères. A paper delivered by Lilienthal at Carnegie Institute of
Technology in April 1960, and subsequently published by Development
and Resources Corporation, bears the title "The Multinational Corporation." The usage was subsequently taken up by *Business Week* in a
special report, "Multinational Companies," in its issue of April 20,
1963.

[15] *Notice of Special Stockholders' Meeting* (October 7, 1959); *Form
10-K for the Fiscal Year Ended December 31, 1962* (filed with the
Securities and Exchange Commission pursuant to Section 13 of the Securities Act of 1934); and 1962 *Annual Report.*

million. It is only when these figures are broken down geographically, however, that the crucial importance of foreign operations becomes clear. As of the end of 1958, the percentage distribution of assets and profits by regions was as follows:

	Assets	Profits
United States and Canada	67	34
Latin America	20	39
Eastern Hemisphere	13	27
Total	100	100

While two thirds of Jersey's assets were located in North America, only one third of its profits came from that region. Or to put the point differently, Jersey's foreign investments were half as large as its domestic investments but its foreign profits were twice as large as its domestic profits. The indicated profit rate abroad is thus four times the domestic rate.

That Jersey's operations are truly world-wide can be gathered from the facts that in 1962 the company sold its products in more than a hundred countries and owned 50 percent or more of the stock in 275 subsidiaries in 52 countries. Table 6 enumerates such subsidiaries by country of organization. Summarizing by regions, we find that Jersey had 114 subsidiaries in the United States and Canada, 77 in Europe, 43 in Latin America, 14 in Asia, 9 in Africa, and 18 elsewhere.

The tremendous variety and scope of Jersey's foreign operations might lead one to suppose that over the years the company has been a large and consistent exporter of capital. Nothing could be further from the truth. Apart from a small initial export of capital many years ago, the expansion of Jersey's foreign assets has been financed from the profits of its foreign operations. Moreover, so great have been these foreign profits that after all foreign expansion needs have been taken care of, there have still been huge sums left over for remittance to the parent company in the United States. Separate figures on the amount of these remittances from foreign profits are not published, but an idea of the orders of magnitude is conveyed by the following figures for 1962. In that year, as already noted,

Table 6

Subsidiaries of Standard Oil

United States	77	Switzerland	2
Canada	37	Uruguay	2
Great Britain	24	Venezuela	2
Panama	17	Algeria	1
France	12	Danzig	1
Bahamas	8	Dominican Republic	1
Italy	6	Egypt	1
Sweden	6	El Salvador	1
Colombia	5	Finland	1
Netherlands	5	Hungary	1
Australia	4	India	1
Brazil	4	Indonesia	1
Chile	4	Kenya	1
Germany	4	Luxembourg	1
Philippines	4	Madagascar	1
Argentina	3	Mexico	1
Denmark	3	New Zealand	1
Ireland	3	Paraguay	1
Japan	3	Peru	1
Netherlands Antilles	3	Republic of Congo	1
Norway	3	Singapore	1
Austria	2	South Africa	1
Belgium	2	Spain	1
Bermuda	2	Surinam	1
Iraq	2	Tunisia	1
Malaya	2		
Morocco	2	Total	275

total profits were $841 million. Of this sum, $538 million were paid out as dividends to stockholders, the vast majority of whom are residents of the United States. The remaining $303 million were added to the company's investments, at home and abroad. Elsewhere in the same Annual Report that records these figures we learn that profits from operations in the United States in 1962 were $309 million. This figure, it will be seen, is $229 million less than the amount of dividends paid. In other words, approximately 40 percent of dividends paid to stockholders plus whatever net investment was made in the United States during the year were financed from the profits of foreign operations. In a word: Standard Oil of New Jersey is a very large and consistent *importer* of capital.

At this point, however, we must pause and ask whether Standard Oil of New Jersey is really an ideal type which helps us to distill the essence of capitalist reality, or whether on the contrary it may not be an exceptional case which we should ignore rather than focus attention on.

Up to the Second World War, it would have been correct to treat Standard Oil as a sort of exception—a very important one, to be sure, exercising tremendous, and at times even decisive, influence on United States world policy. Nevertheless in the multinational scope and magnitude of its operations not only was it far ahead of all the others; there were only a handful which could be said to be developing along the same lines. Many United States corporations of course had large interests in import and export trade, and quite a few had foreign branches or subsidiaries. In neither respect, however, was the situation much different in 1946 from what it had been in 1929. Indeed, direct foreign investments of United States corporations actually declined from $7.5 billion to $7.2 billion, or by 4 percent, between these two dates.[16] Most of the giant corporations which dominated the American economy in those years were, in the words of *Business Week*, "domestically oriented enterprises with international operations" and not, like Standard Oil, "truly world oriented corporations."[17]

A big change took place during the next decade and a half. To quote *Business Week* again, "In industry after industry, U. S. companies found that their overseas earnings were soaring, and that their return on investment abroad was frequently

[16] United States Department of Commerce, Office of Business Economics, *U. S. Business Investments in Foreign Countries: A Supplement to the Survey of Current Business*, Washington, 1960, p. 1.

[17] "Multinational Companies," *Business Week*, April 20, 1963. It is interesting to note that in the United States the business press is often far ahead of the economics profession in recognizing, and even trying to analyze, the latest developments in the capitalist economy.

much higher than in the U.S. As earnings abroad began to rise, profit margins from domestic operations started to shrink. . . . This is the combination that forced development of the multi-national company."[18] As a result, of course, foreign direct investments of American corporations shot up—from $7.2 billion in 1946 to $40.6 billion in 1963, a more than fivefold increase in the years since the Second World War.[19] Parallel to this growth in foreign investments has gone an increase in the sales and profits of foreign branches and subsidiaries. In manufacturing (excluding petroleum and mining), sales of such affiliates amounted to $18.3 billion in 1957 (the first year for which figures are available) and to $28.1 billion in 1962, an increase of 54 percent in six years.[20]

Some idea of the growing relative importance of these foreign operations of American corporations may be gathered from Table 7, which presents data on the sales of foreign manufacturing affiliates, total domestic manufacturing sales, and non-agricultural merchandise exports. (See p. 198 for Table 7.)

It would of course be preferable to compare the foreign and domestic sales and exports of those corporations which have foreign branches or subsidiaries; and it would be still better if we could include the profits of these corporations from foreign and domestic operations respectively. If such data were available, we could form a very clear picture of the degree of involvement of the United States giant corporations in foreign activities. But even the figures presented in Table 7 bear eloquent testimony to the rapid growth of that involvement. In the six years beginning with 1957, the sales of foreign affiliates grew by 54 percent, while total domestic manufacturing sales expanded only 17 percent and non-agricultural exports hardly changed at all.

So much for the record of recent years. If we look ahead, we

[18] *Ibid.*

[19] *Survey of Current Business,* August 1964, p. 10.

[20] Fred Cutler and Samuel Pizer, "Foreign Operations of U. S. Industry: Capital Spending, Sales, and Financing," *Survey of Current Business,* October 1963, p. 19.

Table 7

Growth of Foreign and Domestic Manufacturing
Sales and Merchandise Exports, 1957-1962
(Billions of dollars)

	Sales of Foreign Manufacturing Affiliates	Total Domestic Manufacturing Sales	Merchandise Exports (Excluding foodstuffs)
1957	18.3	341	16.8
1958	n.a.	314	13.8
1959	21.1	356	13.7
1960	23.6	365	16.6
1961	25.6	368	16.9
1962	28.1	400	17.3

n.a. = not available
Sources: Foreign sales, Fred Cutler and Samuel Pizer, "Foreign Operations of
U. S. Industry," *Survey of Current Business,* October 1963; domestic sales
and exports, *Economic Indicators,* current issues.

find that American corporate business, far from regarding its
expansion abroad as having come to an end, is relying heavily
for its future prosperity on the continued penetration of other
countries' economies. "America as the 'land of opportunity' is
beginning to lose that title in the eyes of many U. S. businessmen," says a Special Report in U. S. *News & World Report.*[21]
And the Report goes on to tell why:

These businessmen increasingly are deciding that markets abroad
—not those in this country—offer the biggest potential for future
growth. The feeling grows that the U. S. market, while huge, is
relatively "saturated."

It is overseas that businessmen see the big, untapped market with
hundreds of millions of customers wanting—and increasingly able to
buy—all kinds of products and services.

[21] "For New Opportunities: Now, the Word Is 'Go Abroad,' " U. S.
News & World Report, June 1, 1964. In order to gather material for this
report, "members of the International Staff of U. S. *News & World
Report* talked with scores of U. S. firms abroad. Added material was
gathered from corporations in the U. S. heavily engaged in the foreign
field."

To go after this market, U. S. firms are building and expanding factories all around the world. Since 1958, more than 2,100 American companies have started new operations in Western Europe alone. . . .

All types of businesses—from autos to baby foods—predict a glowing future for markets outside the U. S.

Says L. E. Spencer, president of Goodyear Tire & Rubber Company of Canada: "Foreign markets will expand several times as fast as North American markets over the next 10 years."

From C. C. Smith, vice president of International Business Machines' World Trade Corporation: "The rate of increase in our foreign business is greater than in the U. S. in every major product category. In time, we expect volume to overtake that in the U. S."

Listen to the comment by an official of Colgate-Palmolive Company: "You're in a saturated market here in the U. S., where new products are the only answer to growth. Abroad there are millions of people each year who reach the stage in their cultural, social and economic development where they buy soap, toothpaste, other things we sell."

This flat prediction is made by Fred J. Borch, president of General Electric Corporation: "Regardless of economic or political ups and downs, the most rapidly expanding markets will be abroad in the next 25 years."

Against that background, the survey of U. S. firms abroad turned up these major findings—

1. Foreign sales of U. S. companies are growing much faster than sales of the same companies in this country. Often, the percentage gains are three or four times as great.

2. Profit rates abroad generally are higher than those in similar activities in the U. S. Many firms report a percentage return "twice as high abroad as in America." Most cite lower wage costs overseas —and less competition.

3. Foreign markets usually can best be tapped by an on-the-scene operation, rather than by exporting from the U.S. A plant abroad can avoid tariff and other trade barriers erected against exports from this country. . . .

It thus appears both from the record of the past and from the plans and hopes for the future that American corporate business has irrevocably embarked on the road long since pioneered by Standard Oil. Standard is still the model of a multinational corporation, but it is no longer an exception. It simply shows us in the most developed form what the other giants either already are or are in the process of becoming.

As it happens, the recent history of Standard Oil of New Jersey also supplies us with a textbook example of why multinational corporations are profoundly hostile to the spread of socialism. Before the Cuban Revolution, Jersey was heavily involved in Cuba in several ways. It owned refining facilities on the island and operated an extensive distribution system, involving altogether properties valued at $62,269,000.[22] In addition, Jersey's Cuban subsidiary bought its crude from Creole Petroleum, Jersey's Venezuelan subsidiary, at the high prices maintained by the international oil cartel. The company therefore reaped profits in two countries and on three separate operations—sale of crude, refining of crude, and sale of finished products. As a result of the Revolution, the company's properties in Cuba were nationalized without compensation, and Creole lost its Cuban market. More than $60 million in assets and all three sources of current profit were lost in one blow—and without in any way involving exports from or imports to the United States.

It might be argued that if Jersey and the United States government had pursued different policies toward Cuba, the revolutionary regime would have been glad to continue buying oil from Venezuela, which after all is the nearest and most rational source of supply. This is no doubt true—but with a big proviso. The revolutionary regime would have been glad to continue buying oil from Venezuela, but it would not have been glad to continue paying prices and meeting terms of payment dictated by Standard Oil. And since it could turn to the Soviet Union as an alternative source of supply, it was no longer obliged to go on submitting to the cartel's terms. Hence to remain in the Cuban market, Jersey would at the least have had to cut its prices and offer better credit terms. This not only would have meant less profits on sales to Cuba but would have threatened

[22] Standard and Poor, *Standard Corporate Descriptions*, July 24, 1961.

the whole structure of cartel prices. Jersey and Washington decided instead to make war on the Cuban Revolution.

That what is at stake in the conflict between the United
States and Cuba is not trade between the two countries is confirmed by Cuba's relations with other capitalist countries. Long
after the socialization of the Cuban economy, the Havana government was vigorously promoting its trade with Britain,
France, Spain, Canada, Japan—in short, with any country willing and able to do business with Cuba. It is true, of course, that
Cuba's capacity to export and import has been seriously curtailed by the disorganization and other difficulties of the early
years of the change-over to socialism, but there seems to be no
reason to doubt the Cubans' own contention that in a few years
the island will be a much better trading partner than it was
under the old neo-colonial regime. Nor is there any reason to
doubt that the United States could capture a major share of the
Cuban trade if the blockade were called off and normal relations re-established between the two countries.

But this is not what really interests the giant multinational
corporations which dominate American policy. What they
want is *monopolistic control* over foreign sources of supply and
foreign markets, enabling them to buy and sell on specially
privileged terms, to shift orders from one subsidiary to another,
to favor this country or that depending on which has the most
advantageous tax, labor, and other policies—in a word, they
want to do business on their own terms and wherever they
choose. And for this what they need is not trading partners
but "allies" and clients willing to adjust their laws and policies
to the requirements of American Big Business.

Against this background, one can see that Cuba's crime was
to assert, in deeds as well as in words, her sovereign right to
dispose over her own resources in the interests of her own
people. This involved curtailing and, in the struggle which
ensued, eventually abrogating the rights and privileges which
the giant multinational corporations had previously enjoyed in
Cuba. It was because of this and not because of a loss of trade,

still less because of any irrational fears or prejudices, that the corporations and their government in Washington reacted so violently to the Cuban Revolution.

It might perhaps be thought that since Cuba is a small country, the violence of the reaction was out of all proportion to the damage suffered. But this would be to miss the main point. What makes Cuba so important is precisely that she is so small, plus the fact that she is located so close to the United States. If Cuba can defect from the "free world" and join the socialist camp with impunity, then any country can do so. And if Cuba prospers under the new setup, all the other underdeveloped and exploited countries of the world will be tempted to follow her example. The stake in Cuba is thus not simply the exploitability of one small country but the very existence of the "free world" itself, that is to say, of the whole system of exploitation.

It is this fact that has dictated the Cuban policy of the United States. The strategy has been to damage and cripple the Cuban economy in every possible way, with a threefold objective. First, it is hoped that the Cuban people will sooner or later become disillusioned with their revolutionary leadership, thus setting the stage for a successful counter-revolution. Second, the peoples of the underdeveloped countries are to be taught that revolution does not pay. And third, the burden of supporting the Cuban economy thrown on the rest of the socialist camp, and especially on the Soviet Union as its economically most developed member, is to be maximized so that these other socialist countries may be induced to use their influence to restrain any new revolutions which might place further burdens on their already overstrained economies.

6

This is of course not the only way the "free world" is being defended. The United States failed to understand the nature of the revolution which overthrew the Batista regime in Cuba

until it was too late to keep the revolutionaries from consolidating their power. Every precaution is being taken to see that
the same mistake is not made again. All revolutionaries are
automatically suspect; no regime is too reactionary to merit all-
out United States backing.

Partly, this backing takes the form of so-called economic
aid—in reality handouts to corrupt oligarchies designed to insure their loyalty to Washington rather than to the interests of
their own countries.[23] And partly it takes the form of military
aid, which is predominantly of two types.

First, there is direct participation by United States armed
forces on the territory of the client state: stationing of troops in
bases controlled by the United States (as we saw above, there
are some 275 major base complexes and 1,400 bases either occupied by or prepared for American forces); "emergency" deployment of troops anywhere on the host country's national
territory that the two governments may decide (Lebanon in
the summer of 1958, Thailand in the spring of 1962, the Do-
minican Republic in the spring of 1965); and various kinds of
advisory and training missions accredited to the armed forces
of the clients (in 1957, a total of forty Army, Navy, and Air
Force missions were in Latin America alone, in every country
except Mexico). As South Vietnam shows, training missions
can be quickly and almost imperceptibly transformed into
counter-revolutionary combat forces.[24]

[23] "A lot of the criticism of foreign aid," according to D. A. Fitz-
gerald, a high official in the succession of United States government
agencies in charge of foreign aid from 1948 to 1961, "is because the
critic thought the objective was to get economic growth, and this wasn't
the objective at all. . . . It depends on what the major purpose is, and half
the time the major purpose is to meet a short-term political crisis—and
economic development, if any, is only an incidental result." Interview in
U. S. News & World Report, February 25, 1963, pp. 49, 50.

[24] South Vietnam also shows that in the underdeveloped countries
today reactionary regimes, no matter how lavishly equipped and "advised" by the United States, cannot win wars against dedicated and experienced revolutionary guerrillas. This is not the place to attempt to assess
the implications of this momentous fact. We only record our conviction

The second form of military aid is the provision of material and financial support for the armed forces of the client states. While the dozens of military assistance pacts which the United States has signed with underdeveloped countries around the world are ostensibly designed to meet the "threat" of aggression from the Soviet Union or China, no serious military planner imagines that this is the real purpose. Such a threat, if it really existed, could be countered only by the United States itself, and an attempt to coordinate military strategy with a large number of feeble allies would be a source of weakness rather than strength. The real purpose of this military aid is clearly spelled out by Lieuwen in his pioneer study of the role of the military in Latin America:

Those [military] policies . . . are not designed to meet the military threat of communism, but rather to gain Latin America's friendship, to win its cooperation and support in the United Nations and the Organization of American States. The Rio military alliance, the M[utual] D[efense] A[ssistance] Pacts, the arms grants, the reimbursable aid, the work of the I[nter] A[merican] D[efense] B[oard] and of the military missions—all of these have no great military significance. They are designed, above all, to draw the Latin American officer corps, which exercise great influence over the political scene in most of the republics, closer to the United States, in the hope that they will exclude Soviet influence, give the United States their support, maintain political stability, ensure continued access to strategic raw materials, and provide rights to the use of bases.[25]

To put the matter more bluntly, the purpose of United States military aid to underdeveloped countries is to keep them in the American empire if they are already there and to bring them in if they are not—and in any case to insure that there are no further defections from the "free world." The consequences for

---

that its significance will loom larger and larger as the years go by and that in retrospect the struggle in South Vietnam will be recognized as one of the turning points of the history of the second half of the twentieth century.

[25] Edwin C. Lieuwen, *Arms and Politics in Latin America,* New York, 1960, p. 226.

the recipient countries are tragic. "What we are doing," said
the Colombian statesman Eduardo Santos, "is building up
armies which weigh nothing in the international scale but
which are juggernauts for the internal life of each country.
Each country is being occupied by its own army."[26] And the
same point is made and heavily underlined in a remarkable
study of relations between the United States and Pakistan published by a group of Pakistani students in London:

> In the long run, the worst aspect of military aid lies in the com-
> plete change it produces in the balance of social and political forces
> in favor of conservatism and established vested interests. The
> dragon seeds sown by military aid have produced a fearful crop of
> military officers, with their social roots in the most conservative
> sections of our society, who have learnt to sit in judgment on our
> people. It is an overwhelming force without any countervailing
> force to hold it in check.[27]

This world-wide spawning of little military machines loyal
to Washington does not in any way reduce the need for a big
military machine in the United States itself. As the tide of
revolutionary protest rises in the exploited countries of the
"free world," it is only by increasingly direct and massive intervention by American armed forces that the old order can be
held together a while longer. As the shift to nuclear weapons
and intercontinental missiles proceeds, even the pretense that
the global system of bases is for protection against Russian
aggression is given up. "Little by little," writes Cyrus L. Sulzberger, foreign affairs columnist of the *New York Times*, "the
requirement for bases on the periphery of the NATO area is
dwindling. Medium-range and long-range plus seaborne missiles are changing the emphasis of our counter-strike force. But
the time has not yet come when one can envision the disappearance of all need for U. S. overseas bases; on the contrary."
There follows a revealing analogy with British policy after the

[26] Quoted by Lieuwen, *ibid.*, pp. 237-238.
[27] "The Burden of U. S. Aid," *Pakistan Today*, New Series, No. 1.
Autumn 1961.

Napoleonic Wars, though the naked term "empire" is used only in referring to that bygone era:

> Today Washington stresses preparations to fight limited wars if necessary. These need mobility, the ability to transfer men and supplies from one quarter to the other, using staging points abroad. They also necessitate what is called "forward stockpiling" at strategically important havens.
>
> A study of this particular problem is now under way in the Pentagon. After the Napoleonic Wars, the British Navy made such a study to ascertain London's requisites in defending its vast overseas empire. Later the U.S. Navy made a similar analysis of how to operate globally.
>
> The focus of present Washington research is more on aspects of limited war than total war. . . .
>
> Likewise, the administration sees the possibility we might be engaged in limited wars on other fronts, conflicts similar to that in South Vietnam where we are not belligerents but are increasingly committed. For example, were Iran to be subjected to Russian pressure, initial efforts to aid it might be "limited" rather than "total." To be ready for such actions, the United States must maintain sufficient bases overseas to permit accumulation of stocks for swift reaction by other means than holocaust.[28]

Is not Sulzberger really saying that the United States, like Great Britain in the nineteenth century, needs a global military machine to police a global empire? But, as we know, the United States needs a global military machine also for carrying on its unremitting struggle against the advance of socialism. And the truth is that policing the empire and fighting socialism are rapidly becoming, if they are not already, one and the same. For the threat to the empire comes from revolutionary movements which, like the American Revolution two hundred years ago, are sparked by a deep-seated yearning for national independence and are fueled by an increasingly urgent need for economic development, which experience is proving cannot be achieved by underdeveloped countries today except on the basis of public enterprise and comprehensive planning—in short, only if their nationalist revolutions are also socialist revolutions.

[28] *New York Times*, April 23, 1962.

As these two great socio-political transformations merge into a single process, so likewise does the struggle against them. For the United States to defend its empire today means to fight socialism, not only in the empire but wherever it exists; for socialism is by its very nature an international movement which gains strength everywhere from a success anywhere. Hence all revolutions must be opposed, every source which gives them material or moral aid must be weakened and if possible destroyed. It is this two-sided, world-wide commitment to the political and social status quo which defines and determines the military needs of the United States oligarchy.

7

So much for the American oligarchy's *need* for a military establishment. We must next examine the effect of satisfying this need on the private interests of the members of the oligarchy, and on the stability and cohesiveness of the country's class structure.

It was argued at some length in the last chapter that most governmental activities designed to satisfy collective needs involve either competition with private interests or injury to the class position and privileges of the oligarchy, and that for these reasons opposition is quickly aroused and rapidly reinforced as these activities are extended. The result is that roadblocks are encountered long before socially rational and desirable goals have been attained. How is it with government activities in the military sphere?

To begin with, it is obvious that the building up of a gigantic military establishment neither creates nor involves competition with private enterprise. There are no private military establishments with a vested interest in keeping the government out of their preserves; and the military plays the role of an ideal customer for private business, spending billions of dollars annually on terms that are most favorable to the sellers. Since a large part of the required capital equipment has no alternative use, its cost is commonly included in the price of the end product. The business of producing arms is therefore

virtually <u>risk-free</u>, in spite of which the allowable profit rates
include a generous margin for a mythical risk factor. And the
fact that military procurement officers often look forward to
lucrative employment with arms manufacturers after retirement from the service hardly makes for strictness in their dealings with suppliers.[29]

The results of this system were well illustrated in testimony
before the Senate Investigations Subcommittee dealing with
the profitability of the Boeing Company, one of the country's
largest airplane manufacturers:

Mr. Nunnally [staff accountant] testified that Boeing's government contracts for work on the Bomarc, B-52 and B-54 bombers, KC-
135 tanker and other projects had totaled $11,818,900,000 since
1951. He said the company's costs on the work had totaled $10,911,-
200,000, leaving gross profits of $907,700,000.

He said a year-by-year measurement of the profits against the
company's net investment (net worth plus all borrowed capital)
showed profit percentages ranging from 108.6 percent in 1953 to 36
percent in 1951 and 1960.

Mr. Nunnally said Boeing's profit as measured by the company's
net worth averaged 74.38 percent before payment of taxes and 35.68
percent after taxes on its government contracts and 19.05 percent
after taxes on its combined government and commercial business.

He said this was "almost double" the 10.73 percent average net
profit for all manufacturing industries in the United States computed by government regulatory agencies against net worth in the
same years.[30]

Overall data on the profitability of arms production have
never, to our knowledge, been compiled, and it is possible that

[29] In 1960, according to a subcommittee of the House Armed Services Committee, 720 of the country's largest defense contractors employed 1,426 retired commissioned officers, 251 of them former generals
and admirals. Cited in Oliver C. Cox, *Capitalism and American Leadership*, New York, 1962, p. 118.

[30] *New York Times*, May 23, 1962. Mr. Nunnally also testified that
there was no dispute between him and the company as to the accuracy of
the figures, the *Times* reporter adding that Boeing objected to the "net
investment" yardstick and contended that the rate of profit should be
calculated on sales volume.

Boeing is a specially favored corporation. Be that as it may, there is no doubt that supplying the military is universally regarded as good business: all corporations, big and little, bid for as large a share as they can get. The private interests of the oligarchy, far from generating opposition to military spending, encourage its continuous expansion.

The class interests of the oligarchy work in the same direction. Whereas massive government spending for education and welfare tends to undermine its privileged position, the opposite is true of military spending. The reason is that militarization fosters all the reactionary and irrational forces in society, and inhibits or kills everything progressive and humane. Blind respect is engendered for authority; attitudes of docility and conformity are taught and enforced; dissent is treated as unpatriotic or even treasonable. In such an atmosphere, the oligarchy feels that its moral authority and material position are secure. Veblen, more than any other social scientist, appreciated the importance of this social function of militarism:

The largest and most promising factor of cultural discipline— most promising as a corrective of iconoclastic vagaries—over which business principles rule is national politics. . . . Business interests urge an aggressive national policy and businessmen direct it. Such a policy is warlike as well as patriotic. The direct cultural value of a warlike business policy is unequivocal. It makes for a conservative animus on the part of the populace. During wartime, and within the military organization at all times, civil rights are in abeyance; and the more war and armaments the more abeyance. Military training is a training in ceremonial precedence, arbitrary command, and unquestioning obedience. . . . The more consistent and the more comprehensive this training, the more effectually will the members of the community be trained into habits of subordination and away from that growing propensity to make light of personal authority which is the chief infirmity of democracy. This applies first and most decidedly, of course, to the soldiery, but it applies only in less degree to the rest of the population. They learn to think in warlike terms of rank, authority, and subordination, and to grow progressively more patient of encroachments on their civil rights. . . . Habituation to a warlike, predatory scheme of life is the strongest disciplinary factor that can be brought to counteract the vulgarization of modern life wrought by peaceful industry and the machine process, and to re-habilitate the decaying sense of status and differential dignity. War-fare, with the stress on subordination and mastery and the insistence on gradations of dignity and honor incident to a militant organiza-tion, has always proved an effective school in barbarian methods of thought.[31]

These generalizations, presumably based at least in part on Veblen's observations during the Spanish-American War, have been all too convincingly confirmed by the events of the past two decades when what President Eisenhower, in his poignant Farewell Address, called the military-industrial complex was rising to dominance in American life. Civil liberties indeed fell into abeyance, and dissent from global policies of imperialism and anti-socialism became identified with Communism and hence with treason to the nation.

It would be misleading to leave the impression that only the oligarchy has favored the steady increase in military spending during these years. If one assumes the permanence of monop-oly capitalism, with its proved incapacity to make rational use for peaceful and humane ends of its enormous productive po-tential, one must decide whether one prefers the mass unem-ployment and hopelessness characteristic of the Great Depres-sion or the relative job security and material well-being pro-vided by the huge military budgets of the 1940's and 1950's. Since most Americans, workers included, still do assume with-out question the permanence of the system, it is only natural that they should prefer the situation which is personally and privately more advantageous. And in order to rationalize this preference, they have accepted the official ideology of anti-Communism which appears to justify an unlimited expansion of the military establishment as essential to national survival.

Against this background it is easy to understand why there has been so little political opposition in recent years to expand-

[31] Thorstein Veblen, *The Theory of Business Enterprise*, pp. 391-393.

ing military budgets. In a Congress normally characterized by fierce fighting among lobbies and pressure groups, a majestic unanimity emerges as soon as a request is made for additional billions for the armed services, with Congressmen vying with one another for the honor of proposing the largest increases.[32]

The people's representatives in their enthusiasm even pay little attention to the strictly military rationality of how the money is spent. "My own experience in the Senate," says William Proxmire, Democratic Senator from Wisconsin, "has shown me the painful inability of our democracy to resist the momentum of excessive spending and waste that accompanies our vast military establishment."[33] And he gives a graphic illustration, the Senate's reaction to strong urging by Secretary of Defense McNamara against spending more on B-52 and B-58 bombers than the President had already requested:

> Only three Senators joined me in voting for my amendment, which would have eliminated this appropriation. In the Senate debate, we had made an overwhelming case against spending more than half a billion dollars in this way. Yet some 95 percent of the Senators voting that day rejected the logic of the case, rejected the advice of the President, the Secretary of Defense and his aides, and voted to appropriate the funds. This was more money than was spent in that year by the federal government for medical research; more than was spent for all federal housing programs; more than the budgets allocated to the U.S. Forest Service, the National Park Service, and the Fish and Wildlife Service combined.[34]

No wonder Senator Proxmire concludes that "as a rationalization for federal expenditure, national defense has few peers. Programs that wouldn't get a second look from Congress flit through if they are attached to an armed forces appropriation."[35] The views of Proxmire, reputed to be one of the more

[32] A typical news item: "The military appropriations bill, the largest in American peacetime history, was approved [in the Senate] by a vote of 88 to 0." *New York Times*, June 14, 1962.

[33] "Spendthrifts for Defense," *The Nation*, August 25, 1962, p. 63.

[34] *Ibid.*, p. 64.

[35] *Ibid.*

liberal members of the Senate, might be discounted as likely to be exaggerated. This would hardly apply to Senator Richard B. Russell of Georgia, a conservative Southerner, Chairman of the Senate Armed Services Committee, and often described as the most powerful individual in the Congress. Here is Senator Russell in a colloquy on the Senate floor with Senator Proxmire:

There is something about preparing for destruction that causes men to be more careless in spending money than they would be if they were building for constructive purposes. Why that is so I do not know; but I have observed, over a period of almost thirty years in the Senate, that there is something about buying arms with which to kill, to destroy, to wipe out cities, and to obliterate great transportation systems which causes men not to reckon the dollar cost as closely as they do when they think about proper housing and the care of the health of human beings.[36]

A more devastating condemnation of a whole social order would be hard to imagine. Nor, as we have seen, are the reasons so mysterious as Senator Russell seems to think. The Cold War, the well-known Harvard economist Sumner Slichter explained in 1949, "increases the demand for goods, helps sustain a high level of employment, accelerates technical progress and thus helps the country to raise its standard of living. . . . So we may thank the Russians for helping make capitalism in the United States work better than ever."[37] And a few months later *U.S. News & World Report,* published by the ultra-conservative David Lawrence, spelled out the same idea with brutal candor:

Government planners figure they have found the magic formula for almost endless good times. . . . *Cold War* is the catalyst. Cold War is an automatic pump primer. Turn a spigot, the public clamors for more arms spending. Turn another, the clamor ceases. Truman confidence, cockiness, is based on this "Truman formula." *Truman era of good times,* President is told, can run much beyond 1952. Cold War demands, if fully exploited, are almost limitless.

[36] *Ibid.,* pp. 65-66.
[37] This and the following two quotations are taken from Fred J. Cook's powerful tract *Juggernaut: The Warfare State,* which first appeared as a special edition of *The Nation,* October 20, 1961, p. 300.

U.S. News & World Report was still saying the same thing in 1954. Following news that the United States had exploded the world's first hydrogen bomb, it commented: "What H-bomb means to business. A long period . . . of big orders. In the years ahead, the effects of the new bomb will keep on increasing. As one appraiser put it: 'The H-bomb has blown depression-thinking out the window.'"

Here at last monopoly capitalism had seemingly found the answer to the "on what" question: On what could the government spend enough to keep the system from sinking into the mire of stagnation? On arms, more arms, and ever more arms.

Yet it somehow has not worked out quite this way. The Cold War intensified; the military budget, after a dip at the end of the Korean War, resumed its upward trend. But a sort of creeping stagnation set in all the same.[38]

Why was the military budget not expanded still further? If $50 billion is not enough, why not $60 billion? The Congress, we know, has shown itself ready to vote whatever military appropriations are asked of it, and more. Why did the President not gear his requests to the requirements of a prosperous economy? Why were growth rates allowed to lag, profit margins to sag, unemployment to mount? Evidently, even the amount of military spending is not a perfectly free variable through manipulation of which the leaders of the oligarchy can maintain the right head of steam in the economic engine. Here too, it seems, obstacles and contradictions are in operation.

8

Limitations on the effectiveness of arms spending as an instrument of economic control stem from the nature of the new weapons created by modern science and technology. These limitations are of two kinds, the first economic and the second military.

The economic limitation is, quite simply, that the new tech-

---

[38] This phenomenon is analyzed in the next chapter.

nology of warfare has reduced the power of arms spending to stimulate the economy.

It is a commonplace that warfare is becoming more and more a matter of science and technology, less and less a matter of masses of men and weapons. Rockets and missiles are replacing bombers and rendering fighter planes largely purposeless; huge fleets of surface vessels are obsolete; massed armies are giving way to highly specialized troops wielding an array of fantastically destructive weapons. As a consequence of these changes, there has been a sharp shift in the character of goods and services purchased by military outlays. A much larger proportion goes for research and development, engineering, supervision, and maintenance; a much smaller proportion for the kind of mass-produced military hardware (artillery, tanks, planes, trucks, jeeps, ships) that played the decisive role in two world wars. This change in the composition of military demand means that a given amount of military spending employs far fewer persons today than it used to. In these circumstances, even very large increases in military spending, while enormously profitable to the big corporations, may have relatively little effect on investment and employment.[39] Given the present nature of military demand, it might be wholly impossible to reach a level of full employment by simple increases in the military budget: a bottleneck of specialized scientific and engineering skills could prove to be an insuperable obstacle to further expansion long before the indirect effects of the increased spending had reached the unemployed steel workers of Pittsburgh, the coal miners of Kentucky and West Virginia, the

[39] "The arms budget," writes the distinguished publisher of *Scientific American*, "is losing its potency as an economic anodyne. It is concealing less and less successfully the underlying transformation of our economic system. Progress in the technology of war, as in all other branches of technology, is inexorably cutting back the payroll. With the miniaturization of violence in the step from A-bombs to H-bombs, from manned aircraft to missiles, expenditure on armaments has begun to yield a diminishing economic stimulus." Gerard Piel, "Can Our Economy Stand Disarmament?" *The Atlantic*, September 1962, p. 40.

school dropouts in the slums and ghettos of the big cities all
over the country. Ironically, the huge military outlays of today
may even be contributing substantially to an increase of unemployment: many of the new technologies which are by-
products of military research and development are also applicable to civilian production, where they are quite likely to have
the effect of raising productivity and reducing the demand for
labor.

The second limitation on the use of arms spending as an
economic stimulant derives from the logic of the military situation itself. The piling up of modern weapons of total destruction in an arms race between two evenly matched powers not
only has no rational military purpose—that would perhaps not
matter too much—but actually reduces the chances that the
country could survive a full-scale war. It follows that continued expansion of the military budget is in the strictest sense
irrational: it contradicts the very purpose which the military
establishment is supposed to serve. The situation is well stated
in an article by Jerome B. Wiesner and Herbert F. York:

> Ever since shortly after World War II the military power of the
> U.S. has been steadily increasing. Throughout this same period the
> national security of the U.S. has been rapidly and inexorably dimin-
> ishing. . . .
> From the Soviet point of view the picture is similar but much
> worse. The military power of the U.S.S.R. has been steadily increas-
> ing since it became an atomic power in 1949. Soviet national se-
> curity, however, has been steadily decreasing. . . .
> Both sides in the arms race are thus confronted by the dilemma of
> steadily increasing military power and steadily decreasing national
> security. *It is our considered professional judgment that this
> dilemma has no technical solution.* If the great powers continue to
> look for solutions in the area of science and technology only, the
> result will be to worsen the situation. The clearly predictable course
> of the arms race is a steady open spiral downward into oblivion.[40]

The importance of this statement lies less in what it says—

[40] Jerome B. Wiesner and Herbert F. York, "National Security and
the Nuclear-Test Ban," *Scientific American*, October 1964, p. 8.

others have said much the same thing many times—than in the identity of its authors. Wiesner was the chief scientific adviser to the Kennedy administration and York held the same position under Eisenhower. The fact that they have both signed their names to an article which states unambiguously that the arms race is self-defeating can only mean that this truth has now been digested and absorbed by responsible leaders of the United States oligarchy and that these leaders are ready to steer public opinion in the direction of favoring concrete arms-limitation measures.

Already some cautious steps have been taken. The partial test ban treaty is one, though its significance is largely symbolic. More important is the leveling off of arms spending in the first budget of the Johnson administration, and the articulation by authoritative spokesmen of a hope that a cutback of arms spending by as much as 24 percent as compared to the 1964 level might be possible by 1970.[41] In view of the compelling logic of the situation as set forth by Wiesner and York, there seems to be little reason to doubt the good faith of these prognoses. They signal the end of the illusion that perpetual prosperity can be assured through the unlimited expansion of the arms budget.

They do not mean more than that, however. In particular, they do not mean that the Cold War is coming to an end, that American monopoly capitalism has decided to accept peaceful coexistence, that there will be any let-up in the intensity of the world-wide struggle against socialism, or that genuine disarmament is now in prospect. The real battlefields between capitalism and socialism have for years now been in Asia, Africa, and Latin America—in Korea, Vietnam, Algeria, Cuba, the Congo. The United States has been directly and militarily involved in most of these battles, and there is every reason to think that the leaders of the American oligarchy expect to go on being in-

[41] See the article "Our Defense Needs: The Long View," by Roswell Gilpatric, Deputy Secretary of Defense from 1960 to 1964, in *Foreign Affairs*, April 1964.

volved on an increasing scale in the future. This is the plain meaning of the increasing emphasis within the American military establishment on conventional arms, on building up so-called "counter-insurgency" and "special" forces, on the type of military planning and deployment of troops and supplies highlighted in the quotation from Cyrus Sulzberger on page 206 above.

These activities will continue and grow. They will undoubtedly lead to a long series of catastrophes, crises, and confrontations—of a kind with which we are already all too familiar. What does not seem likely is that they can provide any substitute for the nuclear arms race as an object for military spending. The fateful question "on what?" to which monopoly capitalism can find no answer in the realm of civilian spending has crept subversively into the military establishment itself. From all present indications there is no answer there either.

8

ON THE HISTORY OF MONOPOLY CAPITALISM

"It is not enough," writes Celso Furtado, "to construct an abstract model and provide an explanation of how it operates; it is just as important to demonstrate the explanatory effectiveness of such a model as applied to historical realities."[1] According to our model, the growth of monopoly generates a strong tendency for surplus to rise without at the same time providing adequate mechanisms of surplus absorption. But surplus that is not absorbed is also surplus that is not produced: it is merely potential surplus, and it leaves its statistical trace not in the figures of profits and investment but rather in the figures of unemployment and unutilized productive capacity. If, as most economists and historians seem to agree, we can date the growth of monopoly in the United States from approximately the end of the Civil War, we ought to be able to demonstrate our model's effectiveness in explaining the economic history of the past century.

Now in the analysis of society, even a very good theory is not likely to find direct and obvious confirmation in the historical record. The forces and tendencies which it identifies do not operate in a vacuum, and they may be offset or counteracted for shorter or longer periods by other forces and tendencies which are not encompassed in the theory. No one supposes, for example, that the flight of an airplane refutes the law of gravity. But it is essential that the counteracting forces should also be identified and that the actual course of events be shown to

[1] Celso Furtado, *Development and Underdevelopment*, Berkeley and Los Angeles, 1964, p. 1.

result logically and consistently from the interaction of forces and counterforces. We cannot simply say that the forces which are encompassed in the theory are at work but are negated by unspecified counterforces: this would be to confess the emptiness and uselessness of the theory.

2

If the depressive effects of growing monopoly had operated unchecked, the United States economy would have entered a period of stagnation long before the end of the nineteenth century, and it is unlikely that capitalism could have survived into the second half of the twentieth century. What, then, were the powerful external stimuli which offset these depressive effects and enabled the economy to grow fairly rapidly during the later decades of the nineteenth century and, with significant interruptions, during the first two thirds of the twentieth century?[2] In our judgment, they are of two kinds which we classify as (1) epoch-making innovations, and (2) wars and their aftermaths.

(1) We call "epoch-making" those innovations which shake up the entire pattern of the economy and hence create vast investment outlets in addition to the capital which they directly absorb. Clearly, for an innovation to deserve this designation it must profoundly affect both the location of economic activity and the composition of output. While there is room for argument—and need for study—concerning the impact of innovations in the history of capitalism, we would argue that only three really meet the "epoch-making" tests: the steam engine, the railroad, and the automobile. Each produced a radical alteration of economic geography with attendant internal migrations and the building of whole new communities; each

---

[2] By calling these stimuli "external," we do not mean to imply that they are external in any ultimate sense but only that they are external to that aspect of reality which we have sought to encompass in our theoretical model. They remain external from the point of view of the present analysis because we are not attempting to explain their causes but only to take account of their effects.

required or made possible the production of many new goods and services; each directly or indirectly enlarged the market for a whole range of industrial products.

Both the steam engine and the automobile, it seems clear, opened up outlets for the investment of far more capital than they themselves absorbed. The industry of producing steam engines never bulked large in the economy as a whole, but without the steam engine the great transformation of economic life which we call the industrial revolution would have been impossible. A very large proportion of the capital investment of the late eighteenth and early nineteenth centuries can therefore be attributed to the steam engine. The automobile industry also has had a much greater indirect than direct effect on the demand for capital. The process of suburbanization, with all its attendant residential, commercial, and highway construction, has all along been propelled by the automobile. The petroleum industry, with more capital investment than any other American industry, is in large part a creation of the automobile; and several other major industries (rubber, glass) are similarly dependent. Many service "industries" too have grown up in the wake of the automobile, such as filling stations and repair shops, motels and vacation resorts. Clearly, the amount of capital absorbed by all these outlets exceeds by many times the investment in the automobile industry itself.

The railroad, however, occupies a unique place in the history of capitalism. During the second half of the nineteenth century and the first years of the twentieth century, the building of the railroad network directly absorbed enormous amounts of capital. Census data on the growth of assets from decade to decade suggest that from 1850 to 1900 investment in the railroads exceeded investment in all manufacturing industries combined; and this impression is borne out by the latest calculations of Kuznets.[3] Between 1880 and 1900, the

[3] Simon Kuznets, *Capital in the American Economy: Its Formation and Financing*, Princeton, 1961, p. 198.

percent distribution of net private durable capital formation among Kuznets's four major sectors was as follows:

Agriculture	12.0
Mining	6.5
Manufacturing	31.4
Regulated industries	50.1
Total	100.0

Kuznets does not provide a separate estimate for the railroads, but since they were at that time far and away the largest of the "regulated industries," we are safe in saying that during the last two decades of the nineteenth century, the period when the monopolization process really took hold, somewhere between 40 and 50 percent of private capital formation was in the railroads. This concentration of investment in one industry is surely unrivaled at any time before or since. If we add the indirect effects of the railroad on economic activity and hence on capital investment—undoubtedly comparable in scope and magnitude to the indirect effects of the steam engine and the automobile—we can see that this one innovation quite literally dominated half a century of capitalist development.[4]

Other innovations besides these three have of course had far-reaching economic effects, but we believe that in relation to the problem under consideration—the adequacy of surplus absorption—none comes even close to equal ranking. Electricity would probably be the chief contender, but the investment effects attributable to it have certainly been much

[4] In other respects, too, the railroad played a decisive role in capitalist development. In particular, it was here that the typical unit of enterprise in the monopoly capitalist system, the giant corporation, took on its characteristic form. According to data presented in an 1874 report of a committee of stockholders of the Pennsylvania Railroad (in the Harvard University Library), the Pennsylvania, then as now the country's largest road, had assets of approximately $400 million and in other respects as well conformed closely to the corporate paradigm of Chapter 2 above. It was not until the 1890's that similar corporations began to emerge in industry generally, and by that time the appropriate financial institutions and legal forms had already been fully developed.

smaller than in the case of the railroad and the automobile, both of which it overlaps in time. Electricity is a more efficient and flexible form of power than steam, but the pattern of delivery costs is similar. Hence the crucially important point that electricity did not, like the railroad and the automobile, initiate radical and cumulative alterations in economic geography. Over the years electricity has indeed necessitated the investment of large amounts of capital in central generating stations, and to this extent it has opened up new outlets. But in one of its most important uses, as an illuminant, electricity took the place of gas which, if it had grown in proportion to population and income, would have required a substantial continuing flow of investment. All in all, it would seem that even such a major technological break-through as electricity must have had relatively minor effects on the surplus absorption process; and, as we argued in Chapter 4, this is even more likely to be the case with the types of innovation which are coming out of our scientific and industrial laboratories today.[5] In relation to the surplus absorption process—though not necessarily in relation to such other issues as the potential increase in living standards or the rising productivity of labor—what makes an innovation specially significant is the extent to which it shakes up the whole pattern of economic life. And in this respect the steam engine, the railroad, and the automobile are in a class by themselves.

(2) Before the First World War, the economists' habit of treating wars as mere disturbances with no particular significance for historical trends may well have been largely justified. After all, during most of the nineteenth century (after the Napoleonic Wars), the wars involving the major capitalist countries were few in number, and, with the single exception of the American Civil War, brief in duration and of relatively minor economic impact. It is quite plausible that the economic history of capitalism during this period would not have been

[5] See above, pp. 91-104.

greatly different if these wars had never taken place. (True, this cannot be said of colonial wars, but their importance lay not in their immediate economic impact but in the empires that resulted from them. In this connection, it is therefore more correct to speak of the economic importance of imperialism than of war.)

The experience of the twentieth century has been in a curious way the exact reverse of the nineteenth. That century began with a decade and a half of war, after which peaceful development predominated. The twentieth century began with a decade and a half of (relative) peace, since when the whole world has been continuously under the influence of devastating wars or their aftermaths. Obviously, to treat the economic history of the twentieth century as though wars were mere disturbances in an otherwise peacefully determined course of development would be to abstract from forces which played an essential role in shaping the contours of reality. No one in his right mind would maintain that in the absence of wars the economic history of the twentieth century would have been what it actually has been. Hence we must incorporate wars into our explanatory schema, and this we propose to do by including them, along with epoch-making innovations, as major external stimuli.

From the standpoint of their economic consequences, wars must be divided into two phases, the combat phase and the aftermath phase. Both involve a shaking up of the economy, the more radical, the more total the war and the longer it lasts. It is for this reason that great wars like those of 1914-1918 and 1939-1945 are, economically, similar to epoch-making innovations.

During the combat phase, military demand of course shoots up, resources are shifted to the sectors of the economy catering to it, and civilian demand is curtailed by some combination of price increases and rationing. In the case of durable goods for civilian use (both producer and consumer goods), production may even be halted altogether, with more "services" being squeezed out of existing stocks (multiple shifts, formation of car pools, doubling up in housing, keeping equipment in use after it would normally be scrapped, etc.). Existing plants are converted to war production, and most new investment is similarly channeled. Housing construction is reduced to what is needed for war workers and military personnel. In short, not only does total production rise to the limits set by available resources but the whole pattern of economic life is drastically altered.

This sets the stage for the aftermath phase. The wartime pattern is in the nature of the case temporary, and a reversion to something like the pre-existing state of affairs is bound to follow the end of hostilities. This reversion, however, involves more than a simple retracing of steps. During the combat phase, the existing stocks of civilian capital and durable consumer goods have been used with greater than normal intensity, additions are of negligible magnitude, and even replacement of worn-out items is to a large extent discontinued. Apart from military supplies and the capacity to produce them, society's reproducible wealth tends to shrink, while population growth accentuates the resulting scarcities and shortages. This is the origin of the widespread backlogs of demand which exist at the end of major wars. To a limited extent, these backlogs can be met by converting war factories to civilian use, but much of the preceding investment in war-material capacity is too specialized or wrongly located for civilian uses and has to be scrapped. In this way, investment outlets are created which can absorb large amounts of surplus for several years to come.

This sketch of the combat and aftermath phases could of course be expanded and elaborated. The specific effects of different policies with regard to taxation, money, price control, rationing, etc., could be analyzed; the character of the interlude between the two phases could be explored; the additional effects of wartime destruction in combat zones could be assessed; and so on. But for our purpose, which is simply to account for the broadest outlines of the historic process, it is

enough to know that the two phases exist and that each for a
time exercises a determining influence on the absorption of
surplus—one through the tremendous demands of the military machine, and the other through the backlogs of civilian
demand created during the combat phase.

The question to which we now seek an answer can be formulated as follows: The tendency of monopoly capitalism to
generate more surplus than it can absorb can be neutralized or
even overwhelmed by major external stimuli but will make
itself felt in characteristic ways whenever the stimuli weaken
or disappear. The growth of monopolies may be dated from
about 1870 and has been proceeding, though at an uneven
pace, ever since.[6] We can therefore assume that the tendency
to generate too much surplus has been in operation for some
eight or nine decades and that its strength has been steadily
increasing. To what extent has it been offset by major external
stimuli and to what extent has it risen to the surface and dominated the course of events?

To begin with, there is no evidence that the surplus absorption problem was becoming more difficult before 1900. There

        [6] There is a considerable literature which denies this, much of it
inspired by the well known paper of M. A. Adelman, "The Measurement
of Industrial Concentration," *Review of Economics and Statistics*, November 1951. What may be true is that there has been little change in the
average industrial concentration ratio, defined as the share of a market
controlled by the four (or eight) largest sellers. However, this is a poor
index of monopoly power. For one thing it completely leaves out of
account the learning process, the importance of which we emphasized in
Chapter 2: four companies dominating a market today know how to
maximize their profits much more effectively than did four companies
dominating the same market in 1900. And secondly this ratio applies
only to individual markets and therefore provides no clue to the extent to
which the typical giant corporation has been spreading out to become a
dominant factor in many markets. To illustrate the point, assume an
economy comprising four industries each containing four sellers. In the
first period there are a total of sixteen corporations, four for each market.
In the second period, after a series of mergers, there are four sellers in
each market but only four corporations altogether: each one is now
represented in all four markets. That this represents a vast increase in
monopoly power, despite the stability of the industrial concentration
ratios, seems obvious. We need only add that there is ample evidence that

are no reliable data on unemployment or profit rates, but the rate of capital accumulation, according to Kuznets, was higher in the 1880's and 1890's than in the 1870's.[7] Why did the stormy monopolization drive of this period not show up in increasing surplus absorption difficulties?

The answer, it seems to us, is clear. This was the epoch of the railroad, which absorbed close to half of all private investment during the last two decades of the nineteenth century and opened outlets for a great deal more. That the tendency to excessive surplus generation should be submerged by railroadization seems wholly plausible.

But this raises another question: when should we date the end of the railroad epoch? Here the habit of speaking in terms of decades and centuries, convenient though it often is, could lead us into trouble. It would be tidy if we could confine attention to decade averages and date the end of the railroad epoch at 1900. Examination of year-by-year data, however, clearly points to a different conclusion: there was indeed a marked slowing down of railroad investment during the 1890's, espe-

---

concentration in this overall sense has been increasing. For example, in 1957 a Senate Committee reported the following percentages of total value added by the largest manufacturing companies, comparing 1954 with 1947:

	1947	1954
Largest 50 companies	17	23
Largest 100 companies	23	30
Largest 150 companies	27	34
Largest 200 companies	30	37

(*Concentration in American Industry*, Report of the Subcommittee on Antitrust and Monopoly of the Committee on the Judiciary, U. S. Senate, 85th Cong., 1st Sess., 1957, Table 1.) More recent hearings before the same Committee have brought further confirmation of the trend. Gardiner C. Means testified on July 1, 1964, that the 100 largest manufacturing corporations controlled 58 percent of the land, buildings, and equipment used in manufacturing in 1962, compared with 44 percent in 1929. If current assets such as inventories and receivables are included, the 100 largest firms controlled 49 percent in 1962, compared with 40 percent in 1929. (*New York Times*, July 2, 1964.)

[7] Kuznets's figures on the annual percentage rate of growth of repro-

cially during the long depression from 1892 to 1896, but a strong revival took place about the turn of the century. The real turning point comes with the crisis of 1907 which precipitated a sharp drop in railroad investment, after which it remained permanently at a much lower level. Table 8 compares the periods 1900-1907 and 1908-1915 with respect to the growth of the most important types of railroad capital.

Table 8

Growth of Railroad Capital: Annual Averages
(Thousands of units)

	1900-1907	1908-1915	Percent Change
Miles of track built[a]	5.1	2.8	—45.1
Number of locomotives added[b]	2.3	1.4	—40.5
Number of freight cars added[b]	87.0	43.8	—49.4

[a] Calendar years
[b] Years ending June 30
Source: *Historical Statistics of the United States: Colonial Times to 1957*, 2nd Printing, Washington, 1961, pp. 428-430.

It may also be legitimate to postulate, though we know of no way to prove it statistically, that the new pattern of economic geography and the new composition of national product which the railroad brought into being had become pretty well stabilized by 1907. In other words, the big shake-up which began even before the Civil War, was largely over. If we are right about this, it was in 1907 that the greatest external stimulus in capitalist history lost its tremendous force.

Here we have an ideal opportunity to test our theory. The impetus provided by one epoch-making innovation had petered out. The next epoch-making innovation, the automobile, was

---

ducible wealth for the three decades are as follows: 1869-1879, 4.1; 1879-1889, 4.9; 1889-1899, 4.9. Simon Kuznets, *National Product Since 1869*, New York, 1941, Table IV (p. 228). Steindl, starting from these figures, has estimated the rate of growth of private business capital to have been: 1869-1879, 3.9 percent; 1879-1889, 4.8 percent; and 1889-1899, 4.5 percent. J. Steindl, *Maturity and Stagnation in American Capitalism*, p. 160.

just making its appearance on the economic scene and as yet exerted little or no influence on the economy as a whole. There was still the best part of a decade to go before the United States would become involved in a major war. If the theory is valid, there ought to be unmistakable signs of stagnation during the period 1907-1915.

And indeed there are, though most latter-day economists seem to have ignored them. In the "great debate" over stagnation which took place during the 1930's, we do not recall having encountered any analysis of the 1907-1915 period. This is surprising in a way, since the arguments of "stagnationists" like Hansen and Steindl would have gained much support if they had been able to point to symptoms of stagnation before the First World War.[8] And the counter-argument, heavily stressed by Schumpeter, that one depression, even one as severe as that of the 30's, proves nothing about longer-run trends, would have been effectively answered in advance.[9]

The evidence of stagnation in the years 1907-1915 is of several kinds, and a more detailed study of the period would doubtless produce still more. What follows should be taken as no more than a prelude to a full analysis.

In the first place, the data on the timing of business cycles collected by the National Bureau of Economic Research display a striking change in the pattern of the cycle after 1907. This is shown in Table 9 which relates to the seven full cycles counted by the Bureau from 1890 to 1914.

For the first five cycles, expansions are greater than or about equal to contractions, while for the last two cycles the opposite relation holds. The average length of expansions and contractions is approximately reversed: for the first five, the average expansion is 23.2 months, the average contraction 17.8; for the

[8] Hansen's stagnationist views are largely contained in two volumes of collected essays and reviews: *Full Recovery or Stagnation?* New York, 1938, and *Fiscal Policy and Business Cycles,* New York, 1941; Steindl's in his *Maturity and Stagnation in American Capitalism.*

[9] J. A. Schumpeter, *Business Cycles,* New York, 1939, Volume 2, p. 1036.

Table 9

Pattern of Business Cycles, 1890-1914

	Complete Cycles			Duration in Months	
Number of cycle	Trough	Peak	Trough	Expansion	Contraction
1	May 1891	Jan. 1893	June 1894	20	17
2	June 1894	Dec. 1895	June 1897	18	18
3	June 1897	June 1899	Dec. 1900	24	18
4	Dec. 1900	Sept. 1902	Aug. 1904	21	23
5	Aug. 1904	May 1907	June 1908	33	13
	Average, Cycles 1-5			23.2	17.8
6	June 1908	Jan. 1910	Jan. 1912	19	24
7	Jan. 1912	Jan. 1913	Dec. 1914	12	23
	Average, Cycles 6-7			15.5	23.5

Source: R. A. Gordon, *Business Fluctuations,* New York, 1952, p. 216.

last two, the average expansion is 15.5 months, the average contraction 23.5.

Thorp's well-known *Business Annals* tells a similar story. Of the eighteen years from 1890 through 1907, Thorp gives the unqualified rating of "prosperity" to six, and five more get the rating with some qualification. Of the seven years from 1908 through 1914, none gets an unqualified "prosperity" rating, and only three with qualification.[10] It is interesting that Schumpeter explicitly cited this material from Thorp's *Annals*, for the accuracy and usefulness of which he had a high regard, and stated that it expresses well the difference between two "sub-periods" which he was analyzing, 1898-1907 and 1909-1914. Yet he relegated all this to a footnote, and the passage in the text describing the period is couched in quite different terms, with little apparent relation to Thorp's ratings.[11] This is easy to understand, since in Schumpeter's schema of cycle history

[10] W. L. Thorp, *Business Annals*, New York, 1926, pp. 136-142.
[11] J. A. Schumpeter, *Business Cycles*. Volume 1, p. 427.

the years 1898-1914 are supposed to correspond to the upswing
of a long cycle,[12] and evidence that 1908-1914 was in fact a
period of developing stagnation was not what he most wanted
to emphasize.

Secondly, the most detailed study yet made of the business
cycle that immediately preceded the First World War begins
with a recognition of the special characteristics of the 1907-
1914 period and sets out to explain them.[13] We quote from the
Preface:

This inquiry undertakes to determine the causes that produced
the business depressions of 1910-1911 and 1913 in the United States.
Any such inquiry, however, involves also a discussion of the pre-
mature occurrence of those depressions as related to the normal ebb
and flow of business conditions abroad. It will be remembered that
after the revival of 1909 was well under way, and a buoyant prosperity era was foreshadowed, the onward march of business
progress continued uninterruptedly in Germany, England, and
France—where only a mild reaction took place because of bad
harvests—while in the United States there occurred the unexpected
depression of 1910-1911.
It will be remembered also that when the depression of 1913
occurred in the United States, universal business conditions were
approaching the completion of a prosperity cycle, but that, even so,
while business conditions in Europe were still prospering, this country sank into a state of depression.

Schluter's "explanation" of these facts, running in terms of
the inflexibility of the United States banking and credit machinery, never even comes close to the real problem of lagging
demand, but his factual findings are no less significant on that
account.

[12] Called by Schumpeter the "Kondratieff cycle" after the Russian
economist who first claimed to have discovered a cycle of some fifty years
duration in the nineteenth and early twentieth century history of capitalism. The evidence for the existence of this cycle has always seemed to us
weak and unconvincing, and Schumpeter's ambiguous handling of the
1908-1914 period does nothing to counteract the impression.
[13] W. C. Schluter, *The Pre-War Business Cycle, 1907 to 1914*, New
York, 1923.

The writers of general economic histories have tended to treat the period 1907-1914 in a similar way, though this does not add much to our evidence, since they are quite likely to have relied heavily on Thorp's *Annals* and Schluter's monograph as sources. An example is Faulkner's well-regarded history of the period preceding United States entry into the war:

The upswing of 1909 was of brief duration. It was followed by a depression in 1910-1911, a second upswing in 1912, and a relapse in 1913. The upset of 1907 had proved more fundamental than had been supposed. From that year until America felt the impact of war prosperity in 1915, American economic history was largely one of brief spurts and recessions.[14]

Here the explanation offered for this poor economic performance, that the upset of 1907 had been "more fundamental than had been supposed," is a mere begging of the question. But Faulkner's awareness that the economic performance of the years 1907-1914 was indeed poor may be taken as reflecting the generally accepted state of knowledge among economic historians.

We have reserved for last what seems to us the most telling evidence of growing stagnation in the years 1907-1914. For reasons familiar to the reader, unemployment and underutilization of productive capacity are the surest signs of inadequate surplus absorption. No data on idle capacity exist for the period before the First World War, but there is available a usable series on unemployment going back to 1900.[15] By "usable" we do not mean to imply that the Series gives an accurate picture of the absolute amount of unemployment at any given time or over a period of years. In our judgment, present-day official methods of calculating unemployment seriously understate the

---

[14] H. U. Faulkner, *The Decline of Laissez Faire, 1897–1917*, New York, 1951.

[15] *Historical Statistics of the United States: Colonial Times to 1957*, p. 73. For sources and explanation, see the notes to Series D 46-47 at p. 68.

actual amount; and since the estimates for earlier years have been made on as nearly comparable a basis as possible, to this extent they too must understate the amount.[16] But this does not invalidate their usefulness in comparing one year or period with another. And since it is trends and fluctuations of unemployment rather than the absolute level that interest us here, we believe that the figures can be used with reasonable confidence. Table 10 gives the series from 1900 to 1963, and Chart 3 presents the same data in graphic form. We shall have occasion presently to comment on the later years.

Table 10

Unemployment, 1900-1963
(Percent of Civilian Labor Force)

1900	5.0	1916	4.8	1932	23.6	1948	3.4
1901	2.4	1917	4.8	1933	24.9	1949	5.5
1902	2.7	1918	1.4	1934	21.7	1950	5.0
1903	2.6	1919	2.3	1935	20.1	1951	3.0
1904	4.8	1920	4.0	1936	16.9	1952	2.7
1905	3.1	1921	11.9	1937	14.3	1953	2.5
1906	0.8	1922	7.6	1938	19.0	1954	5.0
1907	1.8	1923	3.2	1939	17.2	1955	4.0
1908	8.5	1924	5.5	1940	14.6	1956	3.8
1909	5.2	1925	4.0	1941	9.9	1957	4.3
1910	5.9	1926	1.9	1942	4.7	1958	6.8
1911	6.2	1927	4.1	1943	1.9	1959	5.5
1912	5.2	1928	4.4	1944	1.2	1960	5.6
1913	4.4	1929	3.2	1945	1.9	1961	6.7
1914	8.0	1930	8.7	1946	3.9	1962	5.6
1915	9.7	1931	15.9	1947	3.6	1963	5.7

Source: For 1900-1957, *Historical Statistics of the United States*, p. 73; for 1958-1963, Council of Economic Advisers, *Economic Indicators*, current numbers.

The chart shows particularly clearly the sharp discontinuity between 1907 and 1908. Apart from the rather special case of 1920-1921, this is the biggest rise in any one year before the

[16] See Philip Eden, "For More Adequate Measurement of Unemployment," *Current Economic Comment* (Bureau of Economic and Business Research, University of Illinois), November 1959.

Chart 3
Unemployment, 1900-1963

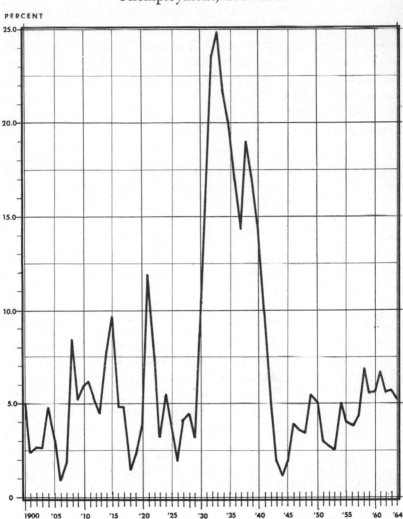

PERCENT

Great Depression and is slightly larger than the average year-to-year rise during the period 1929-1932. What distinguishes the 1907-1908 case from 1920-1921 and likens it to 1929 and the years after is that, following the sharp increase, the rate does not quickly return to the previous level but remains much higher for a period of years. The average rate for the eight years 1900-1907 is 2.9 percent; for the years 1908-1915 it is 6.6 percent. Moreover, from 1900 through 1907, the rate never reached as high as 5 percent; while from 1908 through 1915, it only once dipped under 5 percent. Finally, as the economy headed into what gave every sign of being a serious depression, unemployment rose to 8 percent in 1914 and almost 10 percent in 1915.

All of this constitutes strong evidence that the years after 1907 were characterized by mounting surplus absorption difficulties and the kind of "creeping stagnation" with which we have become familiar in the later 1950's and early 1960's. If there is any other interpretation of these facts, we are certainly ready to consider it on its merits. But until we know what it is, we shall feel justified in concluding that if the First World War had not come along, the decade 1910-1920 would have gone down in United States history as an extraordinarily depressed one. We are not contending that the Great Depression would have occurred a decade and a half early. By 1915, the automobile era was already well under way, and the great shake-up in living patterns and consumption habits which it brought with it would probably have created a boom even if the war had never come. But before this, the country might well have got a good lesson in how profound and pervasive the depressive forces at work in a monopoly capitalist economy are; and certainly the Great Depression, when it did come, could hardly have been so shocking a surprise.

3

But the war did come—in the nick of time; and the picture changed from stagnation to boom. After the Armistice in November 1918, there was a brief and mild "reconversion crisis" which gave way in the spring of 1919 to the aftermath boom. Prices had already climbed sharply during the war, and the first phase of the aftermath boom quickly developed into a speculative mania. The bubble burst in 1922, with wholesale

prices plunging from 154.4 in 1921 to 97.6 in 1922 (1926=
100). But the accompanying depression was as brief as it was
sharp: the aftermath boom was merely interrupted, not
killed. In particular, the backlog demand for housing and other
types of building was still strong and was one of the dominant
features of the economic picture for the next few years. In the
meantime, the first great wave of automobilization, which may
be dated from about 1915 and which rolled on uninterruptedly
during the war, was nearing its peak and producing all its
multifarious by-products and indirect effects: suburbanization, road building, secondary industries, etc. The actual production of automobiles hardly rose above the 1923 level
of 3.6 million cars until 1929 (4.5 million), but the impact of
the automobile is much more accurately indicated by the
rate of growth of the number of cars in operation; and
this remained high throughout the decade. Chart 4 shows
factory sales and registrations—very close to numbers produced and numbers in operation—for the years 1911 through
1962. The tenfold increase in registrations between 1915 and
1929 (from 2.3 million to 23.1 million) gives an indication of
the tremendous impact of the automobile in these years. It is
hence not surprising that when the impetus of the postwar
aftermath subsided—around 1925, the year in which construction reached its maximum—the momentum of automobilization was powerful enough to keep the boom going for several
years more.

An examination of the unemployment figures shows that
surplus absorption was in fact proceeding smoothly (Table 10,
Chart 3). The average for the decade as a whole was 5 percent,
but this is pulled up by the deflationary collapse of 1921. For
the seven years 1923-1929, the average was 3.9 percent, close
to the figure for the years 1900-1907 and certainly low by any
relevant historic standard.

And yet we now know that beneath the prosperous surface
of the 1920's—the much celebrated "New Era"—the seeds of
disaster were busily germinating. A rate of investment which

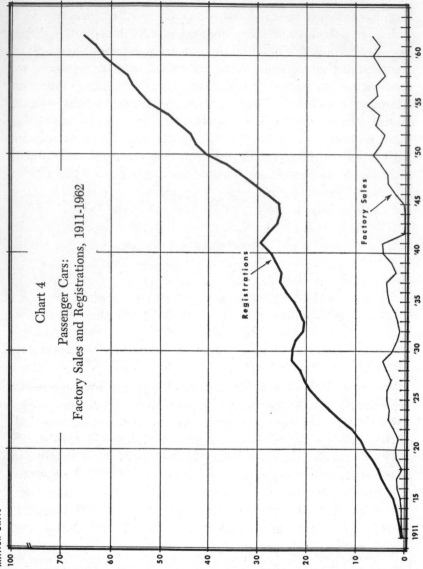

Million Units

Chart 4

Passenger Cars:
Factory Sales and Registrations, 1911-1962

Registrations

Factory Sales

was just sufficient to maintain a reasonable approximation to full employment was considerably higher than would have been required to sustain the economy's rate of growth. As a result, excess capacity accumulated rapidly after 1923. From data presented by Donald Streever in an interesting study of the relation between capacity utilization and investment, we can deduce an index of utilization for the 1920's.[17] Streever constructed an index of capacity for manufacturing and mining for the years 1920-1955, and put alongside it the Federal Reserve Board's index of industrial production. If we divide the FRB index by the capacity index, we have a rough measure of capacity utilization. Table 11 shows the results for the 1920's.

Table 11

Capacity Utilization, 1920-1929
(Percent)

1920	94	1925	91
1921	65	1926	89
1922	80	1927	83
1923	94	1928	82
1924	84	1929	83

Source: Donald Streever, *Capacity Utilization and Business Investment,* University of Illinois Bulletin, Volume 57, No. 55, March 1960, p. 64.

We can see the steady downdrift of capacity utilization—or growth of excess capacity, as the other side of the coin—after 1925. Clearly, the rate of capital investment in the second half of the decade reached an unsustainably high level: surplus absorption proceeded smoothly for the time being, but at the cost of the disastrous collapse of the following years.[18] The precipitous drop in the utilization rate from 1929 to 1930 (from 83 to 66) reflected both the completion of many projects begun in 1928 and the first three quarters of 1929 and also the general

[17] Donald Streever, *Capacity Utilization and Business Investment,* University of Illinois Bulletin, Volume 57, No. 55, March 1960, p. 64.

[18] See pp. 82-88 for the theoretical explanation of this sequence of events.

slump initiated by the drastic cutback in the volume of new projects after the stock market crash of the autumn of 1929.

That Streever's figures reliably reflect what was happening during this period is strongly supported by the well-known Brookings Institution study, *America's Capacity to Produce*, published in 1934.[19] In this first serious study of productive capacity undertaken by American economists, the Brookings investigators concluded that American industry was on the average producing at 83 percent of capacity in 1929, an estimate which precisely coincides with the figure which Streever worked up by an entirely different method.

4

With the onset of the Great Depression, we enter a period which bourgeois economists, with a rare approach to unanimity, have come to regard as a sharp deviation from the country's normal and natural historic path. Two major attempts at explanation were made by American economists, both during the 1930's. Hansen put forward what Schumpeter appropriately dubbed "the theory of vanishing investment opportunity," citing as decisive factors a lower rate of population growth, a capital-saving bias in newer innovations, and the alleged disappearance of the frontier before the turn of the century.[20] This theory had the great merit of attempting to relate the deeply depressed conditions of the 30's to objective historical processes, and it attracted considerable support, especially among the younger economists who were predisposed by Keynesian ideas to look for the causes of depression in the factors influencing the volume of investment.

In opposition to this theory, Schumpeter himself argued, persuasively it seems to us, that none of the factors stressed by Hansen—even granting their reality and relevance, which

[19] E. G. Nourse and associates, *America's Capacity to Produce*, Washington, 1934.

[20] See his *Full Recovery or Stagnation?* and *Fiscal Policy and Business Cycles*, both cited in footnote 8 above.

Schumpeter was by no means willing to do—could, singly or in combination, account for so sudden and unprecedented an experience as the Great Depression. For his part, Schumpeter put forward a quite different theory, made up essentially of two parts. He attributed the severity of the collapse to the coincidence of troughs in the three kinds of cycles which he believed characteristic of the capitalist economy, plus various unique historical events the origins of which he traced back to the war (overexpansion of United States agriculture, weakness in the banking and credit system, the international financial crisis of 1931, etc.). The second part of his theory, which is really the crucial part, sought to explain the weakness and incompleteness of the recovery after 1933 by a political factor, the alleged anti-capitalist bias of the New Deal, not only in its legislation but even more in the spirit with which it administered its legislation.[21]

Schumpeter's theory of the 30's, while of course eagerly welcomed by conservatives and reactionaries (economists as well as others), made little impression on the generation of economists which had come of age since 1929, and may be said to have been given its *coup de grâce* by one of Schumpeter's students and warmest admirers. Arthur Smithies's paper, "The American Economy in the Thirties," delivered at the January 1946 meetings of the American Economic Association (and, ironically, immediately after an analysis by Schumpeter himself of the 1920's), is a relentless exposure of the hollowness of any effort to explain away the Great Depression as a by-product of supposedly radical politics.

Soon after came the postwar boom and the American Celebration. American economists heaved a sigh of relief and promptly relegated the 1930's to the limbo of forgotten nightmares. Josef Steindl's powerful treatise, *Maturity and Stagnation in American Capitalism* (1952), aimed at solving a problem which every serious analyst should have considered a

[21] J. A. Schumpeter, *Business Cycles*, Volume 2, Chapter 15, especially Section G ("The Disappointing Juglar").

standing challenge to his sense of scientific responsibility, was virtually ignored and to this day has not received a fraction of the attention it richly deserves. It may be said without fear of contradiction that the United States economics profession, nay bourgeois economics in general, quite literally has no theory to account for a phenomenon which, as much as any other, has determined the whole course of history during the second third of the twentieth century.

Against this background it seems clear that a central merit of our theory is that it explains the Great Depression, readily and logically, not as the Great Exception but as the normal outcome of the workings of the American economic system. The stagnationist tendencies inherent in monopoly capitalism had already begun to dominate the economic scene in the years after 1907. The war and the automobile submerged them, but only for a time. During the 1930's they rose to the surface, and put their indelible stamp on a whole decade of economic history. Here for the first time we get a crystal-clear view of the system operating with a minimum of external stimuli for an extended period of time, laying bare what Marx called its "law of motion" for all to see. What the economists persist in regarding as a deviation was in fact the realization in practice of the theoretical norm toward which the system is always tending.

Naturally, no general theory such as the one put forward in this book can account for all the details of the historical process. There was nothing "inevitable" about the steepness of the descent after 1929. Here the factors stressed by Schumpeter—apart from his three-cycle scheme, which seems to us to lack a rational foundation—surely played an important role, as did other "accidents" such as the almost unbelievable ineptitude of the policies adopted by the United States oligarchy under the leadership of Herbert Hoover and the Republican Party. What *was* inevitable under the conditions of the time was that the economy should sink, rapidly or slowly, into a state of profound stagnation from which it could make only half-hearted efforts to emerge—until it was once again propelled forward by a powerful enough external stimulus, this time the Second World War.

To avoid misunderstanding, it must be stressed that nothing in the foregoing argument is intended to imply that the force of automobilization was played out by 1929. Obviously, as the upper line in Chart 4 shows, another great wave of automobilization was still to come and was destined to play a large role after the Second World War. But even the vigorous thrust of the automobile during the 20's was, as we have seen, unable to sustain the capital investment boom of that period. And when the depression hit, it did so with such overwhelming force that the further progress of automobilization was effectively arrested for a whole decade. The number of cars on the road actually declined from 1929 through 1933, and it was another three years before the 1929 level was exceeded; from then until the end of the decade, the increase was little more than half what it had been in the comparable period ten years earlier. It was only after the serious erosion of the stock of cars during the war and in the general forward surge of the aftermath boom, that automobilization, with all its multifarious ramifications, could once again become a major stimulus.

How profound the stagnation of the 1930's was—or, looked at another way, how completely the surplus absorption process broke down—can be judged from a number of indicators. First, of course, there was the unprecedented volume of unemployment (Table 10, Chart 3). Whereas the figure averaged 6.6 percent of the labor force in what may be called the years of semi-stagnation from 1908 through 1915, it rose to the staggering average of 18.2 percent in the decade of full-fledged stagnation from 1930 to 1939.

The index of capacity utilization derived from Streever's data tells a similar story. Table 12 continues Table 11 for the 1930's.

Thus the highest utilization rate reached during the 1930's (83 percent in 1937) was barely above the lowest in the 1920's

Table 12

Capacity Utilization, 1930-1939
(Percent)

1930	66	1935	68
1931	53	1936	80
1932	42	1937	83
1933	52	1938	60
1934	58	1939	72

Source: Donald Streever, *Capacity Utilization and Business Investment*, University of Illinois Bulletin, Volume 57, No. 55, March 1960, p. 64.

(82 percent in 1928). The averages are no less striking: 84.5 percent for the 20's falling to 63.4 percent for the 30's.

Even these figures, striking though they are, fail to convey the true depth of the stagnation of the 30's. The figures tell us that in 1939, as the decade came to an end, nearly a fifth of the country's labor force and over a quarter of its productive capacity were idle. From this, one would tend to conclude that output could not have been increased by much more than, say, a third even if additional workers were drawn into the labor force and capital equipment worked with more than normal intensity. And yet during the next few years, under the impact of war and with the inherent restraints of the capitalist market temporarily removed, industrial production more than doubled and real Gross National Product went up by more than two thirds. Moreover, these increases occurred during a period when virtually no net investment was taking place and more than 11 million men in the most productive age groups were being mobilized into the armed forces. While of course neither manpower nor equipment could continue indefinitely to be operated at the wartime pitch of intensity, still we think the tremendous expansion of output achieved between 1939 and 1944 conclusively proves that the official unemployment estimates and the figures on capacity utilization derived by widely accepted statistical methods greatly understate the extent to which human and material resources are underutilized in a monopoly capitalist economy. The bias is a natural one: bourgeois social science is not interested in emphasizing the shortcomings of the private enterprise system nor in revealing, even by implication, how much better a rationally organized and planned socialist economy could perform. The persistence of unemployment and unused capacity cannot be denied, but it can be and is being minimized.

In Chapter 4 we pointed out that an economic upswing, however initiated, generates a rapid increase of surplus, both absolutely and as a proportion of total output. As soon as the investment-seeking part of this rising surplus exceeds available investment outlets, the expansion comes to an end and so does the rise in surplus. And such an upper turning point "may be reached long before full utilization of capacity or full employment is achieved."[22] We are now in a position to see that the business cycle of the 1930's provides a perfect illustration of this proposition. Table 13 shows, for the years 1929-1938, national income, corporate profits after taxes, dividends, undistributed profits, and profits (or losses) as a percent of national income. (The unavoidable use of annual figures—quarterly breakdowns are not available before 1946—somewhat distorts the picture, but the main outlines stand out clearly enough.) As income declines, profits shrink (or losses grow) much faster, and vice versa. Dividends on the other hand are much more stable than either income or profits. As a result, in every year from 1930 through 1936, the corporate system as a whole dipped into capital to pay its shareholders.

The investment-seeking share of profits finally became positive again in 1937; but with no external stimuli operating, investment outlets were practically nonexistent. It was this inability to find outlets for a rising surplus that brought the upswing to a halt and precipitated the sharp recession of the second half of 1937. And all this occurred at a time when some 14 percent of the labor force and 20 percent of productive capacity were still

[22] Above, p. 88.

Table 13

Profits and National Income, 1929-1938
(Millions of dollars)

	National Income	Corporate Profits After Tax	Dividends	Undis- tributed Profits	Profits as Percent of National Income
1929	87,814	8,259	5,813	2,446	9.4
1930	75,729	2,480	5,490	−3,010	3.3
1931	59,708	−1,278	4,088	−5,366	−2.1
1932	42,546	−3,402	2,565	−5,967	−8.0
1933	40,159	−370	2,056	−2,426	−0.1
1934	48,959	972	2,587	−1,615	1.9
1935	57,057	2,194	2,863	−669	3.8
1936	64,911	4,331	4,548	−217	6.7
1937	73,618	4,733	4,685	48	6.4
1938	67,581	2,271	3,187	−916	3.4

Source: *1962 Supplement to Economic Indicators,* Washington, 1962.

idle. What more convincing evidence could there be that monopoly capitalism without external stimuli is powerless to pull itself out of a state of stagnation?

5

The interpretation of the postwar period presents no serious problems for our theory; and the role of the aftermath boom and the vastly increased military budget in sustaining a relatively high level of employment and income has been sufficiently emphasized. But it would be wrong to leave the impression that these have been the only powerful props to the economy in this period: of coordinate importance has been a second great wave of automobilization and suburbanization, fueled by a tremendous growth of mortgage and consumer debt.

Here an interesting and important question arises: Why did the second wave of automobilization occur when it did? Why not in 1937, prolonging the recovery of the 30's and turning it into a full-fledged boom? After all, it was not a matter of any new inventions or technological break-throughs, and people presumably "needed" more automobiles and suburban living as much before the war as they did after.

The answer is that in 1937 people did not have the required purchasing and borrowing power to get things started, while after 1945 they did. During the war, consumers paid off debts and accumulated vast amounts of liquid savings. When they were again free to spend and borrow, they could and did turn their "need" for automobiles and houses in the suburbs into effective demand. And once the wave got fairly started, it built up its own momentum. We have here a classic case of quantity turning into quality. If a few people buy cars and move to the suburbs, that is the end of the matter. But if many do so, all sorts of things become profitable or necessary which otherwise would not have been—shopping centers can stand for what is profitable, schools for what is necessary.[23] A snowball effect is generated which continues to operate until the bottom of the hill is reached, that is, until the internal migration subsides and the requisite new facilities have been provided. At the time of writing, nearly two decades after the war, it is still not possible to say when the whole movement will lose its momentum.[24]

There is thus no mystery about the performance of the United States economy in the postwar period. With the aftermath boom triggering a great upheaval in the living patterns of tens of millions of people, and with arms spending growing

[23] An indication of how many people have been involved is given by population data for what the Bureau of the Census calls Standard Metropolitan Statistical Areas. Between 1950 and 1960 (comparable figures are not available for 1940), the population living in these areas but outside the central cities increased by 36.8 million, just short of 50 percent. This was almost a third more than the total national population increase for the decade.

[24] Of all the numerous factors which have reinforced the second wave of automobilization and suburbanization, one which would have to be carefully analyzed in a full treatment of the subject deserves at least mention in a footnote: the network of federal government policies favoring, and in effect subsidizing, ownership of individual residential units.

nearly fivefold—from $11.4 billion in 1947 to $55.2 billion in 1963—it is probably safe to say that never since the height of the railroad epoch has the American economy been subject in peacetime to such powerful stimuli. What is really remarkable is that despite the strength and persistence of these stimuli, the familiar symptoms of inadequate surplus absorption—unemployment and underutilization of capacity—began to appear at an early stage and, apart from cyclical fluctuations, have been gradually growing more severe. Table 14 tells the essential story.[25]

What needs to be added is that the unemployment situation at the end of the period covered by the table was really considerably worse than the figures indicate. Between 1960 and 1963 there took place a one percent decline in the labor force participation rate, which means that some 1.3 million workers dropped out of the labor force in addition to the normal losses through death and retirement. The main reason for these dropouts is simply that when jobs are scarce many people get discouraged and give up looking for work. If we include the dropouts with those officially counted as unemployed to get a more

[25] The capacity utilization index is constructed using the Federal Reserve Board's index of industrial production as the numerator and the McGraw-Hill index of industrial capacity as the denominator. Of all the capacity estimates now in use by economists and statisticians, those of the McGraw-Hill Economics Department seem to us to be the only comprehensive ones which do not systematically exclude or underestimate what is perhaps the most important aspect of capacity growth since the war: the rising efficiency of a dollar's worth of plant and equipment owing to technological and organizational advances. The McGraw-Hill estimates are derived from direct questionnaires to producers, a procedure with its own difficulties and weaknesses, but one which avoids the downward bias of all the methods which equate capacity with the dollar value of capital stock, however defined.

It is worth noting that the Federal Reserve's estimates of capacity for 17 major materials, which are based largely on engineering data, also avoid the typical downward bias of estimates made by the value-of-capital-stock method. The decline of the weighted average utilization rate in these major materials industries during the 1950's agrees closely with McGraw-Hill estimates for industry as a whole, a fact which tends to support the reliability of the McGraw-Hill method. For a discussion of

Table 14

Capacity Utilization and Unemployment, 1950-1963

	Capacity Utilization (1950=100)	Unemployment as Percent of Labor Force
1950	100	5.0
1951	103	3.0
1952	99	2.7
1953	98	2.5
1954	87	5.0
1955	92	4.0
1956	89	3.8
1957	85	4.3
1958	76	6.8
1959	81	5.5
1960	81	5.6
1961	80	6.7
1962	83	5.6
1963	83	5.7

Sources: For explanation of capacity index, see footnote 25. McGraw-Hill capacity estimates for 1950-1961 from Hearings cited in that footnote, p. 11; for 1962 and 1963, McGraw-Hill press releases of April 26, 1963 and April 24, 1964. Federal Reserve Board index of industrial production and unemployment as percent of labor force from Council of Economic Advisers, *Economic Indicators*, current issues.

accurate idea of the situation, we find that in 1963 unemployment constituted 7.1 percent of the labor force, not 5.6 percent.[26]

these matters, see *Measures of Productive Capacity*, Hearings Before the Subcommittee on Economic Statistics of the Joint Economic Committee, 87th Congress, 2nd Session, May 14, 22, 23, and 24, 1962.

[26] Even this procedure underestimates the real amount of unemployment since there were already in 1960 many people not officially included in the labor force who would have taken jobs had they been available. In a most interesting and valuable study of variations in labor force participation rates ("Cyclical Variation in Civilian Labor Force Participation," *The Review of Economics and Statistics*, November 1964), Kenneth Strand and Thomas Dernburg estimate unemployment as a percentage of what they call the "full employment labor force," that is, the number of

It remains only to note that 1963 was the third year of a sustained upswing. Surely, an economy in which unemployment grows even during the expansion phase of the business cycle is in deep trouble. And with military spending apparently having reached a peak, the pace of automation increasing, and a flood of young people (products of the "baby boom" of the 40's) inundating the labor market, the future of the United States economy hardly looks bright. Developments which in a rational society would make possible a great advance toward abundance for all, under monopoly capitalism constitute a threat to the very livelihood of an ever growing proportion of the working people.

---

persons who would be working or looking for work if the unemployment rate reached 3 percent ("high full employment") or 4 percent ("low full employment"). This percentage they call the "gap unemployment rate." Using the high full employment criterion, they derive the following gap unemployment rates for November of each year from 1953 through 1963 (pp. 388, 390):

1953	5.7	1956	4.8	1959	7.8	1962	10.3
1954	7.6	1957	6.9	1960	8.5	1963	10.4
1955	4.9	1958	8.6	1961	10.0		

Thus "it can be seen that the trend in the gap unemployment rate has been one of fairly steady increase since 1956. . . . Indeed, our analysis suggests that the unemployment situation has deteriorated steadily." (p. 388.) A by-product of Strand's and Dernburg's work is the finding that "the potential labor force in 1975 will be at least four million more than is currently projected by the Bureau of Labor Statistics, and may, quite possibly, be as much as five million higher." (pp. 378-379.)

9

MONOPOLY CAPITALISM AND RACE RELATIONS

The race problem in the United States was not created by monopoly capitalism. It was inherited from the slave system of the Old South. However, the nature of the problem has undergone a transformation during the monopoly capitalist period; and in a world in which the colored races are shaking off the bonds of oppression, it is apparent to everyone that the future of the United States will be deeply, and perhaps decisively, influenced by the further development of relations between the races inside the country.

The most elaborate and widely praised study of the United States race problem is undoubtedly Gunnar Myrdal's *An American Dilemma,* and for this reason it provides an appropriate starting point for our analysis.[1]

The dynamics of race relations in the United States, according to Myrdal, are to be sought in the tension between white prejudice and what he calls the American Creed. Prejudice results in discrimination, segregation, and a generally inferior socio-economic status for Negroes. The Creed expresses the devotion of the whole people to the ideals of freedom and equality. Prejudice, discrimination, and inferiority interact: the more prejudice, the more discrimination; the more discrimination, the more inferiority; the more inferiority, the more prejudice; and so on in a vicious spiral. But it works the other way too. Any measures taken to promote the realization of the Creed will lessen inferiority, diminish prejudice, and counter-

---

[1] First edition, two volumes, New York, 1942; twentieth anniversary edition, one volume, New York and Evanston, 1962.

act discrimination; and this too will be a cumulative process. While self-perpetuating movements in either direction are theoretically possible, Myrdal believed that in practice and in the long run the Creed would dominate, and from this belief he deduced the existence of an underlying meliorative trend. In addition, Myrdal argued that for a variety of reasons wars have a favorable effect on the status of Negroes. Hence, writing in the early phase of the Second World War, Myrdal found a double reason for optimism. In the Author's Preface to the first edition, he wrote—and himself italicized the statement—that *"not since Reconstruction has there been more reason to antic-ipate fundamental changes in American race relations, changes which will involve a development toward the American ideals."*

Twenty years later, writing an additional Preface for the twentieth anniversary edition, Myrdal quoted this statement and added: "A student who has often been wrong in his fore-casts will be excused for pointing to a case when he was right." His close collaborator on the study, Arnold Rose, contributing a Postscript to the anniversary edition, takes a similarly favor-able view of the study's prognosis and foresees an acceleration of the meliorative trend in the future. According to Rose:

There could be no doubt that the races were moving rapidly toward equality and desegregation by 1962. In retrospect, the change of the preceding twenty years appeared as one of the most rapid in the history of human relations. . . . The change had been so rapid and caste and racism so debilitated, that I venture to predict the end of all formal segregation and discrimination within a decade, and the decline of informal segregation and discrimination so that it would be a mere shadow in two decades . . . the dynamic social forces creating inequality will, I predict, be practically elimi-nated in three decades.

Myrdal and Rose thus believe that the race problem in the United States is well on the way to complete solution within the framework of the present social order. But is it? Are the increasing militancy of the Negro liberation movement, the continuing violence of the Southern racists, the uprisings of ghetto dwellers in Northern and Western cities, the growing preoccupation of the whole country with this "dilemma"—are these merely symptoms of progress, as Myrdal and Rose would presumably contend? Or are they the ominous rumblings of a conflict which is growing in scope and bitterness precisely because there is no progress?

Any serious attempt to answer these questions, we believe, must depart from the historical idealism of Myrdal and seek to relate the problem of race relations in the United States to the basic monopoly capitalist structure of American society.

2

Race prejudice as it exists in the world today is almost exclusively an attitude of whites and had its origins in the need of European conquerors from the sixteenth century on to rationalize and justify the robbery, enslavement, and continued exploitation of their colored victims all over the globe.[2] When the slave system was introduced into the American South, race prejudice naturally came with it, and the ideological justification of the system was perhaps elaborated with greater diligence and subtlety there than anywhere else in the world. From colonial times, Americans both North and South have been systematically and continuously subjected to a barrage of propaganda fostering the ideas of white superiority and Negro inferiority.

It was, of course, always easy to adduce evidence purporting to "prove" the white-superiority/Negro-inferiority thesis. Having been enslaved and deprived of all opportunity to share in the benefits of civilized living, Negroes were visibly and undeniably inferior in all respects by which civilized societies judge superiority and inferiority. The argument that this *de facto* inferiority was due to inborn racial characteristics was convincing to those who wanted to believe it. And it was not

---

[2] For excellent treatments of this subject, see Eric Williams, *Capitalism and Slavery*, Chapel Hill, 1944, Chapter 1; and Oliver C. Cox, *Caste, Class, and Race*, New York, 1948, Chapter 16.

only whites who accepted it; many Negroes were successfully brainwashed into believing in the reality of their own inherent inferiority, and this self-depreciation acted as one of the most important bulwarks of the racial system.[3] It should be noted that the slave system, while assiduously fostering the idea of Negro inferiority, does not necessarily imply hatred by whites of Negroes as such. As long as the Negro knew and kept his "place," he was tolerated and even liked by whites. What whites hated was the Negro who believed in and acted on the principle that all men are created equal.

The Civil War was not fought by the Northern ruling class to free the slaves, as many mistakenly believe. It was fought to check the ambitions of the Southern slave-owning oligarchy which wanted to escape from what was essentially a colonial relation to Northern capital. The abolition of slavery was a by-product of the struggle, not its purpose, and Northern capitalism had no intention, despite the interlude of Reconstruction, of liberating the Negro in any meaningful sense. Having subdued the Southern planters, it was glad to have them resume their role of exploiters of black labor whom it could in turn exploit. The notorious compromise of the 1870's was a tacit recognition that the renewed colonial status of the South had been accepted by both sides, with the Southern oligarchy exploiting the Negro and in turn paying tribute to Northern capital for the privilege of doing so.

Under these circumstances, new methods of control over Negro labor were needed to replace slavery, and they were found in various forms of wage labor, sharecropping, and peonage. When Negroes tried to take advantage of their legal

[3] This subject is illuminatingly treated by Harold R. Isaacs who convincingly shows that "the systematic debasement and self-debasement of the Negro . . . has begun with or been underpinned by the image the Negro child has gotten of the naked, uncivilized African." (*The New World of Negro Americans*, New York, 1963, p. 161.) This goes far to explain the enormous psychological significance to American Negroes of the emergence of independent African nations and leaders, and their full acceptance into the comity of nations.

freedom to organize along with poor whites in the Populist movement, the planters answered with violence and the Jim Crow system of legalized segregation. By the turn of the century, the oppression and exploitation of Negroes was probably as bad as it had ever been under slavery, and racist propaganda was at least as virulent—and even more successful in the North because racism no longer had to bear the moral stigma of out-and-out slavery.[4]

Prior to the First World War, Negroes in the United States were overwhelmingly a Southern peasantry. They did begin to move out of the Old South in substantial numbers around 1880, but as late as 1910 the census showed that some 80 percent of the Negro population was still in the former Confederate states and that 90 percent of them lived in rural areas. On the whole Negroes played only a minor role in the Northern economy before 1914.

There, in the course of the nineteenth century, a unique system of supplying the huge demand for labor generated by a rapidly expanding and industrializing economy had taken shape. The lowest rungs of the economic ladder were occupied by successive waves of immigrants, mostly from Europe but also from Asia, Mexico, and Canada. As newcomers arrived to take their place at the bottom, the children and grandchildren of "older" immigrants moved up the ladder to meet the need for semi-skilled, skilled, and white collar workers, with the system of public education playing a key role in preparing them for these higher-paying and higher-status jobs. It is relevant to note that the inferiority-prejudice-discrimination pattern, so much emphasized by Myrdal, operated also in the case of the new immigrants. The reaction of the natives was almost always hostile and sometimes vicious in the extreme. Anne Braden, a

[4] See Rayford W. Logan, *The Negro in American Life and Thought, the Nadir, 1877-1901,* New York, 1954. These last two decades of the nineteenth century were, in Harold Isaacs's words, "the peak years of Western white supremacy all over the world." *The New World of Negro Americans,* p. 119.

gallant fighter for Negro rights in our time, has described what
came to be known as "Bloody Monday" in her home city:

In Louisville, Kentucky, on Monday, August 6, 1855, mobs of men
entered the sections of town occupied by German and Irish immigrants, set fire to stores and houses and, when their occupants tried
to escape, opened up with gunfire and killed them. Even women
with babies in their arms were shot as they fled from burning
houses. The mobs were urged on by the shouting of staid house-
wives and their daughters, wishing that "every German, every Irish-
man and all their descendants were killed."[5]

Prejudice and hostility against the immigrants, bursting out
from time to time in full-scale pogroms, undoubtedly greatly
retarded the upward mobility of the foreign nationality groups.
That these attitudes could not destroy upward mobility altogether was due to two causes, one economic and the other
socio-psychological. On the one hand, there was the rapidly
growing demand for qualified labor, which could be met only
by upgrading. On the other hand, the continuous arrival of new
immigrant groups to occupy the ghettos which the older
groups were vacating enabled the natives (and the older immigrants as they became assimilated) to continue to vent their
feelings of superiority, hostility, and aggression. Irish and
German targets were replaced by Italian and Polish: essential
attitudes and behavior patterns remained unchanged.

The First World War marked the effective end of this system
of provisioning the United States labor market. European immigration was suddenly reduced to a mere trickle, and soon afterwards the demand for labor of all kinds shot up. Part of the
problem was solved through putting the unemployed to work.
As we have already noted, unemployment at 9.7 percent of the
labor force was extremely high in 1915. The figure was reduced
to 1.4 percent by 1918.[6] But this was not enough; it was also
necessary to tap on a large scale the reservoir of surplus manpower which had been building up for some time in the rural
areas, especially in the South.

[5] Anne Braden, *The Wall Between,* New York, 1958, p. ix.
[6] See above, p. 232.

Migrations are nearly always motivated by pushes as well as pulls, and the great migration from rural to urban areas which took place during the First World War was no exception. The push was provided by increasing productivity in agriculture owing to mechanization, more intensive methods of cultivation, and so on. As a consequence, demand for farm labor lagged behind increasing agricultural output and finally reached a census-year peak in 1910, declining thereafter not only relatively to output but absolutely as well.[7] Faced with declining demand for farm labor, the numerous sons and daughters of farmers naturally looked cityward for an opportunity to earn a livelihood. The heavy unemployment which prevailed during the years after 1907 doubtless deterred many from making the move, though a substantial migration was already well under way by that time. The tremendous increase in wartime demand for labor in the cities not only removed this deterrent but substituted for it a powerful magnet. All the conditions for a massive migration were now fulfilled. The United States, having always relied on immigration from abroad, now discovered, quite suddenly as such things go, that it could get along by tapping its own surplus rural manpower just as Europe had been doing since the beginnings of the industrial revolution.

After the war there was no need to return to the old system. The agricultural revolution quickened and high rates of population growth obtained in the rural areas, making available a steady stream of unskilled labor for the cities. In these circumstances, legal restrictions on immigration were a natural sequel. Opposition to immigration began to be voiced as early as the 1880's, but before the war it had never prevailed against the interest of powerful capitalists in having an ample supply

[7] The numbers of gainful workers in agriculture in census years from 1870 to 1930 were as follows (in thousands):

1870	6,850	1910	11,592
1880	8,585	1920	11,449
1890	9,938	1930	10,472
1900	10,912		

Historical Statistics of the United States, Colonial Times to 1957, p. 72.

of cheap labor. Now, with that supply assured from domestic sources, the capitalists themselves joined the opposition, chiefly out of fear that working-class immigrants would infect the United States with the revolutionary virus that had already brought down the capitalist system in Russia and seemed to be threatening the rest of Europe. Immigration was not cut off altogether, but the quota system adopted in 1924 did virtually halt the inflow from the countries of eastern and southern Europe which had been the chief recent sources of unskilled labor. From that time on, most immigrants were persons in higher-status occupations who could be counted upon to become strong defenders of the status quo in their new homeland. Ironically, one important effect of this radical change in the character of the immigrant stream was to reduce the need for upgrading from the ranks of the unskilled and semi-skilled. After 1924, it was tougher for the domestic migrant to the cities to move up the economic ladder than it had been for his counterpart from Europe in the prewar period.

3

From our present point of view, the essential thing is that the shift from external to internal supplying of the demand for unskilled labor meant the urbanization of the Negro. Table 15 shows the net intercensal emigration of Negroes from the Old South during the post-Civil War period.[8]

Negro emigration from the South started before the end of the nineteenth century but took on really mass proportions only during the war decade. There was a decline in the rate of flow during the 1930's, but even the heavy unemployment of that

[8] The source of these figures through the 1940's is *Historical Statistics of the United States, Colonial Times to 1957*, pp. 46-47. They are, as explained at p. 39, refinements of census data, and a strictly comparable figure is not available for the decade of the 1950's. We have arrived at an estimate by reducing the census data for the 1950's (*Statistical Abstract of the United States, 1962*, p. 40) by the same percentage that the compilers of *Historical Statistics* used for reducing the census data for the 1940's.

Table 15

Emigration of Negroes from the Eleven Former
Confederate States, 1870-1960
(In thousands)

1870's	47
1880's	59
1890's	242
1900's	216
1910's	480
1920's	769
1930's	381
1940's	1,260
1950's	1,170

period failed to check the northward movement. The biggest
wave of emigration came with the Second World War and has
continued with but little change ever since.

Almost all of the emigrants from the South settled in the
cities of the North and West. But this was not the only movement of Negroes. Within the South itself, there has been steady
migration from countryside to city. The upshot is that in the
half century between 1910 and 1960, Negroes have been transformed from a regional peasantry into a substantial segment of
the urban working class. The 3-to-1 rural-urban ratio of 1910
has been almost exactly reversed: today three quarters of the
Negro population are city dwellers.

It was of course inevitable that Negroes should enter the
urban economy at the very bottom. They were the poorest,
most illiterate, least skilled on arrival. They were doubly bur-
dened by historic race prejudice and discrimination and by the
prejudice and discrimination that have greeted every group of
impoverished newcomers. The questions we have to ask are:
How have they made out since moving to the cities? Have they
been able to follow in the footsteps of earlier immigrant groups,
climbing the economic ladder and escaping from their original
ghettos?

In answering these questions, we must be careful not to mix up the effects of moving from country to city, a process which has been continuous for more than half a century, with what has happened after arrival in the city. The move from country-side to city has on the average unquestionably meant a higher standard of living for Negroes: if it had not, the migration would have ceased long ago. In other words, the bottom of the urban-industrial ladder is higher than the bottom of the South-ern agricultural ladder, and when Negroes stepped from the one to the other it was a step up. This is not what primarily interests us, however. It was similarly a step up for impover-ished European peasants to leave their homelands and move to the United States: again the proof is that the flow continued until it was cut off by war and legislation. The point is that after they got here, they soon started to climb the new ladder, and fresh immigrant groups took their place at the bottom. What we want to know is whether Negroes have followed the same course, climbing the new ladder after moving to the cities.

A few have, of course, and we shall discuss the role and significance of this minority when we come to the subject of tokenism. But for the great mass of Negroes the answer is, emphatically and unambiguously, no. The widespread opinion to the contrary, to the extent that it has any factual basis, rests on confusing the step from one ladder to the other with a step up the new ladder. This important point was explained to the Clark Committee by Herman P. Miller, Special Assistant to the Director of the Bureau of the Census and one of the country's leading authorities on income distribution:

> We heard this morning from Professor Ginzberg that the Negro made a breakthrough in the 1950's. Senator Javits, in his excellent book, *Discrimination, U.S.A.*, also speaks about the improvement of the economic status of the Negro. Even the Department of Labor refers to the occupational gains that have been made by the Negro in the past 20 years. This is all very true, but I think it can be shown, on the basis of census statistics, that most of the improvement in

occupational status that the Negro has made since 1940 has been through his movement out of sharecropping and agricultural labor in the South and into your Northern industrial areas.

When we look at the figures for the Northern and Central states we find that the occupational status of the Negro relative to the white has not improved appreciably since 1940.[9]

With respect to income, the situation is somewhat more complicated, but no more favorable to the theory that Negroes are moving up the ladder. Miller explained it in his statement prepared for the Clark Committee:

Although the relative occupational status of nonwhites has not changed appreciably in most states since 1940, the income gap between whites and nonwhites did narrow during the Second World War. During the past decade, however, there has been no change in income differentials between the two groups. . . . In 1947, the median wage or salary income for nonwhite workers was 54 percent of that received by the whites. In 1962, the ratio was almost identical (55 percent). . . . In view of the stability of the earnings gap during the postwar period . . . the reduction during the war years cannot be viewed as part of a continuing process, but rather as a phenomenon closely related to war-induced shortages of unskilled labor and government regulations such as those of the War Labor Board designed generally to raise the incomes of lower paid workers, and to an economy operating at full tilt.[10]

It is important to understand that the position of Negroes derives not only from the undoubted facts that on the average they have less education and are concentrated in unskilled or semi-skilled occupations. Even when they have the same amount of schooling as whites, their occupational status is

[9] *Equal Employment Opportunity*, Hearings Before the Subcommittee on Employment and Manpower of the Committee on Labor and Public Welfare, United States Senate, 88th Cong., 1st Sess., on S. 773, S. 1210, S. 1211, and S. 1937; July 24, 25, 26, 29, 31, August 2 and 20, 1963, p. 375. Senator Joseph S. Clark of Pennsylvania is Chairman of this Subcommittee.

[10] *Ibid.*, p. 323. Government statistics customarily distinguish between whites and non-whites rather than between whites and Negroes. Since Negroes constitute more than 90 percent of non-whites, it is legitimate for most purposes to use the two terms interchangeably, as Miller does in his testimony before the Clark Committee.

lower. Even when they do the same work, they are paid less. And in both respects, the relative disadvantage of the Negro is greater the higher you go in the occupation and income scales.

A nonwhite man who has not gone beyond the eighth grade has very little chance of being anything more than a laborer, a porter, or a factory hand. Nearly 8 out of every 10 nonwhite men with eight grades of schooling worked as laborers, service workers, or operatives at the time of the last census. Among whites with the same amount of education, only 5 out of 10 worked at these low-paid jobs.

The nonwhite high school graduate stands a somewhat better chance of getting a well-paid job; but even his chances are not very good. About 6 out of every 10 nonwhite high school graduates were laborers, service workers, or operatives as compared with only 3 out of 10 whites with the same amount of schooling.

Nonwhite college graduates seem to be able to find professional employment in relatively large numbers. About three out of every four were professional or managerial workers—nearly the same proportion as white college graduates. But, there is one big difference. Nonwhites are concentrated in the lower-paid professions. . . .

Nonwhite men earn less than whites with the same number of years of schooling for at least two reasons: (a) they are employed in lower paid jobs; and (b) they are paid less even when they do the same kind of work. The combined impact of these two factors is shown in . . . figures on the lifetime earnings of white and nonwhite men by years of school completed. This table shows that the relative earnings gap between whites and nonwhites increases with educational attainment. The lifetime earnings of nonwhite elementary school graduates is about 64 percent of the white total. Among college graduates nonwhites have only 47 percent of the white total. The fact of the matter is that the average nonwhite with 4 years of college can expect to earn less over a lifetime than the white who did not go beyond the eighth grade.[11]

Negroes have thus not improved their occupational status relative to whites since 1940, nor their income status since the end of the war. Moreover, in certain other key respects their position has been clearly deteriorating. We refer especially to unemployment and the degree of ghettoization.

[11] *Ibid.*, pp. 324-325.

Table 16 presents unemployment rates for whites and non-whites at intervals from 1940 to 1962. Here we see a dramatic worsening of the Negro situation. A breakdown of the global unemployment figures reveals certain characteristic disabilities

Table 16

White and Non-white Unemployment, 1940-1962
(Percent of labor force)

	Total	White	Non-white	Non-white as percent of white
1940	13.3	13.0	14.5	112
1950	4.6	4.1	7.9	176
1960	5.4	4.9	8.5	157
1962	5.6	4.9	11.0	225

Source: For 1940, 1950, and 1960, *U.S. Census of Population, 1960. United States Summary: General Social and Economic Characteristics*, Washington, n.d. For 1962, *Manpower Report of the President*, Washington, 1963, p. 43.

to which Negroes are subject. Some of these were outlined in a statement prepared for the Clark Committee by Under Secretary of Labor John F. Henning:

The unemployment rate for nonwhites as a whole is today over twice as high as for whites—in May [1963], 10.3 percent compared with 5.0 percent. Among married men with family responsibilities, the difference is even wider, 8 percent compared with 3 percent.

The Negro's disadvantage is especially severe when it comes to the better paying, more desirable types of jobs. . . . [A]mong laborers the nonwhite unemployment rate is about one third greater, and in the skilled occupations it is over twice as great.

Today's unemployment strikes hardest at younger workers. In May this year . . . the rate for nonwhite teen-age boys was nearly 25 percent, but 17 percent for white boys. For girls the difference was even wider—33 percent compared with 18 percent.

The nonwhite minorities suffer a disproportionate amount of the hard-core or long-term unemployment. Although they constitute only 11 percent of the work force, they make up 25 percent of all workers unemployed for 6 months or more.[12]

[12] *Nation's Manpower Revolution,* Hearings Before the Subcommittee on Employment and Manpower of the Committee on Labor and

As to the increasing ghettoization of Negroes in cities all over the country, the evidence is conclusive. After exhaustive investigation, the Commission on Race and Housing reported: "Segregation barriers in most cities were tighter in 1950 than ten years earlier. . . . The evidence indicates, on the whole, an increasing separation of racial groups as nonwhites accumulate in the central city areas abandoned by whites and the latter continually move to new suburban subdivisions from which minorities are barred."[13] And a statistical study based on the Censuses of 1940, 1950, and 1960 by Karl E. and Alma F. Taeuber showed, in the words of a *New York Times* report, that "with some notable exceptions, racial segregation, far from disappearing, is on the increase in the United States."[14]

Nor is this only a recent trend. Lieberson has shown, on the basis of intensive statistical processing of census data for ten major cities, that ever since 1910, when the large-scale migration of Negroes to the cities was just getting under way, the extent of their residential segregation has been steadily increasing while that of foreign immigrant groups has been declining.

In summarizing the findings about Negro-European immigrant housing patterns [from 1910 to 1950], we may observe that although at one time certain specific immigrant groups in a city have been somewhat less segregated from Negroes than from native whites, the general summary figures indicate that Negroes and immigrant groups have moved in opposite directions, i.e., declining segregation for immigrants and increasing segregation for Negroes. In terms of sheer magnitude, the Negroes are far more highly segregated than are the immigrant groups. The old-new distinction [between "old" and "new" immigrant groups] which has been so meaningful in earlier analyses is not particularly significant with respect to segregation from Negroes. That is, the old and new immigrants

---

Public Welfare, United States Senate, 88th Cong., 1st Sess., Relating to the Training and Utilization of the Manpower Resources of the Nation, Part 2, June 4-7, 1963, p. 403.

[13] *Where Shall We Live?* Report of the Commission on Race and Housing, Berkeley, 1958, p. 3.

[14] M. S. Handler, "Segregation Rise in U.S. Reported," *New York Times*, November 26, 1964.

are on the average similar in being highly segregated from Negroes.[15]

On the basis of the data presented, which could of course be made much more comprehensive and detailed, the conclusion seems inescapable that since moving to the cities, Negroes have been prevented from improving their socio-economic position: they have not been able to follow earlier immigrant groups up the occupational ladder and out of the ghetto.

4

As always happens in social science, answering one question leads to another. What social forces and institutional mechanisms have forced Negroes to play the part of permanent immigrants, entering the urban economy at the bottom and remaining there decade after decade?[16]

There are, it seems to us, three major sets of factors involved in the answer to this crucially important question. First, a formidable array of private interests benefit, in the most direct and immediate sense, from the continued existence of a segregated subproletariat. Second, the socio-psychological pressures generated by monopoly capitalist society intensify rather than alleviate existing racial prejudices, hence also discrimination and segregation. And third, as monopoly capitalism develops, the demand for unskilled and semi-skilled labor declines both relatively and absolutely, a trend which affects Negroes more than any other group and accentuates their economic and social inferiority. All of these factors mutually interact, tending to push Negroes ever further down in the social structure and locking them into the ghetto.

Consider first the private interests which benefit from the existence of a Negro subproletariat. (a) Employers benefit

[15] Stanley Lieberson, *Ethnic Patterns in American Cities*, New York, 1963, p. 132.

[16] "The Negro population," says the Commission on Race and Housing, "in spite of its centuries of residence in America, has at present some of the characteristics of an incompletely assimilated immigrant group." *Where Shall We Live?* pp. 8-9.

from divisions in the labor force which enable them to play one group off against another, thus weakening all. Historically, for example, no small amount of Negro migration was in direct response to the recruiting of strikebreakers. (b) Owners of ghetto real estate are able to overcrowd and overcharge. (c) Middle and upper income groups benefit from having at their disposal a large supply of cheap domestic labor. (d) Many small marginal businesses, especially in the service trades, can operate profitably only if cheap labor is available to them. (e) White workers benefit by being protected from Negro competition for the more desirable and higher paying jobs. Hence the customary distinction, especially in the South, between "white" and "Negro" jobs, the exclusion of Negroes from apprentice programs, the refusal of many unions to admit Negroes, and so on.[17] In all these groups—and taken together they constitute a vast majority of the white population—what Marx called "the most violent, mean, and malignant passions of the human breast, the Furies of private interest," are summoned into action to keep the Negro "in his place."

With regard to race prejudice, it has already been pointed out that this characteristic white attitude was deliberately created and cultivated as a rationalization and justification for the enslavement and exploitation of colored labor.[18] But in time,

---

[17] "There has grown up a system of Negro jobs and white jobs. And this is the toughest problem facing the Negro southerner in employment." Leslie W. Dunbar, Executive Director of the Southern Regional Council, in testimony before the Clark Committee. *Equal Employment Opportunity*, p. 457.

[18] Among colored peoples, race prejudice, to the extent that it exists at all, is a defensive reaction to white aggression and therefore has an entirely different significance. It may serve to unify and spur on colored peoples in their struggles for freedom and equality, but once these goals have been achieved it rapidly loses its *raison d'être*. As Oliver Cox has pointed out: "Today communication is so far advanced that no people of color, however ingenious, could hope to put a cultural distance between them and whites comparable to that which the Europeans of the commercial and industrial revolution attained in practical isolation over the colored peoples of the world. And such a relationship is crucial for the development of that complex belief in biological superiority and conse-

race prejudice and the discriminatory behavior patterns which go with it came to serve other purposes as well. As capitalism developed, particularly in its monopoly phase, the social structure became more complex and differentiated. Within the basic class framework, which remained in essentials unchanged, there took place a proliferation of social strata and status groups, largely determined by occupation and income. These groupings, as the terms "stratum" and "status" imply, relate to each other as higher or lower, with the whole constituting an irregular and unstable hierarchy. In such a social structure, individuals tend to see and define themselves in terms of the "status hierarchy" and to be motivated by ambitions to move up and fears of moving down.[19] These ambitions and fears are of course exaggerated, intensified, played upon by the corporate sales apparatus which finds in them the principal means of manipulating the "utility functions" of the consuming public.

The net result of all this is that each status group has a deep-rooted psychological need to compensate for feelings of inferiority and envy toward those above by feelings of superiority and contempt for those below. It thus happens that a special pariah group at the bottom acts as a kind of lightning rod for the frustrations and hostilities of all the higher groups, the

---

quent color prejudice which Europeans have been able to attain. Therefore, we must conclude that race prejudice is not only a cultural trait developed among Europeans, but also that no other race could hope to duplicate the phenomenon. Like the discovery of the world, it seems evident that this racial achievement could occur only once." *Caste, Class, and Race,* pp. 348-349. The other side of this coin is, since the colored races obviously can and will attain cultural and technological equality with whites, that the race prejudice of modern whites is not only a unique but also a transitory historical phenomenon. It needs to be added, however, that completely eliminating it from the consciousness of whites, even in a predominantly non-exploitative (that is, socialist) world, may take decades rather than months or years.

[19] The crucial importance of the status hierarchy in the shaping of the individual's consciousness goes far to explain the illusion, so widespread in the United States, that there are no classes in this country, or, as the same idea is often expressed, that everyone is a member of the middle class.

more so the nearer they are to the bottom. It may even be said that the very existence of the pariah group is a kind of harmonizer and stabilizer of the social structure—so long as the pariahs play their role passively and resignedly. Such a society becomes in time so thoroughly saturated with race prejudice that it sinks below the level of consciousness and becomes a part of the "human nature" of its members.[20] The gratification which whites derive from their socio-economic superiority to Negroes has its counterpart in alarm, anger, and even panic at the prospect of Negroes' attaining equality. Status being a relative matter, whites inevitably interpret upward movement by Negroes as downward movement for themselves. This complex of attitudes, product of stratification and status consciousness in monopoly capitalist society, provides an important part of the explanation why whites not only refuse to help Negroes to rise but bitterly resist their efforts to do so. (When we speak of whites and their prejudices and attitudes in this unqualified way, we naturally do not mean all whites. Ever since John Brown, and indeed long before John Brown, there have been whites who have freed themselves of the disease of racial prejudice, have fought along with Negro militants for an end to the rotten system of exploitation and inequality, and have looked forward to the creation of a society in which relations of solidarity and brotherhood will take the place of relations of superiority and inferiority. Moreover, we are confident that the number of such whites will steadily increase in the years ahead. But their number is not great today, and in a survey which aims only at depicting the broadest contours of the current social scene it would be wholly misleading to assign them a decisive role.)

The third set of factors adversely affecting the relative posi-

[20] At this level of development, race prejudice is far from being reachable by public opinion polls and similar devices of "sociometrics" which remain close to the surface of individual and social phenomena. Incidentally, we have here another reason for believing that the eradication of race prejudice from whites will be, even in a rational society, a difficult and protracted process.

tion of Negroes is connected with technological trends and
their impact on the demand for different kinds and grades of
labor. Appearing before a Congressional committee in 1955,
the then Secretary of Labor, James P. Mitchell, testified that
unskilled workers as a proportion of the labor force had declined from 36 percent in 1910 to 20 percent in 1950.[21] A later
Secretary of Labor, Willard Wirtz, told the Clark Committee
in 1963 that the percentage of unskilled was down to 5 percent
by 1962.[22] Translated into absolute figures, this means that the
number of unskilled workers declined slightly, from somewhat
over to somewhat under 13 million between 1910 and 1950,
and then plummeted to fewer than 4 million only twelve years
later. These figures throw a sharp light on the rapid deterioration of the Negro employment situation since the Second
World War. What happened is that until roughly a decade and
a half ago, with the number of unskilled jobs remaining stable,
Negroes were able to hold their own in the total employment
picture by replacing white workers who were moving up the
occupational ladder. This explains why, as Table 16 shows, the
Negro unemployment rate was only a little higher than the
white rate at the end of the Great Depression. Since 1950, on
the other hand, with unskilled jobs disappearing at a fantastic
rate, Negroes not qualified for other kinds of work found themselves increasingly excluded from employment altogether.
Hence the rise of the Negro unemployment rate to more than
double the white rate by the early 1960's. Negroes, in other
words, being the least qualified workers are disproportionately
hard hit as unskilled jobs (and, to an increasing extent, semi-
skilled jobs) are eliminated by mechanization, automation, and
cybernation. Since this technological revolution has not yet run
its course—indeed many authorities think that it is still in its

[21] *Automation and Technological Change*, Hearings Before the Subcommittee on Economic Stabilization of the Joint Committee on the
Economic Report, 84th Cong., 1st Sess., pursuant to Sec. 5(a) of P. L.
304, 79th Cong., Oct. 14, 15, 17, 18, 24, 25, 26, 27, and 28, 1955, p.
264.
[22] *Nation's Manpower Revolution*, Part 1, May 20, 21, 22, and 25,
1963, p. 57.

early stages—the job situation of Negroes is likely to go on deteriorating. To be sure, technological trends are not, as many believe, the *cause* of unemployment: that role, as we have tried to show in earlier chapters, is played by the specific mechanisms of monopoly capitalism.[23] But within the framework of this society technological trends, because of their differential impact on job opportunities, can rightly be considered a cause, and undoubtedly the most important cause, of the relative growth of Negro unemployment.

5

All the forces we have been discussing—vested economic interests, socio-psychological needs, technological trends—are deeply rooted in monopoly capitalism and together are strong enough to account for the fact that Negroes have been unable to rise out of the lower depths of American society. Indeed so pervasive and powerful are these forces that the wonder is only that the position of Negroes has not drastically worsened. That it has not, that in absolute terms their real income and consuming power have risen more or less in step with the rest of the population's, can only be explained by the existence of counteracting forces.

One of these counteracting forces we have already commented upon: the shift out of Southern agriculture and into the urban economy. Some schooling was better than none; even a rat-infested tenement provided more shelter than a broken-down shack on Tobacco Road; being on the relief rolls of a big city meant more income, both money and real, than subsistence farming. And as the nation's per capita income rose, so also did that of the lowest income group, even that of unemployables on permanent relief. As we have seen, it has been this shift from countryside to city which has caused so many

[23] Under socialism there is no reason why technological progress, no matter how rapid or of what kind, should be associated with unemployment. In a socialist society technological progress may make possible a continuous reduction in the number of years, weeks, and hours worked, but it is inconceivable that this reduction should take the completely irrational form of capitalist unemployment.

observers to believe in the reality of a large-scale Negro break-through in the last two decades. Actually, it was an aspect of a structural change in the economy rather than a change in the position of Negroes within the economy.

But in one particular area, that of government employment, Negroes have indeed scored a breakthrough, and this has un-questionably been the decisive factor in preventing a cata-strophic decline in their relative position in the economy as a whole. Table 17 gives the essential data (all levels of govern-ment are included).

Table 17

Non-white Employment in Government, 1940-1962
(Figures are for April, in thousands)

	1940	1956	1960	1961	1962
Government employees, total	3,845	6,919	8,014	8,150	8,647
Non-white government employees	214	670	855	932	1,046
Non-white as percent of total	5.6	9.7	10.7	11.4	12.1

Source: United States Department of Labor, *The Economic Situation of Negroes in the United States,* Bulletin S-3, Revised 1962, p. 8.

Between 1940 and 1962, total government employment somewhat more than doubled, while non-white (as already noted, more than 90 percent Negro) employment in govern-ment expanded nearly five times. As a result non-white em-ployment grew from 5.6 percent of the total to 12.1 percent. Since non-whites constituted 11.5 percent of the labor force at mid-1961, it is a safe inference that Negroes are now more than proportionately represented in government employment.[24]

Two closely interrelated forces have been responsible for this relative improvement of the position of Negroes in govern-ment employment. The first, and beyond doubt the most im-portant, has been the increasing scope and militancy of the

[24] If the data were available to compare income received from gov-ernment employment by whites and non-whites, the picture would of course be much less favorable for Negroes since they are heavily concen-trated in the lower-paying categories. But here too there has been im-

Negro liberation movement itself. The second has been the need of the American oligarchy, bent on consolidating a global empire including people of all colors, to avoid as much as possible the stigma of racism. If American Negroes had passively accepted the continuation of their degraded position, history teaches us that the oligarchy would have made no concessions. But once seriously challenged by militant Negro struggle, it was forced by the logic of its domestic and international situation to make concessions, with the twin objectives of pacifying Negroes at home and projecting abroad an image of the United States as a liberal society seeking to overcome an evil inheritance from the past.

The oligarchy, acting through the federal government and in the North and West through state and local governments, has also made other concessions to the Negro struggle. The armed forces have been desegregated, and a large body of civil rights legislation forbidding discrimination in public accommodations, housing, education, and employment, has been enacted. Apart from the desegration of the armed forces, however, these concessions have had little effect. Critics often attribute this failure to bad faith: there was never any intention, it is said, to concede to Negroes any of the real susbstance of their demand for equality. This is a serious misreading of the situation. No doubt there are many white legislators and administrators to whom such strictures apply with full force, but this is not true of the top economic and political leadership of the oligarchy— the managers of the giant corporations and their partners at the highest governmental levels. These men are governed in their political attitudes and behavior not by personal prejudices but by their conception of class interests. And while they may at times be confused by their own ideology or mistake short-run for long-run interests, it seems clear that with respect

provement. A study made by the Civil Service Commission showed that between June 1962 and June 1963 Negro employment in the federal government increased by 3 percent and that "the major percentage gains had been in the better-paying jobs." *New York Times,* March 4, 1964.

to the race problem in the United States they have come, perhaps belatedly but none the less surely, to understand that the very existence of their system is at stake. Either a solution will be found which insures the loyalty, or at least the neutrality, of the Negro people, or else the world revolution will sooner or later acquire a ready-made and potentially powerful Trojan horse within the ramparts of monopoly capitalism's mightiest fortress. When men like Kennedy and Johnson and Warren champion such measures as the Civil Rights Act of 1964, it is clearly superficial to accuse them of perpetrating a cheap political maneuver. They know that they are in trouble, and they are looking for a way out.

Why then such meager results? The answer is simply that the oligarchy does not have the power to shape and control race relations any more than it has the power to plan the development of the economy. In matters which are within the administrative jurisdiction of government, policies can be effectively implemented. Thus it was possible to desegregate the armed forces and greatly to increase the number of Negroes in government employment. But when it comes to housing, education, and private employment, all the deeply rooted economic and socio-psychological forces analyzed above come into play. It was capitalism, with its enthronement of greed and privilege, which created the race problem and made of it the ugly thing it is today. It is the very same system which resists and thwarts every effort at a solution.

6

The fact that despite all political efforts, the relative economic and social position of Negroes has changed but little in recent years, and in some respects has deteriorated, makes it a matter of great urgency for the oligarchy to devise strategies which will divide and weaken the Negro protest movement and thus prevent it from developing its full revolutionary potential. These strategies can all be appropriately grouped under the heading of "tokenism."

If we are to understand the real nature of tokenism, it is necessary to keep in mind certain developments within the Negro community since the great migration from the Southern countryside got under way. As Negroes moved out of a largely subsistence economy into a money economy and as their average levels of income and education rose, their expenditures for goods and services naturally increased correspondingly. Goods were for the most part supplied by established white business; but segregation, *de jure* in the South and *de facto* in the North, gave rise to a rapidly expanding demand for certain kinds of services which whites would not or could not provide or which Negroes could provide better. Chief among these were the services of teachers, ministers, doctors, dentists, lawyers, barbers and beauty parlors, undertakers, certain kinds of insurance, and a press catering to the special needs of the segregated Negro community. Professionals and owners of enterprises supplying these services form the core of what Franklin Frazier called the black bourgeoisie.[25] Their ranks have been augmented by the growth of Negro employment in the middle and higher levels of the civil service and by the rapid expansion of the number of Negroes in the sports and entertainment worlds. The growth of the black bourgeoisie has been particularly marked since the Second World War. Between 1950 and 1960 the proportion of non-white families with incomes over $10,000 (1959 dollars) increased from 1 percent to 4.7 percent, a rate of growth close to three times that among whites. During the same years, the total distribution of income among Negro families became more unequal, while the change among white families was in the opposite direction.[26]

The theory behind tokenism, not often expressed but clearly deducible from the practice, is that the black bourgeoisie is the

[25] E. Franklin Frazier, *Black Bourgeoisie: The Rise of a New Middle Class in the United States*, Glencoe, Illinois, 1957.

[26] All data from Herman P. Miller, *Trends in the Income of Families and Persons in the United States: 1947 to 1960*, Bureau of the Census Technical Paper No. 8, Washington, 1963, Table 9, pp. 168-189. The measure of inequality used by Miller is the so-called Gini coefficient

decisive element in the Negro community. It contains the intellectual and political elite, the people with education and leadership ability and experience. It already has a material stake in the existing social order, but its loyalty is doubtful because of the special disabilities imposed upon it solely because of its color. If this loyalty can be made secure, the potential revolutionizing of the Negro protest movement can be forestalled and the world can be given palpable evidence—through the placing of loyal Negroes in prominent positions—that the United States does not pursue a South African-type policy of *apartheid* but on the contrary fights against it and strives for equal opportunity for its Negro citizens. The problem is thus how to secure the loyalty of the black bourgeoisie.

To this end the political drive to assure legal equality for Negroes must be continued. We know that legal equality does not guarantee real equality: the right to patronize the best hotels and restaurants, for example, means little to the Negro masses. But it is of great importance to the well-to-do Negro, and the continuation of any kind of disability based solely on color is hateful to all Negroes. The loyalty of the black bourgeoisie can never be guaranteed as long as vestiges of the Jim Crow system persist. For this reason we can confidently predict that, however long and bloody the struggle may be, the South will eventually be made over in the image of the North.

Second, the black bourgeoisie must be provided with greater access to the dominant institutions of the society: corporations, the policy-making levels of government, the universities, the

---

which increased for non-white families from .402 in 1950 to .414 in 1960, while for white families it was declining from .372 to .357.

Apart from the direction of change, the greater degree of income inequality for non-whites which these figures indicate should not be interpreted to mean that there is really a greater degree of equality of material circumstances among whites than among Negroes. In the upper reaches of the social structure, income is less significant than property; and while we know of no data on Negro property ownership, it seems beyond doubt that the disparity between Negroes and whites in this regard is immeasurably greater than in incomes.

suburbs. Here the oligarchy is showing itself to be alert and adaptable. A *New York Times* survey found that:

Business and industry here, in the face of the civil rights revolution, have been reassessing their employment policies and hiring Negroes for office and other salaried posts that they rarely held before.

Many national concerns with headquarters in New York City have announced new nondiscrimination policies or reaffirmed old ones. Personnel officers are taking a new look at their recruiting methods and seeking advice from Negro leaders on how to find and attract the best qualified Negroes.

On a nationwide basis, about 80 of the country's largest companies enrolled under Plans for Progress of the President's Committee on Equal Opportunity have reported substantial increases in the hiring of Negroes for salaried positions. . . .

The latest figures for the 80 companies that filed reports in the last year . . . showed that non-whites got 2,241 of the 31,698 salaried jobs that opened up. This represented an increase of 8.9 percent in the number of jobs held by nonwhites in those companies.[27]

The same thing has been happening in government, as already noted; and in addition to being hired in larger numbers in the better-paying grades, Negroes are increasingly being placed in executive jobs at or near the cabinet level, in federal judgeships, and the like. And as Negroes are brought into the economic and political power structure, they also become more acceptable in the middle- and upper-class suburbs—provided of course that their incomes and standard of living are comparable to their neighbors'.

Not many Negroes are affected by these easings of the barriers separating the races at the upper economic and social levels—in fact, it is of the essence of tokenism that not many should be. But this does not deprive the phenomenon of its importance. The mere existence of the possibility of moving up and out can have a profound psychological impact.

Third, the strategy of tokenism requires not only that Negro leadership should come from the black bourgeoisie but that it

[27] *New York Times*, November 12, 1963.

should be kept dependent on favors and financial support from the white oligarchy. The established civil rights organizations— the National Association for the Advancement of Colored People, the Urban League, and the Congress of Racial Equality—were all founded on a bi-racial basis and get most of their funds from white sources; they therefore present no potential threat. But it is always necessary to pay attention to the emergence of new and potentially independent leaders. Where this occurs, there are two standard tactics for dealing with the newcomers. The first is to co-opt them into the service of the oligarchy by flattery, jobs, or other material favors. Noel Day, a young Boston Negro leader who ran for Congress in the 1964 election, comments on this tactic:

Although the system is rotten it is nevertheless marvellously complex in the same way as the chambered Nautilus, beautiful in its complexity. The co-opting begins at birth; the potential for co-optation is built into the system. It is part of what we are taught is good. We have been taught to feel that the couple of thousand dollars a year more is what is desirable. The Negro and most other minority groups have been taught to desire entrance into the mainstream, they have not been taught to look to themselves and develop any sense of pride or prestige within their group, they have been taught to aspire to become mainstream Americans. In the case of the Negro, to aspire to become white. . . . One way of becoming white is by having a higher salary, or a title or a prestige position. This is not a very simple thing, but it is one of the evil beauties of the system. It has so many built-in checks and controls that come into operation— some of these are vitiating the energy of the freedom movement already. The official rhetoric has changed—in response to the dislocations and pressures we are witnessing an attempt at mass co-optation similar to the mass co-optation of the labor movement. The reaction of American business, for instance, is fantastic. The integration programs of some of the major companies are quick and adept—the fact that the First National Bank of Boston two months ago had about fifty Negro employees and now has over a thousand. Under pressure by CORE, they gave in to CORE's demands within *two weeks. Two months later* one of their top personnel men came into my office and said—now we are really concerned about developing a program for dropouts. What he was saying is that they are so adaptable, so flexible, in maintaining the balance of American business, in substituting reform as an antidote to revolution, that they will even go beyond the demands of the civil rights movement.[28]

If co-optation fails, the standard tactic is to attempt to destroy the potentially independent leader by branding him a Communist, a subversive, a trouble-maker, and by subjecting him to economic and legal harassments.

The reference in Noel Day's statement to developing a program for dropouts points to a fourth aspect of tokenism: to open up greater opportunities for Negro youths of all classes who because of luck, hard work, or special aptitudes are able to overcome the handicap of their background and start moving up the educational ladder. For a "qualified" Negro in the United States today, there is seemingly no limit to what he may aspire to. A report in the *New York Times* states:

Dr. Robert F. Goheen, president of Princeton University, said yesterday that the competition among colleges and universities for able Negro students was "much more intense" than the traditional competition for football players. . . . Dr. Goheen said: "It certainly is very clear that the number of able colored who have also had adequate educational opportunities is very small. And we find we are all extending our hands to the same relatively few young men and women."[29]

Here we can see as under a magnifying glass the mechanics of tokenism. With the country's leading institutions of higher learning falling over themselves to recruit qualified Negro students—and with giant corporations and the federal government both eager to snap them up after graduation—the prospects opened up to the lucky ones are indeed dazzling. But as President Goheen stresses, their number is very small, and it can only remain very small as long as the vast majority of Negroes stay anchored at the bottom of the economic ladder.

[28] "Symposium: New Politics," *Studies on the Left*, Summer 1964, pp. 44-45.
[29] *New York Times*, October 21, 1963.

The fact that the great mass of Negroes derive no benefits from tokenism does not mean that they are unaffected by it. One of its purposes, and to the extent that it succeeds one of its consequences, is to detach the ablest young men and women from their own people and thus to deprive the liberation movement of its best leadership material. And even those who have no stake in the system and no hope of ever acquiring one may become reconciled to it if they come to believe there is a chance that their children, or perhaps even their children's children, may be able to rise out of their own degraded condition.

7

It would be a great mistake to underestimate the skill and tenacity of the United States oligarchy when faced with what it regards—and in the case of race relations, rightly regards— as a threat to its existence. And it would be just as serious a mistake to underestimate the effectiveness, actual and potential, of the strategy of tokenism. Yet we believe that in the long run the real condition of the Negro masses will be the decisive factor. If some improvement, however modest and slow, can be registered in the years ahead, a well conceived policy of tokenism may be enough to keep Negroes from developing into monopoly capitalism's "enemy within the gates." But if the trends of the recent past continue, if advances are canceled out by setbacks, if the paradox of widespread poverty and degradation in the midst of potential abundance becomes ever more glaring, then it will be only a matter of time until American Negroes, propelled by the needs of their own humanity and inspired by the struggles and achievements of their brothers in the underdeveloped countries, will generate their own revolutionary self-consciousness.

If this assessment of the situation is correct, it becomes a matter of great importance to know whether the kinds of reforms which are possible within the framework of the existing system—the kinds advocated by the established civil rights organizations and their white supporters—are likely to yield any real benefits to the Negro masses.

It seems clear to us that the answer is negative; that the chief beneficiaries of reforms of this type are the black bourgeoisie; and that, regardless of the intentions of their sponsors, their objective effect is merely to supplement the policy of tokenism.

This might be thought not to be the case with prohibitions against discrimination in the hiring of labor, which unquestionably helped open up many new jobs to Negroes during the war. In a period of heavy and growing unemployment, however, no such effect can be expected. Even if color is not the reason, Negroes will be discriminated against because of their inferior qualifications. Only those with special talents or training will benefit, and they are already set apart from the ghettoized masses.

Nor can the ghetto dwellers hope to gain from anti-discrimination measures in the field of housing. The only kind of housing that would benefit them would result from construction on a large scale of low-rent units for those who most need it where they need it. Under existing conditions, there is no chance that such housing could be integrated. Attempts to build low-rent housing in marginal neighborhoods and to keep it occupied on a bi-racial basis necessitate the enforcement of so-called "benevolent quotas"—in other words require that Negro occupancy be kept low and hence that few Negroes benefit. As to the prevention of discrimination in the sale of private housing, either by law or by judicial nullification of restrictive covenants, this certainly helps well-to-do Negroes to move into previously all-white neighborhoods. As far as low-income Negroes are concerned, however, the most that can be said is that it facilitates expansion of the ghetto itself through what has been called the "invasion-succession sequence." In this strictly limited sense, anti-discrimination measures do help low-income Negroes: after all, they have to live somewhere. But it does nothing to raise their status or to promote racial integration in the lower reaches of the social structure.

With appropriate modifications, the story is not different in the case of school integration. Where neighborhoods are racially mixed, school integration follows naturally and is unquestionably good for all concerned. But this affects few Negroes, mostly of the higher-income group. The real problem is the ghetto schools. Some upgrading of schools attended by ghetto dwellers may be achieved by placing them on the margins of the ghetto and drawing school districts so as to include both black and white areas. But this does not touch the problem of the ghetto schools themselves, and here all the forces of tradition, inertia, prejudice, and privilege come into play to block or abort attempts at reform. Programs of driving a certain number of Negro children by bus from ghetto areas to white schools elsewhere merely evade the problem, and there is considerable evidence that they increase the insecurity and self-distrust of the children involved.[30]

There is really no mystery about why reforms which remain within the confines of the system hold out no prospect of meaningful improvement to the Negro masses. The system has two poles: wealth, privilege, power at one; poverty, deprivation, powerlessness at the other. It has always been that way, but in earlier times whole groups could rise because expansion made room above and there were others ready to take their place at the bottom. Today, Negroes are at the bottom, and there is neither room above nor anyone ready to take their place. Thus only individuals can move up, not the group as such: reforms help the few, not the many. For the many nothing short of a complete change in the system—the abolition of both poles and the substitution of a society in which wealth and power are shared by all—can transform their condition.

Some will say that even if this is true, it does not mean that the Negro masses will necessarily become aware of the causes of their degradation, still less that they will achieve a revolu-

[30] See A. James Gregor, "Black Nationalism: A Preliminary Analysis of Negro Radicalism," *Science & Society*, Fall 1963, pp. 427-431. Gregor also presents valuable evidence on the negligible importance to the Negro masses of anti-discrimination programs in housing.

tionary self-consciousness. May they not be blinded by the mystifications of bourgeois ideology and paralyzed by a leadership drawn from the tokenized elite? After all, there have always been oppressed classes and races, but the achievement of revolutionary self-consciousness is a rare historical event. Why should we expect American Negroes to do what so few have done before them?

There are, we believe, two reasons, equally compelling.

First, American Negroes live in a society which has mastered technology and advanced the productivity of labor beyond anything dreamed of even a few years ago. True, this has been done in search of profits and more perfect means of destruction, but the potential for human abundance and freedom is there and cannot be hidden. Poverty and oppression are no longer necessary, and a system which perpetuates them cannot but appear to its victims ever more clearly as a barbarous anachronism.

Second, the tide of world revolution against imperialist exploitation, which in our time is simply the international face of monopoly capitalism, is flowing strong, much too strong to be turned back or halted. Already, the rise of independent African nations has helped to transform the American Negro's image of himself. As Africans—and Asians and Latin Americans—carry their revolutions forward from national independence to socialist egalitarianism, the American Negro's consciousness will be transformed again and again—by his own knowledge and experience and by the example of those all over the world who are struggling against, and increasingly winning victories over, the same inhuman system of capitalist-imperialist oppression.

The Negro masses cannot hope for integration into American society as it is now constituted. But they can hope to be one of the historical agents which will overthrow it and put in its place another society in which they will share, not civil rights which is at best a narrow bourgeois concept, but full human rights.

10

ON THE QUALITY
OF MONOPOLY CAPITALIST SOCIETY

The purpose of the preceding discussion has been not only to advance the understanding of the working principles of the contemporary American economy but also to gain insight into the forces that mold the lives, shape the minds, and determine the development of individuals in our society. This insight is pressingly needed today. Disorientation, apathy, and often despair, haunting Americans in all walks of life, have assumed in our time the dimensions of a profound crisis. This crisis affects every aspect of national life, and ravages both its socio-political and its individual spheres—everyman's everyday existence. A heavy, strangulating sense of the emptiness and futility of life permeates the country's moral and intellectual climate. High-level committees are entrusted with the discovery and specification of "national goals" while gloom pervades the printed matter (fiction and non-fiction alike) appearing daily in the literary marketplace. The malaise deprives work of meaning and purpose; turns leisure into joyless, debilitating laziness; fatally impairs the educational system and the conditions for healthy growth in the young; transforms religion and church into commercialized vehicles of "togetherness"; and destroys the very foundation of bourgeois society, the family.

Some critics may object that these phenomena are nothing new, that they have always characterized capitalism or perhaps even human society in general. Others may feel that they represent inevitable by-products of modern industrial civilization, unavoidable attributes of the "affluent society," inescapa-

281

ble costs of economic progress. One thing must be made clear at the outset: we are not insisting that the condition which we are analyzing is brand new, nor that it necessarily constitutes a deterioration by comparison with the state of affairs twenty or fifty years ago. It is our strong impression—shared by thoughtful observers of the most divergent persuasions—that the crisis has never been so sharp and all-pervasive, and that matters have recently been going from bad to worse. But we are aware that we are moving here in an area in which precise or even approximate measurements and proofs are hard to come by. It may be useful to indicate briefly the reasons for this difficulty.

Statistical information on social developments is either scanty or ambiguous.[1] Consider for instance an index of social malaise such as the number of suicides. Apart from the incompleteness of the relevant data, it is obvious that their value depends on how the deaths in question are reported. Thus at a time when self-destruction was thought of as a serious blemish on the reputation of the surviving family, many a suicide was reported as death due to heart attack or other natural causes. As the social attitude toward suicide has changed and the reluctance to admit its occurrence has subsided, more suicides are reported and registered as such. This change in reporting would tend to give an impression of deterioration where actually there may have been none. Further on suicide, it is often held that its incidence among Negroes in the United States is markedly lower than among whites. To the extent, however, that the authorities in general, but primarily in the southern states, consider a Negro hardly worth bothering with and therefore make little effort to establish the cause of his death, the statistics on suicide among Negroes understate to an unknown degree the number of suicides among Negroes.

[1] The scantiness is due largely to the reluctance of reporting and statistics-gathering agencies to disclose many processes that reflect negatively on the existing social order; the ambiguity to many conceptual and theoretical problems which could be brought nearer adequate solution only if "behavioral science" would devote its energies to important issues rather than to the trivia which so conspicuously dominate the field.

Or take another example: the question whether juvenile delinquency presents a more serious problem than in the past. A definitive answer would depend first of all on the official definition of juvenile delinquency and whether it has changed in the course of time. If the definition has narrowed, if many misdemeanors are now considered "minor mischiefs" which earlier would have been thought of as acts of delinquency, then clearly recent statistics are not comparable with those of an earlier period.[2] The answer depends, further, on the extent to which the resources of law enforcement agencies as well as their diligence and vigilance have changed. Is a larger or a smaller proportion of "delinquents" apprehended and prosecuted by the police and the juvenile courts than, say, fifty years ago? And apart from the quantitative aspect of the matter, there is a qualitative one: have the nature and the motivation of the delinquent act greatly changed? For it obviously makes a lot of difference whether the delinquent acts consist of murder, rape, narcotics addiction and peddling, or of petty thievery, unauthorized driving, and precocious drinking. On all these important questions there is a lack of comprehensive and reliable information, and statistically supportable conclusions are therefore impossible to reach.

Let us present one more example. There is incontrovertible evidence that since the Second World War the proportion of marriages ending in divorce (or in legal and/or actual separation) has been markedly increasing.[3] The conclusions to be drawn from this are, however, ambiguous. We ourselves think that this development reflects not merely the obvious tendency to a progressive disintegration and breakdown of the bourgeois family but also people's growing loneliness and misery; but there is no way of proving the validity of this opinion. Indeed

[2] A similar consideration makes it impossible to compare the social class incidence of juvenile delinquency. What in the case of a middle- or upper-class boy or girl is considered an act of exuberance or a "prank" would in the case of a working-class or a Negro youngster be treated as a manifestation of delinquency.

[3] Incidentally, even the information in this area is deficient with regard to the "poor man's divorce," i.e. simple desertion.

the very opposite conclusion might be justified: that the in-creasing proportion of broken marriages indicates an improve-ment rather than a deterioration of the human condition. People have gained more freedom, and instead of suffocating in the clutches of unhappy marriages are now more capable of rearranging their lives according to their real needs. There is much force in this reasoning, which is only seemingly incom-patible with our own view, and it certainly comes nearer the truth than the conventional image of the typical American's "happy family life" which is supposed to provide the ideal framework for the flowering of individuality, morality, and order. In any case the argument in question is sufficiently cogent to make it impossible to employ the ratio of divorces to marriages as a valid index of people's happiness and welfare.

In the face of these obstacles, we have decided here to re-frain from making intertemporal comparisons with regard to some very important areas. We have arrived at this decision reluctantly, because we are convinced of the indispensability of viewing the phenomena in historical perspective; further-more it is our considered opinion that our impressions, al-though statistically unprovable, are substantially correct. Nevertheless, in order to keep the discussion on substantive issues, we shall confine ourselves to an outline of conditions which exist at the present time, leaving open the question whether they are different, better, or worse than conditions which existed at earlier periods.

This abstention from historical comparisons is unnecessary and indeed would be wholly inadmissible with regard to certain measurable aspects of social reality. Thus we can cer-tainly give quantitative expression to the crucial fact that our society is very much richer now than at any previous time. Productivity and per capita output and income are much higher than ever before; and the gap between what is and what *could* be has never been so glaring as it is now. On this even the most meticulous purists in the field of national output and income measurement could do no more than raise questions about the exact amount by which output and income have risen, or the precise extent to which achievement has fallen short of potentiality. And these doubts about specific magnitudes, however legitimate, do not affect the nature of our argument and have no bearing on its validity. For the crucially important finding is that monopoly capitalism, for all the productivity and wealth which it has generated, has utterly failed to provide the foundations of a society capable of promoting the healthy and happy development of its members.

2

When a draft of this chapter was being prepared for publication in 1962,[4] it seemed important to devote considerable space to proving the falsity of the then fashionable view that poverty was disappearing from the American scene. Even a year later, this would have been unnecessary. The publication, also in 1962, of Michael Harrington's book *The Other America* successfully focused the spotlight of publicity on the problem of poverty, and since then the outpouring of literature on the subject, both in book form and in the mass media, has been phenomenal. Finally, with President Johnson's declaration of a "war on poverty" in his January, 1964, State of the Union Message, the whole world was officially informed not only that poverty exists in the United States but that it is one of the country's most critical political issues. For our present purposes we need do no more today than record a few of the readily available statistics which demonstrate the failure of monopoly capitalism in purely economic terms. But before we do so, it will be useful to ask how it happened that poverty which only a few years ago had been written off as practically a thing of the past, suddenly came to occupy the center of the political stage.

There are, we believe, two parts to the explanation. First, as Marx pointed out in *Capital* and as the experience of the subsequent century of capitalist development has confirmed again and again, capitalism everywhere generates wealth at one pole

[4] *Monthly Review*, July-August, 1962.

and poverty at the other. This law of capitalist development, which is equally applicable to the most advanced metropolis and the most backward colony, has of course never been recognized by bourgeois economists. They have rather propagated the apologetic notion that a levelling-up tendency is inherent in capitalism.

This is where the second part of the explanation becomes relevant. At the root of capitalist poverty one always finds unemployment and underemployment—what Marx called the industrial reserve army—which directly deprive their victims of income and undermine the security and bargaining power of those with whom the unemployed compete for scarce jobs. Now during the Second World War, unemployment was really wiped out for a few years. While more than ten million men in the most productive age groups were being mobilized into the armed forces, total production was being expanded by two thirds or more. Under these circumstances, every physically able person, regardless of color, age, or sex, could get a job; and overtime became the rule rather than the exception. With several members of each family employed, family incomes in the lower-income brackets increased sharply. It would of course be wrong to say that poverty was eliminated during the war, but the improvement of living standards of poor people all over the country was nothing short of dramatic. And these favorable conditions for the underprivileged and disadvantaged continued, though in a weakened form, through the aftermath boom and the prosperity of the early 1950's, rooted in the Korean War and the huge military budgets which accompanied and followed it. For more than a decade, poverty in the United States receded and then was held at bay, while the economy as a whole expanded under the extraordinary demands of wars, hot and cold.

Bourgeois ideologists, wearing the blinkers provided by orthodox economic theory, naturally misinterpreted these developments completely. Here at last, they exulted, was capitalism behaving as they expected it to. The past was forgotten, especially the recent past of the Great Depression; the lessons of more than a century were ignored; the future was charted as an extrapolation of the wholly untypical years surrounding the greatest war in history. Hence the American Celebration, with its complacent assurance that poverty in this most affluent of societies would soon be no more than an unpleasant memory.

But capitalism's basic law of motion, temporarily thwarted, soon resumed its sway. Unemployment crept steadily upward, and the character of the new technologies of the postwar period sharply accentuated the disadvantages of unskilled and semi-skilled workers. Those at the bottom of the economic ladder who had been, in relative terms, the chief beneficiaries of wartime full employment now found themselves doubly hard hit.

By the end of the 1950's the real state of affairs could no longer be concealed: it was impossible to continue to believe in the existence of a meliorative trend which, given time, would result in the automatic liquidation of poverty. Not only was poverty still with us, as it always had been; there was evidence on all sides, but especially in the decaying centers of the big cities, that it was spreading and deepening. Affluence began to appear for what it is—not the cure for poverty but its Siamese twin.

A changed view of, and attitude toward, poverty now became inevitable. From being a passing nuisance, it suddenly became once again, as it had been before the war, a problem. The first fruit of this change was the new literature of poverty, the second its reappearance on the political stage. Johnson's "war on poverty" is in truth but a variation on a familiar theme. Herbert Hoover, running in 1928 as the Republican candidate for the presidency, declared that "we shall soon with the help of God be within sight of the day when poverty will be banished from this nation." And his successor, Franklin D. Roosevelt, vowed to change the situation in which "one third of a nation" was ill housed, ill clad, and ill fed.

We now know that neither God nor FDR managed to turn

the trick, and there is little reason to assume that Lyndon Johnson can do better. In the meantime, however, we can ask what are the dimensions of the problem his "war on poverty" is intended to cope with.

To answer this question we must of course first define poverty. Bourgeois theorists frequently throw up their hands at this point. Poverty, they say, is a relative matter, and everyone is entitled to define it as he sees fit. Some even go so far as to argue that since the poorest American—say, an unemployable living on public welfare in Mississippi—undoubtedly disposes over more income than an average worker or peasant in many underdeveloped countries, there really is no poverty in the United States. To a Marxist, however, such subjective judgments are at best meaningless and at worst deliberately misleading. Every society has its own standards for measuring poverty; and though these standards may not be precisely quantifiable, they are nevertheless real, objective facts. What is involved here is essentially the concept of the conventional subsistence minimum which plays such an important part in Marx's theory of wages and surplus value. Unlike the classical economists, Marx did not think of the subsistence minimum as being physiologically determined. The worker's "natural wants, such as food, clothing, fuel, and housing vary according to the climatic and other physical conditions of his country," he wrote. "On the other hand the number and extent of his so-called necessary wants . . . are themselves the product of historical development and depend, therefore, to a great extent on the degree of civilization of a country."[5] The subsistence minimum thus varies historically, but at any given time and place it can be identified and approximately measured. From this flows logically the definition of poverty as the condition in which those members of a society live whose incomes are insufficient to cover what is for that society and at that time the subsistence minimum.

[5] *Capital*, Volume 1, Part 2, Chapter 4, Section 3.

It is evidently reasoning like this—though obviously not derived from Marx—which underlies the work of the Bureau of Labor Statistics in defining "modest but adequate" budgets for working-class families. If we equate these budgets with the conventional subsistence minimum, we can say that all whose incomes fall below the levels so delimited are living in poverty.

By this criterion, how much poverty was there in the United States in 1959, the year to which the latest census data apply?

In that year a "modest but adequate" level of living cost a family between $5,370 (Houston) and $6,567 (Chicago) in 20 large American cities.[6] At the same time, 20 percent of the families in the country had incomes of less than $2,800 a year; another 20 percent had incomes between $2,800 and $4,800; and still another 20 percent had incomes between $4,800 and $6,500.[7]

How can we avoid the conclusion that, *by the standards of American capitalist society itself*, close to half the people are living in poverty?

3

Let us now turn to another facet of contemporary American reality. What is the state of housing in this country, where the production of steel, concrete, aluminum, glass, and other building materials is by far the largest in the world?

In the 1960 Census of Housing, of the country's 53 million occupied housing units, 8.8 million (16.6 percent) are classified as lacking private toilet or bath or running water.[8] Nearly two thirds of these dwellings are what the Census refers to as "deteriorating" or "dilapidated."[9] The median number of per-

[6] *Statistical Abstract of the United States*, 1963, p. 359.

[7] Herman P. Miller, *Rich Man, Poor Man*, New York, 1964, p. 7.

[8] Computed from U. S. Department of Commerce, Bureau of the Census, *1960 Census of Housing: Advance Reports Housing Characteristics*, April 1961.

[9] "*Deteriorating* housing needs more repair than would be provided in the course of regular maintenance. It has one or more defects of an

sons living in a housing unit is estimated to be 2.9. Since the median is the value above which half of the observations lie and below which half of the observations lie, and since the dwellings of the poor are typically more crowded than those of the better off, we can hardly take this figure as an appropriate one for estimating the number of individuals living in substandard quarters. Yet even using it, we arrive at 25.5 million people. The magnitude of the problem is certainly not overstated by one specialist in the field who wrote that "one in ten American families occupies a dilapidated dwelling; an even larger proportion of units still lack commonplace sanitary facilities."[10]

This refers to the population as a whole. The living conditions of non-whites are much worse. Of 5.1 million housing units inhabited by non-whites, some 2.3 million (45 percent) lack private toilet or bath or running water; and the proportion of deteriorating and/or dilapidated units is markedly larger than for the entire country. As the number of people per housing unit is usually much higher among non-whites than among whites, it is safe to estimate that at least half of the non-white population lacks adequate housing.

Matters appear in an even more somber light when attention is focused not on national aggregates but on cities. Writing in 1957, the editors of *Fortune* magazine reported:

> The slum problem in our great cities is worsening. Today some 17 million Americans live in dwellings which are beyond rehabilitation —decayed, dirty, rat infested, without decent heat or light or plumbing. The problem afflicts all our metropolitan cities, but it is most severe in the biggest, richest, most industrialized cities.[11]

---

intermediate nature that must be corrected if the unit is to continue to provide safe and adequate shelter. . . . *Dilapidated* housing does not provide safe and adequate shelter." *Ibid.*, p. 2.

[10] Chester Rapkin, "Some Effects of Economic Growth on the Character of Cities," *American Economic Review*, May 1956, p. 295.

[11] William H. Whyte, Jr., and others, *The Exploding Metropolis*, p. 93.

Actually, the view that conditions are worst in the biggest cities seems to be little more than a reflection of the old romantic notion that the big city is the source of all social evil. According to a more systematic study than that of the *Fortune* editors: "In very broad, general terms, it can . . . be stated that there is a configuration of blight prevalent in virtually all cities. . . . There is no correlation with population size. In short, the problem is clearly not limited to metropolitan centers. All cities, large and small, suburban city, core city, and independent city, are involved."[12]

Thus, for example, in 1950 in Robbins, Illinois, with a population of 4,766, 85.6 percent of all dwelling units were dilapidated, lacking running water, toilet, or bath; while in the metropolitan area of Indianapolis, inhabited by 551,777 people, the comparable figure was 31 percent. In Cambridge, Massachusetts (1960 population, 120,740), it was found in 1958 that "57 percent of Cambridge housing at the present time is substandard; 22 percent of the housing actually beyond rehabilitation."[13]

To be sure, in large metropolitan centers this cancerous blight is most spectacular and its impact on people's lives particularly striking.

New York is a sprawling, voracious monster of a city. It covers 315 square miles; it is crammed with some 8 million people. At least a million, a full eighth of its total population, live in packed squalor, six and ten to a room, in slum tenements so rat infested that on the average one hundred persons a year are badly chewed and, so far this year, two have been actually gnawed to death. Symbolically, perhaps there are in New York more rats than people—an estimated 9 million of them.[14]

In a more statistical vein, a *New York Times* reporter stated in 1958:

[12] Reuel Hemdahl, *Urban Renewal*, New York, 1959, p. 46.
[13] Cambridge Civic Association, *Civic Bulletin*, November 1958.
[14] Fred J. Cook and Gene Gleason, "The Shame of New York," *The Nation*, October 31, 1959.

An estimated 400,000 of the 2,250,000 dwelling units [in New York] are in slum buildings. About 282,000 of these fall short of the U. S. Census Bureau's standard housing requirements in that they lack private toilet or bath, are "cold water flats" or have no running water, or are in a bad state of physical deterioration. Another 118,-000, though meeting the Census Bureau's low structural requirements, are so overcrowded and so violate the city's health, sanitary or occupancy standards as to warrant their inclusion in any slum count.[15]

But as Edward J. Logue, the Development Administrator of New Haven, Connecticut, has remarked:

Perhaps we need fewer statistics and instead a few good old-fashioned walking tours: walks through the slums, up the stinking stairways into the overcrowded, shabby rooms; walks through the run-down commercial areas, taking care to glance above the first-floor store fronts at the dusty windows of the deserted upper floors; walks through the oil-soaked, dreary factory lofts built before the assembly line was ever heard of. The filth, the misery and the danger are all there—easy to see and, once seen, impossible to forget.[16]

The dates of the foregoing quotations—from ten to fifteen years after the war—give the lie to the widely held opinion that a major improvement in housing has taken place during the "affluent" postwar period. The opposite has been the case: whatever efforts have been undertaken by governments— federal, state, and local—to cope with the housing situation have not only failed to reach the roots of the problem; they have actually led to a further aggravation of what was already a severe national crisis. As a result, matters have gone from bad to worse: slums and blight, instead of contracting, have spread. New York, the best known case in point, in the years 1950-1958

has completed or got under way thirteen projects with federal aid. They involve clearance of 227 acres of slums and the replacement of 20,437 bad housing units with 21,820 new units in addition to such

[15] *The New York Times,* November 30, 1958.
[16] "Urban Ruin—Or Urban Renewal?" *The New York Times Magazine,* November 9, 1958.

embellishments as the Coliseum and the Lincoln Square cultural center. The net gain of 1,383 apartments is small in the face of the housing shortage. . . . The overall program . . . would redevelop a total of 906 slum acres over the next decade and provide 65,000 new apartments . . . This ambitious program would . . . clear only about one eighth of the existing slum acreage, without necessarily halting the formation of new slums.[17]

"The truth is," remarks Mr. Logue in the previously cited article, "that all that has been accomplished with the $20 or $30 million doled out to New York yearly from limited federal funds has been far from enough just to keep even in the struggle against spreading blight."

It is of the utmost importance to understand the reasons for this state of affairs. Some liberal critics of the status quo blame it on people's insufficient awareness of the prevailing situation, resulting in too skimpy appropriations of governmental funds to the so-called "public sector." Others blame the chaotic overlapping of local authorities, the nearly complete immunity of municipal governments from genuine democratic control, the resulting graft and corruption among city officials, and the notorious responsiveness to pressure groups among legislators on all levels. There is truth in all of these strictures, which yet hardly scratch the surface of the problem. To begin with, there are probably more competent, unselfish, and dedicated men and women working in city planning and housing than in most other fields of public and private endeavor. If graft and corruption continually thwart their efforts and lead them to produce results which are the opposite of what was intended, then this phenomenon has to be explained rather than simply taken for granted and attributed to the "human nature" of legislators and administrators. Moreover, it is misleading to argue that inadequate support for the public sector as a whole is a major cause of the tragic condition of housing. Quite apart from the fact that the military establishment, which belongs to the public sector, can surely not be considered to have been treated as an

[17] Charles Grutzner, *The New York Times*, November 30, 1958.

unwanted stepchild, it is far from certain that such resources as are placed at the disposal of government are so allocated as to promote the public welfare.[18] A strong case can be made for the proposition that governmental expenditures on highways—also a part of the public sector—have been excessive rather than insufficient.

Thus the key to the puzzle must be sought elsewhere. As a first step it may be useful to view the process by which so-called urban renewal projects are actually carried out. Oversimplifying but not omitting any of the important links in the chain, we can describe the process briefly as follows: The city government designates an area within its boundaries as in need of redevelopment. A Local Public Agency (LPA)—the exact nature of which varies from state to state and to a certain extent within states—buys up the land and buildings within the designated area, using the power of eminent domain and paying prices based on appraised values which in turn are determined by the existing state of the area. Existing structures are demolished, and the land is sold to developers who undertake to build up the area anew.[19] The character of the renewal project is generally worked out between the LPA and the developers, and some special conditions in addition to existing zoning regulations and building codes may be imposed upon the developers. Public housing authorities, local government agencies, hospitals, and the like, may be brought into the project; but in general both the intent and the effect of urban renewal legislation—federal, state, and local—is that deteriorating or otherwise undesirable areas should end up as valuable assets in the hands of prosperous private enterpreneurs.

Those who are versed in the "economics of graft" will easily recognize the possibilities for corruption in this scheme. First, since typically the entire map of a city is dotted with more or

[18] These subjects are discussed at length in Chapters 6 and 7 above.
[19] It is primarily in helping to carry the losses which the municipal governments incur in these transactions that federal grants-in-aid and hence a degree of federal control enter the picture.

less extensive districts of slums and blight, there is always a wide range of alternatives when it comes to choosing the next renewal area. Obviously, the responsible authorities are in a position to allow the decision to be influenced by many weighty considerations. One could be, for instance, the municipal authorities' preference for decorum and display, which would suggest giving high priority to the clearance of areas which offend the sensitivities of the town's power elite and its domestic and foreign visitors—without necessarily containing the city's worst slums. Such areas can usually be found near the choicest parts of the city; developers are likely to be interested in them; and their renewal therefore appears most attractive not only on political and public relations grounds but also because of comparative inexpensiveness to the municipal treasury. Or the initiative may come directly from real estate interests. An area may appear for any number of reasons (proximity to "good" neighborhoods, natural setting, availability of transportation facilities) to a construction firm as a good site for new housing, and its bid may convince the authorities of the urgency of designating it as a renewal-worthy slum area. In general it is clear that in making their choices those to whom the power of decision is entrusted are subject to strong pressures to take into account not merely the housing needs of the ill housed but also other interests of an entirely different kind.

Similar considerations apply to the second step, the selection of the firm to which the contract is to be awarded. Despite the emphasis placed on secret competitive bidding as the controlling principle, the evidence is overwhelming that the function of this principle is to obscure rather than define the motives for the choices which are actually made. Political connections with machine-ridden municipal administrations, outright bribery, the "cutting in" of important officials in various deals—these and similar unsavory practices are daily reported in the press as playing a major part in securing the coveted contracts. It can easily be imagined how much opportunity there is for corruption and nepotism when, in addition to the actual dollars and cents appearing on the bid, the bidding firms' credit standing, reputation, and other vaguely defined characteristics can be—and indeed probably must be—taken into account in making the final awards. If it is considered, furthermore, that the redeveloper's profits depend largely on the specific terms of the contract which have to be bargained out with the responsible officials, it is not surprising that honesty and civic responsibility are not among the outstanding virtues of those connected with urban renewal programs. For they too—to borrow a remark of Oscar Wilde's—can resist anything but temptation.

Urban renewal projects typically involve the eviction from their homes of hundreds or thousands of families, usually poor and often entirely or predominantly Negro (hence the bitter identification, among Negroes, of urban renewal with "Negro removal"). What happens to them?

Legally, Local Public Agencies are responsible for providing relocating services and finding alternative "decent, safe, and sanitary housing." But in practice, despite the well-intentioned efforts of many professional city planners and community action groups, the evicted inhabitants are all too often left to their own devices. They scurry around looking for another dwelling, double up with others, crowd entire families into single boarding-house rooms or subdivided apartments, and thus transfer to other parts of the city the slum conditions from which they have just been removed. And in the process the friendships and personal ties which in their old surroundings eased the burdens of life and provided a minimum of comfort and security in times of adversity are destroyed. "As the program now operates," concludes a comprehensive study of the subject published in 1960, "the truly indigent are not aided by urban renewal, and many of them are made more miserable by being uprooted from their familiar neighborhoods into other districts where they have no ties or affections"—and where, we may add, they usually have to pay more for less space.[20] Nor

[20] Edward Higbee, *The Squeeze: Cities Without Space*, New York, 1960, p. 83.

have matters improved much since 1960. A detailed survey of relocation studies published late in 1964 concluded, among other things:

In addition to the personal disruptions caused by forced relocation, the vast majority of displaced families incur increased housing costs, often of substantial proportions and irrespective of housing improvements or the family's financial capabilities. It appears further that those most likely to benefit by relocation are families having adequate financial and personal resources, who would probably upgrade their housing voluntarily within a short time. Those with least resources for mobility and for coping with change are most adversely affected by relocation. It is likely, too, that the reports of local public authorities on relocation understate the adverse impact of the relocation process.[21]

And now we come to the final act of the urban renewal drama. With the buildings in the development area erased and the inhabitants dispersed, the lucky contract holder embarks upon his project, the purpose of which of course is to maximize the return on his investment. The city planners working for the LPA may have succeeded in writing certain restrictions into the contract, hoping to prevent the worst abuses of private land development. But they can hope to do little more. Profits are not made by building sound, low-rent (or low-priced) housing for low-income families. They can be made only from constructing and leasing or selling luxury apartment buildings, skyscrapers for commercial use, or private houses for middle- and upper-class residents. Accordingly, "slum clearance under present rules should be labeled properly as slum relocation or

[21] Chester Hartman, "The Housing of Relocated Families," *Journal of the American Institute of Planners*, November 1964, p. 266. It should be added that the only thing which is really new about urban renewal is the name. "No matter how different the reasons may be," wrote Friedrich Engels nearly a century ago, "the result is everywhere the same: the most scandalous alleys and lanes disappear to the accompaniment of lavish self-glorification by the bourgeoisie on account of this tremendous success, but—they appear again at once somewhere else, and often in the immediate neighborhood." *The Housing Question*, in Marx and Engels, *Selected Works in Two Volumes*, Volume 1, Moscow, 1950, p. 550.

slum shifting. It is not true urban renewal. Instead of being social uplift programs as sometimes depicted, the big renewal projects in residential areas have been called land grabs aided by government subsidies and the powerful privilege of eminent domain."[22] None of this has any relation to solving the country's housing crisis—providing decent shelter for the nation's underprivileged third. The exact reverse is true. As James Marston Fitch has aptly said:

> Many . . . urban renewal projects seem . . . to be merely clusters of upper-class apartment houses. Even when these projects are not touched with scandal or the suspicion of profiteering, there must be grave doubts about the wisdom of clearing slums only to replace them with luxury housing. The pattern of giant towers standing in landscaped deserts is class architecture of the most blatant sort.[23]

What are the chances that a better showing will be made in the years ahead? Unfortunately, very poor indeed. Not that there is any lack of knowledge of what ought to be done or any deficiency of means to do it. On these points, the report of the Commission on National Goals, appointed by President Eisenhower during his second term of office, is explicit:

> There will have to be about ten million additional homes in the United States by 1970, and there ought to be up to ten million more to replace seriously substandard dwellings and the large number normally lost for other reasons. . . . Two million dwellings per year is about 40 percent higher than the record output in 1950 and over 60 percent more than the annual average for the decade. But this volume, plus rehabilitation and services, is well within the prospective capacity of the construction industry. . . . This rate of construction cannot be achieved if the market for new housing remains limited to

[22] Higbee, *The Squeeze,* p. 86. It should be noted in passing that the government subsidies referred to include not only federal grants-in-aid but also outlays on new schools, roads, parks, etc., which the municipal authorities provide at public expense for the new residents of the redevelopment areas.

[23] "In Defense of the City," an address before the Academy of Political Science at the Spring Meeting on "The Urban Problems," April 29, 1960. The Academy of Political Science, Columbia University, 1960, p. 10.

the top 30 or 40 percent of the population (less in high-density development), with a tiny volume of public housing (2½ percent of new construction in 1959) at the bottom.[24]

What this means, of course, is that the indicated rate of construction will *not* be attained. At no time in the history of capitalism have the lower-income groups provided a market for new housing, and the record of the postwar years has proved that this is as true in the era of "affluence" as it was in earlier periods of "scarcity." And there is not the slightest prospect that public housing will take on serious proportions as long as political power remains concentrated in the hands of a moneyed oligarchy. What parades as urban renewal, as we have seen, has more to do with housing the rich than the poor. What can be expected in the 1960's is a continuation of the trends of the preceding years of the Great American Celebration: more and more sumptuous residences for the upper class; better houses for the middle class; and no improvement, indeed over wide areas spreading blight and slums, for the underprivileged majority.

There was a time when it could be argued that society lacked the resources to solve the housing problem, that the deprivation of the many for the benefit of the few was the price of civilization and progress. That argument has long since lost its force. As Mrs. Wurster says in the passage just quoted, the provision of the needed houses is today "well within the prospective capacity of the construction industry." What is required now is "only" the will to use this capacity in the interests of the poor rather than in the interests of the rich. No more *talk* about the affluent society, the welfare state, wars on poverty, and the like; no more hypocritical legislation to enrich the land speculators and real estate operators; no more investiga-

[24] Catherine Bauer Wurster, "Framework for an Urban Society," *Goals for Americans: The Report of the President's Commission on National Goals,* New York, 1960, pp. 234-235. In preparing her memorandum, Mrs. Wurster was advised by a panel of outstanding authorities in the field.

tions to prove what has already been proved a hundred times—
what is now needed is genuine planning and resolute action to
rehouse the majority of the American people. Such planning
and such action, however, will never be undertaken by a government run by and for the rich, as every capitalist government
is and must be. To demand these things from a capitalist government is to demand that it cease to be capitalist.

4

Two developments which profoundly affect the quality of
present-day American society must now be considered. One is
the spectacular spread of suburbia, and the other the no less
dramatic congestion, and in some areas threatened breakdown,
of the country's transportation system. These developments are
of course closely related to the housing problem; indeed the
spread of blight and slums and the growth of suburbs are but
two sides of the same coin. As street after street and neighborhood after neighborhood fall prey to squalor, overcrowding,
and dilapidation, their relatively well-to-do inhabitants move
elsewhere. And since land values in the cities' better districts
are high, and apartments and single-family dwellings accordingly expensive, indeed out of reach of all but the truly rich,
middle-class families with children in need of living space go
out of town. As a result there has taken place since the war a
massive internal migration involving the construction of nearly
15 million one-family houses—mostly in suburban areas. This
tremendous expansion of suburban living has probably contributed more than any other factor to the emergence of the
image of American well-being in the years following the Second World War. The suburban house with its electric kitchen
and washing machine; multiple bathrooms; rumpus, family,
and TV rooms; backyard, front lawn, and two-car garage has
become the symbol and the showpiece of America's affluent
way of life. Exhibitions abroad which are calculated to impress
foreigners with the accomplishments of the United States invariably present a facsimile of some such "home" as their *pièce
de résistance*.

It would be a major error, however, to believe that all of suburbia consists of luxury housing of this kind. While "there is no doubt that suburbanization is a cream-separation process whereby the better paid middle class is floated off by itself where it spends less on public welfare and more on its own desires,"[25] there are tremendous qualitative differences both between suburbs and within suburbs. Some suburbs that sprang up in the last couple of decades or greatly expanded, in relative proximity to larger cities, consist wholly or partly of commodious, well-built houses situated on sizable lots and providing their occupants with living quarters of a kind until recently accessible only to the top layers of the ruling class. These residences are clustered in "exclusive" neighborhoods, enjoy good public services, spacious and well-equipped schools, recreation facilities, and the like. This concentration of the expensive houses of the rich produces what might be called a "secondary cream-separation process" by which the upper and upper-middle income strata remove themselves into splendid isolation from the rest of the middle class inhabiting the bulk of suburbia.

The dwellings of the latter social group, a large majority of suburban housing, are for the most part shoddily constructed tract houses erected on minimum-size lots with low life-expectancy and correspondingly high maintenance costs. The widely advertised fact that a considerable proportion of these houses are owned by their occupants should not be taken too seriously. As Higbee points out, "ownership" of a home is today "but a thin veil of modesty hiding an all too naked long-term loan."[26] And the servicing of the loan, the payment of high (and sharply regressive) real estate taxes, of bills for utilities and continually recurring repair jobs by carpenters, plumbers, roofers, and electricians claim a major share of the "owner's" income.[27] With repairs being frequently postponed and ne-

[25] Higbee, *The Squeeze*, p. 100.
[26] *Ibid.*, p. 40.
[27] See Glen H. Beyer, *Housing: A Factual Analysis*, New York, 1958, p. 163.

glected, with dilapidation setting in at an early stage, the sub-urban subdivisions and developments, crowded into small areas and provided with minimal community services, rapidly deteriorate and display a strong tendency to evolve into a suburban variety of slum and blight.

Still, as far as housing in the narrowest sense is concerned, the move to even one of the less desirable suburban locations represents a significant advance in the physical well-being of middle-class families (in particular their women and children) which were previously suffocating in dingy, stuffy, and crowded urban dwellings. Some fresh air, a few trees and plants, an additional couple of hundred square feet of floor space, and the opportunity for children to play outdoors, all constitute an improvement over the confined existence in con-gested urban communities. Yet before even this partial balance can be struck in favor of the suburbs, consideration must be given to one feature of suburban life which affects primarily the breadwinning member of the family. This is the acute and ever sharpening crisis of transportation.

The part played by the evolution of transportation facilities in the shaping of American life has been both decisive and paradoxical. Until the First World War, the settlement of out-of-town areas by people working in urban centers was more or less closely circumscribed by the structure of the railroad net-work. With the railroads limited to providing station-to-station service and readily accessible only from relatively short dis-tances on both sides of the tracks, these areas of necessity re-mained quite restricted. It was not until the massive spread of the automobile in the 1920's that remote locations could be turned into sites of large suburban settlements. And the uneven but incessant proliferation of the automobile has been the principal force promoting the spectacular expansion of sub-urbia and the equally dramatic transformation of the city itself. As we saw in Chapter 8, the number of passenger cars regis-tered in the United States rose from 8 million to 23 million during the booming decade of the '20s, increased only slightly (by a little over 4 million) in the depressed decade preceding the outbreak of the Second World War, and then leaped to 40 million in 1950 and to over 65 million in 1962.

The overall economic impact of this development has been dealt with in Chapter 8. The point to be stressed here is its immediate effect on the transportation and working and living conditions both in the cities and in the suburbs. It is in this regard that the dialectic of the process is most striking. By radically "negating" the slowness of the horse-pulled carriage as well as the rigidity of the track-bound train, the automobile made it possible to expand tremendously the city's residential hinterland. Direct motoring or combining driving a car with riding a train enabled people to move to places within a radius of as much as fifty miles from their work, with the result that in a few decades some of the most populous and economically developed parts of the country were transformed into vast areas of continuous urban and suburban settlement.

The "negation of the negation" was not long in coming. Just as when everyone follows the example of a man in a crowd who climbs on a chair to get a better view, with the result that no one can see more than before but the whole crowd has exchanged standing on firm ground for balancing on a shaky foundation, so the proliferation of the automobile is all but annulling, in many parts of the country, the initial advantage enjoyed by the early owner. The sequence of events assumes the stringency of inescapable fate. As the car- and smog- and noise-infected city becomes increasingly uninhabitable, the number of people moving out of town increases, and with them the number of automobiles which they rely on for daily commuting to work. The roads and highways become congested to the point of strangulation, the problem of parking facilities grows all but insoluble, and the automobile turns into the very opposite of what it was originally intended to be: from a means of rapid transportation into an insuperable obstacle to traffic.

Thus to the suburbanite who was originally lured out of the city by the availability of speedy and convenient transportation, going to work and returning home become increasingly time-consuming, tedious, and nerve-wracking. And "once parking fees and tolls for highways, bridges, and tunnels are added to personal expenditures for automobiles, the total amount spent by Americans for motor transportation comes up to a substantial and increasing part of their personal incomes."[28] Nor is the automobile as a source of pleasure what it used to be. With the spread of surburbia, ever longer distances need to be travelled before anything worth reaching can be reached. The best cars in the world have no place to go; the most super superhighways in the world lead nowhere.

The rapid progression of the automobile toward self-frustration involves much more than the automobile itself. In the process it has been dealing mortal blows in various directions. It forces the earmarking of an ever-increasing volume of resources to the construction of additional highways, with this entire gigantic effort being continually overtaken by the even more sweeping expansion of traffic. It necessitates a steadily growing allotment of space to parking facilities, with the result that "the more space is provided cars in cities, the greater becomes the need for use of cars, and hence for still more space for them."[29] It diverts a growing number of commuters from the railroads thus leading to more expensive and progressively worse railroad passenger service, which in turn augments the number of cars on the roads. And it undermines in the same way (and with the same effect) whatever rapid transit systems exist (or existed) in the cities, so that "many experts feel that it is too late to save public transportation in America."[30]

The outcome for people living in city and suburb is truly dramatic. The automobile—conceived, born, reared in the city and having in turn given birth to the suburb—is now devour-

[28] Jean Gottmann, *Megalopolis: The Urbanized Northeastern Seaboard of the United States,* New York, 1961, p. 679.

[29] Victor Gruen, as quoted in Jane Jacobs, *The Death and Life of Great American Cities,* New York, 1961, p. 351.

[30] Gottmann, *Megalopolis,* p. 658 n.

ing its parent and its offspring alike. Having appeared as
harbinger of a new freedom—the freedom of movement—it is
reducing mobility within cities and rendering life in the suburbs a traumatic experience for all who must commute to and
from their work. As in the case of much technological progress
under capitalism, the fruits of the automobile are turning out
to be the opposite of its immense potentialities. Instead of making the country of its emergence and mass adoption a better
place to live in, it leads thoughtful observers to remark: "It can
justifiably be said that our country in many respects is becoming less and less *habitable*. The meaning of the word 'habitable'
can be simply defined. It connotes a living place that is practical for the purposes of both work and leisure, that is healthful
and that, finally, contributes to a sense of happiness."[31]

5

"Not by bread alone. . . ." Most of those who do more than
simply take the structure and the values of monopoly capitalist
society for granted, who reflect on its *raison d'être* and seek to
defend it against socialist criticism, have lately been pivoting
their case on this society's allegedly superior capacity to satisfy
the spiritual and cultural needs of its members.[32] This is undoubtedly a weighty argument which calls for careful scrutiny.
Fortunately, the task is greatly facilitated by the fact, percep-
tively observed by the First Official United States Education
Mission to the USSR, that "the educational system of any

[31] Fairfield Osborn, in a Foreword to Edward Higbee's *The Squeeze:
Cities Without Space*.

[32] In this regard, the defense of capitalism and the attack on socialism
have made a 180° turn. Not very long ago, prominent social scientists
and economists argued that a socialist economic system based on public
ownership of the means of production and comprehensive economic
planning might be most desirable on cultural and ethical grounds but
would be completely unworkable economically: bereft of the institutions
of private property, deprived of the benefits of the profit motive, and left
without guidance by the competitive market, such an economic organization would necessarily lapse into a state of chaos. How different from the
story one reads nowadays!

people or country is one of the most brilliantly illuminating facets of a culture."[33] Bearing this in mind, we devote the remainder of this chapter to an examination of education in the United States today.

What is the state of the American educational system? Its official purposes and aims have often been stated. According to the Dethrick Report, "our system is designed to give young people the know-how to help them to excel in their best fields of endeavor as *free individuals*. We look for the creative spark in every child and try to teach our youngsters how to think independently, and how to work to develop their talents for a useful happy living in a way of life which they may choose for themselves."[34] And Dr. John W. Gardner, President of the Carnegie Corporation of New York and the Carnegie Foundation for Advancement of Teaching, who, as "one of the country's most respected educational leaders," was entrusted by the President's Commission on National Goals with writing the report on education, proclaims that "a society such as ours, dedicated to the worth of the individual, committed to the nurture of free, rational, and responsible men and women, has special reasons for valuing education. Our deepest convictions impel us to foster individual fulfillment. We wish each one to achieve the promise that is in him. We wish each one to be worthy of a free society, and capable of strengthening a free society."[35] In fact, much of the current talk about "people's capitalism," about the emergence of a classless society in the United States, is based on the view that the American educational system, by increasingly providing all citizens with equal opportunity to receive a good education, is eliminating the class barriers of old.[36]

A number of important assertions are involved here: let us

[33] *Soviet Commitment to Education*, U. S. Department of Health, Education and Welfare, Bulletin 1959 No. 16, Washington, 1959, p. 116. This document is henceforth referred to as the Dethrick Report.

[34] Dethrick Report, p. 116.

[35] *Goals for Americans*, p. 81.

[36] "A number of influential voices have been advising us that whatever social classes we ever had are now indeed withering away. We are

begin with the purely material, economic aspects of the matter. Professor Trace is right, we believe, in stressing that "the school with the newest building, the most spacious library, the most modern gymnasium, the brightest classroom, the smallest classes, the shiniest equipment, and the hottest lunch program may still be a school in which very little learning is going on."[37] Nevertheless, it is important to know what volume and proportion of available resources a society places at the disposal of its educational establishment, and to what extent these resources provide equal educational opportunity for all.

In 1960 the aggregate national outlay, public and private, on education on all levels amounted to approximately $23.1 billion. This figure has to be considered in relation to other magnitudes. For one thing, in that year this total spending on education constituted 5½ percent of the country's National Income. Now, Dr. Gardner is undoubtedly right in saying that "even if we knew exactly where Soviet education was going, the information would be of limited relevance. It is impossible to evaluate an educational system apart from the society which it both reflects and serves."[38] Nevertheless it is surely significant that the total cost of education in the Soviet Union in the late 1950's was authoritatively estimated at between 10 and 15 percent of National Income.[39] And with a per capita income at most half as high as that of the United States, this commitment to education involves a far heavier burden on the Soviet people.

But what conveys perhaps an even clearer notion of the rela-

---

being told that the people of our country have achieved unparalleled equality." Vance Packard, *The Status Seekers*, New York, 1959, p. 4. "The organization of a market capable of absorbing the machine's inexhaustible output has abolished classes and greatly reduced the differences between individuals and groups." August Heckscher, *Goals for Americans*, p. 131.

[37] A. S. Trace, Jr., *What Ivan Knows That Johnny Doesn't*, New York, 1961, p. 5.

[38] John W. Gardner, "Foreword," James B. Conant, *The American High School Today*, New York, Toronto, London, 1959, p. xi.

[39] Dethrick Report, p. 31.

tive weight accorded by our society to education is a juxtaposition of the support which it receives with the resource allocations for other purposes. Thus in 1960, the military establishment cost more than twice as much as the entire educational effort. An amount nearly equal that allotted to the military establishment went to buy the services of financial institutions, stockbrokers, real estate agents, investment counselors, and the like; and the acquisition, maintenance, and operation of automobiles came to over $37 billion—not counting some $10 billion expended for highway construction. Advertising expenditures at the same time were nearly three times as high as all the budgets of our institutions of higher learning taken together.

The United States Office of Education reports that schools are accommodating some 1.7 million pupils above their normal capacity, with the result that many classrooms are seriously overcrowded and multiple-shift operations cannot be avoided. In addition, about 2 million children attend schools that are in unsatisfactory condition. At a time when states and localities are spending less than $3 billion a year for school construction, it is estimated that no less than $6 billion will be needed annually during the 1960's to eliminate existing shortages and to keep pace with rising school enrollments.

All this is serious enough, but its effects on the educational system are minor as compared to those which result from the dismally low salaries which our society accords the men and women to whom it entrusts the education of its youth. In 1957, the median annual rate of pay for full-time teachers in urban public schools was $4,324. Since the average rate of pay is reported to have increased by $424 between 1957 and 1959,[40] and since it is likely that a similar increase took place during the next two years, it would seem probable that by 1961 the median salary had risen to somewhere around $5,000.[41] Thus

[40] Helene T. Lesansky, "Salaries of City Public School Teachers, 1957-1959," United States Department of Labor, Bureau of Labor Statistics, *Monthly Labor Review*, March 1961, pp. 259 ff.

[41] These figures refer to urban teachers; the salary level of rural teachers is much lower.

even after the post-Sputnik "leap forward" of instructional salaries, one half of the country's teachers received less, and at least one third much less, than what could be considered a living wage.

Aggregative information on both school facilities and teachers' salaries of course conceals important regional and social differentials. Taking 80 percent of the inadequate average expenditure per pupil in elementary and secondary public schools ($341 in 1958) as a benchmark, the Committee for Economic Development found that "'eleven states fell below this 80 percent floor in 1957-58—most of them far below it. The states are Mississippi, Alabama, Arkansas, Tennessee, Kentucky, South Carolina, North Carolina, Georgia, West Virginia, Virginia, Maine. The eleven states had 22 percent of the nation's public school enrollment."[42]

The social differentiation within the educational system is perhaps even more striking than the regional differentiation, and it flatly contradicts all the talk about the "classlessness" of our society and the equality of opportunity which it is supposed to provide for all. The moneyed oligarchy which sits on top of the social pyramid does not, for the most part, send its boys and girls to public schools at all, but rather to exclusive private institutions. The list of these private schools, like the list of the wealthy families which patronize them, is relatively short: their total student body is some 60,000 to 70,000. Their facilities are usually first rate, their staffs carefully selected and relatively well paid—the average expenditure per student is estimated to be well above $1,000 per year[43]—and their grad-

[42] Ralph Lazarus, *We Can Have Better Schools*, Committee for Economic Development, New York, 1960, p. 14. It should be noted that a number of other states such as Idaho, Hawaii, Oklahoma, Utah, and Florida are not much above the miserable standards of the Deep South where Mississippi brings up the rear with an annual outlay of $174 per pupil.

[43] Boarding schools providing tuition, room, and board cost approximately $2,500 per academic year, not counting clothing expenses, pocket money, and fares.

uates (particularly boys) usually continue their education in one of the ranking private colleges. The social function of these schools and colleges is of the utmost importance. As Mills has said, "If one had to choose one clue to the national unity of the upper social classes in America today, it would best be the really exclusive boarding school for girls and prep school for boys."[44]

But for the bourgeoisie as a whole, the large stratum of the middle class which for one reason or another does not wish or cannot afford to send its youngsters to private schools, the "cream separation process" takes place within the public school system itself. In the words of a distinguished educator, "there is concrete evidence which demonstrates beyond reasonable doubt that our public-school system has rejected its role of facilitating social mobility and has become in fact an instrument of social and economic class distinction in American society."[45] Indeed, as Professor Sexton shows in her remarkable book, "in the schools of modern America we still find that children from 'comfortless cabins,' or to shift time and locale, from 'urban slums' cannot compete with the children of the elite. This is true not necessarily because of any deficiency of talent or ability but because society being dominated by elites has given their children a head start and, following the lead as always, the schools have compounded the advantage by providing them with superior educational services of every conceivable variety."[46]

Let us have a look at a few ingredients of this educational mix, as yet confining attention exclusively to the economic aspects of the problem. When it comes to aggregate expenditures, we can do no better than reproduce the relevant passage from a recent authoritative report:

---

[44] C. Wright Mills, *The Power Elite*, p. 64.
[45] Kenneth B. Clark's Foreword to Patricia Cayo Sexton, *Education and Income: Inequalities of Opportunities in Our Public Schools,* New York, 1961, p. ix.
[46] *Ibid.,* p. xvii.

The contrast in money available to the schools in a wealthy suburb and to the schools in a large city jolts one's notions of the meaning of equality of opportunity. The pedagogic tasks which confront the teachers in the slum schools are far more difficult than those which their colleagues in the wealthy suburbs face. Yet the expenditure per pupil in the wealthy suburban school is as high as $1,000 per year. The expenditure in a big city school is less than half that amount. An even more significant contrast is provided by looking at school facilities and noting the size of the professional staff. In the suburb there is likely to be a spacious modern school staffed by as many as 70 professionals per 1,000 pupils; in the slum one finds a crowded, often dilapidated and unattractive school staffed by 40 or fewer professionals per 1,000 pupils.[47]

Other inequalities are no less significant. Reporting on her investigations in "one of the largest cities in the country and by many standards the most prosperous," Professor Sexton presents a vast body of illuminating information. In the lower-income group, about one half of all schools have no proper facilities for scientific studies; only 2 percent of the schools in the upper-income bracket suffer from such a deficiency. Whatever may be the general level of qualification and competence of American teachers—and we shall return to this presently—apprentice and substitute teachers are certainly not the best qualified and most experienced. And yet it is precisely in the lower-income half of the schools, where the need for well trained and experienced teachers is highest, that one finds that the percentage of classes taught by so-called ESRP's (Emergency Substitute in Regular Position) is more than three times greater than in the schools catering to upper-income pupils. Similarly, medical care at school is provided most unevenly. Although rheumatic fever, strep throat, diphtheria are considerably more frequent among lower-income children than among those from well-to-do families, the pupils of lower-income background receive markedly less medical attention than those attending upper-income schools. According to Professor Sexton:

[47] James Bryant Conant, *Slums and Suburbs: A Commentary on Schools in Metropolitan Areas*, New York, Toronto, London, 1961, p. 3.

What may be the most flagrant example of unequally distributed school services . . . is to be found in the free-lunch program. . . . In the lowest-income group, among children who are likely to be in greatest need of balanced, wholesome meals at lunchtime and who are most likely to be undernourished and ailing, almost half (42 percent) go to schools where free meals and free milk are not available. . . . In addition to being denied *free* lunches where need is obvious, children attending schools without lunchrooms are also denied the subsidies that are being put into the *paid* lunch program. Children in upper-income schools, where hot lunches are usually provided, can buy lunches as cheaply as can be made for them at home. In addition, these children are being fed wholesome, balanced meals; they are saved the time and inconvenience of going home for lunch. . . . In low-income areas, where members often work and are not home at lunchtime, children may not eat "lunch" at all.[48]

This account refers to elementary schools. When it comes to high schools, which play a major part in determining the adolescent's future life, the situation is more complex and even more dramatic. Since high schools are generally much larger than elementary schools and draw their pupils from wider geographical areas, they tend to include a more representative cross section of the community. This is less true of cities, however, where there is a need for more than one high school. Here the differentiation and discrimination pattern is similar to that prevailing in elementary schools. In such places, "the districts . . . are selective by social class, and every city has its neighborhoods—or at least suburbs—where two-thirds or more of the kids are college-bound. . . . All larger cities also run district high schools in wretched slums, where no more than a handful of the kids have even considered the possibility of college education, and the academic options are severely restricted."[49] The purely material differences between those high schools serving upper- and lower-income groups respectively are no less striking than in the case of elementary schools. They can be seen in the quality and safety of the buildings, in the avail-

[48] Sexton, *Education and Income,* pp. 134-135.
[49] Martin Mayer, *The Schools,* New York, 1961, pp. 323-324.

ability of various facilities, in the selection of teachers, as well as in the distribution of scholastic awards and scholarships of all kinds.

In smaller school districts which maintain only one high school catering to the needs of an entire town plus possibly some outlying suburban or rural settlements, the discriminatory process unfolds within the school itself. "In some ways," writes Professor Sexton, "high schools reveal the operation of the social class system better than elementary schools do. . . . All elementary-school children, regardless of origins and aspirations, study much the same subjects and proceed through the same curriculum. It is only at the high-school level that they begin to go their separate ways. In the high schools students are very methodically sorted out into various categories —like mail in a post office—depending on the school's appraisal of their destination in life."[50] As a result of this sorting, students get assigned to one of the three typically available curricula or, as they are frequently called, "tracks" or "lanes": college-preparatory, general, and vocational. "Placement in these curricula may determine the student's entire future life. If a student is placed, for example, in a general or vocational curriculum (at ages ranging from twelve to fourteen), he will have great difficulty qualifying for college entry or remaining in college should he be admitted. His chances therefore, of moving into professional or highly skilled jobs will be similarly limited."[51]

The relation between the social class into which the pupil is born and the high school track or lane into which he is shunted by school administrators, counselors, and teachers is thoroughly explored in Arthur B. Hollingshead's classic study of "Elmtown," which he describes as a "typical Middle Western community."[52] The results of his research leave no room for doubt that upper-class pupils have an incomparably better

[50] Sexton, *Education and Income*, p. 152.
[51] *Ibid*.
[52] *Elmtown's Youth: The Impact of Social Classes on Adolescents*.

chance of being admitted to and succeeding in the college-preparatory curriculum than the children of lower-income families. Quite apart from the fact that the former group is in general better looked after at home and therefore better able to fulfill the school requirements, every possible privilege and favor facilitates the school career of a boy or girl from a "good family." Hollingshead cites instance after instance of such discriminatory treatment. Thus

it seems reasonable to assume that, if a teacher recognizes that a pupil is doing poor work or failing work, she will give him aid out of class, but what seems reasonable is not what happens; on the contrary, the students reported for poor and failing work are not listed as having received help outside of class. For instance, 27 percent of the class II's were reported at one time or another for poor or failing work, and 92 percent of the class V's; the other classes were distributed between these extremes; conversely, 63 percent of the class II's received aid outside of class, but only 8 percent of the class V's.[53]

What is perhaps even more significant is that even in respect to the enforcement of discipline and the grading of school work —operations which one would expect to find conducted with the greatest impartiality—both administrators and teachers tend to apply standards which vary according to the class position of the students. "It is believed widely in classes IV and V," Hollingshead reports, "and to a somewhat lesser extent in class III, that the grades a student receives are determined by the position of his parents in the social structure rather than by his ability or his industriousness. This belief is not without foundation, as is generally the case when one encounters a persistent belief illustrated by one story after another, over a number of years of questionable grading practices in relation to children of prominent families."[54] Hollingshead concludes:

[53] *Ibid.*, p. 179. In Hollingshead's classification class I is the socially highest, class V the lowest.

[54] *Ibid.*, p. 181. See also the significant discussion of "Discipline," pp. 185-192.

It is clear that, on the average, the higher an adolescent's class position, the better his chances are to receive high grades. Conversely, the lower one's position in the prestige structure, the more likely the adolescent is to receive low grades. To be sure, a real differential factor in the home environment may be conditioning the child's responses to the school situation in each class, but this does not invalidate the relationship between class and grade.[55]

These facts are of course well known to people with practical experience in the educational system. But far from arousing indignation, they are usually accepted as proof of the "obvious" —that upper-class students are more intelligent and academically talented than their lower-class schoolmates. What is really proved is something quite different: that the ruling class under monopoly capitalism has been successful, like earlier ruling classes, in instilling into the minds of the ruled the belief that the wealth and privileges of the few are based on natural, inborn superiority. Since this belief runs directly counter to the most hallowed of all articles of the American Creed—that all men are created equal—it needs to be carefully nurtured and buttressed. This assignment has been, so to speak, handed to the public school system which has cheerfully accepted it and efficiently carried it out. And for this purpose no weapon has been so widely and effectively utilized as the so-called IQ test. "Just as the right to rule was given to kings by God," writes Professor Sexton, "so is the right to rule given to upper classes by 'nature' and by virtue of what they presume to be their superior IQ's."[56]

Yet these tests do not actually measure innate ability. In the words of one student of the problem:

The typical intelligence test includes questions calling for the recall of information. Some questions call for arithmetic reasoning, others call for the understanding of spatial relationships. Many of the questions test the extent of the child's vocabulary. Printed tests, which the child must read, inevitably measure his skill in reading. Now it is obvious that recall of information, arithmetic reasoning,

[55] *Ibid.*, p. 173.
[56] Sexton, *Education and Income,* p. 51.

understanding of spatial relationships, extent of vocabulary, and skill in reading are all products of *learning*. Every intelligence test therefore measures how much the child has learned. But how much a child learns depends in part on how much opportunity he has had to learn. . . . A major fact about children . . . is that their environments *are not the same*. They have not all had the same experiences, and they have not all had the same opportunities to learn.[57]

Many similar statements could be cited from authorities in the United States, Britain, and other countries. Indeed, the consensus is by now overwhelming that "there is no doubt whatever about the 'class-bias' displayed by intelligence-test scores, from Binet to the present, and at both ends of the range."[58]

With the class bias of IQ and similar tests having thus been demonstrated, their protagonists defend them nonetheless on pragmatic grounds. Granting the inability of the tests to establish anything concerning innate capacities, they insist on their usefulness and desirability for the prediction of the pupil's future academic career. This undoubtedly is a cogent argument, which deserves to be taken seriously. Indeed, it comes much closer to the nub of the matter than the pleas of liberal school reformers who would seek to raise even the lowest test scores by skillful teaching, or the more radical-sounding demand of others that the tests be entirely abolished. For measuring, as they do, socio-economic background rather than natural endowments, and serving, as they also do, to forecast more or less reliably the student's school achievements, the test scores assume a significance which transcends by far the realm of the educational system. They constitute in fact eloquent testimonials to the degree of socio-economic inequality and discrimination in a profoundly class-split society. Complaining about the "unfairness" of the tests, demanding remedial measures within the educational system to improve their outcome, or

[57] Irving Adler, *What We Want of Our Schools: Plain Talk on Education from Theory to Budgets,* New York, 1957, pp. 71-72.

[58] Mayer, *The Schools,* p. 107.

calling for their outright discontinuation is like seeking to improve or destroy a camera because it turns out pictures of an ugly reality. To be sure, the reality which the IQ and kindred scores depict is not the reality of differing natural, innate human capacities, gifts, and potentialities. To have exposed as a fallacy this claim of Binet, Terman, and others is undoubtedly an important contribution of the modern "anti-IQ-test" movement. To go beyond it, however, and to deny that the test scores mirror more or less adequately the reality of human capacities, gifts, and opportunities *within* the prevailing socio-economic order amounts to substituting one fallacy for another, misses the crux of the problem, and inevitably leads to a superficial meliorism as a way of dealing with a profound human predicament the roots of which reach as deep as those of the capitalist system itself.[59]

This predicament, it is important to understand, affects not only the low-IQ children of the underprivileged classes but also the young of the upper strata themselves. It relates to the quality of the education which the schools and colleges purvey to all American youth, both privileged and underprivileged. The justified and indeed imperative insistence on the doubly tragic condition of those who are discriminated against should not be allowed to promote by implication the notion that what the upper classes receive is *good* education.

Nothing could be further from the truth. If the object of an educational system—to paraphrase the excellent statement of Robert Maynard Hutchins—should be to help people develop their highest powers, to become as intelligent as they can,[60]

[59] A sweeping denial of the validity and usefulness of IQ tests can also lead to a misapprehension of their potential function in a rational socialist society. For it is in such a society, in which the socio-economic opportunities for learning become at least approximately equal, that investigations of innate ability by means of tests of the IQ type can be meaningfully undertaken. Such estimates may then, but only then, become useful tools, facilitating a more appropriate organization of the educational process and providing each child with a better chance to follow his or her natural interests and propensities.

[60] Robert M. Hutchins, *The Higher Learning in America*, New

and if "the only way to develop the abilities of a child up to the limits of his powers is to strive constantly to develop his powers beyond the limits of his present abilities,"[61] then the schools of this country today perform nearly the opposite of their proper task. This can be seen on all levels of the educational system—elementary, secondary, college, university— and "one thing only prevents our established system of education from crumbling into the dust and ashes of the minds that devised it, and that is the stubborn virtue of individual teachers."[62] The evidence for this is so overwhelming that the difficulty lies not in assembling it but in limiting a brief account to the indispensable minimum.

As far as the elementary level is concerned, a recently published survey reports that 35 percent of all American youth are seriously retarded in reading, while an additional 40 percent are not reading as well as they might. The following is described as typical of the situation in the country's elementary schools: The first-grade pre-primer contains only 15 different words. A second pre-primer presents only 26 additional words, to be followed by a primer with 80 new words and a reader with 114 further words. Thus the successful beginning reader knows 235 different words, and a nine-year old at the end of the third grade "knows" or rather recognizes 1,342 words. These words are combined again and again to make up the texts, which thus involve endless and tedious repetition which cannot help stunting the child's interest in and desire for further reading.[63] To be sure, some additional vocabulary is acquired by some pupils at some schools by the age of 9; but this is the standard which prevails in elementary instruction.

Haven and London, 1962. See especially the Preface to the paperbound edition.

[61] Adler, *What We Want of Our Schools,* p. 91.

[62] Eric Linklater, *Laxdale Hall,* as quoted in Albert Lynd, *Quackery in the Public Schools,* New York, 1953, p. x.

[63] See Charles C. Walcutt, ed., *Tomorrow's Illiterates: The State of Reading Instruction Today,* Boston, 1961, passim.

Lest it be thought that this standard is dictated by the "natural order of things," and kept down by the innate abilities of children in general, it is instructive to look at the comparable practice in the schools of the Soviet Union. This is facilitated by the study of Trace.[64] Whereas, to repeat, the American child at the end of the third grade is familiar with fewer than 1,500 words, the Soviet third-grade reader *Rodnaya Rech* (Native Language) works with approximately 8,000 words; and whereas the fourth-grade American reader includes 532 words not taught in the preceding books, the corresponding Soviet textbook has a vocabulary of approximately 10,000 words, that is, adds about 2,000 words to those employed in the preceding reader.

The picture is the same if we turn from vocabulary—the simplest yardstick for the measurement of achievement in reading—to the content of what our elementary school children are given to read. In this country, "The selections in elementary school readers for the early grades deal chiefly with cardboard boys and girls who participate in trivial episodes involving mommies and daddies, baby sitters and visiting aunts, grandfathers who own farms, mailmen, corner cops and corner grocers, and other assorted people in a hypothetical and sterilized community." And the authors of the texts which are confined to an intellectual pauper's language are either the compilers of the readers themselves or "unimaginative or unknown children's writers who know all about the rules of vocabulary control." Comparable Soviet readers, on the other hand, consist to a preponderant extent of writings (prose and poetry) by such outstanding Russian authors as Tolstoy, Turgenev, Pushkin, Korolenko, Nekrasov, Gorky, and others. Summing up, Trace writes: "I should like very much to be able to say that there is available among American basal readers a series with selections even remotely comparable in difficulty, in literary quality, and in informational value to those in the

[64] *What Ivan Knows That Johnny Doesn't*, passim; for the information presented in the text, see in particular pp. 30-51.

Rodnaya Rech readers, but I know of none. About the best one can say of these basal readers is that some are worse than others; but not much worse, because they are all bad." Thus, far from making the child as intelligent as he can be, far from striving constantly to develop his powers beyond the limits of his present ability, what our elementary schools are "working on" is to compress the child's intellect to "an oversimplified, exclusively middle-class idealization, almost always unrelated to real life"[65]—or, in Mortimer Smith's brutal but apt expression, to "diminish the child's mind."

So much for the elementary schools. As we climb the ladder to higher levels, the situation becomes perhaps somewhat more complex but by no means better. To be sure, it constitutes a major achievement under advanced capitalism that child labor has been greatly curtailed, if not entirely eliminated, and that nearly all children under 14, and over 90 percent of adolescents in the 14-to-17 age group are enrolled in school. The feasibility of such a nearly comprehensive school coverage indicates, as it were, the existing potentialities of education, and provides a concrete demonstration of what could be accomplished in a rationally ordered society. As matters stand, however, these statistics tend to convey an impression which is most deceptive. They suggest that educational accomplishment can be measured in quantitative terms; that the number of pupils enrolled, the number of years of schooling, and the number of hours of instruction per week provide meaningful indices of the magnitude and achievements of the educational effort.

And yet when it comes to what is crucial, the quality of education, the following statement summarizes probably as well as any the existing state of affairs:

There is a sort of Gresham's Law at work in American education. Levels are dropping off along the line. An average mark of 85 percent today is equivalent to the bare average passing mark of 60 percent a generation ago—indicative of the general downgrading of state requirements for the high-school diploma. Increasingly, the

[65] *Ibid.*, pp. 21, 28, and 29.

high schools must teach elementary subjects because the elementary schools have failed to do so. The colleges must give remedial courses in high school—sometimes even elementary school—subjects because freshman cannot spell, write grammatically, express themselves, or . . . because so many of them are mathematical illiterates. Each year we take pleasure in the greater number of American children going to school longer and reaching higher levels of education. But simultaneously the higher levels become lower so we end up where we began a hundred years ago—with an elementary-vocation education for the majority and a poor college-preparatory course for a minority of students.[66]

This finding is corroborated by so many different and independent surveys and studies that its accuracy cannot be doubted. Thus in 1960, Project Talent, a vast national testing program involving 450,000 students, showed that 99 percent of all high school students cannot write a five-minute theme without mistakes in English. William A. Gorham, the supervisor of the test, concluded that the results are "a sad commentary on our high school products."[67] Nor is this malaise confined to English. In the words of the Council for Basic Education:

How can we expect the high school student to master foreign languages if he has never learned in elementary school the rudiments of the structure of his own language? How can he understand history if he has no sense of chronological progression of events; or understand what is happening in other countries if he has no sense of geographical significance or location? How can he understand higher mathematics or the new physics if arithmetic has been taught primarily for its social utility, as something that comes in handy when you want to make change or fill out your income tax? Above all, how can he understand and enjoy good books, or express himself with simple clarity in writing, if he has never learned to read properly or how to write?[68]

At the same time the curricula of high schools are stuffed

[66] H. G. Rickover, *Education and Freedom,* New York, 1959, p. 145.
[67] Council for Basic Education, *Bulletin,* December 1960, p. 8.
[68] Council for Basic Education, *Bulletin,* January 1960, p. 8.

with courses in photography, woodshop, adjustment to family living, how to deal with the problem of going steady, dating, typing, speech, driving, retail selling, and so forth and so on. As Hutchins put it with characteristic pithiness, "American educational standards have collapsed . . . and specialism, vocationalism and triviality have taken over."[69]

It would take us too far afield to try to discuss in detail the kind of education provided by colleges and universities. What Thorstein Veblen observed some forty-five years ago applies with multiplied force to the present: "Whatever may have been true for the earlier time, when the American college first grew up and flourished, it is beyond question that the under-graduate department which takes the place of the college today cannot be rated as an institution of the higher learning."[70] This is recognized by former President Conant of Harvard, who states that "a bachelor's degree has long since lost any meaning as a mark of scholastic attainment or the completion of a course of formal academic training."[71] The truth is that the colleges have too often turned into mere extensions of high schools, partly seeking to make up for the most glaring deficiencies of elementary and secondary education, and partly providing their clients with four more years of the same. To some extent this is undoubtedly due, as noted by the education editor of the *New York Times,* to the fact that "even the educational policies and power of the universities are, in the last analysis, at the mercy of the elementary and high schools."[72] More significant, however, is the fact that the forces which determine the quality of our educational system are as actively at work on the college level as they are in the

[69] Hutchins, *The Higher Learning in America,* p. xiii.

[70] Thorstein Veblen, *The Higher Learning in America: A Memorandum on the Conduct of Universities by Business Men,* New York, 1918; cited from the third printing, Stanford, California, 1954, p. 24.

[71] James Bryant Conant, *The American High School Today: A First Report to Interested Citizens,* New York, Toronto, London, 1959, p. 6.

[72] Fred M. Hechinger, *The Big Red Schoolhouse,* Garden City, New York, 1962, p. 17.

lower stories of the structure. As a result, to quote a recent monumental study of American higher learning, "a close look at the college-educated people in the United States is enough to dispel any notion that our institutions of higher learning are doing a good job of liberal education."[73]

Nor should this be a cause for wonderment. In most colleges of the country, good and bad alike, the first half of the curriculum—usually referred to as the lower division, or the program of general studies—is devoted to what by all reasonable standards should properly constitute high school or even elementary school subjects. As can be imagined, this effort is almost inevitably doomed to failure. It is a labor of Sisyphus to try to undo in two academic years the habits of thought, the attitude toward intellectual work, and the mode of study acquired in the course of twelve years of elementary and secondary schooling. That such is actually the case can be seen on all sides. As far as English is concerned, a vast proportion of college graduates remain not only ignorant of the contents, trends, and meaning of English and American literature (not to speak of world literature), but also incapable of stylistically and orthographically acceptable writing.[74] And the situation is particularly striking, and fatal, in an area which must certainly be regarded as the backbone of all humanist education: history. Here a one-year cram course "covering" the entire time span from prehistoric man to the latest presidential election is superimposed on such historical bits and pieces as may have

[73] Nevitt Sanford, ed., *The American College: A Psychological and Social Interpretation of the Higher Learning,* New York, London, 1962, p. 10.

[74] "Without the least exaggeration I can say that, as a teacher of graduate students in English, there is not one single assumption I can make about either knowledge or skill already acquired. I cannot assume a single book read by everyone in my class; I cannot assume knowledge of the simplest Bible story or myth or fairy tale or piece of children's literature." William Riley Parker, Professor of English, Indiana University, as quoted in Council for Basic Education, *Bulletin,* December 1961, p. 10.

been acquired in the hodge-podge courses called "social studies" taught in elementary and secondary schools. Considering that these survey courses on the History of Western Civilization, or whatever similar title they may happen to be listed under, are customarily taught by poorly qualified, inexperienced teaching assistants and instructors—who indeed could be really well qualified for an assignment of this kind?—and are based on inevitably pedestrian textbooks and voluminous compendia comprising a few assorted pages by every "great" author from Socrates to Toynbee, the question may well be asked whether a better way could possibly be devised to destroy in the student any interest in history and any capacity for historical thought? And the picture is hardly improved by throwing into the "general studies" hopper a couple of elementary courses providing a smattering of ignorance in social or natural sciences. What "education" of this kind conveys to its recipients is a pretense of knowledge and understanding where none actually exists, a pretense which readily develops into an effective bar to learning and thus becomes more destructive than ignorance itself.

The transition from the lower to the upper division of the college involves a certain break. The "make-up" program, to counter the inadequacy of the pre-college education, is supposed to be completed in the first two years; the function of the next two is more diversified. A sizable proportion of future college graduates—probably as many as a third—continue through the upper division without any specific occupational objective. Coming for the most part from upper- and middle-class families, "too old to play and too young to work," the boys from this group seek the bachelor's degree as an indispensable mark of social status and as a prerequisite for any kind of white collar employment in the business world, while to the girls attendance at college is the best avenue to a suitable marriage. Not interested in any particular field of specialization, most of these students tend to choose what campus opinion considers to be "cinch majors," and to limit their exertions to whatever minimum may be required to secure gentlemen's passing grades. Interspersed with various athletic and social activities, this upper division program consisting of a number of courses the contents of which are banished from the student's mind immediately upon completion of the final examination, and calling for very little reading (frequently nothing but textbooks), adds little to what has already been acquired. This is true for the very best colleges in the country; what is achieved in the overwhelming majority is markedly less. And to all of them Hutchins' remark applies: "One of the easiest things in the world is to assemble a list of hilarious courses offered in the colleges and universities of the United States. Such courses reflect the total lack of coherent, rational purpose in these institutions."[75]

It could perhaps be argued that in the case of this "gentleman" third of the student population all this does not much matter—the students are interested only in the bachelor's degree and nothing else. But the situation becomes truly dramatic when what amounts to approximately another third of the college graduates are considered: those who go through college in order to embark upon the difficult and responsible career of teaching and/or educational administration in the elementary and secondary schools. What kind of education do our educators get? A harsh answer to this question was given by Lawrence A. Kimpton during his tenure as Chancellor of the University of Chicago: "The schools of education that train teachers and generate the curriculum for the secondary schools are upon the whole a pretty shabby lot, very often divorced from the main body of the university and with dubious standards and frail contents."[76] And another observer sums up his extensive studies of our teachers' education by stating that "there is increasing evidence to show that the teacher-training institutions—which have in the words of the Harvard Report,

[75] Hutchins, *The Higher Learning in America,* p. xiii.
[76] Quoted in Council for Basic Education, *Bulletin,* February 1960, p. 5.

'taught everything except the indispensable thing, the love of knowledge'—are providing us with teachers who are our most poorly educated citizens."[77] This finding is corroborated by a series of tests and surveys ranking different college departments by the general intelligence of the students who choose them as fields of concentration. All of these studies show education to be at bottom of the distribution. "An obvious explanation for this ordering is that it reflects the varying difficulty of the subjects as they are usually taught at the undergraduate level. The order has, in fact, been found to be substantially correlated with the reputations for difficulty that these fields enjoy among undergraduate students."[78] Nor could it be otherwise: the curriculum of an aspiring teacher or school administrator is filled with an entire gamut of courses the intellectual vacuity, triviality, and tedium of which are proverbial. Instruction in subject matter cultivates pretentious ignorance, "like the summer course in one teachers' college which deals with World Literature from ancient times to the twentieth century —all in thirty days."[79] And the preoccupation with how to teach pushes all concern with what to teach into the background. The compulsion to take these assorted courses, "workshops," and seminars in order to be eligible for certification assures the schools of education of a captive audience, and "in this fact friendly critics see tendencies toward what would promptly be stamped as a crass and vulgar racketeering in less humane activities."[80]

The nature and quality of education for educators can be

[77] Mortimer Smith, *The Diminished Mind: A Study of Planned Mediocrity in Our Public Schools*, Chicago, 1954, p. 87.

[78] Carl Bereiter and Mervin B. Freedman, "Fields of Study and the People in Them," in Nevitt Sanford, ed., *The American College*, p. 564.

[79] Mortimer Smith, *The Diminished Mind*, p. 93.

[80] Edgar W. Knight, "The Obligation of Professional Education to the Schools," *School and Society*, October 6, 1951 (as quoted in Smith, *The Diminished Mind*, pp. 91-92, where the information is supplied that the writer was until his death in 1953 Kenan Professor of Educational History at the University of North Carolina).

assessed by getting an idea of the basis on which the highest educational degrees are conferred. Thus the country's leading school of education, Teachers' College of Columbia University, awarded doctorates of education to candidates who presented dissertations on the following topics:

The Cooperative Selection of School Furniture to Serve the Kindergarten through Third Grade Program in the Garden City Public Schools.

A Guide for Initiating School Camping with Special Reference to Bronxville.

A Suggested Methodology to Formulate a Composite Ideal Image of the Professional Nurse.

A History of Competitive Rowing in Colleges and Universities of the United States of America.

At Michigan State University, dissertations submitted in fulfillment of the requirements for the highest degree in education included the following:

An Evaluation of Thirteen Brands of Football Helmets on the Basis of Certain Impact Measures.

An Investigation of Various Methods Used in Football-Helmet Evaluation.

A Study of the Personality Differences Between a Group of Women Who Had Participated in Sewing Classes in an Adult Education Program and a Group of Their Friends and Neighbors Who Had Not Participated in Any Adult Education Activities.

The University of North Dakota conferred its highest degree in education for a thesis entitled *Selected Major Issues in Teaching First-year Typewriting;* while the weighty purpose of a doctoral study at the University of Indiana was "to determine what influence the teachers' and pupils' use of laughter and smiling may have upon teacher effectiveness."[81]

---

[81] Council for Basic Education, *Bulletin,* January, March, November, 1960; May, December, 1961. The United States cultural impact on the "free world" is suggested by the following observation: "We saw a not irrelevant UPI dispatch the other day from Japan, which country has . . .

It might be objected that these cases are deplorable exceptions. Unfortunately, such an objection is unwarranted. For one thing, the utterly inane listings in the announcements of courses offered, and of dissertations accepted, by schools of education could be readily multiplied. But even more important is the fact that it is often precisely what Ricardo called the "strong case" and what in common parlance is likely to be dismissed as "exaggeration" that throws the most light on a phenomenon under investigation. The strong case, the exaggeration, calls attention to underlying conditions which might otherwise go unnoticed. And so it is here: they enable us to see the school of education as what it is, "the intellectual slum of the campus and a legitimate target for faculty jokes."[82]

Little needs to be said about the instruction received in the upper division of college by the nearly 15 percent of the student body who concentrate in the field of "business and commerce." Providing training in accounting, marketing, advertising, typewriting, and similar subjects, this is a strictly vocational course which has no connection with humanist education and which in the view of many has no place in the curriculum of a liberal arts college. It is, in fact, offered primarily by state and municipally supported institutions, with the more reputable private institutions priding themselves on not stooping to programs of this kind.[83] These business and commerce branches of the colleges may or may not serve as useful stepping stones to employment in business—there is consider-

---

been liberally supplied with American guidance. Apparently they have learned their lessons well, for the newspaper account stated that Assistant Professor Tosie Otsuka of Shimane University has just received her doctor's degree with a thesis on the subject of Dish Washing." *Ibid.*, March 1961.

[82] *Ibid.*, February 1960, p. 5.

[83] With somewhat less than full consistency, these same elite educational establishments maintain graduate schools of business. Despite the fact that their curricula have in recent years been fancied up by inclusion of courses in economic theory, statistics, "managerial science," and the like, their *raison d'être* within the framework of a university is hardly less dubious than that of their undergraduate counterparts in the colleges.

able doubt on the point, even among businessmen—but by no stretch of the imagination can it be maintained that the information and skills which they purvey widen the horizons or enhance the intellectual powers of their students.

The remaining one sixth or so of college students spend their junior and senior years on pre-professional subjects of various kinds. In the case of many, their training terminates with a bachelor's degree in engineering, applied science, agronomy, and the like. Others go on to graduate studies in the professional schools (law, medicine, etc.) or in the graduate schools of arts and sciences where for the most part they prepare themselves to become teachers and researchers in colleges and universities or to assume research or administrative posts in government agencies, private foundations, and industrial laboratories. Whatever the goal of their studies in the junior and senior years, the instruction received by this segment of the student body is considered by experts in the various fields to be fair to excellent depending on the institution in question. Here, it is generally conceded, American education is at its best.

And yet one cannot but have strong reservations about the quality of the education received even by this privileged group. There is an increasing tendency for specialization to start early and to pre-empt more and more of the student's time and energy. Jibes about specialists who know more and more about less and less strike close to home, and laments over the deepening gulf that separates the sciences from the humanities are all too well founded. As is inevitable within the general framework of monopoly capitalism, even the very best products of the educational system tend to be "science barbarians" and "high-IQ imbeciles." This is not to say that the American educational system does not turn out thoughtful and truly educated people. Their number is, however, distressingly small, and they attain a level of intellectual excellence not because but in spite of the educational system, not as a result of but in a bitter struggle with the prevailing cultural and intellectual climate. That they succeed testifies that even under the most adverse circumstances mankind's striving for knowledge and understanding cannot be entirely thwarted. Their existence under present conditions provides a hint of what a good educational system could accomplish in a good society.

In sum, the state of education is dismal for the nation as a whole. Few of those who complete twelve years of public education emerge as more than half-way literate and educated—not to speak of the large proportion of the dropouts who never graduate from high school. Nor is it significantly different with the luckier ones who are able to make their way up to and through college. At best a tiny minority of college students receive what can truly be considered a rational and rigorous humanist education, and there is "much evidence that colleges rarely succeed in bringing about important changes in attitudes or values and that the main effect of four years of college is to make students more like one another."[84] As Hutchins inquires on the basis of rich experience and extensive study: "Why are the graduates of the great universities indistinguishable, even by their grammar, from the mass of the population who have never had their advantages? Their grammar may perhaps be accounted for by the deficiencies of the American schools, the ineradicable marks of which are borne by our fellow countrymen to their dying day. But what about the intellectual interest, the willingness and ability to reason, the independence of thought and character . . . ?"[85]

None of these essential traits of an educated person are acquired by the overwhelming majority even of that narrow elite of the university graduates who succeed in reaching the heights of the academic ladder and end up with doctorates (and eventually professorships) in bona fide academic fields. In fact, the chances are large that the stresses and strains of the hard work associated with achievement in the exacting areas of

[84] P. E. Jacob, *Changing Values in College*, New York, 1957, as quoted in Nevitt Sanford, ed., *The American College*, p. 13.
[85] *Freedom, Education and the Fund: Essays and Addresses, 1946-1956*, New York, 1956, p. 76.

mathematics, sciences, and technology deprive even the academically most distinguished products of our university education of opportunities for developing the fundamental qualities which Hutchins rightly associates with being educated. In our entire educational system, from bottom to top, there is little room for the formation and cultivation of the *intellect,* for the emergence and flowering of the individual who is capable of an intelligent, critical approach to the surrounding world, who was taught and has learned to think of the present as history. And the vast majority, those who receive nothing but a perfunctory secondary education or manage to procure an indifferent college degree, go into life unable to think clearly, knowing less and less about more and more, and void of all respect for the intellect and for the accumulated knowledge and wisdom of mankind.

The burst of anxiety over the educational system which was triggered off by the Soviet Union's launching its Sputnik in the autumn of 1957 is itself an aspect of the social condition which the state of education faithfully mirrors. With a few notable exceptions, those who have joined the parade of critics of American education are least of all concerned with its "intellectual and moral degradation"—to use an expression of Hutchins.[86] Their preoccupation is not with the massive and cruel destruction of human abilities and potentialities which the educational system both reflects and helps to perpetuate. Only some twenty-five years ago, when the educational situation was hardly better than it is today, "government and business were largely indifferent to education. They did not finance it, because they saw no reason why they should. Their only interest . . . was in keeping teachers from arousing the students to any desire for social change."[87] What today supplements this interest in preserving the status quo is the mounting awareness of the urgent requirements of the military and corporate juggernauts that dominate American society. These re-

[86] *Ibid.,* p. 16.
[87] Hutchins, *The Higher Learning in America,* p. x.

quirements do not call for a more rational and humanist education of the people—indeed, they militate against it. What they do demand is an adequate supply of suitably qualified technical personnel and a satisfactory number of first-rate scientists. To secure both it is not necessary to educate the masses; an appropriate training of the most promising, high-IQ minority is all that needs to be organized.[88]

Accordingly, the emphasis of the present drive to raise educational standards in schools and colleges centers primarily on the so-called "gifted" child. Although "this 'gifted'-child program is servicing upper-income groups almost exclusively,"[89] our educational statesmen do not hesitate to recommend it as the most promising avenue to an educational "breakthrough." Thus the distinguished authors of the recent Rockefeller Brothers Fund report on education speak about "our" commitment to the "dignity of the individual," to his "intellectual, moral and spiritual growth," to "equal opportunity for all"—only to end up with the lament "that our society has given too little attention to the individual of unusual talent or potentialities." This deficiency is to be mended now by the "pursuit of excellence," and for the benefit of those who may suspect that this "pursuit" will erect an unsurmountable bar to the education of the common man it is added: *Our conception of excellence must embrace many kinds of achievement at many levels. . . .* There is excellence in abstract intellectual activity, in art, in music, in managerial activities, in craftmanship, in human relations, in

---

[88] The exploitation of the fruits of the current "scientific-industrial revolution," both in industry and in the military establishment, does not seem to depend on the improvement of the literacy and skills of the entire labor force, but rather on the availability of a relatively small number of highly trained scientists and engineers and of a narrow stratum of qualified mechanics and foremen. The skill requirements for the ordinary worker may, in fact, be declining as his task becomes increasingly routinized and reduced to the simplest operations. See the illuminating discussion of this problem in James R. Bright, *Automation and Management*, Boston, 1958, pp. 176 ff.

[89] Sexton, *Education and Income*, p. 60.

technical work."[90] Could there be a better formula for letting the ditchdigger "pursue excellence" in digging ditches, while conferring further privileges on the already privileged few?

It is to the credit of President Conant, who has conducted a comprehensive inquiry into the state of the educational system, to have admitted frankly that his interest is in the 15 to 20 percent of all high school students whom he classifies as "academically talented." Having established that "the percentage of young men who are preparing to be doctors, lawyers, engineers, scientists, scholars and teachers of academic subjects is about the same in this country as in Europe . . . something like 6 percent of an age group,"[91] he lavishes all his attention and solicitude on this elite. The "academically talented," he feels, should be given a break: they should be more challenged, their program of academic subjects should be intensified and broadened, they should be taught more foreign languages, and they should be induced to work harder at school.[92]

To the remaining 80 to 85 percent, Conant's approach is quite different. His prescription for the plebs is "meaningful sequences of courses leading to the development of marketable skills." These courses should be designed with the help of "advisory committees composed of representatives of management and labor," and while the students enrolled should also get some instruction in English, social studies, and the like, no

[90] Rockefeller Brothers Fund, Inc., *The Pursuit of Excellence: Education and the Future of America*, Garden City, New York, 1958, Chapters 1 and 2. The last sentence is to be found on p. 16.

[91] Conant, *The American High School Today*, p. 3.

[92] We are not suggesting that severe selectivity and even programs for so-called gifted children may not be indicated under certain circumstances. Thus a poor society, just emerging from the state of backwardness, may be unable to afford high quality mass education. But surely if the Soviet Union can economically sustain "mass education very nearly at the level of excellence of the European upper-track secondary school and scholastically well above the level of the usual American college-preparatory high school" (Rickover, *Education and Freedom*, p. 177), the United States could support, in material terms, an even more ambitious educational system without resorting to educational rationing.

undue stress is to be placed in their curricula on academic subjects. In fact, as far as these students are concerned, the existing educational system is found to be on the whole satisfactory. What worries Conant about these boys and girls whose years at high school are spent on taking courses in stenography, typing, the use of clerical machines, home economics, building trades, retailing, and automobile servicing is not that they are not receiving any real education, but that a large proportion of them—and a majority of the Negroes—find no employment upon dropping out or graduating from high school.

As I write in June, 1961, the unemployment rate nationwide is something over 7 percent for all age brackets, but unemployment among youth under twenty-one years of age is about 17 percent, or more than twice the nationwide rate for all workers. These young people are my chief concern, especially when they are pocketed together in large numbers within the confines of the big city slums. What can words like "freedom," "liberty," and "equality of opportunity" mean to these young people? With what kind of zeal and dedication can we expect them to withstand the relentless pressures of communism?[93]

It is not that "these young people," as well as those who are more fortunate in finding employment, remain illiterate and ignorant that seems to be Conant's "chief concern"—it is only their possibly weakening resistance to Communism, their possibly turning into "social dynamite."

Once more, it is to Conant's credit to have presented clearly and without embellishments the ruling class's real interest in the state of education. His brutal realism certainly sheds much more light on the prevailing condition than all the verbiage about the "dignity of the individual" and the "spiritual elevation of free men." And yet it is shattering testimony to our society's cultural bankruptcy when a former president of one of the country's greatest universities unceremoniously disposes of 80 to 85 percent of the nation as "ineducable"—declaring with

[93] Conant, *Slums and Suburbs*, p. 34.

equal readiness that "a sense of distasteful weariness overtakes me" when it is suggested that we need to say what we mean by education. Conant, for his part, is "ready to define education as what goes on in schools and colleges."[94] If this is not an utter, unqualified repudiation of the entire humanist tradition of mankind, then pray what is?

[94] Quoted in Council for Basic Education, *Bulletin*, January 1960, p. 3.

11

THE IRRATIONAL SYSTEM

It is of the essence of capitalism that both goods and labor power are typically bought and sold on the market. In such a society relations among individuals are dominated by the principle of the exchange of equivalents, of *quid pro quo*, not only in economic matters but in all other aspects of life as well.

Not that the principle of equivalent exchange is or ever has been universally practiced in capitalist society. As Marx showed so convincingly in the closing chapters of the first volume of *Capital*, the primary accumulation of capital was effected through violence and plunder, and the same methods continue in daily use throughout capitalism's dependent colonies and semi-colonies. Nevertheless the ideological sway of *quid pro quo* became all but absolute. In their relations with each other and in what they teach those over whom they rule, capitalists are fully committed to the principle of *quid pro quo*, both as a guide to action and as a standard of morality.

This commitment reflected an important step forward in the development of the forces of production and in the evolution of human consciousness. Only on the basis of equivalent exchange was it possible to realize the more rational utilization of human and material resources which has been the central achievement of capitalism.[1] At the same time, it must never be forgotten that the rationality of *quid pro quo* is specifically capitalist rationality which at a certain stage of development becomes

[1] Max Weber went so far as to celebrate the introduction of double-entry bookkeeping, that classical outgrowth of the *quid pro quo* principle, as marking a major milestone of social history.

incompatible with the underlying forces and relations of production. To ignore this and to treat *quid pro quo* as a universal maxim of rational conduct is in itself an aspect of bourgeois ideology, just as the radical-sounding assertion that under socialism exchange of equivalents can be immediately dispensed with betrays a utopian view of the nature of the economic problems faced by a socialist society.[2]

But even during the life span of capitalism itself, *quid pro quo* breaks down as a rational principle of economic and social organization. The giant corporation withdraws from the sphere of the market large segments of economic activity and subjects them to scientifically designed administration. This change represents a continuous increase in the rationality of the parts of the system, but it is not accompanied by any rationalization of the whole. On the contrary, with commodities being priced not according to their costs of production but to yield the maximum possible profit, the principle of *quid pro quo* turns into the opposite of a promoter of rational economic organization and instead becomes a formula for maintaining scarcity in the midst of potential plenty. Human and material resources remain idle because there is in the market no *quid* to exchange

[2] Marx emphasized in his *Critique of the Gotha Program* that the principle of equivalent exchange must survive in a socialist society for a considerable period as a guide to the efficient allocation and utilization of human and material resources. By the same token, however, the evolution of socialism into communism requires an unremitting struggle *against* the principle, with a view to its ultimate replacement by the ideal "From each according to his ability, to each according to his need." In a fully developed communist society, in which social production would be organized as in one vast economic enterprise and in which scarcity would be largely overcome, equivalent exchange would no more serve as the organizing principle of economic activity than at the present time the removal of a chair from one's bedroom to one's sitting room requires charging the sitting room and crediting the bedroom with the value of the furniture. This is obviously not to imply that the communist society of the future can dispense with rational calculation; what it does indicate is that the nature of the rationality involved in economic calculation undergoes a profound change. And this change in turn is but one manifestation of a thoroughgoing transformation of human needs and of the relations among men in society.

against the *quo* of their potential output. And this is true even though the real cost of such output would be nil. In the most advanced capitalist country a large part of the population lives in abysmal poverty while in the underdeveloped countries hundreds of millions suffer from disease and starvation because there is no mechanism for effecting an exchange of what they could produce for what they so desperately need. Insistence on the inviolability of equivalent exchange when what is to be exchanged costs nothing, strict economizing of resources when a large proportion of them goes to waste—these are obviously the very denial of the rationality which the concept of value and the principle of *quid pro quo* originally expressed.

The obsolescence of such central categories of bourgeois thought is but one symptom of the profoundly contradictory nature of monopoly capitalism, of the ever sharpening conflict between the rapidly advancing rationalization of the actual processes of production and the undiminished *elementality* of the system as a whole.[3] This conflict affects all aspects of society. While rationality has been conquering ever new areas of consciousness, the inability of bourgeois thought to comprehend the development of society as a whole has remained essentially unchanged, a faithful mirror of the continuing elementality and irrationality of the capitalist order itself.

Social reality is therefore conceived in outlived, topsy-turvy, and fetishistic terms. Powerless to justify an irrational and inhuman social order and unable to answer the increasingly urgent questions which it poses, bourgeois ideology clings to concepts that are anachronistic and moribund. Its bankruptcy manifests itself not so much in the generation of new fetishes and half-truths as in the stubborn upholding of old fetishes and half-truths which now turn into blatant lies. And the more these old fetishes and half-truths lose whatever truth content

---

[3] Throughout this chapter we use the words elemental and elementality to characterize a society which is governed as though by great natural forces, like wind and tide, to which men may seek to adjust but over which they have no control.

they once possessed the more insistently they are hammered, like advertising slogans, into the popular consciousness.

The claim that the United States economy is a "free enterprise" system is a case in point. At no time was enterprise really free in the sense that anyone who wanted to could start a business of his own. Still the concept conveyed an important aspect of the truth by pointing up the difference between the relative freedom of competitive capitalism on the one hand and the restrictions imposed by the guild system and the mercantilist state on the other. Having long ago lost this limited claim to truthfulness and referring as it now does to the freedom of giant corporations to exercise undisturbed their vast monopoly powers, "free enterprise" has turned into a shibboleth devoid of all descriptive or explanatory validity.

Of a similar nature is the incessant repetition that the political regime in the United States today is a democracy. In the United States, as in all other capitalist countries, the property-less masses have never been in a position to determine the conditions of their lives or the policies of the nation's government. Nevertheless as long as democracy meant the overthrow of monarchial despotism and the ascent to power of a relatively numerous bourgeoisie, the term focused attention on a major change in the life of society. But what is left of this truth content in a society in which a tiny oligarchy resting on vast economic power and in full control of society's political and cultural apparatus makes all the important political decisions? Clearly the claim that such a society is democratic serves to conceal, not to reveal, the truth.

Or consider religion which still bulks large in the dominant ideology. That the religious perception of the world is and always has been false consciousness need not be belabored, nor that Christianity and other organized creeds have served to rationalize and justify conquest, exploitation, and inhumanity. And yet there is no doubt that in the past religious consciousness has partaken of truth by fostering the development of knowledge and the arts of civilization. It was the Roman Catholic Church which acted as the guardian of language, scholarship, and historical thought in Europe's darkest centuries; and modern science took shape in a centuries-long struggle between faith and reason. How different is the role of religion today! The more obviously it has succumbed to rationalism and the more manifestly it has ceased to exercise influence on people's thoughts and actions, the more strident has become the sales effort for this ingredient of the dominant ideology. The slogan "Jesus Saves" on innumerable roadside billboards, the massive advertising activities of neighborhood churches, the cartelized exhortations to join any of the ubiquitously available ecclesiastical institutions, the spiritual messages poured into millions of homes by the mass media of press and airwaves—all these have little to do with people's faith and morals, and still less with their perception of reality. What are being offered for sale in the religious marketplace are recipes for acquiring the "power of positive thinking" or attaining "peace of mind"—on the same footing as liquor and tranquilizing pills, ocean cruises and summer resorts.

Bourgeois ideology is no longer a world outlook, a *Weltanschauung*, which attempts to discern order in the existing chaos and to discover a meaning in life. It has turned into a sort of box of assorted tools and gimmicks for attaining the central goal of bourgeois policies. And this goal—which in its younger days the bourgeoisie defined in terms of material progress and individual freedom—is more and more explicitly limited to one thing only: preservation of the status quo, alias the "free world," with all its manifest evils, absurdities, and irrationalities.

It is of course impossible to advance a reasoned defense of this status quo, and indeed the effort is seldom made any more. Instead of taking the form of a demonstration of the rationality and desirability of monopoly capitalism, the defense increasingly focuses on the repudiation of socialism which is the only real alternative to monopoly capitalism, and on the denunciation of revolution which is the only possible means of achieving socialism. All striving for a better, more humane, more rational society is held to be unscientific, utopian, and subversive; by the same token the existing order of society is made to appear not only as the only possible one but as the only conceivable one. *maybe it is*

The contradiction between the increasing rationality of society's methods of production and the organizations which embody them on the one hand and the undiminished elementality and irrationality in the functioning and perception of the whole creates that ideological wasteland which is the hallmark of monopoly capitalism. But we must insist that this is not, as some apologists of the status quo would have us believe, "the end of ideology"; it is the displacement of the ideology of rising capitalism by the ideology of the general crisis and decline of the world capitalist order. That its main pillar is anti-Communism is neither accidental nor due to a transient conjunction of political forces, any more than is the fact that the main content of the political and economic policies of modern capitalism is armaments and Cold War. These policies can only be *anti;* there is nothing left for them to be *pro*.

2

Adam Smith saw in the division of labor the key to the wealth of nations, and he was of course right. Many before and after him saw a darker side, and they were right too. In Marx's words, "the division of labor seizes upon not only the economic but every other sphere of society and everywhere lays the foundation of that all-engrossing system of specializing and sorting men, that development in a man of one single faculty at the expense of all other faculties, which caused A. Ferguson, the master of Adam Smith, to exclaim: 'We make a nation of helots, and have no free citizens.' "[4]

The great social critics of the nineteenth century, from Owen and Fourier through Marx and Engels, were all moved by a sense of outrage at this profoundly dehumanizing effect of

[4] *Capital,* Volume 1, Chapter 14, Section 4.

the capitalist division of labor. And much as their visions of the
good society differed, they all had one thing in common: conditions must be created to foster the development of whole
human beings, "free citizens," in possession of all their faculties
and capable of realizing their full potentialities. Some thought
in romantic terms, of a return to a supposedly lost Golden Age.
Others, of whom Marx and Engels were by far the most influential, saw the solution in the maximum development through
scientific and technological advance of the productivity of
human labor. As Marx expressed it in a well known passage in
the *Critique of the Gotha Program,* it would be only

when the enslaving subordination of the individual to the division of
labor, and with it the antithesis between mental and physical labor,
has vanished; when labor is no longer merely a means of life but has
become life's principal need; when the productive forces have also
increased with the all-round development of the individual, and all
the springs of cooperative wealth flow more abundantly—only then
will it be possible completely to transcend the narrow outlook of
bourgeois right and only then will society be able to inscribe on its
banners: From each according to his ability, to each according to his
needs!

Marx thought that such a high degree of labor productivity
could be realized only in a "higher stage of communist society."
We can now see that this was an illusion, that from the point of
view of raising the productivity of labor, capitalism had a
much greater potential than Marx, or for that matter contemporary bourgeois social scientists, imagined. The giant corporation has proved to be an unprecedentedly effective instrument
for promoting science and technology and for harnessing them
to the production of goods and services. In the United States
today the means already exist for overcoming poverty, for supplying everyone with the necessities and conveniences of life,
for giving to all a genuinely rounded education and the free
time to develop their faculties to the full—in a word for escaping from that all-engrossing system of specializing and sorting
men of which Marx wrote.

In fact, of course, nothing of the sort has happened. Men are still being specialized and sorted, imprisoned in the narrow cells prepared for them by the division of labor, their faculties stunted and their minds diminished. And a threat to their security and peace of mind which already loomed large in Marx's day has grown in direct proportion to the spreading incidence and accelerated speed of technological change under monopoly capitalism.

Modern industry never looks upon or treats the existing form of a production process as final. The technical basis of industry is therefore revolutionary, while all earlier modes of production were essentially conservative. By means of machinery, chemical processes, and other methods, it leads to continual changes not only in the technical basis of production, but also in the function of the laborer, and in the social combinations of the labor-process. At the same time, therefore, it revolutionizes the division of labor within the society, and incessantly transfers masses of capital and of work-people from one branch of production to another. Large-scale industry by its very nature therefore necessitates changes in work, variability of function, universal mobility of the laborer; on the other hand, in its capitalistic form, it reproduces the old division of labor with its ossified particularities. We have seen how this insurmountable contradiction robs the worker's situation of all peace, permanence, and security; how it constantly threatens, by taking away the instruments of labor, to snatch from his hands his means of subsistence, and, by suppressing his particular subdivided task, to make him superfluous. We have seen, too, how this contradiction works itself out through incessant sacrifices by the working class, the most reckless squandering of labor power, and the devastations caused by social anarchy.[5]

To bring this statement up to date one need only add that the scale of industry has grown incomparably bigger during the past century, that with the advent of automation and cybernation its technical basis has become far more revolutionary, and that the suppression of particular subdivided tasks has never taken place in so many areas of industry and with such startling speed. If it were not for the expansion of jobs in the

[5] *Capital*, Volume 1, Chapter 13, Section 9.

so-called service sector of the economy (including government), the plight of the worker who must sell his labor power in order to earn his livelihood would indeed be desperate.

While the growth of the service sector has partially compensated for the job-destroying effects of modern technology, it and related developments have added a new dimension to the dehumanization of the labor process under capitalism. There is no need to repeat here what has been so much emphasized in earlier chapters, that a large and growing part of the product of monopoly capitalist society is, judged by genuine human needs, useless, wasteful, or positively destructive. The clearest illustration is the tens of billions of dollars worth of goods and services which are swallowed up every year by a military machine the only purpose of which is to keep the people of the world from solving their problems in the only way they can be solved, through revolutionary socialism. But it is not only those who man and supply the military machine who are engaged in an anti-human enterprise. The same can be said in varying degrees of many millions of other workers who produce, and create wants for, goods and services which no one needs. And so interdependent are the various sectors and branches of the economy that nearly everyone is involved in one way or another in these anti-human activities: the farmer supplying food to troops fighting against the people of Vietnam, the tool and die makers turning out the intricate machinery needed for a new automobile model, the manufacturers of paper and ink and TV sets whose products are used to control and poison the minds of the people, and so on and on and on.

"There is," Paul Goodman writes, " 'nearly full employment' (with highly significant exceptions), but there get to be fewer jobs that are necessary and unquestionably useful; that require energy and draw on some of one's best capacities; and that can be done keeping one's honor and dignity."[6] Goodman is certainly right to stress that this "simple objective fact" is impor-

---

[6] *Growing Up Absurd,* New York, 1960, p. 17.

tant in explaining the troubles of young people in this society. But it is more than that: it is important in explaining the alienation from work, the cynicism, the corruption which permeate every nook and cranny of monopoly capitalism and which anyone with a sense of history cannot fail to recognize as characteristic features of a society in full decline.

3

Asked if he liked his job, one of John Updike's characters replied, "Hell, it wouldn't be a job if I liked it." All but a tiny minority of specially lucky or privileged workers would undoubtedly agree. There is nothing inherently interesting about most of the narrowly sub-divided tasks which workers are obliged to perform; and with the purpose of the job at best obscure and at worst humanly degrading, the worker can find no satisfaction in what his efforts accomplish. As far as he is concerned, the one justification is the paycheck.

The paycheck is the key to whatever gratifications are allowed to working people in this society: such self-respect, status, and recognition by one's fellows as can be achieved depend primarily on the possession of material objects. The worker's house, the model of his automobile, his wife's clothes—all assume major significance as indexes of success or failure. And yet within the existing social framework these objects of consumption increasingly lose their capacity to satisfy. Forces similar to those which destroy the worker's identification with his work lead to the erosion of his self-identification as a consumer. With goods being sought for their status-bearing qualities, the drive to substitute the newer and more expensive for the older and cheaper ceases to be related to the serviceability of the goods and becomes a means of climbing up a rung on the social ladder.

In this way consumption becomes a sort of extension and continuation of the process of earning a livelihood. Just as the worker is always under pressure to get ahead at the expense of his fellows at the shop or office, so the consumer pursues the same goals at the expense of his neighbors after work. Neither worker nor consumer is ever really satisfied; they are always on the lookout for a new job, always wanting to move to a better neighborhood. Work and consumption thus share the same ambiguity: while fulfilling the basic needs of survival, they increasingly lose their inner content and meaning.

Nor are matters any better when it comes to another aspect of the worker's non-work life—the expenditure of leisure time. Leisure has traditionally been thought of as serving the purpose of "recreation," that is to say the revival and refocusing of mental and psychic energies from their compulsory commitment to work to genuinely interesting pursuits. Now, however, the function of leisure undergoes a change. As Erich Fromm has observed, leisure becomes a synonym of time spent in passivity, of idleness. It no longer signifies doing what a person *wants* to do, as distinct from doing, at work, what he *must* do; to an ever increasing extent it means simply doing nothing. And the reason for doing nothing is partly that there is so little that is humanly interesting to do, but perhaps even more because the emptiness and purposelessness of life in capitalist society stifles the desire to do anything.

This propensity to do nothing has had a decisive part in determining the kinds of entertainment which are supplied to fill the leisure hours—in the evenings, on weekends and holidays, during vacations. The basic principle is that whatever is presented—reading matter, movies, radio and TV programs—must not make undue demands on the intellectual and emotional resources of the recipients: the purpose is to provide "fun," "relaxation," a "good time"—in short, passively absorbable amusement. Even the form and organization of the material is affected. The show is continuous, the movie theater can be entered at any time; the book can be read from front to back or from back to front; skipping a few installments of a serial does not matter; the TV can be switched from channel to channel without loss of coherence or comprehension.

Other forms of "killing time"—what a revealing expression! —are hardly more exacting. Being a sports fan does not involve participation in any activity or acquiring any skill. Events are provided for all seasons, and it is not even necessary to attend in person since giant corporations find it a profitable form of advertising to sponsor radio and TV broadcasts of games and matches. Elaborate statistical records are compiled and regularly published in specialized books and periodicals, enabling even fans who have never played a game in their lives to discuss the various teams and players with all the assurance of experts. Being interested at different times of the year in the sports appropriate to the season turns into something people have in common. Like the largely imaginary good and bad points of different makes and models of automobiles, the strengths and weaknesses of teams and players become topics of conversation which the inherent triviality of the theme transforms into mere chatter.[7]

Perhaps nothing is more symptomatic of the part played by leisure in daily life than this degeneration of conversation into chatter. Like friendship, conversation presupposes the existence of some common purposes, interests, and activities. Friendship implies an emotional commitment; conversation demands an intellectual effort. When these preconditions do not exist—when people exist together but do not relate to one another in any fundamental way—both friendship and conversation are bound to atrophy. When people have nothing to say, "small talk" becomes the order of the day. As the word friend fades and comes to designate someone whom one happens to have met, it applies to a multitude of acquaintances and to no one in particular. Social gatherings are motivated less by a desire to be with other people than by fear of being alone. People's unrelatedness at these gatherings is often and characteristically dissolved in alcohol.

The satisfaction derived from this kind of conviviality is

[7] This community of interest creates bonds of pseudo-solidarity not only within social classes but also across class lines, and in this way performs an important ideological function. As fans of the Detroit baseball or hockey teams, the president of General Motors and the floor-sweeper in a GM factory are brought together as equals.

fleeting; the hangover is inevitable. Although suffocating in his solitude, the individual does not overcome it, as David Riesman has observed, by becoming a particle in a crowd. The misery of loneliness and the horror of togetherness produce an attitude of ambivalence between involvement and withdrawal. Leaving one party with the thought that he might as well have stayed at home, he goes to another thinking that he might as well be there. Thus he is drawn into an uninterrupted whirl of socializing—on different levels and scales of course, depending on class, status, and income—or concluding, as Arthur Miller has put it, that if one has to be alone one may as well stay by oneself, he turns into a recluse, spending hours on end "working around the house," mowing the lawn, pottering in the backyard. Brooding and muttering to himself, he turns on the radio, listens to a scrap of news or a singing commercial, switches over to the TV to see the end of a Western, leaves both and looks absent-mindedly at the newspaper filled with accounts of crime and scandal—in short, shifts restlessly from one way of doing nothing to another way of doing nothing, all the while longing for and dreading the beginning of the work week when he will start longing for and dreading the coming of the weekend.

In these conditions the sensation produced by leisure is closely related to that experienced at work—grinding, debilitating boredom. Only it must be added that the boredom lived through in the hours and days of free time can be even more oppressive than that endured during the work week. In the case of work it appears to be natural, an aspect of the grim necessity to earn one's bread in the sweat of one's brow. All of human history has taught people to take it for granted that physical suffering and psychic distress are the price of survival. And as long as scarcity dominated the human condition, this calculus, cruel as it undoubtedly was in the light of the idleness and luxury enjoyed by the privileged few, appeared cogent and convincing to the have-nots. For them every shortening of the work day, every reduction in the work week were precious steps in the direction of freedom.

Today we must ask what remains of that cogency, of that progress toward freedom when the torture of work buys a longer span of non-work which is itself robbed of all joy, which turns into an extension of work itself, into the emptiness, tedium, and torpor of modern leisure? What rationality is left in bearing the self-denial, the repression, the compulsion of work when what follows at the end of the working day and the working week is the barren desert of boredom that is free time in this society?

4

With the increasing specialization and rationalization of the part processes of the capitalist enonomy, calculation has come to pervade all aspects of life. The individual is pressed from the very beginning into one of the available prefabricated molds—depending on the social class and stratum to which he, or rather his family, belongs—and the normal outcome is a standardized, rationalized human product systematically checked by means of statistical quality controls administered by innumerable testing services from nursery school on. This "product's" reactions and responses become increasingly automatic and predictable. Smiling is to be expected from receptionists and airline hostesses, from sales clerks and gas station attendants—regardless of their mood, their physical condition, their attitude toward the other party. A sustained display of cheerfulness is a necessity in dealing with workers and employees, suppliers and customers—equally regardless of the content and meaning of these dealings as such. Similarly, whether a person, a landscape, a musical composition is judged beautiful depends not on its specific characteristics but on its market success, relation to the latest fad, cost, newness, its capacity to purvey "fun" and "relaxation."

In the absence of spontaneous identification with people and things, pretense, that strange homage paid to outdated beliefs and ideals, has become a ubiquitous substitute. Like Pavlov's dog reacting to the sound of the bell, one snaps to pretended attention on prescribed occasions; manifests pretended interest in a book or a conversation; displays pretended concern over political developments at home or abroad; expresses pretended pleasure or sorrow in connection with happenings in the lives of others; exhibits pretended joy on fixed dates such as Christmas, birthdays, anniversaries.

This mechanism for covering up unrelatedness and lack of emotional commitment seems to work, to provide for a more or less smooth flow of human coexistence. It assures superficial politeness in dealings among people; enforces the maintenance of certain behavioral norms; keeps churches, charitable organizations, and clubs going; and provides the basis for much of society's cultural activity. Its limitations, however, are becoming increasingly apparent and tend to an ever greater extent to reduce its effectiveness.

As pretense penetrates into every corner of society, it becomes harder and harder to take it at face value. As people come to recognize that what they are confronted with *is* pretense, the content of what is pretended becomes irrelevant and what is experienced is merely the act of pretending itself. As he who is smiled at becomes aware of the artificiality, insincerity, indeed compulsiveness of the smile, it ceases to signify human friendliness, benevolence, and warmth. It is reciprocated by an equally artificial, insincere, compulsive counter-smile, with the two facial expressions cancelling out and leaving behind the mutual indifference which they were supposed to disguise.

In much the same way, as it becomes clear to an artist that the reception accorded his work has little relation to his talent and insight and instead merely reflects people's compulsive urge to pretend whatever attitude may be in fashion, his very creativity turns into a pretense. He tries to evoke the pretended preference of the public, with the result that one pretense negates the other: the artist has nothing to communicate to his public, while the public provides no inspiration to the artist. This rupture of the bond between art and society deprives art of the possibility of availing itself of its own medium of telling the truth and robs society of one of the few means by which throughout history it has been able to apprehend the truth.[8]

But where the mechanism of pretense tends to break down entirely and ceases to perform the function of making possible the maintenance of basic human contacts is in the realm of the relations between the sexes. Here pretense is least capable of serving as a substitute for spontaneity, for here spontaneity and the capacity for emotional engagement are not merely components of the relation—they are its very essence. Here pretense, even without being sensed as such, cannot conceal the repression of libidinous drives and the inability to experience sensual gratification. Here all efforts to keep up the appearances of affection, of enjoyed togetherness, of family bliss inevitably fail to hide what Marx saw as the alienation of man from himself and what Freud later called the "affect-crippledness" of the individual.

The phenomenon itself is of course not of recent origin. Repression has always marked the exploitation of man by man. Curbing the striving for freedom, subduing the aversion to toil and self-denial, destroying the sense of compassion and solidarity with fellow men, repression has forced man into molds making him fit to exploit and be exploited. As Freud put it, "it is impossible to ignore the extent to which civilization is built up on renunciation of instinctual gratifications, the degree to which the existence of civilization presupposes the non-gratification (suppression, repression, or something else?) of powerful instinctual urgencies."[9] Soc as superego

For many centuries the forces of repression derived much of

[8] Where the pretense is openly dropped and an attempt is made to convey a truthful image of reality, even the language of art is forsaken. Reality is depicted in its stark nakedness, unmediated by artistic imagination which, like all forms of spontaneity, becomes increasingly unattainable. This can be clearly seen, for example, in the writings of Henry Miller, in the plays of Tennessee Williams and Edward Albee, and in much modern painting and music.

[9] Sigmund Freud, *Civilization and Its Discontents*, London, 1955, p. 63.

their formidable power from two sources which remained relatively invariant. One was the state of constricting scarcity which was—in the conditions of the time, rightly—considered to be an inescapable fact of nature. The incidence of burdens imposed by that scarcity was of course open to question and criticism: the injustices associated with it gave rise to almost continuous popular protest; convincing arguments could be and were advanced to show that in a different social order the dire effects of scarcity could be mitigated. But the existence of scarcity could not be denied. And the recognition of its existence necessarily implied the recognition of the inevitability of life-long labor and bare subsistence standards of living for the vast majority of mankind.

The other source of fuel for the engine of repression is closely related to the first: the people's unquestioning belief in the basic principles underlying the taboos and prohibitions, the rules and regulations governing the behavior of men in society. These principles, elaborated by society's cultural and religious apparatus, transmitted from one generation to the next, internalized and appearing as an immutable aspect of "human nature," coagulated into a conscience, a superego, ever watchful and sternly punishing violators of its precepts with bitter feelings of guilt. Society thus acquired what might be called a psychic police force effectively upholding spiritual "law and order."

What distinguishes our time from all earlier epochs is that by now in the advanced capitalist countries the mechanism of repression has accomplished its historical mission. The work discipline and self-denial which it imposed made possible the massive accumulation of capital and with it the building up of an enormously productive industrial apparatus. The development of automation and cybernation in the last two decades signals the end of the long, long era in which the inevitability of scarcity constituted the central fact of human existence. There can be no doubt that the continued acceptance of that inevitability under conditions such as prevail in the United

States today is false consciousness *par excellence*. It now serves only to maintain and support an oppressive social order, and its sway over the minds of people reflects nothing but the anachronistic prevalence of an outlived ideology.

The same historical processes which have made it objectively possible to eliminate scarcity have greatly contributed to weakening society's psychic police force. The advance and spread of rationality resulting from and in turn causing the spectacular progress of science and technology have fatally undermined faith in many of the basic moral principles guiding men's conduct. Rendered obsolete by profound changes in economic reality and corroded by rational criticism in all its forms, these principles can no longer carry the weight of the repressive structure which they have traditionally been called upon to support.

This progressive erosion of the economic and ideological foundations of repression has led in advanced capitalist countries to consequences which are as complex and contradictory as they are important. On the one hand the most immediate and obvious manifestations of repression have markedly contracted and dissolved; sexual relations in and out of wedlock are freer; the availability and widespread use of inexpensive contraceptives have gone far toward liberating women from domestic slavery; and the upbringing of children is in some respects more sensible and sensitive.

On the other hand the weakening of the mechanism of repression has led to no less pronounced negative consequences. The old moral code, largely enforced by the individual's conscience, is in obvious and precipitous decline. But monopoly capitalism has proved totally incapable of generating a new morality to guide men's conduct in an age of potential plenty. As a result the burden of protecting society against destructive conduct has fallen increasingly on pressures external to the individual—on economic rewards and penalties, and above all on the police and the courts. That these external pressures have been incapable of taking the place of an effective moral code is

obvious in a thousand ways, large and small. Crime rates, for
example, have risen far more rapidly than population.[10] But
perhaps even more symptomatic (and terrifying) is the ever
increasing extent to which violence saturates the very atmosphere of the most advanced capitalist country. City dwellers,
reports the *New York Times* (May 20, 1963), "are afraid to use
their parks even during daylight." And police departments in
New York and elsewhere issue special pamphlets containing
such advice to citizens as to walk only where the streets are
lighted, to double-lock all doors at night, and never to open
doors when there is a knock without prior identification of the
caller. "Even in Philadelphia, the city of brotherly love," says
Philadelphia's former Mayor Richardson Dilworth, "I wouldn't
consider going out on the streets at night except in a taxi with
locked doors."[11]

Such is the inevitable fate of a society without faith and
without morals—and without the ability to provide its members with ways of using their energies for humanly interesting
and worthy purposes.

5

It was one of Freud's major insights that civilization rests not
only on the repression of libidinous drives but also, and no less
importantly, on their being channeled in significant volume
toward creative ends—the process which he called sublimation. As the need for repression wanes and the mechanism of
repression breaks down, it seems clear that civilization can
flourish only if the channels of sublimation are continuously
widened and deepened, only if people can find ever new outlets
for their latent energies which also provide genuine sources of
gratification. And yet under monopoly capitalism the exact

[10] The *New York Times* of October 11, 1962, quotes J. Edgar
Hoover, Director of the Federal Bureau of Investigation, to the effect
that crimes more than doubled since 1946 and increased five times as fast
as population between 1957 and 1962.
[11] *New York Times*, March 17, 1965.

opposite happens: the whole vital process of sublimation is in danger of collapsing. How else is it possible to interpret the loss of meaning attaching to work, the stultifying boredom of leisure, the degeneration of what goes by the name of culture, the withering away of political activity as a struggle over the course to be travelled by society?

Under these circumstances it is easy to understand why sexuality has again come to the fore as the increasingly predominant means of satisfying libidinous drives. In the official ideology the resurgence of sexuality takes the form of insistence that happiness is to be found within one's four walls, in the arms of one's spouse, and in togetherness with one's family. This resurgence is no less evident in the national culture and in the sales effort's incessant appeal to sexuality as the wellspring of pleasure—to be obtained by buying an automobile or a cake of soap, taking a trip, acquiring a new dress or piece of jewelry.

But this "reprimitivization" does not work. There is an essential asymmetry in the processes involved: taboos and sublimations are essential to the curbing and reorienting of libidinous energies, but the weakening of the taboos and the choking of the channels of sublimation do not automatically lead to the redirection of libidinous drives toward their original biological ends. On the contrary, the effect is merely to carry further the destruction of man's psychic capacity for direct gratification of libidinous needs. The seeming possibilities so lavishly proffered by the renewed emphasis on sexuality remain essentially unseizable: anaesthetized man suffers from a sort of psychic castration, from an inability to experience psychic catharsis through sexual activity. Though much that used to be forbidden is now allowed, what is now allowed has ceased to be the same as what used to be forbidden. Yielding to the attacks of rationalism, the prohibitions and injunctions of old have fallen into abeyance, but not before they have emptied the activities they were supposed to prevent of their emotional content and thus deprived them of their meaning and power to gratify. The similarity to what has been happening in the economic realm is striking: the rationalization of the mode of functioning of both the human and the economic units of this society proceeds in step with the fading away of any meaningful purpose. The "atrophy of sexual life" of which Freud spoke is not the atrophy of sexual activity; it is the atrophy of that activity's psychic content and meaning.

As so often happens, appearances are misleading. Just as the drivenness of Don Juan and Messalina is now recognized as a sign not of an exuberant *joie de vivre* but of persistent failure to achieve sexual satisfaction and a resulting restless search for partners who could help them to attain what for them was unattainable, so this society's obsession with sexuality must be recognized not as reflecting a general increase of sexual gratification but as a clear sign of sexual malfunctioning. This malfunctioning may take the form of impairment of the technical capacity for sexual activity. But it is important to understand that it need not take this form and may equally well express itself in the absence or significant reduction of the ability to experience psychic release through sexual activity. As originally pointed out by Freud and later emphasized and elaborated by Wilhelm Reich, the two are by no means identical: technical potency can and frequently does coexist with psychic, orgastic impotence which in turn gives rise to all sorts of neurotic disorders.

The most important consequence of sexual malfunctioning is that it plays havoc with the "inner world" which is supposed to reconcile man with the dreariness and oppressiveness of the outer world. Instead of helping him to overcome his incapacity for human relatedness, for love and solidarity, sexuality is transformed into a source of tension and frustration. Once again we meet the paradox of partial rationality advancing along with total irrationality. Increasing knowledge undermines old taboos and inhibitions, reduces ignorance and fear, makes possible an increase in the volume of sexual activity. At the same time the gap between the apparent satisfaction of sexual demands and the gratification derived from sexual activity grows, and the suffering which is caused by psychic inadequacy becomes more debilitating and harder to bear. "The increase of knowledge about the sexual life had affected women for the worse rather than for the better," writes Dr. Dingwall, a British student of American society. "For the more she knew, the more she suspected that she was being cheated."[12] And he goes on to draw the inescapable conclusions that "the lack of full sexual satisfaction is at the core of the discontent manifested by so many American women" and that it has "its repercussions in every department of life."[13]

The department of life most immediately affected is of course the realm of marital relations. Psychically damaged by their sexual malfunctioning, both partners to the marriage tend to lapse into a state of emotional misery which at once bars them from giving each other what they need and from understanding the causes of their troubles. Both husband and wife feel "cheated" and tend to blame the other partner. What Freud called the "earlier overestimation of the sexual object" yields to its aggressive disparagement. What was once admired now turns into a source of irritation and annoyance, resulting in quarrels and recriminations over matters quite unrelated to the real problem. The hostility displayed on such occasions generates feelings of guilt and remorse; these feelings lead to reconciliations; and the reconciliations start the whole vicious cycle over again.

The fact that the man can obtain a measure of somatic release of tension through sexual relations, while this possibility is much more limited for the woman, tends to reinforce in the wife a sense of being abused and exploited. This in turn gives rise to a persistent demand that the husband at least live up to his obligations in other areas of marital life. He, on the other hand, suffering from a nagging uncertainty whether it might

[12] Eric John Dingwall, *The American Woman: A Historical Study,* London, 1956, p. 220.
[13] *Ibid.,* p. 222.

not indeed be his own exceptional inadequacy which is responsible for his wife's unhappiness, succumbs to the pressure. He redoubles his efforts to provide for the family, attempts to be as useful as possible around the house, and goes into debt to satisfy her whims. He puts his woman on a pedestal and does all he can to placate her by being continuously at her beck and call—only to discover that all his efforts are in vain, that nothing he can give can satisfy her wants, and that instead of winning her affection he merely loses her respect.

There are many ways in which individuals seek to escape from the predicament, the differences depending on such factors as economic and social status, religious and ethnic background, and particular personality traits. The notion, for the most part illusory, that a change of partners will provide an effective remedy leads in some strata of society to a proliferation of extra-marital relations and to a large and ever increasing frequency of family break-ups through divorce, separation, or desertion. The rapidly rising divorce rate has led the Family Service Association of America to declare that "family breakdown [is] America's No. 1 social problem."[14]

Where for economic or religious reasons divorce is avoided and husband and wife stay together, the atmosphere in the family is frequently that of frigidity or undisguised hostility. People with little or no economic freedom of movement, subdued by the unrelenting necessity to earn a living and provide for their children, resign themselves to their fate. With their incapacity to live matched only by the objective impossibility of changing their lives, they bear their misery to the bitter end and live out their days with their abilities and creative potentialities never discovered and never developed. For many, alco-

---

[14] Quoted from *Family Service Highlights,* the Association's journal, in the *New York Times,* November 12, 1961. At about the same time, Professor Judson T. Landis of the University of California was expressing the view that the deterioration of family life in California, in many respects a bellwether state, had reached "frightening proportions," with "50 marriages (it's 55 in San Francisco) in 100 ending on the rocks." *San Francisco Chronicle,* November 2, 1961.

hol is the only solace; for some, suicide provides a desperate escape.

The economically more fortunate often expect relief through changes in external circumstances. Driven by another illusory notion, that the emotional catharsis which eludes them can somehow be captured in a different setting, they move to new houses, surround themselves with expensive gadgets, take frequent trips abroad. Continuously looking for some new way to overcome their emotional starvation, these are the prototypes of the proverbially restless American consumer, always receptive to new fads and fashions, to new products and models—and to new tranquilizers and pain-killers.[15]

A different course is pursued by what may be called the "hi-fi set," drawn from members of the professions, workers in the entertainment and mass communications industries, college and university teachers and students. Owing to their educational backgrounds and the nature of their occupations, these people are likely to be especially sensitive to the contradiction between the relaxation of repression and the growing obstacles which monopoly capitalist society puts in the way of the gratification of emotional drives. Their response to the crisis is often a frantic effort to find a solution on the individual plane through what may perhaps be called a measure of "resublimation." Undertaken deliberately, this attempt has all the earmarks of occupational therapy. Taking up painting or interior decorating; turning into a connoisseur of rare *objets d'art;* amassing musical records (frequently pointedly limited to one particular country or one historical period)—such are the characteristic expressions of this "cultural" drive. Its artificiality is usually quite transparent. The books are likely to remain unopened to adorn the tastefully designed bookshelves; the

---

[15] It is essentially the same vain chase after a will-o'-the-wisp—only in the opposite direction—which sends the so-called beatniks looking for emotional fulfillment through renunciation of the "square" way of life with its comforts and amenities, and through the adoption instead of a way of life characterized by eccentricity, promiscuity, and narcotics.

this because of emotional stress · because we're not used to being · alone & with quiet · it scares us

continuous running of the technically superb record player suggests not so much love of music as dread of silence; poring over the catalogues of antiquarians and art dealers or selecting new fabrics to redecorate the living room can hardly do more than provide a temporary escape from the necessity of being alone with one's thoughts and feelings. The contrived sources of gratification are as barren as the missing ones they are designed to replace.

Where the impact of the quest for substitute gratifications is most strongly felt and also most important is in the realm of relations between parents and children. The belief that difficulties between husband and wife will be alleviated by their joint responsibility and affection for the young is all but universally held. Yet in practice the arrival of children, far from solving all problems, usually compounds and complicates them. While having children is a matter of fulfillment and pride, the burdens and obligations which they impose limit the parents' freedom and add to the already formidable stresses and strains under which they live. And if it comes to the break-up of the marriage, the presence of children makes the separation emotionally more traumatic and economically more difficult.

Such unpleasant facts disappear from the commonly accepted stereotype of family life in the United States today. There the children appear elevated on a pedestal even higher than that occupied by the woman. They are constantly showered with attention and favors, and a large and growing proportion of the family income is devoted to satisfying their wants. And yet this idolization of the child, emphasized as it is by the dominant ideology and exploited by the ever present sales effort, far from demonstrating that the country is a children's paradise, points rather to the problematic nature of the child's position in society and of the parents' relations with their children. For, themselves emotionally starved and debarred from giving each other what they need, torn between the natural and socially approved love for children and the often irresistible temptation to hold them at least partly responsible for the inability to break out of the confining misery

The woman whose role is to work in the home, her only function is childcare may overdo her job

of their own lives, the parents are in no position to satisfy the emotional needs of the children or to arrive at healthy relations with them.

This ambivalence adds to the tension which dominates the atmosphere within the family, a tension which may express itself in stormy conflicts or silent hostility or contrived "togetherness." The child, ever sensitive to his environment, is inevitably affected to the depths of his being. The unrelatedness of the parents molds his own personality; the affect-crippledness of one generation becomes an "inherited" characteristic maiming and destroying the life of the next.

In a small, though unfortunately increasing, minority of cases, the frustration of the parents takes the form of uncontrolled aggressiveness breaking through all inhibitions and resulting in unimaginable brutality to children.[16] More often it expresses itself in permissiveness which is usually only a thin disguise for lack of interest and concern with the development of the children. Encouraged to spend hours in front of the TV set or to do whatever they please, the main demand on the children is that they leave their parents alone. Always in the way, always being shunted off into someone else's care, the children are made to feel unwanted, a mere source of bother and expense.

For the most part, however, the parents' inability to feel spontaneous affection for their children, clashing as it does with ideological norms and the demands of conscience, creates painful sensations of guilt which the parents try to assuage by leaning over backwards to give their children the symbols of love and affection. That this solicitude is contrived, that it does not emanate from genuine warmth and empathy for the child can be sensed at every step—above all by the child himself, the most efficient and reliable of lie detectors.

[16] "Scores of cases now before juvenile authorities throughout Northern California indicate the savage abuse parents are inflicting on their children. In San Francisco alone, cases of cruelty to children have more than tripled in the last two years, and since the first of January the pattern of parental violence seems to be accelerating at an even greater pace." *San Francisco Chronicle*, April 5, 1961.

Being surrounded by sham is thus the child's daily experience. Registering everything that happens in his environment, mimetic from his earliest days, he is as much influenced by the parents' attitude toward each other as he is by their attitude toward himself. Even when receiving all the outward manifestations of love, he cannot but be profoundly affected by the grown-ups' unrelatedness to each other: under the most favorable circumstances the world of the child cannot be insulated from the freezing temperature of the world of adults. The aimless drift of the parents' life, their tensions, frustrations, and boredom cannot fail to imprint themselves on the child's character and development. Thus the parents shape their children to their own likeness. Just as the parents have lost faith in society, ceased to believe in its ideology, become hostile toward their work and toward each other, so the children lose faith in their parents and see through the hypocrisy of their precepts and admonitions. All find themselves together in a jungle in which there is no love and no trust, no purpose worth striving for and no ideal worth fighting for.

6

This state of affairs cannot be changed by wishing or incantation. Declarations that what the United States needs is a "spiritual revival" or a clarification of "national goals" are as symptomatic of the pathological condition they are directed against as of a profound inability to comprehend its nature and origins. When a writer as sensitive and observant as Paul Goodman truthfully states that "our society cannot have it both ways: to maintain a conformist and ignoble system *and* to have skilled and spirited men to man the system with," only to conclude that "if ten thousand people in all walks of life will stand up on their two feet and talk out and insist, we shall get our country back," one gets the full measure of the failure of even our best social critics to face up to the real character and dimensions of the crisis of our time.[17]

[17] *Growing Up Absurd,* New York, 1960, p. 14 and p. xvi.

For behind the emptiness, the degradation, and the suffering which poison human existence in this society lies the profound irrationality and moral bankruptcy of monopoly capitalism itself. No outraged protests, no reforms within the monopoly capitalist framework can arrest the decay of the whole. And as becomes clearer every day, this decay makes increasingly problematical the rationality of even the most spectacular advances in scientific knowledge and technical and organizational skills. Improvements in the means of mass communication merely hasten the degeneration of popular culture. The utmost perfection in the manufacture of weapons of destruction does not make their production rational. The irrationality of the end negates all improvements of the means. Rationality itself becomes irrational. We have reached a point where the only true rationality lies in action to overthrow what has become a hopelessly irrational system.

Will such action be forthcoming in sufficient volume and intensity to accomplish its purpose? The future of the United States and of monopoly capitalism obviously depends on the answer. So also, though more indirectly, does the future of mankind itself for a long time to come.

The answer of traditional Marxian orthodoxy—that the industrial proletariat must eventually rise in revolution against its capitalist oppressors—no longer carries conviction. Industrial workers are a diminishing minority of the American working class, and their organized cores in the basic industries have to a large extent been integrated into the system as consumers and ideologically conditioned members of the society. They are not, as the industrial workers were in Marx's day, the system's special victims, though they suffer from its elementality and irrationality along with all other classes and strata—more than some, less than others.

The system of course has its special victims. They are the unemployed and the unemployable, the migrant farm workers, the inhabitants of the big city ghettos, the school dropouts, the aged subsisting on meager pensions—in a word, the outsiders, those who because of their limited command over purchasing power are unable to avail themselves of the gratifications, such as they are, of consumption. But these groups, despite their impressive numbers,[18] are too heterogeneous, too scattered and fragmented, to constitute a coherent force in society. And the oligarchy knows how, through doles and handouts, to keep them divided and to prevent their becoming a lumpen-proletariat of desperate starvelings.[19]

If we confine attention to the inner dynamics of advanced monopoly capitalism, it is hard to avoid the conclusion that the prospect of effective revolutionary action to overthrow the system is slim. Viewed from this angle, the more likely course of development would seem to be a continuation of the present process of decay, with the contradiction between the compulsions of the system and the elementary needs of human nature becoming ever more insupportable. The logical outcome would be the spread of increasingly severe psychic disorders leading to the impairment and eventual breakdown of the system's ability to function even on its own terms.[20]

But as we emphasized in Chapter 7, advanced monopoly capitalism does not exist in isolation, and any speculation

[18] See the discussion of the dimensions of poverty in the United States today, above pp. 285-289.

[19] These are of course the objectives of the Johnson administration's so-called war on poverty.

[20] That we may already be entering such a stage is suggested by the findings of the so-called Midtown Manhattan Study, by far the most thorough investigation yet undertaken of the mental health of a large population sample. Based on eight years of research in a relatively well-to-do, all-white area in New York City, and referring only to adults between ages 20 and 59, this Study found that only 18.5 percent of the sample could be classified as Well, i.e., free from significant symptoms. The Mild and Moderate levels of symptom formation accounted for 36.3 and 21.8 percent of the sample respectively. The Marked, Severe, and Incapacitated were 13.2, 7.5, and 2.7 percent respectively. Thus over four fifths of the sample were found to be suffering from some identifiable form of mental disturbance, and nearly a quarter were "in the impaired range of the mental health continuum." Leo Srole and others, *Mental Health in the Metropolis: The Midtown Manhattan Study*, New York, Toronto, London, 1962, p. 342.

about its future which takes account only of its inner laws and tendencies is certain to be misleading. The United States dominates and exploits to one extent or another all the countries and territories of the so-called "free world" and correspondingly meets with varying degrees of resistance. The highest form of resistance is revolutionary war aimed at withdrawal from the world capitalist system and the initiation of social and economic reconstruction on a socialist basis. Such warfare has never been absent since the Second World War, and the revolutionary peoples have achieved a series of historic victories in Vietnam, China, Korea, Cuba, and Algeria. These victories, taken together with the increasingly obvious inability of the underdeveloped countries to solve their problems within the framework of the world capitalist system, have sown the seeds of revolution throughout the continents of Asia, Africa, and Latin America. Some of these seeds will sprout and ripen rapidly, others slowly, still others perhaps not until after a long period of germination. What seems in any case clear is that they are now implanted beyond any prospect of extirpation. It is no longer mere rhetoric to speak of the world revolution: the term describes what is already a reality and is certain to become increasingly the dominant characteristic of the historical epoch in which we live.

The implications of this fact for the future of monopoly capitalism are only beginning to become apparent. The ruling class of the United States understands, instinctively and through experience, that every advance of the world revolution is a defeat—economic, political, and moral—for itself. It is determined to resist such advances wherever they may threaten, by whatever means may be available; and it counts on its enormous superiority in the technology of warfare to bring it victory. But the truth is that in this struggle there can be no real victories for the counter-revolutionary side. Underlying the revolutionary upsurge are real economic, social, and demographic problems; and it is the very nature of counter-revolution to prevent these problems from being rationally attacked, let alone solved. Counter-revolution may win, indeed already has won, many battles, but the war goes on and inexorably spreads to new peoples and new regions. And as it spreads so does the involvement of the United States.

No one can now foresee all the consequences for the United States of this increasing commitment to the cause of world counter-revolution, but equally no one can doubt that it will profoundly affect the inner as well as the outer course of events. In the long run its main impact may well be on the youth of the nation. The need for military manpower seems certain to rise sharply; it may soon be normal for young Americans to spend several years of their lives, if they are lucky enough to survive, fighting in the jungles and mountains of Asia, Africa, and Latin America. The psychic stress and physical suffering experienced by them and their families will add a new dimension to the agony inflicted by an anti-human social order. Will the effect be merely to hasten the process of decay already so far advanced? Will the shock perhaps awaken more and more people to the urgent need for basic change? Or will, as some believe, the increasingly evident hopelessness of its cause lead the American ruling class to the ultimate irrationality of unleashing nuclear holocaust?

That no one can now answer these questions means that all the options are not foreclosed, that action aimed at altering the course of events has a chance to succeed. There are even indications, especially in the Negro freedom movement in the South, in the uprisings of the urban ghettos, and in the academic community's mounting protest against the war in Vietnam, that significant segments of the American people are ready to join an active struggle against what is being cumulatively revealed as an intolerable social order. If this is so, who can set limits to the numbers who may join them in the future?

But even if the present protest movements should suffer defeat or prove abortive, that would be no reason to write off permanently the possibility of a real revolutionary movement in the United States. As the world revolution spreads and as the socialist countries show by their example that it is possible to use man's mastery over the forces of nature to build a rational society satisfying the human needs of human beings, more and more Americans are bound to question the necessity of what they now take for granted. And once that happens on a mass scale, the most powerful supports of the present irrational system will crumble and the problem of creating anew will impose itself as a sheer necessity. This will not happen in five years or ten, perhaps not in the present century: few great historical dramas run their course in so short a time. But perhaps even fewer, once they are fairly started, change their nature or reverse their direction until all their potentialities have been revealed. The drama of our time is the world revolution; it can never come to an end until it has encompassed the whole world.

In the meantime, what we in the United States need is historical perspective, courage to face the facts, and faith in mankind and its future. Having these, we can recognize our moral obligation to devote ourselves to fighting against an evil and destructive system which maims, oppresses, and dishonors those who live under it, and which threatens devastation and death to millions of others around the globe.

APPENDIX

ESTIMATING THE ECONOMIC SURPLUS

By Joseph D. Phillips

The problem of estimating the volume of economic surplus produced by the American economy is complicated by a dearth of statistical data that can be used directly for the purpose. It has been necessary to rely primarily upon figures developed for the national income accounts of the United States Department of Commerce. Many of these data are rather crude approximations—for example, the estimates of income of unincorporated enterprises. More serious are the differences between the categories employed in the national income accounts and those implied in the concept of economic surplus. These differences have necessitated a number of rough adjustments in the available data.

The method employed in making the estimates of economic surplus has been to proceed from the more commonly recognized elements of surplus to those less commonly included, although it has not been feasible to follow this procedure throughout. Thus the initial step was to incorporate in the economic surplus the elements of property income contained in the national income accounts. Several of these required adjustments to make them approximate the concepts employed here; these are explained below.

Next, the volume of various types of what may be called wasteful expenditures incurred in the business process was estimated. From the standpoint of the individual firm many of these expenditures appear to be necessary business expenses, but from the standpoint of the economy they constitute forms of waste. They have therefore been incorporated in the economic surplus.

The third major category of surplus for which estimates were made was that absorbed by government. All government expenditure is included in economic surplus. Thus the criterion is not whether the government expenditure is in some sense necessary or useful.

The totals of these three major categories of economic surplus—property income, waste in the business process, and government expenditure—were then added together to obtain our grand totals. It should be noted, however, that these totals still do not include all elements of surplus. Some could not be estimated on a year-by-year basis because of inadequate data. One of these elements is the penetration of the productive process by the sales effort, but some data for recent years have been assembled to indicate its order of magnitude. Another element which might reasonably be incorporated in the surplus, but is omitted here, is the output foregone owing to the existence of unemployment.[1]

1. Property Income

Corporate profits were taken after corporation income taxes had been deducted and after allowance for inventory valuation adjustment. (See Table 18.[2]) The adjustment for excessive depreciation charges was made after the profit income of unincorporated enterprises had been added to corporate profits to obtain total business profits.

A. Income of Unincorporated Enterprises

The general problem here is whether to treat income of un-

[1] The Conference on Economic Progress estimated the output loss for the years 1953-1960 from this source at $262 billion in 1959 dollars. *Jobs and Growth*, Washington, 1961, p. 33.

[2] All tables are at the end of the Appendix.

incorporated enterprises as profit or as labor income or as a
mixture of both. At least one study has treated it in its entirety
as labor income.[3] This procedure seems unjustified for our purpose. Data obtained from tax returns and from the census show
that a considerable number of unincorporated enterprises employ a number of workers and obtain sizable profits. On the
other hand, it would be inappropriate to consider all income of
unincorporated enterprises as profit income since no deduction
is made in arriving at the total of income of unincorporated
enterprises for salaries of owners, who in many cases are the
sole workers in their firms.

One suggested solution to this problem is to estimate the
element of labor income in this category of income by multi-
plying the average earnings of employees by the number of
active proprietors of unincorporated enterprises, both figures
being taken separately for each major industrial division. The
difference between this estimate of labor income of proprietors
and total income of unincorporated enterprises is then classed
as property income.[4]

Another approach to the problem has been offered by Denison. He argues that

the best way to approach that question [the proportion of the income of unincorporated enterprises which represents a return for
labor input] may be to assume that the total return for labor, including the labor of employees, owners, and family workers, comprises
the same proportion (about three-fourths) of total income originating in unincorporated firms as it does in corporations, where the
problem is minimal.

Such an assumption . . . would imply in 1952 an average return to
proprietors of nonfarm unincorporated business about two-thirds as
high as the average compensation of paid employees in the business

[3] Jesse V. Burkhead, "Changes in the Functional Distribution of Income," *Journal of the American Statistical Association*, June 1953, pp.
192-219.

[4] Edward C. Budd, "Treatment of Distributive Shares," in *A Critique
of the United States Income and Product Accounts: Studies in Income
and Wealth*, Volume 22, pp. 356-357. Budd's estimate of property
income of unincorporated enterprises in 1952 amounted to 26.7 percent
of the total income of such enterprises.

economy as a whole. It would also imply that in the aggregate little more than half of nonfarm proprietors' income represents a return for labor. If these ratios should seem low, it is well to remember that most nonfarm proprietors are in firms whose total net income per proprietor is much below average employee earnings, and that the bulk of total proprietors' income is accounted for by the larger firms, where property income may predominate.[5]

This solution has been adopted here. The percentage of income originating in corporations that went to employees in each year was considered the measure of the labor component in the income originating in sole proprietorships and partnerships. From the remainder, the net interest originating in sole proprietorships and partnerships was subtracted to obtain our estimates of profits of unincorporated business. (See Table 19.) And these were added to corporate profits to obtain unadjusted totals of business profits before the adjustment for excessive depreciation charges was made.

B. Excessive Depreciation Charges

One adjustment which needs to be made in the profits figures given in the national income accounts arises from excessive depreciation charges. The authors of U. S. Income and Output acknowledge this possibility:

Profits are obviously hard to measure with precision. Difficulties associated with the making of proper allowance for depreciation should be mentioned specifically. The profit ratios [profit as percent of income originating in corporations] charted here are based upon calculations employing the depreciation concepts which have been used in corporate tax returns. These are not necessarily the most appropriate for economic analysis. For instance, they reflect changes in the tax laws, such as the special amortization provisions enacted in 1950 and the legalization of alternative formulae which permitted accelerated depreciation under the Revenue Code of 1954. Profit ratios adjusted to eliminate the effects of these changes might be higher by one or two percentage points for 1957 [from about 20 percent to about 21 or 22 percent], and would show a somewhat

[5] Edward F. Denison, "Income Types and the Size Distribution," *American Economic Review*, May 1954, p. 256.

different movement over the past few years. The broad pattern of
downdrift since 1951 . . . would remain, however, and no change in
the interpretation of it would seem to be called for.[6]

They go on to argue, however, that for some purposes depreciation charges have been inadequate:

The fact that tax depreciation is based on original cost values
introduces an additional element that requires consideration, especially in problems involving long-term comparisons. For many objectives of economic analysis, it would be preferable to value depreciation in terms of current replacement cost. Generally speaking,
this change of method would raise depreciation and reduce profits
relatively more in the postwar period than during the 1920's.[7]

This latter point is based on the argument that the cost of
replacing equipment and structures in periods of inflation is
greater than current depreciation charges, which are related to
original cost of these assets. Eisner has challenged this argument:

(1) Increase in prices may not be sufficient to wipe out the excess
of depreciation allowances over replacement requirements caused
by growth in the real volume of investment.
(2) The extent of price increase necessary to cancel the effects of
growth in the real volume of investment is a function of the rate of
growth of investment (in monetary terms, which is a product of the
real growth and the change in prices), the length of life of assets,
and the period of amortization. Illustrative examples reveal that
only when prices increase somewhat faster than real investment do
replacement requirements approach the magnitude of depreciation
allowances.
We may conclude that the phenomenon of growth places on
shaky ground those who would argue that depreciation allowances
are insufficient to meet replacement requirements. To the extent that
replacement requirements may offer a criterion for the size of depreciation allowances a contrary hypothesis would appear appropriate. Perhaps depreciation allowances are too high and net profits, as
well as net income and net investment, are understated by conventional accounting practices! And perhaps our traditional analyses of

[6] United States Department of Commerce, *U. S. Income and Output,*
Washington, 1958, p. 15.
[7] *Ibid.,* p. 16.

the distribution of "income" overlook, consequently, a substantial component of the social product which accrues to business enterprises in the form of generous depreciation allowances.[8]

Eisner also points out that "It may be quite possible, in spite of inflated prices, to replace old assets with new ones whose dollar cost per unit of productive capacity or output is less than that of the cheaper but less efficient assets being replaced." Furthermore, he notes that the basic relevance of replacement requirements to the consideration of depreciation allowances may be questioned. "Many accountants will insist that depreciation accounting is merely a device for allocating original cost and is entirely unrelated to replacement requirements."[9]

Eisner has argued elsewhere that the changes made in the Internal Revenue Code of 1954 which provide explicitly for (a) the "declining balance" method of charging depreciation, at a rate up to twice that of the straight-line method, and (b) the "sum of the years' digits" method cannot fail to have a tremendous effect upon corporate tax payments through their effect upon the computation of corporate profits. These alternative formulas permitted accelerated depreciation.[10] He estimated roughly that by 1960 the Treasury would be losing about $3 billion a year as a result of the 1954 changes in the law, assuming that the changes in tax liabilities had no effect on the amount of gross national product. This figure implies an estimate of nearly $6 billion in excess depreciation from this source for 1960. It thus implies that, as a result of the 1954 changes alone, business profits in 1960 should be higher by nearly $6 billion than they were reported to be.

The soundness and conservatism of his predictions, Eisner contended in 1959, were confirmed by the estimates and re-

[8] Robert Eisner, "Depreciation Allowances, Replacement Requirements and Growth," *American Economic Review*, December 1952, p. 831.

[9] *Ibid.*, p. 820.

[10] Robert Eisner, "Depreciation Under the New Tax Law," *Harvard Business Review*, January-February 1955, pp. 66-74.

ports of actual corporate depreciation charges made by the Treasury and Commerce Departments and by the staff of the Joint Economic Committee. Treasury Department reports indicated that total depreciation and accelerated amortization deductions of corporations rose from $12 billion in 1953 to $17.6 billion in 1956. Estimates of the Department of Commerce showed corporate depreciation and amortization rising from $11.8 billion in 1953 to $19.7 billion in 1957, and the staff of the Joint Economic Committee estimated a further rise to $21.3 billion by 1958. When depreciation deductions of unincorporated enterprises were added, the rise in depreciation deductions between 1953 and 1958 was estimated to entail an annual loss to the Treasury by 1958 of over $5 billion in tax revenues. This "includes the direct effects of the rate of growth of gross capital additions, aside from the results of changes in depreciation methods," but the part of the loss "which can be ascribed specifically to the change in depreciation methods is undoubtedly more than the $2.5 billion" which Eisner predicted for 1958 on the basis of a 4 percent assumed growth in the rate of gross capital additions.[11] Thus by 1958 excess depreciation charges from this source had already approached $6 billion and would increase rapidly thereafter.

These estimates are indicative of the amount of excess depreciations from only one source, the 1954 changes in the Internal Revenue Code. There is some basis for inferring that there has long been a tendency for American business to exaggerate depreciation expense. In view of Fabricant's estimate that the average life span of a capital asset in the United States is about thirty years, which was supported by oral estimates which Domar obtained from the Department of Commerce, it would seem that even before the 1954 changes the Internal Revenue Code permitted depreciation at a more rapid rate

[11] Robert Eisner, "Effects of Depreciation Allowances for Tax Purposes," *Tax Revision Compendium*, printed for the House Committee on Ways and Means, Washington, 1959, Volume 2, p. 794.

than practice with respect to replacement justified.[12] For
many types of equipment the Code allowed depreciation on
the basis of life spans of less than thirty years.

One attempt to estimate "real depreciation in the USA" is
that of the Soviet economist M. Golanskii:

American statistics greatly overestimate the cost of replacement
for wear and tear of fixed capital. In addition to depreciation, this
item [capital consumption allowances] includes in it the cost of
replacement of accidental losses of fixed capital and investments,
which are treated as current expenses. . . . Nor is it possible to use
official depreciation data. Depreciation represents the sum of money
required to renew the value of the wear and tear of fixed capital.
What is meant is the fixed capital actually participating in the process of material production. But American statistics, ignoring the
distinction between productive and unproductive spheres, include in
depreciation of fixed capital the wear and tear on dwellings and
other buildings and property which do not participate in production.

Besides the fixed capital replacement fund is greatly exaggerated
by overstatement of the depreciation rates. . . .

Obviously, data containing such extensive distortions cannot serve
as a correct indication of the depreciation of fixed assets . . . [their
use] leads to the national income being underestimated by many
billions of dollars.

Lack of appropriate statistics makes it impossible for us to remove
from the official depreciation total the indicated elements of surplus
value. However, a rough estimate of the real value of depreciation
of fixed capital in the sphere of material production may be made on
the basis of the depreciation data available for U.S. manufacturing
industries. The share of depreciation in the value of the final product
of manufacturing industry is taken by us tentatively as being equal
to the share of depreciation in the final product of all spheres of
material production. . . . The lowest (4 percent) percentage of
depreciation in the value of final product of U.S. manufacturing
industry was recorded in 1947. This percentage, which most ac-

[12] Solomon Fabricant, *Capital Consumption and Adjustment*, New
York, 1938, p. 34; Evsey D. Domar, *Essays in the Theory of Economic
Growth*, New York, 1957, p. 158n. Domar points out that it is possible
the average life span has been declining over time because of the increasing importance of equipment as compared with structures among the
depreciable assets of firms.

curately reflects the real wear and tear of fixed capital, is taken by us as an indication of the share of depreciation in the value of the final material product in the U.S. for the entire period under consideration.[13]

Golanskii arrives at the following depreciation estimates (in millions of dollars), which are here compared with Department of Commerce totals for the same years:

Year	Golanskii	Department of Commerce[14]
1929	$ 2,838	$ 7,698
1947	6,532	12,150
1950	7,831	18,042
1955	10,425	28,110

It is not feasible to apply Golanskii's method of estimation to other years, since some of the steps by which he estimated final material product, particularly those relating to indirect taxes, are not fully explained. However, we have expressed his depreciation estimates as percentages of gross private investment in producers' durable equipment and nonresidential construction for the corresponding years. The percentages range between 25 and 26.8 percent. They thus correspond rather closely to Domar's estimate of 28 percent for Soviet D/G (the ratio of depreciation to gross investment).[15] If we take 26 percent of total gross private investment in producers' durable equipment and nonresidential construction from 1929 to 1963 as the basis for our estimate of depreciation, we get a total of $204,350 million in depreciation for this period of thirty-five years.

[13] "Methods Employed to Recalculate the National Income of the U.S.A.," *Problems of Economics,* March 1960, pp. 57-63, translated from *Mirovaia Economika i Meghdunarodnye Otnochentia,* Number 11, 1959.

[14] *National Income,* 1954 ed., pp. 162-163; *Survey of Current Business,* July 1957, pp. 8-9. These were the sources used by Golanskii, which we have therefore used for comparative data, although the depreciation estimates have since been revised.

[15] *Essays in the Theory of Economic Growth,* p. 160. Domar cites Norman Kaplan's estimates of Soviet investment (*Soviet Capital Formation and Industrialization: A Rand Corporation Study* [P 277], Santa

Another estimate was obtained by expressing the total of Golanskii's estimates of depreciation for 1929, 1947, 1950, and 1955 as a percentage of the corresponding total of the revised Department of Commerce estimates of depreciation for those years after deducting depreciation on owner-occupied dwellings and institutional depreciation. This amounted to 48.2 percent, which produced an estimate of $257,655 million in depreciation for the period 1929-1963 when applied to the Department of Commerce total of depreciation, adjusted as indicated above, for the same period.

The larger of these two estimates was adopted as the total of business depreciation for the period 1929-1963. This total was distributed by years in accordance with an index which reflected the distribution by years of the Department of Commerce depreciation series, adjusted to eliminate depreciation on owner-occupied dwellings and institutional depreciation and to reduce the influence of the changes in the Internal Revenue Code of figures for 1954 and subsequent years.[16]

The estimates of depreciation obtained in this manner were then subtracted from the aggregate net receipts of business firms to obtain our estimates of business profit before taxes. (See Table 18.)

Monica, California, 1952) to show that Soviet D/G in current prices averaged between 12 and 25 percent over the period 1930-1950, but he considers the range not very meaningful because of sharp inflations. Domar therefore develops his own estimate of Soviet D/G on the basis of Kaplan's estimate of the real rate of growth of Soviet investment and his own estimate of the average life span of Soviet investment assets.

[16] The latter adjustment was made by subtracting from the Department of Commerce series Eisner's estimate of the excess depreciation made possible in each of these years by the use of the "sum of the year's digits" method in place of "straight-line" method of depreciation. The amounts subtracted appear in Joint Committee on the Economic Report, *Federal Tax Policy for Economic Growth and Stability*, Washington, 1955, Column 6, Table 4, p. 520. Eisner later indicated that these estimates had proved to be conservative. *Tax Revision Compendium*, p. 794.

C. Rent, Interest, and Other Property Income

Another category listed in the national income accounts which is customarily classified as property income is the rental income of persons. In recent years, as in the 1930's, more than half of this type of income, as it appears in the national income accounts, has consisted of imputed net rent from owner-occupied dwellings. It does not seem appropriate to include this element in the economic surplus, and it was therefore subtracted from the rental income of persons to obtain the adjusted rental income that was incorporated in the estimates of economic surplus.

Interest constitutes another element of property income. In our estimates net interest, rather than personal interest income, was included in the economic surplus. Personal interest income, as it appears in the national income accounts, combines net interest (which excludes government interest payments) and interest payments by government. Since all expenditures by government are later incorporated in our estimates of economic surplus, net interest paid by government is excluded from our interest component to avoid double counting.

The only other element of income which needs to be considered here is the compensation of corporate officers. A significant part of this income represents a share of profits, although it is not explicitly treated as such. In our estimates one-half of total compensation of corporate officers in each year was included in the economic surplus of the year. These estimates appear in Table 20.

2. Waste in the Business Process

It is essential that some allowance be made for the elements of economic surplus which take the form of waste in the business process, and Table 22 includes estimates for some of these. In general, the largest part of this waste is associated with the process of selling the output of business. This includes much of such expenditures as advertising, market research, expense account entertaining, the maintenance of excessive numbers of sales outlets, and the salaries and bonuses of salesmen. Closely related are outlays for such activities as public relations and lobbying, the rental and maintenance of showy office buildings, and business litigation.

Estimates of the costs of distribution have been obtained for the years beginning with 1929. To do this, we applied Barger's estimate of the value added by distribution (percent of retail value of all commodities retailed) in 1929 to retail sales for the years 1929 to 1934, his estimate for 1939 to sales for the years 1935 to 1945, and his estimate for 1948 to sales for the years 1946 to 1963.[17] Since profits, both corporate and noncorporate, and net interest from trade have already been incorporated in our estimates of surplus, a proportionate share of these has been subtracted from our estimates of value added in distribution. The part of the remaining costs of distribution considered surplus was arrived at arbitrarily by adding to surplus 35 percent of the residual costs for each year. Corporate advertising by other than trade corporations has also been included in economic surplus.

In addition to the part of economic surplus consumed in distribution, a considerable segment is used up in the costs associated with the finance, insurance, real estate, and legal services industries.[18] The profits, rent, and net interest arising in these industries have already been included in our measures of economic surplus. The largest remaining element is employee compensation. This element was also considered part of the economic surplus. No attempt was made to incorporate that

[17] Harold Barger, *Distribution's Place in the American Economy Since 1869*, pp. 57-60. His percentages do not include freight charges between producer and initial distributor, but do include transportation charges between initial distributor, subsequent distributors, and consumers. The figure for 1929 was 36.6 percent, for 1939, 37.3 percent, and for 1948, 37.4 percent.

[18] Even in the most rationally conducted economy there would of course be some costs arising from the need for financial settlements between enterprises and for the services of lawyers rendering legal aid to people or helping settle controversies between economic units. However, these costs would still be defrayed out of economic surplus.

part of the income of unincorporated enterprises in these industries which we treated as a labor return to their proprietors.

3. Surplus Absorption by Government

The estimates of absorption of surplus by government were
based on total government expenditures. From these were subtracted federal grants-in-aid to state and local governments
(because otherwise they would appear twice—as federal expenditures and as state and local expenditures). These estimates are set forth in Table 21.

Final estimates appear in Table 22. These estimates of total
surplus, when expressed as percentages of gross national
product (Chart 5, p. 382), have been running higher in recent
years than in the periods before or immediately after the
Second World War.

4. Penetration of the Productive Process by the Sales Effort

Only very rough estimates can be made of the amount of
economic surplus used up because of the penetration of the
sales effort into the productive process itself. Here we are dealing with such costs as the expenses of changing models of
automobiles and other durable consumer goods when no
fundamental change in quality or usefulness is involved, with
costs of providing superfluous product variation and differentiation, and with similar outlays. That such phenomena constitute a significant characteristic of the American economy is
acknowledged by many business executives. A survey conducted by the *Harvard Business Review* among its subscribers
revealed that of 3,100 replies to a questionnaire asking whether
"planned obsolescence" was felt to be a problem, about two
thirds were in the affirmative.[19]

Testimony before the Kefauver Committee during its investigation of administered prices in the automobile industry indi-

[19] John B. Stewart, "Problems in Review: Planned Obsolescence,"
Harvard Business Review, September-October 1959, p. 14.

Chart 5
Surplus as Percent of Gross National Product

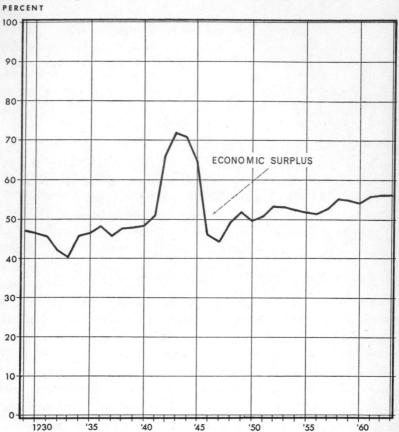

cated that a "significant portion of the automobile industry's
overhead costs arise from an emphasis upon style, rather than
price, competition." Theodore O. Yntema, vice president of the
Ford Motor Company, estimated that Ford's normal expenditures for model changes in all automotive lines would cost $350
million a year, although in 1957 such costs ran to $440 million.
These figures covered styling, engineering, and the purchase of
special commercial tools, but did not include any allowance for
facilities expenditures or rearrangement costs for the model
changeover. Frederick Donner, of General Motors, testified

that design changes for automobiles and trucks in his firm cost "on the order of $500 million a year." The Chrysler representative stated that they had averaged something over $200 million a year in the cost of bringing their new models to market. The three leading automobile manufacturers were thus spending together some $1 billion a year to introduce their new models.

The extent to which styling costs have risen is indicated in a chart submitted by the Ford Motor Company depicting the change in its tool amortization, engineering, and styling costs from 1948 to 1957. These costs, after holding stable from 1948 to 1951, doubled between 1951 and 1953 and in 1957 were 6½ times the 1948 level. The ratio of model-change costs to sales was about 2½ times greater in 1957 than in 1948.

Another indication of the rise in styling costs appears in the amortization costs of special commercial tools. These include the tools and dies ordered for the production of particular model lines, and they are amortized as production costs over the model run for which they are acquired. The total of this cost item for the three leading automobile manufacturers rose from about $182 million in 1950 to $762 million in 1957. Some of this rise was due to inflation, but the greater part was the result of greater complexity and more frequent changes of models. The dependence of these costs on style changes was indicated by Yntema when he testified that 72 percent of the special tooling costs of the 1955 Ford line, which he used as an example, was for body and front-end components, which are most susceptible to style obsolescence. Chassis tooling accounted for 12 percent and engine tooling the remaining 16 percent. And of these 1955 tools only 3.5 percent, by cost, were still in use on the 1958 models.[20]

Information on the penetration of the sales effort into the

[20] All the above data are from *Administered Prices: Automobiles*, Report of the Subcommittee on Antitrust and Monopoly of the Committee on the Judiciary, U. S. Senate, 85th Congress, 2nd Session (1958), pp. 121-123. For a discussion of the costs to the economy as a whole of automobile model changes, see Chapter 5 above, pp. 135-138.

productive process in other industries is more difficult to obtain. Emphasis on style changes in order to convince buyers that their older models are obsolete is characteristic of most other consumer durables industries and is reflected in frequent, sometimes annual, model changes. However, model changes in these other consumer durables are generally less expensive to design, engineer, and put into production. Since the cost of making model changes in the automobile industry amounts to something over $1 billion a year, a rough estimate of $500 million per year for model-change costs in all other consumer durables industries, which together account for about one and a half times as much consumer expenditure as automobiles, seems reasonable.

These estimates do not include any allowance for the labor, material, and other costs involved in adding the chrome, the fins, and similar frills to each unit after the model change has been made. Nor do they include any allowance for the costs arising from excessive product variation and differentiation. These costs might run two or three times as much as model-change costs. It is not unlikely that the various costs associated with the penetration of the sales effort into the production process account for 10 to 20 percent of what consumers spend on durable goods.

In the nondurable consumer goods industries the additional production costs associated with style changes are generally much smaller in relation to other costs of production or to sales than with consumer durable goods. However, the widespread product variation and differentiation found also in these industries are manifestations of the "interpenetration effect" in the productive process. It seems reasonable to suppose that these factors account for not less than 5 percent of consumer expenditures on the products of these industries.

Thus the total of costs arising from the penetration of the sales effort into the productive process must amount to something on the order of 10 percent of consumer expenditures on commodities.

Table 18[21]

Elements of Profit Income in Economic Surplus
(Millions of dollars)

	Corporate profits after taxes	Profit income of unincorporated enterprises	Total business profits, unadjusted (1)+(2)	Official depreciation estimates, all business	Aggregate net receipts (3)+(4)	Adjusted depreciation estimates	Total business profits, adjusted (5)—(6)
	(1)	(2)	(3)	(4)	(5)	(6)	(7)
1929	$ 8,731	$ 5,449	$14,180	$ 6,627	$20,807	$ 3,556	$17,251
1930	5,740	3,512	9,252	6,660	15,912	3,578	12,334
1931	1,136	1,148	2,284	6,493	8,777	3,482	5,295
1932	—2,355	—822	—3,177	5,995	—2,818	3,217	—399
1933	—2,513	—797	—3,310	5,612	—2,302	3,011	—709
1934	347	911	1,258	5,531	6,789	2,967	3,822
1935	1,967	2,129	4,096	5,593	9,689	3,004	6,685
1936	3,593	2,957	6,550	5,616	12,166	3,018	9,148
1937	4,702	3,591	8,293	5,811	14,104	3,121	10,983
1938	3,234	2,635	5,869	5,836	11,705	3,136	8,569
1939	4,248	3,181	7,429	6,004	13,433	3,225	10,208
1940	6,286	4,553	10,839	6,170	17,009	3,313	13,696
1941	6,901	7,036	13,937	6,872	20,809	3,688	17,121
1942	8,263	10,010	18,273	7,878	26,151	4,226	21,925
1943	9,707	11,608	21,315	8,485	29,800	4,557	25,243
1944	10,084	11,726	21,810	9,334	31,144	5,014	26,130
1945	7,724	10,909	18,633	9,695	28,328	5,205	23,123
1946	8,177	11,183	19,260	7,468	26,728	4,012	22,716
1947	12,343	12,696	25,039	9,314	34,353	4,999	29,354
1948	18,365	15,767	34,132	11,186	45,318	6,007	39,311
1949	17,851	13,699	31,550	13,016	44,566	6,987	37,579
1950	17,798	16,017	33,815	14,210	48,025	7,627	40,398
1951	18,507	17,682	36,189	16,208	52,397	8,702	43,695
1952	18,213	16,058	34,271	18,077	52,348	9,703	42,645
1953	17,092	14,793	31,885	20,020	51,905	10,749	41,156
1954	16,523	13,600	30,123	21,888	52,011	11,426	40,585
1955	21,299	16,251	37,550	24,290	61,840	12,022	49,818
1956	20,763	15,512	36,275	26,447	62,722	12,589	50,133
1957	20,747	14,948	35,695	28,972	64,667	13,296	51,371
1958	18,509	14,291	32,800	30,422	63,222	13,539	49,683
1959	24,004	16,882	40,686	32,131	72,817	13,922	58,895
1960	22,201	15,452	37,653	33,577	71,230	14,164	57,066
1961	21,868	15,506	37,374	34,740	72,114	14,356	57,758
1962	25,261	16,334	41,595	38,366	79,961	15,872	64,089
1963	26,277	16,652	42,929	40,009	82,938	16,380	66,558

[21] Sources for Tables 18-22 are listed on pp. 390-391.

Table 19

Estimates of Profit Income of Unincorporated Business
(Millions of dollars)

	Income originating in unincorporated business	Percent of income originating in corporations going to employees	Labor income arising in unincorporated business (1) × (2)	Income originating in unincorporated business, other than labor income (1)−(3)	Net interest originating in unincorporated business	Profits of unincorporated business (4)−(5)
	(1)	(2)	(3)	(4)	(5)	(6)
1929	$23,941	74.6	$17,860	$ 6,081	$ 632	$ 5,449
1930	20,052	78.7	15,781	4,271	759	3,512
1931	15,912	87.9	13,987	1,925	777	1,148
1932	10,838	101.0	10,946	−108	714	−822
1933	10,564	101.6	10,733	−169	628	−797
1934	12,515	88.3	11,051	1,464	553	911
1935	16,330	83.8	13,685	2,645	516	2,129
1936	17,155	80.0	13,724	3,431	474	2,957
1937	20,175	79.9	16,120	4,055	464	3,591
1938	18,359	83.0	15,238	3,121	486	2,635
1939	19,285	80.9	15,602	3,683	502	3,181
1940	21,230	76.2	16,177	5,053	500	4,553
1941	27,632	72.7	20,088	7,544	508	7,036
1942	37,005	71.7	26,533	10,472	462	10,010
1943	43,045	72.2	31,078	11,967	359	11,608
1944	45,938	73.8	33,902	12,036	310	11,726
1945	48,629	77.0	37,444	11,185	276	10,909
1946	56,963	79.9	45,513	11,450	267	11,183
1947	57,978	77.5	44,933	13,045	349	12,696
1948	64,253	74.8	48,061	16,192	425	15,767
1949	58,863	75.9	44,677	14,186	487	13,699
1950	62,684	73.6	46,135	16,549	532	16,017
1951	70,238	73.9	51,906	18,332	650	17,682
1952	71,933	76.7	55,173	16,760	702	16,058
1953	71,859	78.4	56,337	15,522	729	14,793
1954	71,353	79.9	57,011	14,342	742	13,600
1955	74,722	77.2	57,685	17,037	786	16,251
1956	79,020	79.2	62,584	16,436	924	15,512
1957	81,091	80.2	65,035	16,056	1,108	14,948
1958	82,992	81.4	67,555	15,437	1,146	14,291
1959	86,360	79.0	68,224	18,136	1,254	16,882
1960	88,013	80.9	71,203	16,810	1,358	15,452
1961	81,228	81.3	74,168	17,060	1,554	15,506
1962	95,725	81.0	77,537	18,188	1,854	16,334
1963	99,106	81.0	80,276	18,830	2,178	16,652

Table 20

Other Forms of Property Income
(Millions of dollars)

	Total business profits, adjusted	Rental income of persons	Net interest	Profit element in compensation of corporate officers	Total property income
	(1)	(2)	(3)	(4)	(5)
1929	$17,251	$2,703	$ 6,445	$1,668	$ 28,067
1930	12,334	2,352	5,985	1,570	22,241
1931	5,295	1,721	5,839	1,349	14,204
1932	−399	1,190	5,434	1,066	7,291
1933	−709	876	5,042	977	6,096
1934	3,822	801	4,869	1,086	10,578
1935	6,685	766	4,751	1,172	13,374
1936	9,148	792	4,741	1,356	16,037
1937	10,983	924	4,708	1,404	18,019
1938	8,569	1,200	4,636	1,295	15,700
1939	10,208	1,309	4,604	1,348	17,460
1940	13,696	1,410	4,490	1,475	21,071
1941	17,121	1,773	4,544	1,736	25,174
1942	21,925	2,490	4,291	1,845	30,551
1943	25,243	2,722	3,658	1,872	33,495
1944	26,130	2,734	3,342	1,880	34,086
1945	23,123	2,750	3,185	2,059	31,117
1946	22,716	3,580	3,113	2,571	31,980
1947	29,354	4,055	3,792	3,013	40,214
1948	39,311	4,535	4,179	3,366	51,391
1949	37,579	4,974	4,773	3,371	50,697
1950	40,398	5,250	5,469	3,803	54,920
1951	43,695	5,435	6,272	4,061	59,463
1952	42,645	5,724	7,084	4,169	59,622
1953	41,156	5,610	8,196	4,338	59,300
1954	40,585	5,563	9,145	4,503	59,796
1955	40,818	5,279	10,381	5,178	70,656
1956	50,133	5,249	11,716	5,500[a]	72,598
1957	51,371	5,511	13,427	5,900[a]	76,209
1958	49,683	5,221	14,827	6,200[a]	75,931
1959	58,895	5,181	16,384	6,700[a]	87,160
1960	57,066	5,329	18,050	7,000[a]	87,445
1961	57,758	5,239	20,100	7,300[a]	90,397
1962	64,089	5,232	22,084	7,800[a]	99,205
1963	66,558	5,368	24,392	8,300[a]	104,618

[a] Estimated.

Table 21

Surplus Absorption by Government
(Millions of dollars)

	Federal government expenditures	State and local government expenditures	Total governmental expenditures, (1)+(2)	Federal grants-in-aid to state and local governments	Surplus absorbed by government (3)−(4)
	(1)	(2)	(3)	(4)	(5)
1929	$ 2,645	$ 7,699	$ 10,344	$ 117	$ 10,227
1930	2,766	8,381	11,147	125	11,022
1931	4,183	8,448	12,631	313	12,318
1932	3,188	7,553	10,741	134	10,607
1933	3,986	7,192	11,178	502	10,676
1934	6,394	8,069	14,463	1,633	12,830
1935	6,527	8,519	15,046	1,706	13,340
1936	8,501	8,105	16,606	724	15,882
1937	7,225	8,366	15,591	764	14,827
1938	8,451	8,916	17,367	778	16,589
1939	8,955	9,555	18,510	988	17,522
1940	10,089	9,235	19,324	857	18,467
1941	20,539	9,021	29,560	807	28,753
1942	56,141	8,779	64,920	888	64,032
1943	85,972	8,369	94,341	942	93,399
1944	95,585	8,434	104,019	947	103,072
1945	84,826	8,987	93,813	870	92,943
1946	37,104	11,098	48,202	1,108	47,094
1947	31,135	14,414	45,549	1,738	43,811
1948	35,414	17,567	52,981	1,986	50,995
1949	41,599	20,156	61,755	2,228	59,527
1950	41,027	22,428	63,455	2,339	61,116
1951	58,045	23,790	81,835	2,478	79,357
1952	71,613	25,447	97,060	2,635	94,425
1953	77,715	27,136	104,851	2,811	102,040
1954	69,570	30,053	99,623	2,882	96,741
1955	68,915	32,713	101,628	3,050	98,578
1956	71,844	35,715	107,559	3,257	104,302
1957	79,721	39,638	119,359	4,086	115,273
1958	87,921	44,108	132,029	5,445	126,584
1959	91,417	46,957	138,374	6,727	131,647
1960	93,064	49,984	143,048	6,301	136,747
1961	102,602	54,413	157,015	7,241	149,774
1962	110,424	57,341	167,765	8,000	159,765
1963	115,176	61,966	177,142	9,134	168,008

Table 22

Total Economic Surplus and Its Major Components
(Millions of dollars)

	Total property income	Waste in distribution	Corporate advertising other than by trade corporations	Surplus employee compensation		Surplus absorbed by government	Total surplus	Surplus as per cent of GNP
				Finance, insurance and real estate	Legal services			
	(1)	(2)	(3)	(4)	(5)	(6)	(7)	(8)
1929	$ 28,067	$ 5,714	$1,799	$ 2,989	$124	$ 10,227	$ 48,920	46.9
1930	22,241	5,050	1,277	2,808	131	11,022	42,529	46.7
1931	14,204	4,477	1,118	2,527	132	12,318	34,776	45.6
1932	7,291	3,572	797	2,145	126	10,607	24,538	41.9
1933	6,006	3,177	638	1,939	118	10,676	22,644	40.4
1934	10,578	3,473	797	2,031	116	12,830	29,825	45.9
1935	13,374	3,988	828	2,111	121	13,340	33,762	46.6
1936	16,037	4,488	932	2,313	126	15,882	39,778	48.1
1937	18,019	4,982	1,015	2,524	135	14,827	41,502	45.7
1938	15,700	4,636	933	2,460	138	16,589	40,456	47.5
1939	17,460	4,946	970	2,522	142	17,522	43,562	47.8
1940	21,071	5,288	1,023	2,599	144	18,467	48,592	48.3
1941	25,174	5,991	1,095	2,752	151	28,753	63,916	50.8
1942	30,551	6,028	1,056	2,864	150	64,032	104,681	65.8
1943	33,495	6,547	1,223	3,013	149	93,399	137,826	71.6
1944	34,086	7,423	1,335	3,166	159	103,072	149,241	70.6
1945	31,117	8,507	1,351	3,436	169	92,943	137,523	64.4
1946	31,980	11,012	1,616	4,307	184	47,094	96,193	45.7
1947	40,214	13,097	2,037	4,722	209	43,811	104,090	44.4
1948	51,391	14,458	2,295	5,295	228	50,995	124,662	48.1
1949	50,697	15,059	2,486	5,554	242	59,527	133,565	51.7
1950	54,920	16,050	2,739	6,159	265	61,116	141,249	49.6
1951	59,463	17,928	3,064	6,747	294	79,357	166,863	50.7
1952	59,622	19,049	3,454	7,344	325	94,425	184,219	53.1
1953	59,300	20,088	3,787	7,991	358	102,040	193,564	53.0
1954	59,796	20,280	4,026	8,720	386	96,741	189,949	52.3
1955	70,656	21,635	4,530	9,535	421	98,578	205,355	51.7
1956	72,598	22,391	4,918	10,393	459	104,302	215,061	51.3
1957	76,209	23,946	5,432	11,134	496	115,273	232,490	52.5
1958	75,931	24,191	5,597	11,905	542	126,584	244,750	55.1
1959	87,160	25,608	6,191	13,006	601	131,647	264,213	54.7
1960	87,445	26,636	6,578	13,948	670	136,747	272,024	54.1
1961	90,397	26,469	6,779	14,972	730	149,774	289,121	55.7
1962	99,205	28,380	7,200[a]	15,835	809	159,765	311,194	56.0
1963	104,618	29,749	7,700[a]	16,780	870	168,008	327,725	56.1

[a] Estimated.

Sources for Tables in Appendix

Table 18

(1) 1929-1955: U. S. Office of Business Economics, *U. S. Income and Output*, Washington, U. S. Government Printing Office, 1958, line 18 minus line 20, Table I-8, pp. 126-127.
1956-63: *Survey of Current Business*, July, 1964, line 18 minus line 20, Table 2, p. 8.
(2) Table 19, Col. (6).
(4) 1929-45: U. S. Office of Business Economics, *National Income, 1954 Edition*, Washington, U. S. Government Printing Office, 1954, line 3, Table 4, pp. 164-165, minus line 12 and line 14, Table 39, p. 214.
1946-55: *U. S. Income and Output*, line 5, Table V-1, p. 188, minus line 12 and line 14, Table VII-17, p. 229.
1955-58: *Survey of Current Business*, July, 1961, line 1, Table 59, p. 29, plus line 1, Table 60, p. 30, minus line 12 and line 14, Table 73, p. 33.
1959-63: *Survey of Current Business*, July, 1964, line 1, Table 61, p. 32, plus line 1, Table 47, p. 28, minus line 12 and line 14, Table 72, p. 35.
(6) See text.

Table 19

(1) 1929-1955: *U. S. Income and Output*, line 15, Table I-12, pp. 134-135.
1956-58: *Survey of Current Business*, July, 1961, line 13, Table 9, p. 11.
1959-63: *Survey of Current Business*, July, 1964, line 13, Table 8, p. 13.
(2) 1929-55: *U. S. Income and Output*, line 4 divided by line 3, Table I-12, pp. 134-135.
1956-58: *Survey of Current Business*, July, 1961, line 4 divided by line 3, Table 9, p. 11.
1959-63: *Survey of Current Business*, July, 1964, line 4 divided by line 3, Table 8, p. 13.
(5) 1929-55: *U. S. Income and Output*, line 24, Table I-12, pp. 134-35.
1956-58: *Survey of Current Business*, July, 1961, line 22, Table 9, p. 11.
1959-63: *Survey of Current Business*, July, 1964, line 22, Table 8, p. 13.

Table 20

(1) Table 18, Col. (7).
(2) 1929-1955: *U. S. Income and Output*, line 17, Table I-8, pp. 126-127, minus line 5, Table VII-17, p. 229.
1956-1958: *Survey of Current Business*, July, 1961, line 17, Table 2, p. 6, minus line 5, Table 73, p. 33.
1959-1963: *Survey of Current Business*, July, 1964, line 17, Table 2, p. 8, minus line 5, Table 72, p. 35.
(3) 1929-1955: *U. S. Income and Output*, line 25, Table I-8, pp. 126-127.
1956-1963: *Survey of Current Business*, July, 1964, line 25, Table 2, p. 8.
(4) 1929-1955: *U. S. Income and Output*, line 6, Table I-12, pp. 134-135, divided by 2.
1956-1963: Estimated from data in *Statistics of Income, Corporation Income Tax Returns*, 1955 to 1961-62.
(5) Sum of Cols. (1) through (4).

Table 21

(1) 1929-1945: *National Income, 1954 Edition*, line 2, Table 9, p. 172.
1946-1955: *U. S. Income and Output*, line 21, Table III-1, p. 164.

1056 1958: *Survey of Current Business*, July, 1961, line 21, Table 20, p. 16.

1959-1963: *Survey of Current Business*, July, 1964, line 21, Table 19, p. 18.

(2) 1929-1945: *National Income, 1954 Edition*, line 18, Table 9, p. 172.

1946-1955: *U. S. Income and Output*, line 24, Table III-2, p. 165.

1956-1958: *Survey of Current Business*, July, 1961, line 24, Table 21, p. 17.

1959-1963: *Survey of Current Business*, July, 1964, line 24, Table 20, p. 19.

(4) 1929-1945: *National Income, 1954 Edition*, line 13, Table 9, p. 172.

1946-1955: *U. S. Income and Output*, line 23, Table III-2, p. 165.

1956-1958: *Survey of Current Business*, July, 1961, line 23, Table 21, p. 17.

1959-1963: *Survey of Current Business*, July, 1964, line 23, Table 20, p. 19.

Table 22

(1) Table 20, Col. (5).

(2) See text.

(3) *Statistics of Income, Corporation Income Tax Returns*, Annual, 1929 to 1961-1962. Advertising expenditures of all active corporations minus those of wholesale and retail corporations (expenditures of the latter two groups reflected in estimates of Col. 2, this table). Fiscal year figures attributed to calendar years in which first part of fiscal year fell. Figures for 1962 and 1963 projected.

(4) 1929-45: *National Income, 1954 Edition*, line 44, Table 14, p. 168-79.

1946-55: *U. S. Income and Output*, line 44, Table VI-1, p. 200.

1956-58: *Survey of Current Business*, July, 1961, line 41, Table 48, p. 26.

1959-63: *Survey of Current Business*, July, 1964, line 44, Table 50, p. 29.

(5) 1929-45: *National Income, 1954 Edition*, line 76, Table 14, pp. 178-79.

1946-55: *U. S. Income and Output*, line 76, Table VI-1, p. 200.

1956-58: *Survey of Current Business*, July, 1961, line 73, Table 48, p. 26.

1959-63: *Survey of Current Business*, July, 1964, line 76, Table 50, p. 29.

(6) Table 21, Col. (5).

(7) Sum of (1) through (6).

(8) Col. (7) divided by GNP:

1929-55: *U. S. Income and Output*, line 1, Table I-17, pp. 138-39.

1956-58: *Survey of Current Business*, July, 1961, line 1, Table 1, p. 6.

1959-63: *Survey of Current Business*, July, 1964, line 1, Table 1, p. 8.

AUTHOR INDEX

Adams, Walter, 65n
Adelman, M. A., 225n
Adler, Irving, 316n, 318n

Baran, Paul A., 5n, 8n, 12n
Barger, Harold, 380n
Bator, F. M., 147n, 151n, 152, 163n, 174n
Bauman, Jacquelin, 100n
Bereiter, Carl, 326n
Berle, A. A., Jr., 21, 34
Beyer, Glen H., 301n
Boulding, K. E., 149n
Braden, Anne, 253-254
Bright, James R., 332n
Budd, Edward C., 371n
Burkhead, Edward C., 371n
Burnham, James, 34, 190
Burns, Arthur R., 60
Burns, James MacGregor, 164

Cairncross, A. K., 105
Cary, William L., 150n
Chamberlin, E. H., 55, 117, 123n
Cheskin, Louis, 120-121
Clark, Kenneth B., 310n
Compton, William H., 46n
Conant, James Bryant, 307n, 311n, 322, 333-335
Cook, Fred J., 212n, 291
Cox, Oliver C., 178n, 208n, 251n, 264n
Cutler, Frederick, 107n, 197n, 198n

Day, Noel, 275-276
Dempsey, David, 33n
Denison, Edward F., 371-372
Dernburg, Thomas, 247n
Dingwall, Eric John, 357
Domar, Evsey, 81n, 376n, 377
Dreiser, Theodore, 33n
Duesenberry, James S., 14n, 60n, 68n

Earley, James, 23-27, 40, 48, 67
Eden, Philip, 232n
Eisner, Robert, 373-375
Elliott, Osborn, 37n
Engels, Friedrich, 5, 177n, 179n, 297n

Fabricant, Solomon, 375-376
Faulkner, H. U., 231
Ferguson, A., 231
Fisher, Franklin M., 135-138
Fitch, James Marston, 298
Fleming, D. F., 185n, 186n, 188
Frazier, Franklin E., 272
Freedman, Mervin B., 326n
Freud, Sigmund, 351, 354, 356, 357
Fuller, J. G., 30n
Furtado, Celso, 218

Galbraith, J. K., 70, 74, 154n, 160-161
Gardner, John W., 306-307
Gilpatric, Roswell, 216n
Gleason, Gene, 291n
Golanskii, M., 376-378
Goodman, Paul, 344, 362
Gordon, R. A., 229
Gorham, William A., 321
Gottman, Jean, 304n
Graham, Robert E., Jr., 100n
Gray, Horace M., 65n
Greenewalt, Crawford H., 45n, 46n, 48
Gregor, James A., 279n
Griliches, Zvi, 135-138
Gruen, Victor, 304n
Grutzner, Charles, 293n

Hechinger, Fred M., 322n
Hamberg, Daniel, 130n, 145n
Handler, M. S., 262n
Hansen, A. H., 89, 92, 160n, 228, 238-239
Harrington, Michael, 285

392

SUBJECT INDEX

No attempt has been made to include all appearances of such terms as "capitalism," "monopoly capitalism," "corporation," and "surplus," since these relate to the essential subject matter of the book and occur so frequently that a listing would be useless. It is hoped nevertheless that the entries included may provide certain helpful leads.

MONTHLY REVIEW

an independent socialist magazine
edited by Paul M. Sweezy and Harry Magdoff

Business Week: ". . . a brand of socialism that is thorough-going and tough-minded, drastic enough to provide the sharp break with the past that many left-wingers in the underdeveloped countries see as essential. At the same time they maintain a sturdy independence of both Moscow and Peking that appeals to neutralists. And their skill in manipulating the abstruse concepts of modern economics impresses would-be intellectuals. . . . Their analysis of the troubles of capitalism is just plausible enough to be disturbing."

Bertrand Russell: "Your journal has been of the greatest interest to me over a period of time. I am not a Marxist by any means as I have sought to show in critiques published in several books, but I recognize the power of much of your own analysis and where I disagree I find your journal valuable and of stimulating importance. I want to thank you for your work and to tell you of my appreciation of it."

The Wellesley Department of Economics: " . . . the leading Marxist intellectual (not Communist) economic journal published anywhere in the world, and is on our subscription list at the College library for good reasons."

Albert Einstein: "Clarity about the aims and problems of socialism is of greatest significance in our age of transition. . . . I consider the founding of this magazine to be an important public service." (In his article, "Why Socialism" in Vol. I, No. 1.)

DOMESTIC: $7 for one year, $12 for two years, $5 for one-year student subscription.

FOREIGN: $8 for one year, $14 for two years, $6 for one-year student subscription. (Subscription rates subject to change.)

116 West 14th Street, New York, New York 10011